INTRODUCTIONS TO OLDER LANGUAGES

W. P. LEHMANN
Founding Editor

AN INTRODUCTION TO

old french

WILLIAM W. KIBLER

The Modern Language Association of America
New York   1984

MLA and the MODERN LANGUAGE ASSOCIATION are
trademarks owned by the Modern Language Association of America.
For information about obtaining permission to reprint material from
MLA book publications, send your request by mail (see address below),
e-mail (permissions@mla.org), or fax (646 458-0030).

Library of Congress Cataloging-in-Publication Data

Kibler, William W., 1942-
An introduction to Old French.
(Introductions to older languages ; 3)
Bibliography: p. Includes index.
1. French language—To 1500—Grammar.   2. French
language—To 1500—Readers. I. Title.   II. Series.
PC2823.K52 1984   447'.01   83-19368
ISBN-13: 978-0-87352-291-5
ISBN-10: 0-87352-291-5
ISBN-13: 978-0-87352-292-2 (pbk.)

ISSN 1099-0313
Tenth printing 2012

Published by The Modern Language Association of America
26 Broadway, New York, New York, 10004-1789
www.mla.org

contents

abbreviations and symbols

Abbreviations

Insofar as possible I have avoided abbreviations in the text proper. The following occur chiefly in charts, tables, and examples:

d.o.	direct object	obj.	object
Engl.	English	OP	oblique plural
f.	feminine	OS	oblique singular
Fr.	French	perf.	perfect
fut.	future	pl.	plural
FP	feminine plural	prep.	preposition
FS	feminine singular	pres.	present
i.o.	indirect object	pret.	preterite
impers.	impersonal (verb)	sg.	singular
lit.	literally	S	strong
m.	masculine	W	weak
MS	manuscript	1	first person
neg.	negative	2	second person
NP	nominative plural	3	third person
NS	nominative singular		

A list of abbreviations used in the Glossary appears on pp. 297–98.

Symbols

The International Phonetic Alphabet is used in the phonology sections. Phonemic transcriptions of sounds or words are enclosed by /   /. Words in capitals (e.g., MŪRŬS) are Latin etyma. The following additional symbols are employed:

> developed to
< developed from
/ alternating with (or) separates two lines of verse
– long vowel (Latin)
˘ short vowel (Latin)
ˌ open vowel (Vulgar Latin/Gallo-Roman)
. close vowel (Vulgar Latin/Gallo-Roman)

Asterisks (*) before words in the grammar sections identify words found in the reading selections in the volume. Asterisks before words in the phonology sections indicate hypothetical or unattested forms.

select bibliography

Short Titles of Old French Works Cited

Aucassin. *Aucassin et Nicolette*. Ed. Mario Roques. Classiques Français du Moyen Âge, 41. Paris: Champion, 1969.

Béroul. Béroul. *Le Roman de Tristan*. Ed. [L. M. Defourques]. Classiques Français du Moyen Âge, 12. Paris: Champion, 1962.

Brut. Wace. *Le Roman de Brut*. Ed. Ivor Arnold. Paris: Société des Anciens Textes Français, 1938.

Charrete. Chrétien de Troyes. *Lancelot; or, The Knight of the Cart (Le Chevalier de la Charrete)*. Ed. William W. Kibler. Garland Library of Medieval Literature, 1. New York: Garland, 1981.

Charroi. *Le Charroi de Nîmes*. Ed. Duncan McMillan. Paris: Klincksieck, 1972.

Cligés. *Cligés*. Ed. Alexandre Micha. Vol. 2 of *Les Romans de Chrétien de Troyes*. Classiques Français du Moyen Âge, 84. Paris: Champion, 1957.

Colin Muset. *Les Chansons de Colin Muset*. Ed. Joseph Bédier. Classiques Français du Moyen Âge, 7. Paris: Champion, 1938.

Couronnement. *Les Rédactions en vers du Couronnement de Louis*. Ed. Yvon G. Lepage. Textes Littéraires Français, 261. Genève: Droz, 1978.

Eneas. *Eneas, roman du XIIe siècle*. Ed. J. L. Salverda de Grave. Classiques Français du Moyen Âge, 44 and 62. Paris: Champion, 1964–68.

Erec. *Erec et Enide*. Ed. Mario Roques. Vol. 1 of *Les Romans de Chrétien de Troyes*. Classiques Français du Moyen Âge, 80. Paris: Champion, 1963.

Fierabras. *Fierabras*. Ed. A. Kroeber and G. Servois. Les Anciens Poëtes de la France, 4. Paris: Vieweg, 1860.

Floovant. *Floovant*. Ed. H. Michelant and F. Guessard. Les Anciens Poëtes de la France, 1. Paris: Vieweg, 1858.

Gaydon. *Gaydon*. Ed. F. Guessard and S. Luce. Les Anciens Poëtes de la France, 7. Paris: Vieweg, 1862.

Huon. *Huon de Bordeaux*. Ed. Pierre Ruelle. Université de Bruxelles, Travaux de la Faculté de Philosophie et Lettres, 20. Bruxelles: Presses Universitaires de Bruxelles, 1960.

Joinville. Jehan, seigneur de Joinville, *La Vie de Saint Louis*. Ed. Noel Corbett. Sherbrooke, Ont.: Naaman, 1977.

Marie. *Les Lais de Marie de France*. Ed. Jean Rychner. Classiques Français du Moyen Âge, 93. Paris: Champion, 1968.

Mort Artu. *La Mort le roi Artu*. Ed. Jean Frappier. Textes Littéraires Français, 58. Genève: Droz, 1964.

Perceval. *Le Roman de Perceval; ou, Le Conte du Graal*. Ed. William Roach. Textes Littéraires Français, 71. Genève: Droz, 1959.

Piramus. *Piramus et Tisbé*. Ed. F. Branciforti. Biblioteca dell' "Archivum Romanicum," 57. Firenze: Leo Olschki, 1959.

Prise. *La Prise d'Orange*. Ed. Claude Régnier. Paris: Klincksieck, 1970.

Raoul. *Raoul de Cambrai*. Ed. P. Meyer and A. Longnon. Paris: Société des Anciens Textes Français, 1882.

Roland. *The Song of Roland, an Analytical Edition*. Vol. 2 of *Oxford Text and English Translation*. Ed. Gerard J. Brault. University Park: Pennsylvania State Univ. Press, 1978.

St. Nicholas. Jehan Bodel, *Le Jeu de saint Nicolas*. Ed. Albert Henry. Textes Littéraires Français, 290. Genève: Droz, 1981.

Thomas. *Les Fragments du roman de Tristan de Thomas*. Ed. Bartina H. Wind. Textes Littéraires Français, 92. Genève: Droz, 1960.

Troie. Benoit de Sainte-Maure. *Le Roman de Troie*. Ed. L. Constans. 6 vols. Paris: Société des Anciens Textes Français, 1904–12.

Vie de Saint Thomas. Guernes de Pont-Sainte-Maxence. *La Vie de Saint Thomas Becket*. Ed. Emmaneul Walberg. Classiques Français du Moyen Âge, 77. Paris: Champion, 1964.

Villehardouin. Geoffroy de Villehardouin, *La Conquête de Constantinople*. Ed. Jean Dufournet. Paris: Garnier-Flammarion, 1969.

Yvain. *Les Romans de Chrétien de Troyes*. Vol. 4 of *Le Chevalier au Lion (Yvain)*. Ed. Mario Roques. Classiques Français du Moyen Âge, 89. Paris: Champion, 1960.

Anthology

Aspland, C. W. *A Medieval French Reader*. Oxford: Clarendon, 1979. All citations from this anthology are noted in the text by the selection number followed by a comma.

Dictionaries

Bloch, Oscar, and Walther Von Wartburg. *Dictionnaire étymologique de la langue française*. 6th ed. Paris: Presses Universitaires de France, 1975.

Godefroy, Frédéric. *Dictionnaire de l'ancienne langue française et de tous ses dialectes du IXe au XVe siècle*. 10 vols. Paris: 1880–1902. Rpt. Paris: Librairie des Sciences et des Arts, 1938.

Greimas, A. J. *Dictionnaire de l'ancien français jusqu'au milieu du XIVe siècle*. Paris: Larousse, 1968.

Tobler, Adolf, and E. Lommatzsch. *Altfranzösisches Wörterbuch*. Berlin: Weidmannsche Buchhandlung; Wiesbaden: Franz Steiner, 1925– . Currently through the letter *T*.

Von Wartburg, Walther. *Französisches Etymologisches Wörterbuch*. Bonn: Fritz Klopp; Basel: Helbing Lichtenhahn; Leipzig: B. G. Teubner; Basel: Zbinden, 1928– .

Principal Grammatical and Phonological Works Consulted

Anglade, Joseph. *Grammaire élémentaire de l'ancien français*. Paris: Armand Colin, 1965.

Bourciez, E., and J. Bourciez. *Phonétique française: Etude historique*. Paris: Klincksieck, 1974.

Einhorn, E. *Old French: A Concise Handbook*. Cambridge: Cambridge Univ. Press, 1974.

Foulet, Lucien. *Petite syntaxe de l'ancien français*. Classiques Français du Moyen Âge, 2nd ser. 3rd ed. Paris: Champion, 1928.

Gossen, Charles Théodore. *Grammaire de l'ancien picard*. Bibliothèque Française et Romane, ser. A, no. 19. Paris: Klincksieck, 1970.

Ménard, Philippe. *Syntaxe de l'ancien français*. Vol. 1 of *Manuel du français du moyen âge*. Ed. Yves Lefèvre. New rev. ed. Bordeaux: Société Bordelaise de Diffusion des Travaux de Lettres et Sciences Humaines, 1973.

Moignet, Gérard. *Grammaire de l'ancien français: Morphologie—syntaxe*. Paris: Klincksieck, 1973.

Pope, Mildred K. *From Latin to Modern French with Especial Consideration of Anglo-Norman*. Manchester: Manchester Univ. Press, 1934.

Raynaud de Lage, Guy. *Introduction à l'ancien français*. 3rd ed. Paris: Société d'Edition d'Enseignement Supérieur, 1962.

Schwan, E., and D. Behrens. *Grammaire de l'ancien français*. Trans. Oscar Bloch. Rpt. ed. Bruxelles: Editions Libro-Sciences S.P.R.L., 1970.

Sneyders de Vogel, Kornelis. *Syntaxe historique du français*. 2nd ed. The Hague: J. B. Wolters, 1927.

Voretzsch, Carl. *Einführung in das Studium der altfranzösischen Sprache zum Selbstunterricht für den Anfänger*. 6th ed. Halle: Niemeyer, 1932.

Wagner, R. L. *L'Ancien français: Points de vue, programmes*. Paris: Larousse, 1974.

Other Linguistic and Literary Studies

Batany, J. "Ancien français, méthodes nouvelles." *Langue Française* 10 (1971): 31–52.

———. *Français médiéval*. Collection Études, 66. Paris: Bordas, 1972.

Bruneau, Charles. "La Champagne, dialecte ancien et patois moderne." *Revue de Linguistique Romane* 5 (1929): 71–175.

Duby, Georges. *Medieval Marriage: Two Models from Twelfth-Century France*. Trans. E. Forster. Baltimore: Johns Hopkins Univ. Press, 1978.

Dufournet, Jean. Pref. to *Aucassin et Nicolette*. Paris: Garnier-Flammarion, 1973.

Fouché, Pierre. *Phonétique historique du français*. 2nd ed. 3 vols. Paris: Klincksieck, 1966.

———. *Morphologie historique du français: Le Verbe*. New ed. Paris: Klincksieck, 1967.

Foulet, Alfred, and Mary Blakely Speer. *On Editing Old French Texts*. Lawrence: Regents Press of Kansas, 1979.

Foulet, Lucien. "L'Accent tonique et l'ordre des mots. Formes faibles du pronom personnel après le verbe." *Romania* 50 (1924): 54–93.

———. "L'Extension de la forme oblique du pronom personnel en ancien français." *Romania* 61 (1935): 257–315, 401–63; 62 (1936): 27–91.

Frank, Grace. *The Medieval French Drama*. Oxford: Clarendon, 1954.

Gossen, Carl Theodor. *Französische Skriptastudien, Untersuchungen zu den nordfranzösischen Urkundensprachen des Mittelalters*. Osterreichische Akademie der Wissenschaften, Philosophisch-Historische Klasse, 253. Wien: Hermann Böhlaus Nachf., 1967.

———. "Remarques sur la déclinaison en ancien picard." *Travaux de Linguistique et de Littérature* 9 (1971): 197–207.

Imbs, Paul. "Prolégomènes à une étude de l'expression de la vitesse en ancien français." In *Mélanges G. Straka*. Lyon: Société de Linguistique Romane, 1970, 2: 151–66.

Moignet, Gérard. "Sur le système de la flexion à deux cas de l'ancien français." In *Mélanges P. Gardette*. Strasbourg: *Travaux de Linguistique et de Littérature*, 1966, 339–56.

Price, G. "Contribution à l'étude de la syntaxe des pronoms personnels sujets en ancien français." *Romania* 87 (1966): 476–504.

———. "Quel est le rôle de l'opposition *cist/cil* en ancien français?" *Romania* 89 (1968): 240–54.

———. "La transformation du système français des démonstratifs." *Zeitschrift für Romanische Philologie* 85 (1969): 489–505.

Rickard, Peter. "*(Il) estuet, (il) convient, (il) faut* and Their Constructions in Old and Middle French." In *The French Language: Studies Presented to Lewis Charles Harmer*. London: Harrap, 1970, 65–92.

Ritchie, R. L. Graeme. *Recherches sur la syntaxe de la conjonction "que" dans l'ancien français depuis les origines de la langue jusqu'au commencement du XIIIe siècle*. Paris: Champion, 1907.

Rohlfs, Gerhard. *Vom Vulgärlatein zum Altfranzösischen*. Tübingen: Niemeyer, 1963.

Rothwell, W. "The Hours of the Day in Medieval French." *French Studies* 13 (1959): 240–51.

Södergaard, O. "Etude syntactique sur l'ancien français *onques*." *Studia Neophilologica* 33 (1961): 69–79.

Tilander, Gunnar. "Un Problème syntaxique de l'ancien français: Je lui donne = Je le lui donne." *Romania* 63 (1937): 31–47.

Tobler, Adolf. *Mélanges de grammaire française*. Trans. M. Kuttner and L. Sudre. Paris: Picard, 1905.

Von Wartburg, Walther. *La Fragmentation linguistique de la Romania*. Bibliothèque Française et Romane, ser. A, 13. Paris: Klincksieck, 1967.

Woledge, Brian. "Notes on the Syntax of Indeclinable Nouns in 12th-Century French." In *The French Language: Studies Presented to Lewis Charles Harmer*. London: Harrap, 1970, 38–52.

———. "Un Scribe champenois devant un texte normand." In *Mélanges Jean Frappier*. Genève: Droz, 1970, 2: 1139–54.

ïṇtroдuсtïoṇ

The language generally known today as Old French was in actuality a series of more or less distinct stages of several highly differentiated dialects current from the ninth century until the late fifteenth century. It was referred to by contemporary writers as *romanz* or *lingua romana rustica* to distinguish it from the great cultural language of the Middle Ages, Latin or *lingua latina*.

The earliest extant text, the *Strasbourg Oaths*, was written down sometime shortly after 842. This and the only other known text of the ninth century, the *Sequence of Saint Eulalia* (c. 881), were still quite close to Latin in their syntax and lexicon, and they certainly do not represent the language as it was spoken. This early period was sparse in texts, and it is not until the cultural reawakening of the twelfth century that one finds significant work in the vernacular. This "twelfth-century renaissance" produced literary texts of the highest quality in a number of genres: lyric poetry, epic, romance, drama, beast fable, and historiography. Texts from this period, extending roughly from 1100 to 1285, are remarkably homogeneous in their syntax and morphology. The language in which they were composed, although quite diversified in dialect, is usually distinguished by two traits: the existence of a two-case declension system for nouns, adjectives, and articles and the maintenance of hiatus, particularly in verbal forms.

Although there is strong evidence that the declension system was lost early in spoken Old French, the written texts attempt to maintain it at least until the late thirteenth century. When the two-case system falls into disuse and the hiatus is no longer maintained (e.g., *j'ai veü* > *j'ai vu*; *armeüre* > *armure*; *porriëz* > *porriez*), we can no longer properly speak of Old French; this stage of language development is usually referred to as

Middle French. Thus, for the purposes of this grammar, Old French is that stage of the French language reflected in texts of the twelfth and thirteenth centuries; very early Old French and Middle French are excluded from consideration.

Old French is a descendant of the spoken Latin that was carried into Gaul by the invading Roman troops of Julius Caesar between 58 and 51 B.C. In Gaul, this "Vulgar" Latin, mixed with the native Celtic "substratum," eventually became two distinct languages. Old French (*langue d'oïl*) was spoken north of a line running approximately from the mouth of the Loire eastward following the river to north of Bourges, then turning southward to Saint Etienne; from there it ran northeastward to the Alps. South of that line was spoken the language now known as Occitan (*langue d'oc*) or Provençal. The line of demarcation between these two major language areas moved somewhat southward during the course of the Middle Ages. Old French and Occitan differ in morphology, syntax, and vocabulary, as well as in phonology. Two major dialect groups lie on the border between the regions of Oc and Oïl. To the east, in an area including the cities of Geneva, Grenoble, and Lyon, was spoken a series of intermediary dialects known collectively as Franco-Provençal. To the west, in the areas of Saintonge, Aunis, Poitou, and Angoumois, was spoken a border dialect that in the twelfth and thirteenth centuries was more akin to Occitan than to Old French. This dialect is sometimes referred to as Southwestern.

As mentioned initially, Old French is itself composed of a number of distinct dialects, the most important of which are Picard and Walloon in the northeast, Lotharingian, Champenois and Burgundian in the east, Norman in the northwest, Anglo-Norman in England, and Francien in the central region of the Ile-de-France (see map on endpapers). A weak central monarchy after the collapse of Charlemagne's empire, political division of the area by the feudal system, and poor or nonexistent interregional communications all fostered dialectal fragmentation. The *romanz* spoken by the Burgundians in southeastern France was phonologically quite different from that spoken by the Picards in the north, which in turn was distinct from the Anglo-Norman spoken in Britain.

Although we cannot determine how comprehensible any of these dialects was to the speakers of the other dialects, there are clear indications that, by the early thirteenth century, the dialect known as Francien was beginning to predominate, for both political and practical reasons. Beginning shortly after 1200, the Capetian monarchy under Philippe Auguste began to reassert its primacy over the feudal lords; the language of its capital, Paris, had no highly idiosyncratic traits and was a politically expedient choice. In addition, increasing commercial activities, more frequent travel (particularly on pilgrimages, a popular form of medieval tourism), and bureaucratic centralization all favored the cultivation of a mutually comprehensible dialect.

Thus, out of the diversity of Old French, we can identify a period (c. 1100–1285) and a dialect (Francien) that, more than any others, typify "Old French" and constitute the basis of a grammar of the language. It would be nearly impossible, however, to find a text from this period that is purely Francien in the sense of reflecting uniquely Francien phonological, morphological, and lexical traits. All texts from the Old French period are to some degree "contaminated" by traits from dialects other than the one in which they were principally composed, and one of the significant traits of Francien was its receptivity to other dialectal characteristics.

In the first fifteen chapters of the grammar, the student is introduced to Francien through a study of Marie de France's *lai* "Fresne" (see Reading and Textual Analysis, Selection 1a). The final eight chapters present reading selections in two other major literary dialects of Old French, Anglo-Norman and Picard.

Although some slight morphological and lexical differences can be noted between dialects, by far the most significant distinctions are phonological, that is, related to the sound system of the language and to the notation of those sounds through spelling. As Old French developed from spoken or "Vulgar" Latin, the sounds of the language evolved in a gradual, unconscious, and systematic manner. The study of the historical evolution of those sounds and their differentiation into diverse dialects is known as phonology. In traditional grammars of Old French, phonology is generally the first section, upon which all else is predicated, but some recent popular grammars omit phonology altogether. I have found it a valuable pedagogical tool, and for that reason I have chosen to include it in special sections at the end of each chapter. If one is interested principally in acquiring a reading knowledge of Old French, these sections can be skipped, since the grammar sections of each chapter, which cover morphology and syntax, are self-contained. The phonology sections provide more detailed grammatical explanations that are particularly valuable when one is confronted with texts written in dialects other than Francien.

Following the annotated reading selections, the body of each chapter presents Old French morphology and syntax. Instead of introducing these in two separate sections, as previous Old French grammars have, I have sought to present morphological and syntactical problems in the order in which difficulties present themselves in the texts considered. I have begun with what will seem most foreign and puzzling to the contemporary student familiar with modern English and French.

This book has grown out of my classroom experience with the language over the past twenty years, as both student and teacher. It would not have been possible without the important grammars that preceded it, for it both imitates their better points and attempts to avoid their worst. In particular I should like to acknowledge my debt to the following texts, which were constantly at my side while I prepared my own grammar: Mildred K. Pope, *From Latin to Modern French*; Gérard Moignet, *Grammaire de l'ancien français*; E. Einhorn, *Old French: A Concise Handbook*; Philippe Ménard, *Syntaxe de l'ancien français*; E. Bourciez and J. Bourciez, *Phonétique française: Etude historique*; Kornelis Sneyders de Vogel, *Syntaxe historique du français*; Lucien Foulet, *Petite syntaxe de l'ancien français*; Guy Raynaud de Lage, *Introduction à l'ancien français*; R. L. Wagner, *L'Ancien Français*; and Karl Voretzsch, *Einführung in das Studium der altfranzösischen Sprache zum Selbstunterricht für den Anfänger* (see select bibliography).

In preparing this book, I have tried to keep in mind the contemporary English-speaking public, with all its strengths and weaknesses. Frequently lacking a firm basis in linguistics and a solid knowledge of Latin, the modern student is unprepared to deal with the complexity of many of the texts I have listed, whereas other grammars are so abbreviated or laconic that they are useless without an experienced teacher at hand. I have therefore tried to provide a text that is suitable for persons wishing to learn Old French on their own, as well as for those enrolled in one- or two-semester courses in the language at the college or university level.

As often as possible, I have selected examples of morphological and syntactical structures from the readings at the beginning of each chapter. All such passages are identified by a chapter number and a line number separated by a colon, thus: 7:229. Since the short texts in this volume did not always provide useful examples, and since instructors may wish to supplement the materials here with further readings, I have chosen additional examples from C. W. Aspland's excellent new anthology, *A Medieval French Reader*. All readings from Aspland are identified by a section number and a line number separated by a comma, thus: 7, 229. Citations from this volume are all © C. W. Aspland and are reprinted by permission of Oxford University Press. Examples from sources other than Aspland or the reading selections are identified by a short title keyed to the bibliography.

Each example is translated. Particularly in the early chapters, a rough word-for-word translation often precedes a smoother English rendering. Translations from the *Song of Roland* are based upon Gerard J. Brault's translation; all others are my own.

A complete glossary of every form found in the twenty-three readings is provided. Aspland's *Reader* also has a detailed glossary. A student looking for a complete dictionary should consider A. J. Greimas, *Dictionnaire de l'ancien français jusqu'au milieu du XIVe siècle*, which is concise, accurate, and relatively inexpensive. In the library one should consult A.

Tobler and E. Lommatzsch, *Altfranzösisches Wörterbuch* (in publication since 1925 and now complete through the letter *T*) or F. Godefroy, *Dictionnaire de l'ancienne langue française et de tous ses dialectes du IXe au XVe siècle.*

This grammar could never have been completed without the encouragement and suggestions of a number of colleagues and friends, and it is a pleasure to be able to thank them here. Hans-Erich Keller and Thelma S. Fenster read the entire typescript with extreme care and offered many valuable suggestions for improvement. My colleagues Michael Gagarin, Cheryl Demharter, and James F. M. Stephens weeded a number of inconsistencies out of the phonology sections. I am especially grateful to Helen-Jo Jakusz Hewitt of the Linguistics Research Center, who was of inestimable help in preparing the computerized glossary. The generosity of the Research Institute of the University of Texas provided me with two very competent and cheerful research assistants, Karen Kelton and Margaret Knott, who did most of the initial typing and final proofreading of the typescript. Finally, I should like to express my thanks to W. P. Lehmann, the general editor of the MLA series of introductory texts to older languages, whose faith in the project never faltered. For the strengths of this grammar, may they share the credit; for its weaknesses, may they take no blame.

Third Printing

In making the revisions for the second and third printings, I profited greatly from suggestions by Rupert Pickens, Robert F. Cook, and Joseph Duggan and especially from the lists of corrigenda carefully prepared by Jonathan Beck and Samuel N. Rosenberg in conjunction with their reviews for *Romance Philology* and *Speculum.*

William W. Kibler

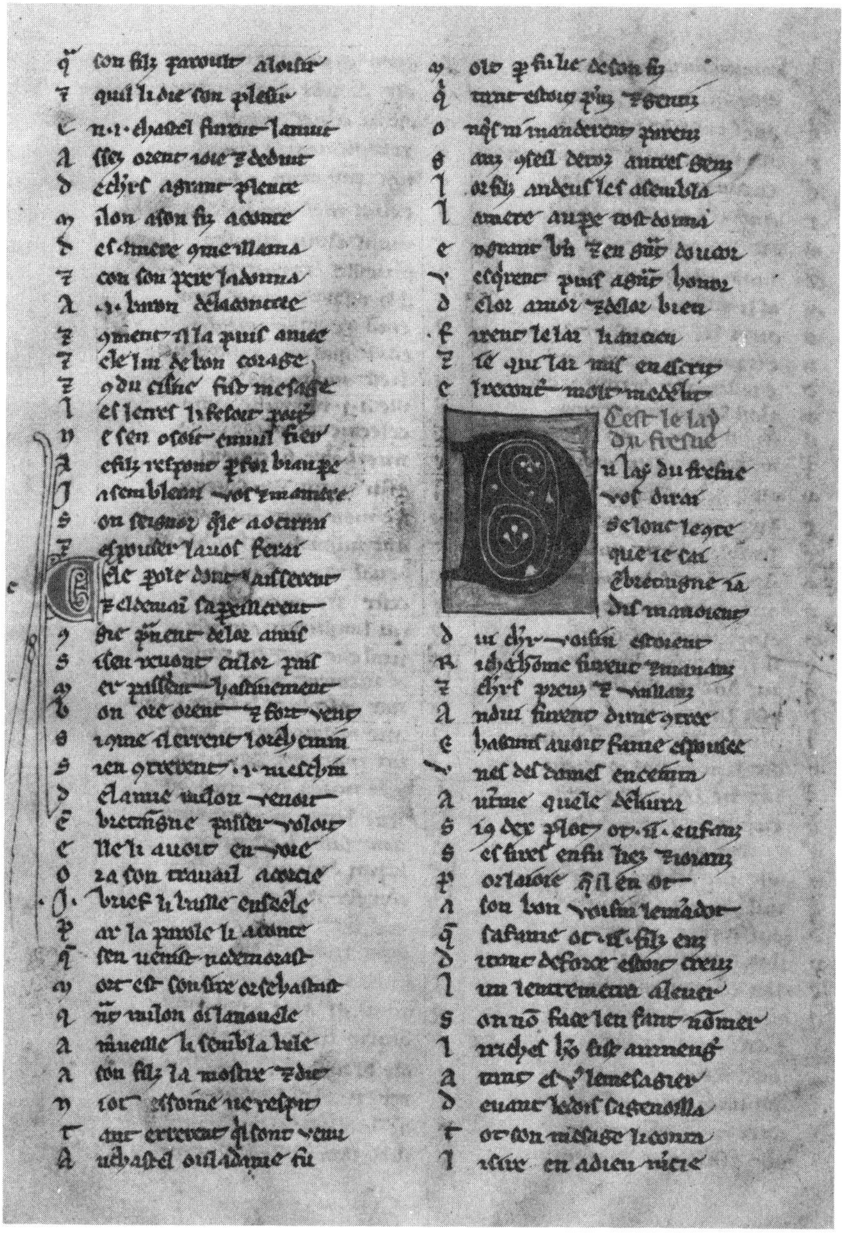

Illustration 1

The opening lines of "Fresne" (manuscript f. fr. 1104, folio 39v, Bibliothèque Nationale, Paris)

chapter 1

Reading and Textual Analysis, Selection 1a

Chapters 1 through 15 present a complete *lai*, "Le Fresne" 'The Ash Tree' by Marie de France. Marie's biography is sketchy, for all that we know about her must be gleaned from her own writings. It is generally agreed that the same "Marie" is responsible for three very different late twelfth-century works signed with this forename: the *Lais* (probably composed in the 1160s), the *Fables* (between 1167 and 1189), and the *Espurgatoire Saint Patriz* (after 1189). In the fourth line of the epilogue to the *Fables* she refers to herself as follows:

> Marie ai num, si sui de France
> (My name is Marie, and I am from France)

and her near-contemporary Denis Piramus calls her *dame Marie*. The *nobles reis* to whom Marie dedicated her *lais* (Prologue, line 43) has been identified with virtual unanimity as Henry II Plantagenet, who ruled England from 1154 to 1189. This information indicates that, although she was probably born into the French aristocracy, she lived most of her life in England and frequented courtly circles there. A number of theories have identified her with various historical Maries, but none has gained universal acceptance.

Although Marie de France probably wrote in "standard" literary Francien with Norman influences, the principal manuscripts of her works were produced by Anglo-Norman scribes. One of the important manuscripts of her *Lais*, however, that in the Bibliothèque Nationale in Paris (ms. nouv. acq. fr. 1104), is in Francien. It was copied down around the middle of the thirteenth century. The version of "Fresne" presented in the first fifteen chapters of this grammar is newly edited from that manuscript (see illustration).

1:0	C'est le lay du Fresne.
1:1	Du lay du Fresne vos dirai
1:2	Selonc le conte que je sai.
1:3	En Bretaigne jadis manoient
1:4	Dui chevalier; voisin estoient.
1:5	Riche homme furent et mananz
1:6	Et chevaliers preuz et vaillanz.
1:7	Andui furent d'une contree.
1:8	Chascuns avoit fame espousee.
1:9	Unes des dames enceinta.
1:10	Au terme qu'ele delivra,
1:11	Si con Deus plot ot deus enfanz.
1:12	Ses sire en fu liez et joianz.
1:13	Por la joie que il en ot
1:14	A son bon voisin le mandot
1:15	Que sa fame ot deus filz eüz,
1:16	De tanz enfanz estoit creüz;
1:17	L'un li trametra a lever,
1:18	Son non face l'enfant nommer.
1:19	Li riches hom sist au mengier,
1:20	Atant es vos le mesagier!
1:21	Devant le dois s'agenoilla;
1:22	Tot son mesage li conta.
1:23	Li sire en a Dieu mercïé;
1:24	Un bon cheval li a donné.

1:9   *unes*: nom. sg. *-s* by analogy with masc. declension.

1:14 *mandot*: 3 imperf. ind.; western and southwestern dialects, incl. Norman and Anglo-Norman. See Phonology 19.

1:17 *lever*: 'to raise; stand up; build.' Also, as here, 'to hold up (a child or convert) over the baptismal font and, thereby, serve as godparent.'

---

1. A Grammar of Old French: Tendencies versus Rules

No attempt was made to compose a grammar of French until well into the Renaissance, and even then the earliest grammars treated French as a version of Latin, attempting at first to relate its morphological and syntactical systems to those of the classical language. Since there were no written grammatical "rules" for Old French, each writer was theoretically free to manipulate the lexicon as he or she saw fit. In practice, of course, this was not the case, because beyond certain (albeit unexpressed) limits comprehensibility was prejudiced.

Thus, in spite of the great dialectal diversity outlined in the Introduction, there is a remarkable conformity in Old French syntax. Even the morphological traits that distinguish one dialect from another do not compromise the two-case system or the verb conjugations. It is only in phonology that the dialectal distinctions are critical. Consequently, once one has mastered those phonetic traits that distinguish one dialect from another, it is relatively easy to shift from a text in, say, Francien to one in Picard, Anglo-Norman, or even Lotharingian.

In a language as diverse as Old French, with no written grammatical rules, however, some writers inevitably invented constructions that were not typical of the grammar as a whole. All that we can hope to do here is to define tendencies that reflect the most frequently employed syntactical and morphological patterns and to recognize all the while that these tendencies were not universal.

Within the work of a single writer, within a single text, and sometimes even from one line to the next, tendencies vary. Even a trait that we have already identified as characteristic of Old French—the presence of the two-case system—was sometimes obviated, as in these lines in "Fresne":

> Riche homme furent et mananz
> Et chevaliers preuz et vaillanz. (1:5–6)
> Rich men (they) were and powerful
> And knights bold and brave.

In the first line, *Riche homme* (NP) is correctly employed as a predicate nominative of the verb "to be" (*furent*, preterite), yet in the second line *chevaliers* and the accompanying adjectives, including *mananz* in the first line, with precisely the same function, are incorrectly given oblique plural forms (see 5.15). Since these incorrect forms are not confirmed by the meter or rhyme, however, they must be attributed to the scribe of ms. 1104 rather than to Marie.

2.   Syntax: Basic Observations

Two basic tendencies or rules govern Old French syntax. First, the verb is the principal element or "heart" of the sentence, and all other elements are secondary to it. Second, an unstressed or weak particle (with the exception of articles) cannot begin a sentence. What readers of modern English or French consider to be "normal" word order—subject/verb/complement (S/V/C)—is not always the practice in Old French.

2.1. Word order: the place of the verb. Word order in Old French is flexible, with other sentence elements (subject, complements) revolving around the predominant verb. The centrality of the verb is stressed in the most common type of independent sentence in Old French, that with a medial verb. Sentences with medial verbs are of two types:

S/V/C	Ses	sires est	liez	et	joianz (1:12)
	Her husband (lord)	is	happy	and	joyful
C/V/S	En Bretaigne jadis manoient / Dui chevalier (1:3–4)
	In Britain formerly lived / Two knights
	Two knights once lived in Britain

The predominance of the verb is also underscored in verb-initial sentences. This is the normal order for questions and interpolations:

> "Dame," fet il (2:45)
> "Milady," said he

This order is also found in declarative sentences when the complement is unstressed:

> Voit le Guillelmes (8, 251)
> Sees it William
> William sees it

The order S/C/V is the usual order for subordinate clauses:

> La fame au chevalier s'en rist,
> Qui joste lui au mengier sist (2:25–26)
> The wife of the knight smiled
> Who beside him at meal sat
> The knight's wife, who was seated beside him at table, smiled

> La gent qui en la meson erent (2:49)
> The people who in the house were
> Those who were in the house

> Ne nos ne l'aviens veü,
> Que fame deus enfanz eüst (3:82–83)
> Nor we not it have seen,
> That (a) woman two children would have
> Nor have we ever seen that a woman would bear two children

In principal clauses it is the normal order when the complement is a pronoun, but it can also occur when the complement is a noun. If the verb is in a compound tense, the complement is generally placed between the auxiliary and the past participle:

> E Huon ad l'espee treite (7, 39)
> And Hugh drew his sword.

The final two word-order mutations, V/C/S and C/S/V, are relatively rare in Old French.

2.2. Postpositioning or "inversion." A corollary of the basic tendency just stated—that the verb is the central element of the sentence—is the observation that the verb group is preceded by only one of the noun groups (subject, direct or indirect object, adverb, circumstantial complement, attribute). Rarely will this be the subject pronoun. All other groups will follow the verb.

Two frequent word orders in principal sentences involve postpositioning the subject: C/V/S and V/S/C. Any type of complement placed initially causes inversion, but by far the most common are direct objects and the various adverbial complements:

DIRECT OBJECTS:

> L'un   li   trametra   a lever (1:17)
> (The) one to him will send (he) to raise up
>   (over the baptismal font)
> He will send him one to be his godson
>
> Sa preude fame enhaï (il) (2:61)
> His good wife hated   (he)
> He hated his good wife

(For the regular omission of the postpositioned subject pronoun, see 7.25.)

MOST ADVERBS AND ADVERBIAL PHRASES:

> "Si   m'   aït   Dieus" (2:31)
> So   to me   may help   God
> "So help me God"
>
> Ore est sa voisine vengiee. (3:68)
> Now is her neighbor avenged.

Conjunctions, as well as a limited number of adverbs (*car* 'for, because'; *neporquant, neporec* 'nevertheless'; *onques* 'ever, never'; *certes* 'indeed'; *sanz faille* 'surely'), do not generally require postpositioning of the subject. Likewise, there is no inversion in subordinate clauses after conjunctions and relative pronouns:

> Car ele ert fainte et orgueilleuse (2:27)
> For she was deceitful and proud

"Certes, vus le savrez!" (18:18)
"Indeed you will know it!"

Que sa fame ot deus filz eüz (1:15)
That his wife had two sons had
That his wife had had two sons

2.3. Unstressed elements. Unstressed elements, generally the direct and indirect object pronouns (see 7.24.2), are part of the verb group, and their presence before the verb proper does not violate the principle that only one noun group precedes the verb group:

"Si m' aït Dieus" (2:31)
So to me may help God
"So help me God"

L'un li trametra a lever (1:17)
(The) one to him will send (he) to raise up
He will send him one to be his godson

It is, indeed, to avoid the presence of unstressed elements at the beginning of the sentence that word orders such as that in line 2:31 are so common in Old French. For special forms used in postpositioning, see 7.24.3.

3. Articles: Forms

Articles are unstressed elements in the noun group. There are two articles in Old French, the definite article and the indefinite article. They may be masculine or feminine, singular or plural, nominative or oblique.

THE DEFINITE ARTICLE			THE INDEFINITE ARTICLE		
	Masculine	*Feminine*		*Masculine*	*Feminine*
NS	li	la	NS	uns	une
OS	le	la	OS	un	une
NP	li	les	NP	un	unes
OP	les	les	OP	uns	unes

Articles agree in gender, number, and case with the nouns they determine.

3.1 Article elision. Being unstressed, the definite articles frequently became so unemphatic that they were pronounced as part of the word that preceded or followed. When the following noun begins with a vowel or non-Germanic (nonaspirate) *h*, the oblique singular forms of the definite articles, both masculine and feminine, generally combine with it by elision:

> le un : l'un (1:17)
> le enfant : l'enfant (1:18)
> la abaesse : l'abaesse (5:154)

The feminine nominative singular form *la* elides, but the masculine nominative singular *li* does not:

> la aventure : l'aventure (14:496)
> li arcevesques : li arcevesques (11:369)

(In cases of apparent elision in the nominative singular, e.g., *l'arcevesques* (16:16), one is probably confronting a substitution of *le* for *li* due to loss of the declension system. See 3.8 and 4.11.)

The plural definite articles never elide:

> li enragié (16:14)
> li alquant (17:21)
> les huis (6:183)
> les armes (20:24a)

3.2. Article enclisis. When the following noun begins with a consonant, the unstressed definite article frequently combines with the preceding prepositions *a*, *de*, and *en* by a process known as **enclisis.**

Enclisis of masculine singular *le*:

> a le : al, au (16:11; 1:10)
> de le : del, dou, du (1:1; 8:278)
> en le : el, ou, on, eu, u (4:130)

Enclisis of the masculine and feminine plural article *les*:

> a les : as, aus (13:461)
> de les : des (1:9)
> en les : es (11:383)

Note that the feminine definite article *la* does not combine by enclisis:

> a la damoisele (8:282)
> de la meschine (11:373)
> en la coudre (10:347)

For a more complete listing of Old French enclitic forms, see 13.51.

Phonology 1

In studying the phonological development from Latin to Old French, we must consider three important series of changes: those of the late Latin period (until the end of the fifth century), those of the Gallo-Roman period (from the late fifth century to the appearance of the first text in Old French, the *Strasbourg Oaths* of 842), and from the mid-ninth century to the early twelfth century. During each of these periods the changes occurred gradually and imperceptibly to contemporaries; only when presented in summary form do they appear significant and far-reaching. The changes that took place in the first period happened throughout the Roman Empire, and most of them are therefore common to all the Romance languages. It was during the second and third periods that the French language truly began taking shape. Political instability, social and economic deprivations, foreign invasions, and poor local communications fostered rapid linguistic development until the mid-twelfth century, when, under the comparative tranquillity of Capetian rule, the language became relatively stable. Phonetic changes were fewer and less frequent over a period of some two hundred years—the period of Old French.

This and the following phonology section present the principal sounds of Latin, Vulgar Latin, and Old French and the notations to be employed. Phonology Sections 3 through 5 cover the most significant linguistic changes of the Vulgar Latin period, and Phonology Sections 6 through 10 summarize the important changes in the French vowel system that took place during the Gallo-Roman and early Old French periods, when the language we know as Old French was effectively forged. Phonology Sections 11 through 15 examine the development of consonants. The final eight phonology sections treat Old French dialects, with special emphasis on Anglo-Norman (16–19) and Picard (20–23).

Rules of phonology, or for that matter of anything else in Old French, are descriptive rather than prescriptive. There are always numerous exceptions to the "rule" that reveal new principles and tendencies to specify and explain. Our presentation of the phonological development from Latin to Old French is deliberately simplified for the sake of clarity and to emphasize those aspects that help to explain the grammatical evolution of the language. For a much more detailed account, the interested student is encouraged to consult M. K. Pope, *From Latin to Modern French with Especial Consideration of Anglo-Norman*, and E. and J. Bourciez, *Phonétique française: Etude historique*.

Since we lack access to native speakers of Old French, we cannot hope to acquire a perfect understanding of its pronunciation. Moreover, in the course of several centuries and over widely diversified regions, pronunciation tended to vary. This variance, indeed, accounts for most of the dialect distinctions outlined in the Introduction. Nevertheless, comparative Romance phonology, our knowledge of the sounds of Latin and modern French, rhyme studies, and the like can help us to approximate the spoken sounds of Old French.

Before examining in more detail the consonant and vowel systems of Old French, the student should be aware of a few basic guides to pronunciation. All letters that were written represented phonemes, with the following exceptions:

(a)   final -*nt* of the third person plural verbal ending -*ent* (e.g., *furent*, 1:7; *estoient*, 1:4) was not pronounced after the late thirteenth century.

(b)   *s* interior before consonants other than *p*, *t*, *c* *(=k)* (thus, *s* was pronounced in *chascuns* and *espousee*, 1:8, but not in *Fresne* or *esligier*).

(c)   *h* in words of Latin origin (*homme*, *heritage*). Note that in words of Germanic origin the initial *h* was pronounced (*hauberc*, *haitiez*).

(d)   "etymological letters" added by learned scribes, generally in imitation of Latin spellings (*t* in *et*, *p* in *sept*, *c* in *dict*), were not pronounced.

There was word stress (as in modern English) rather than only sentence stress (characteristic of modern French).

chapter 2

Reading and Textual Analysis, Selection 1b

"Le Fresne" is found in a collection of moderate-length narrative poems by Marie de France known as the *Lais*. The word *lai* is used in Old French with several quite different meanings. The most common are the following:

(a) a short narrative poem in octosyllabic rhymed couplets of the twelfth or early thirteenth century treating legendary material ostensibly of Celtic origin;

(b) a lyric poem characterized in the twelfth century by a large number of strophes, then popularized in the Middle French period as a fixed-form poem of twelve strophes, of which only the first and last might have the same form;

(c) a "legacy poem" in which the poet distributes ironic gifts to his friends, acquaintances, and enemies (usually in reference to François Villon's *Le Lais*, 1456).

The etymon for (a) and (b) is thought to be Old Irish LAID 'a song.'

Although their origins are obscure and the subject of scholarly debate, the *lais* of type (a), which alone interest us here, likely began as brief narrative or lyric poems with Celtic themes, carried about by Breton or other Celtic bards and translated into and performed in the language of their audiences, usually French. The word soon came to refer to any narrative poem whose subject matter was ostensibly Celtic. Marie de France may have been the first non-Celt to compose poems in this manner, if we can accept what she tells us in the general prologue to her collection: "I thought of writing some good story, translating it from Latin into French; but this would have been of little value to me: so many others have done this! I thought about the *lais* that I had heard. . . . I had heard many of them and did not wish to forget or neglect them. I put them in rhyme and made poems (*ditié*); often have I performed them to the accompaniment of a *vielle*" (Prologue, lines 28–33, 39–42).

Although she may well have originally heard all the *lais* she composed performed by Celtic bards, several of them, including "Le Fresne," do not have specifically Celtic themes.

2:25	La fame au chevalier s'en rist,
2:26	Qui joste lui au mengier sist,
2:27	Car ele ert fainte et orgueilleuse
2:28	Et mesdisante et envïeuse.
2:29	Ele parla molt folement
2:30	Et dit, oiant toute la gent:
2:31	"Si m'aït Dieus, molt me merveil
2:32	Ou cil preudons prist cest conseil,
2:33	Qui a mandé a mon seignor
2:34	Sa honte et sa grant desonor,
2:35	Que sa fame a eüz deus fiz:
2:36	Et il et elle en sont honniz.
2:37	Nos savon bien qu'il i afiert:
2:38	C'onques ne fu ne ja nen iert
2:39	Ne n'avendra cele aventure
2:40	Qu'a une seule porteüre
2:41	Une fame deus enfanz ait,
2:42	Se dui homes ne li ont fait."
2:43	Ses sires l'avoit regardee;
2:44	Molt durement l'avoit blasmee:
2:45	"Dame," fet il, "lessiez ester!
2:46	Ne devez mie issi parler!
2:47	Veritez est que ceste dame
2:48	A molt esté de bone fame."
2:49	La gent qui en la meson erent
2:50	Cele parole raconterent;
2:51	Assez fu dite et conneüe,
2:52	Par toute Bretaingne seüe;
2:53	Molt en fu la dame haïe,
2:54	Puis en dut estre maubaillie.
2:55	Totes les fames qui l'oïrent,
2:56	Povres et riches, l'enhaïrent.
2:57	Cil qui le mesage ot porté
2:58	A son seignor a tout conté.

2:59   Quant il l'oï dire et retrere,
2:60   Dolenz en fu, ne sot que fere;
2:61   Sa preude fame enhaï
2:62   Et durement la mescreï;
2:63   Et molt la tenoit en destroit,
2:64   San ce qu'ele nu deservoit.

2:33   *qui*: antecedent is *preudons*, not *conseil*.
2:37   *qu'il*: unexpressed antecedent in OF; mod. F *ce qu'il*.
2:42   *homes*: NP, *-s* by analogy with OP.
2:43   *sires*: NS, *-s* by analogy with Class II nouns.
2:49   *la gent . . . erent*: the sg. noun *gent* is often perceived in a collective sense as a plural and therefore takes a plural verb (see 2.5.2).
2:54   *dut estre*: for the imminent aspect of *devoir*, see 21.92.
2:62   *durement*: adverb of degree, see 19.82.

---

4. Article Usage

Articles in Old French indicate the degree of generality or particularity of the nouns they determine. There are two series of articles: indefinite and definite. Note that articles are regularly omitted when the noun is not particularized.

4.1. Indefinite articles. The indefinite article (in spite of its name) applies to a distinct individual or object; it is used in the singular to introduce and particularize a noun not previously mentioned:

> d'*une* contree (1:7)
> from a (certain) land (Here = "from the same land")
> la dame avoit *une* meschine (4:99)
> the lady had a serving-girl (as yet unmentioned)
> *un* bon cheval (1:24)
> a (particular) good horse

As the table in 1.3 indicates, the indefinite article has a plural. The form is rare in Old French, but it is used with a collective value to refer to pairs or series:

unes chauces 'a pair of breeches'
uns sollers 'a pair of shoes'

uns ganz 'a pair of gloves'
unes noveles 'tidings, news'
unes letres 'a letter'—understood as the message composed of the individual letters
uns si tres grans souspirs (5, 147) 'several very deep sighs one after another'

or for plurals that have no singular:

unes forces 'a pair of scissors'

4.2. Definite articles. Definite articles give a slight stress to nouns. They distinguish something that has already been introduced into the discourse:

La dame qui si mesparla (3:65)
The lady who thus had spoken ill (and who was heavily implicated in the discourse throughout reading selection 1a).

They are also used to indicate those objects and beings whose presence necessarily follows from the context:

Atant es vos *le* mesagier! (1:20)
Behold the messenger (arrives)!

The messenger has not specifically been introduced, but his presence is implied in the verb *mandot* in line 1:14. Similarly, in line 1:21, *le dois* has not been specifically introduced, but its presence is inferred from the context: "a noble meal." Thus, when an author refers to her (or his) source, this implied text will be referred to as

le conte que je sai. (1:2)
the tale that I know.

True to its origin (from the Latin demonstrative ILLE, see Phonology 7), the Old French article could function as a demonstrative when followed by a noun used absolutely to denote possession:

Criant l'enseinne al rei baron,
La Loowis, le fiz Charlun.   (7, 80–81)
Shouting the battle cry of the baron king,
That of Louis, Charlemagne's son.

Aimi! sire, ostés vo cheval!
A poi que il ne m'a blechie.
Li Robins ne regiete mie
Quant je vois aprés se karue.   (22, 73–76)

Heavens! Sir, remove your horse!
He's almost injured me.
Robin's (horse) doesn't kick
When I follow his plough.

4.3. Omission of articles. When a noun is used in an indeterminate or general sense or when there is no need to particularize it, the article may be omitted. Thus, the indefinite article is omitted in the following instances, in which the nouns refer to women and men in general, not to a woman or a man in particular:

> ... onques ne fu ... / ... Que fame deus enfanz eüst (3:81–83)
> ... never was it ... / ... That (a) woman would bear two children

> D'enfant ocirre n'est pas gas. (4:98)
> To kill (a) child is no joke.

Likewise, when a noun is qualified by words such as *tel* 'such,' *autre* 'other, another,' or *meïsmes* 'same, self,' the indefinite article is omitted:

> De tel homme puet en parler. (3:89)
> Of such (a) man can one speak.

Plural nouns, which by virtue of their plurality tend to be general, are often devoid of articles:

> voisin estoient (1:4)
> they were neighbors

> Riche homme furent et mananz
> Et chevaliers preuz et vaillanz. (1:5–6)
> They were powerful and well-to-do men
> And bold and brave knights.

Proper names, being highly particularized by nature, do not need articles to determine them further, but they may have them:

> le Fresne (7:229)   la Coudre (15:524)
> al Satan (18:1)   du Fresne (1:1)

Similarly, nouns used in direct address, which at that moment function as proper nouns, need no article:

> "Dame," fet il. (2:45)
> "Milady," said he.

Abstract nouns, which evoke general concepts, are not subject to particularization:

> Jamés honor ne pris n'avrai. (3:74)
> Never shall I have esteem or honor.

Certain syntactical situations—conditionals, interrogatives, and negatives—are indeterminate and easily omit articles.

In accord with the distinctions to be outlined in 6.18, nouns modified
by other nominal determiners cannot take articles:

> ceste parole (3:78) (demonstrative adjective)
> sa voisine (3:68) (weak possessive)
> de tanz enfanz (1:16) (quantitative determiner)

5. Old French Nouns

Old French nouns are distinguished by gender, number, and case. They
may be either masculine or feminine, singular or plural, nominative or
oblique.

5.1. Gender. For nouns referring to animate beings, gender corresponds naturally to the sex of the being: for example, *li chevaliers* (m.) 'the
knight'; *la fame* (f.) 'the wife, woman'; *li chevaus* (m.) 'the horse'; *la vache* (f.)
'the cow.' The feminine is often "marked" by a final *-e*, which in Old
French was pronounced as well as written:

MASCULINE	FEMININE
li voisins, le voisin 'neighbor'	la voisine
li amis, l'ami 'friend'	l'amie
li filz, le filz (fiz) 'son'	la fille 'daughter'
li meschins, le meschin 'youth'	la meschine 'young woman'
li damoisiaus, le damoisel 'young man'	la damoiselle 'young lady'

The feminine may also be distinguished by the suffix *-esse*—*li abes, l'abbé*
'the abbot'/*l'abaesse* 'the abbess'; *li cuens, le conte* 'the count'/*la contesse* 'the
countess'—or by some other distinguishing suffix—*li emperere, l'empereor*
'the emperor'/*l'empereriz* 'the empress.'

For inanimate objects and words referring to abstract concepts, the
gender is determined; it does not correspond to any readily recognizable
criteria. Words thus determined are said to have **grammatical gender**, as
opposed to **natural gender**, discussed above. Such nouns are masculine or
feminine because for the most part they were so already in Classical or
Vulgar Latin, out of which Old French developed:

MASCULINE   **FEMININE**

le lai 'the lay'   la contree 'the country, land'
le fresne 'the ash tree'   la foiz 'the time, occasion, instance'
le nom 'the name'   la joie 'the joy'

5.2. Number. Most nouns can be either singular or plural. Plural is generally marked for the masculine by a combination of the article and the ending and for the feminine by the article and -*s*:

SINGULAR   **PLURAL**

le conte 'the account, story'   les contes
le cheval 'the horse'   les chevaus
la fame 'the woman'   les fames
li cuens 'the count'   li conte
l'enfant 'the child'   les enfanz

Certain nouns occur primarily in plural forms although they have a singular meaning; their plurality is internal, residing in the nature of the notion expressed:

les braies 'pants'
les noces 'wedding'
les forces 'scissors'
les mors 'mores, manners'
les guernons 'moustache'

Most of these words are also attested in the singular: *braie, noce, guernon.*
Collective nouns, which are morphologically singular, frequently take plural verbs:

> La gent qui en la meson erent (2:49)
> The people (sg.) who in the house were (pl.)
> The people who were in the house
>
> par ou la gent venoient (6:179)
> through which the people (sg.) came (pl.)

The converse is also common in Old French: multiple subjects are often coordinated with a singular verb if the subject closest to the verb is in the singular:

> li sire i vint et ses amis (11:368)
> The lord and his friends came there

> Li cris et le noise ala par tote le terre (21:35a)
> The hue and cry went throughout the land

It is even possible to coordinate one noun with both a singular verb and a plural verb:

> Si vous vueil proier, com mon pere,
>   Qu'el soit leüe,
> Qu'autre *gent* n'en *soit deceüe*
> Qui n'*ont* encore *aperceüe*
>   Tel tricherie. (21, 244–48)
> And I wish to beg you, as my father,
>   That it be read,
> So that others might not be deceived
> Who have not yet noticed
>   Such trickery.

5.3. Case. There are two cases in Old French: nominative and oblique. The nominative indicates the subject of the clause (and any words qualifying or in apposition to this subject) or the person addressed; the oblique is used in all other instances. The masculine nominative is marked in the determining article by an -*i* in both the singular and plural:

NOMINATIVES

li sire (1:23) 'the husband, the lord' (m. sg.)
li hom (1:19) 'the man' (m. sg.)
Dieus (2:31) 'God' (m. sg.)
dui chevalier (1:4) 'two knights' (m. pl.)
voisin (1:4) 'neighbors' (m. pl., in apposition to the unexpressed subject pronoun *il*)
sa fame (1:15) 'his wife, woman' (f. sg.)
Dame (2:45) 'My Lady' (f. sg.; person addressed)

OBLIQUES

le conte (1:2) 'the account' (m. sg., obj. of the prep. *selonc*)
deus enfanz (1:11) 'two children' (m. pl., dir. obj.)
fame (1:8) 'wife' (f. sg., dir. obj.)
la joie (1:13) 'the joy' (f. sg., obj. of prep.)
deus filles (3:70) 'two daughters' (f. pl., dir. obj.)

Phonology 2

Although the Old French speaker of the twelfth century produced a great number of sounds that had not been present in Latin, the scribes continued to use Latin symbols instead of inventing new symbols for the new sounds. As a result, some letters might represent different sounds in Old French than they had in Latin (e.g., *c, g*), some letters were combined to approximate the new sounds (e.g., the diphthongs, triphthongs, and digraphs), some letters were modified (*w, v, j*), and many letters stood for more than one sound (*c, g, x, e, o*).

Therefore, before studying the phonological history of Old French, one should understand its orthographic system—that is, the values assigned to the letters, both individually and in combination. In presenting Old French phonology, we use the International Phonetic Alphabet, which should be familiar to most users of this grammar.

Representation of consonants in Latin and Old French

Latin consonants were represented by the following nineteen signs: *b, c, d, f, g, h, i, k, l, m, n, p, q, r, s, t, u, x, z.* Of these, the semivowel, semiconsonant *i* is transcribed *j* in many Old French texts when it functions as a true consonant. The semivowel, semiconsonant *u* (pronounced /w/ in the classical period) was replaced by *v* in Old French when it functioned as a true consonant. *k*, an equivalent of *c*, was rare in both Latin and Old French. All the other consonants carried over into Old French, but they did not always represent the same sound they had in Latin.

Many of these consonants represent approximately the same sounds in Old French as in Latin or modern English: *b, d, f, k, l, m, n, p, t, v.*

The following consonants require brief special consideration: *c, g, h, j, q, r, s, x, z.*

c, which in all positions in Latin represented the velar plosive /k/ (English *cat*), came to represent a dental affricate /ts/ (English *its*) preceding *e* and *i* in Old French, before finally coming to represent the dental fricative /s/ by the end of the Old French period. In Old French *c* retained the phonemic value /k/ before *a, o, u*.

Similarly, the Latin velar /g/ (English *go*) became /dʒ/ (English *judge*) preceding *e* and *i* in Old French, before becoming the palatal fricative /ʒ/ (French *je*). Followed by *a, o, u* it remained /g/.

Latin *h* was silent and was generally lost in Vulgar Latin. Although it was sometimes restored in spelling, it was not pronounced in Old French:

ome or *home* 'man.' Germanic *h*, introduced in the early Old French period, was aspirate in Old French.

j before any vowel was the equivalent of *g* before *e* or *i* (i.e., /dʒ/).

qu was pronounced /kw/ in Latin but became a digraph for /k/ in Old French (see below).

r was slightly trilled in Old French, somewhat as in Spanish today, rather than pronounced like the /ʁ/ of modern French or the retroflex /r/ of American English.

s between vowels represents /z/ (English *rose*).

The dental fricative /s/ was notated *ss* or *c* (rarely *x*).

x in Latin represented the combination /k+s/; it may represent the same sound in Old French, but when final it was frequently a scribal notation for -*us*. Thus, *Kex* is pronounced /keus/, never /kɛks/.

z was pronounced /ts/ when final and /dz/ before a vowel. Like the other affricates, /ts/ (spelled *c*), and /dʒ/ (spelled *g* or *j*), it lost its dental element in the course of the thirteenth century and became a pure fricative (/z/before a vowel, /s/ when final).

Consonant digraphs in Old French

A combination of two or more letters that represents a single phoneme is called a digraph. The following consonant digraphs are conventional in Old French:

ch, pronounced /tʃ/ (English *church*, *chief*) in the twelfth century, then /ʃ/ (French *chemise*, *champagne*) in the thirteenth;
gn (or *ng* when final), pronounced /ɲ/ (English *canyon*);
ill (or *il* when final), pronounced /λ/ (Italian *figlio*);
gu used before *e* or *i* to represent /g/;
ss used to represent /s/ between vowels;
qu used for /k/ in a number of words.

Only the first three represent new sounds.

The following table represents Old French consonant phonemes, listed horizontally according to manner of production and vertically by point of articulation:

	velars	palatals	prepalatals	dentals	labiodentals	bilabials
plosives	k			t		p
	g			d		b
affricates			č	ts		
			ǰ	dz		
fricatives	h		ʃ	s	f	w
			ʒ	z	v	
vibrants		λ	r	l		
nasals		ɲ		n		m

Within groups, the **unvoiced consonants** (produced without vibration of the vocal cords) are placed above the **voiced**.

chapter 3

Reading and Textual Analysis, Selection 2

Like many of Marie's twelve *Lais*, "Le Fresne" is set *en Bretaigne* 'in Brittany,' which Marie also refers to as *Bretaigne la Menur* 'Minor' or 'Small Britain' to contrast with *Bretaigne la Majur* 'Great Britain.' Breton cities are mentioned prominently in several *lais*: Nantes in "Chaitivel," Saint-Malo in "Laustic," and Dol-de-Bretagne in "Fresne." The action of "Lanval" occurs in England proper, which Marie refers to as *la tere de Logre* (the name of Arthur's mythical kingdom), whereas "Yonec" and "Milun" are set in *Suhtwales* 'South Wales.' The lay of the "Deus Amanz" 'Two Lovers' takes place on a hillside in Normandy, not far from present-day Rouen.

This second section of "Le Fresne" illustrates the proverb of lines 87–88: "He who slanders and lies about another, cannot see beyond the nose on his face."

3:65	La dame qui si mesparla
3:66	En l'an meïsmes enceinta.
3:67	De deus enfanz est enceintiee;
3:68	Ore est sa voisine vengiee.
3:69	Desqu'a son terme les porta;
3:70	Deus filles ot. Molt li pesa,
3:71	Molt durement en fu dolente;
3:72	A soi meïsmes se demente:
3:73	"Lasse," fet ele, "que ferai?

3:74   Jamés honor ne pris n'avrai.
3:75   Honie sui, c'est veritez.
3:76   Mes sire et toz mes parentez
3:77   Certes jamés ne m'ameront
3:78   Des que ceste parole orront,
3:79   Car je meïsmes me jujai;
3:80   De totes fames mesparlai.
3:81   Dont ne di ge c'onques ne fu,
3:82   Ne nos ne l'avïens veü,
3:83   Que fame deus enfanz eüst,
3:84   Se deus hommes ne conneüst?
3:85   Or en ai deus; ce m'est avis,
3:86   Sor moi en est torné li pis.
3:87   Qui sor autrui mesdit et ment
3:88   Ne set mie qu'a l'ueil li pent;
3:89   De tel homme puet en parler,
3:90   Qui mieus de lui fet a löer.
3:91   Por moi desfendre de honnir
3:92   L'un des enfanz m'estuet murdrir.
3:93   Mieus le voil vers Dieu amender
3:94   Que moi honnir ne vergonder."

3:66   *meïsmes*: note the nonorganic adverbial -*s* (see 14.56.2).
3:81   *dont/donc* (see 20.87.4).
3:87–88 Proverbial expression, equivalent to English "He cannot see beyond the end of his nose."

---

6. Noun Declensions

The two-case noun declension system is one of the most characteristic traits of Old French. In written texts, both literary and official, it is well maintained until the fourteenth century in the northern, eastern, and central dialects. In the western dialects, it is already in jeopardy by the late twelfth century. It is in ill repair in the *Song of Roland*, an Anglo-Norman text of the early twelfth century, whereas in the romances of Chrétien de Troyes, from Champagne in the third quarter of that same century, it is very well preserved. The conservative tendencies of Old French scribes no doubt preserved the declension system longer in the written language than in the spoken idiom. Yet even within a single dialect, individual texts and authors vary widely in their respect for the declension system.

The classification system used here represents general characteristics from a historical perspective; the actual morphosyntactic state of a particular work can only be derived from a detailed descriptive grammar of that work.

6.1. Noun inflection: feminine nouns, Class I. Feminine Class I nouns do not have a true declension since there is no morphological distinction between the nominative and oblique cases in the singular or plural. The plural is distinguished from the singular by having a final -s. To maintain the parallel with other noun classes, however, the following "declension" is given:

NS   la fame
OS   la fame
NP   les fames
OP   les fames

Most feminine nouns ending in unstressed -e are of this class.

6.2. Noun inflection: masculine nouns, Class II. Masculine nouns of this class are distinguished by having final -s (or, for orthographic reasons, -z) in the nominative singular and oblique plural, contrasting with no ending in the oblique singular and nominative plural:

NS   li voisins   li sergenz   li pailes
OS   le voisin   le sergent   le paile
NP   li voisin   li sergent   li paile
OP   les voisins   les sergenz   les pailes

Most masculine nouns are of this class, as are all infinitives used as nouns:

NS   li mengiers
OS   le mengier
NP   li mengier
OP   les mengiers

7. Noun Inflection: Class Ia and IIa Nouns

Feminine nouns with so-called masculine endings (that is, without the characteristic feminine -*e*) and masculine nouns ending in unstressed -*e* were frequently declined as hybrids. In the nominative singular, the feminine nouns often have the masculine nominative singular -*s* (or -*z*), whereas the masculine nouns sometimes lack this ending:

7.1. Class Ia (feminine hybrids).

NS   la riens
OS   la rien
NP   les riens
OP   les riens

The following are the most common nouns of this class; they do not have a final mute ("feminine") -*e*:

*amor 'love'   *mer 'sea'
*beauté 'beauty'   *merci 'mercy'
char(n) 'flesh'   *mort 'death'
cité 'city'   *nef 'ship'
clamor 'clamor'   noif 'snow'
color 'color'   *nuit 'night'
*cort 'court'   ost 'army'
crestienté 'Christianity'   *peor 'fear'
dolor 'sorrow'   *raison 'speech'
foi 'faith'   *rien 'thing, person'
*fin 'end'   saison 'season'
flor 'flower'   *tor 'tower'
*gent 'people'   valor 'worth'
*(h)onor 'honor'   verdor 'greenness, verdure'
loi 'religion'   *vertu 'strength, virtue'
*main 'hand'   virginité 'virginity'
*maison 'house'   *volonté 'will, desire'

*In this list and following lists, words preceded by asterisks are in the texts reproduced in this volume. Words are given in the oblique singular form and in their most frequently encountered spelling. However, the student should bear in mind at all times that variation in spelling is the rule rather than the exception in Old French.

7.2. Class IIa (masculine hybrids).

NS   li pere
OS   le pere
NP   li pere
OP   les peres

The following are the most common nouns of this class; most have a final unstressed -*e*:

*archevesque 'archbishop'   *maistre 'master'
compere 'friend, crony'   parastre 'stepfather'
ermite 'hermit, recluse'   *pere 'father'
eschipre 'sailor'   prince 'prince'
frere 'brother'   vavasor 'vavasor'
*gendre 'son-in-law'   ventre 'belly, abdomen'
livre 'book'   *vespre 'evening'

8. Breakdown of the Declension System

Already in the twelfth century, and regularly by the thirteenth century, analogy with the far more important Class I and Class II nouns began to break down Classes Ia and IIa. The feminine nouns of Class Ia tended to eliminate the morphological opposition distinguishing the two singular cases, generally by eliminating the -*s* from the feminine nominative:

NS   la cité
OS   la cité
NP   les citez
OP   les citez

but also, occasionally, by extending the -*s* to the oblique:

NS   la beautés
OS   la beautés
NP   les beautés
OP   les beautés

In "Le Fresne," for example, we find:

> La gent (NS, Class Ia) qui en la meson erent
> Cele parole raconterent.   (2:49–50)
> The people who in the house were
> This speech recounted.
> Those who were in the house repeated what he had said.

Masculine nouns of Class IIa, however, tended to acquire the morphological opposition -s/- characteristic of masculine singular nouns of Class II:

NS   li livres
OS   le livre
NP   li livre
OP   les livres

9. Auxiliary Verbs: *Avoir* and *Estre*.

The two verbs of greatest frequency in any Old French text are *avoir* 'to have' and *estre* 'to be.' In addition to their usual meanings (the third singular present occurs in lines 3:75, 3:85; the imperfect indicative in 4:99–100; the preterite in 3:71), they are combined with the past participles of all other verbs to form compound tenses (see, e.g., 3:67, 3:86, 4:124, 4:132). Compound tenses will be discussed in detail in 7.28.

The following table presents a complete paradigm of these verbs in the simple tenses, using the forms in which they most frequently occur. In some early texts and in the Anglo-Norman dialect, the diphthong -oi- (in the infinitive of *avoir*, the present subjunctive and imperative of *estre*, and the conditional and imperfect indicative of both verbs) was written -ei-.

AVOIR   ESTRE

PRESENT INDICATIVE

sg. 1 ai   sui
    2 as   es, iés
    3 a   est
pl. 1 avons   somes, esmes
    2 avez   estes
    3 ont   sont

PRESENT SUBJUNCTIVE

sg.	1 aie	soie
	2 aies	soies
	3 ait, aie	soit
pl.	1 aiiens, aions	soiiens, soions
	2 aiiez, aiez	soiiez, soiez
	3 aient	soient

IMPERFECT INDICATIVE

		type I	*type II*
sg.	1 avoie	iere, ere	estoie
	2 avoies	ieres, eres	estoies
	3 avoit	iere, ere	estoit
		iert, ert	
pl.	1 aviiens, avïons	eriiens, erïons	estiiens, estïons
	2 aviiez, avïez	eriiez, erïez	estiiez, estïez
	3 avoient	ierent, erent	estoient

IMPERFECT SUBJUNCTIVE

sg.	1 eüsse	fusse
	2 eüsses	fusses
	3 eüst	fust
pl.	1 eüssiens, eüssons	fussiens, fussons
	2 eüssiez, eüssez	fussiez, fussez
	3 eüssent	fussent

PRETERITE

sg.	1 oi	fui
	2 eüs, oüs	fus
	3 ot, out	fu
pl.	1 eümes, oümes	fumes
	2 eüstes, oüstes	fustes
	3 orent, ourent	furent

AVOIR	ESTRE

IMPERATIVE

sg.	2	aie(s)	soies
pl.	1	aiiens, aions	soiiens, soions
	2	aiiez, aiez	soiiez, soiez

PRESENT PARTICIPLE

aiant   estant

PAST PARTICIPLE

eüz, oüz   esté

FUTURE

		type I	type II	type I	type II	type III
sg.	1	avrai	arai	ier, er	estrai	serai
	2	avras	aras	iers, ers	estras	seras
	3	avra	ara	iert, ert	estra	sera
pl.	1	avrons	arons	iermes, ermes	estrons	serons
	2	avrez	arez	————	estrez	serez
	3	avront	aront	ierent, erent	estront	seront

CONDITIONAL

		type I	type II	type I	type II
sg.	1	avroie	aroie	estroie	seroie
	2	avroies	aroies	estroies	seroies
	3	avroit	aroit	estroit	seroit
pl.	1	avriiens, avrïons	ariiens, arions	estriiens, estrions	seriiens, serïons
	2	avriiez, avrïez	ariiez	estriiez	seriiez, serïez
	3	avroient	aroient	estroient	seroient

Phonology 3

Representation of vowels in Latin and Old French

Latin has five vowels: A, E, I, O, U. Although their **quantity** is seldom indicated in Latin manuscripts, modern editors often mark them either long (‾) or short (˘). Vulgar Latin had the same vowels, but they are now distinguished by editors for **quality** rather than quantity by subscripts to indicate closed pronunciation (.) or open pronunciation ( ). The semi-vowel, semiconsonant *yod* /j/ is notated *j* or *i*; it represents a palatalized fricative corresponding to the initial sound of the English *yacht* or *yes*.

Latin had three diphthongs: AU, AE, OE. Only the first was retained in Vulgar Latin.

Old French monophthongs

Early twelfth-century Old French had thirteen monophthongs, distributed as follows:

	front	central	back
high	/i/ /y/		/u/
mid	/e/ /ø/		/o/ /õ/
	/ɛ/ /ē/	/ə/	
			/ɔ/
low		/a/	/ã/

For the problem of the nasalized vowels, see Phonology 8.

Equivalent pronunciations and orthographic representations are listed in the following table:

PHONETIC SYMBOL	NEAREST MODERN EQUIVALENT	ORTHOGRAPHY
/i/	Engl. *knee*	i, y
/y/	Fr. *mur*	u
/u/	Fr. *tour*	ou, o, u
/e/ *or* /e̞/	Fr. *dé*	é, ai, e
/ø/	Fr. *peu, fleur*	ue, eu, ueu

PHONETIC SYMBOL	NEAREST MODERN EQUIVALENT	ORTHOGRAPHY
/o/ *or* /o̩/	Fr. *mot*	o
/õ/	Fr. *son*, but with *n* sounded	on, om
/ẽ/	Fr. *sain*, but with *n* sounded	en, em
/ɛ/ *or* /ẹ/	Engl. *ten*	e
/ə/	*a* of Engl. *about*	e
/ɔ/ *or* /ọ/	Engl. *port*	o
/ã/	Fr. *an*, but with *n* sounded	an, am
/a/	Engl. *ah*	a

The acute accent is a modern spelling convention employed by editors of Old French texts only over the final syllable of a word, to distinguish tonic from weak *e*. The only other modern orthographic conventions regularly found in Old French texts are ç to represent /s/ and a diaresis over certain vowels to indicate that they are in hiatus rather than part of a diphthong. Thus:

$$\text{peü} = /\text{pə-y}/, \text{ not } /\text{pø}/$$
$$\text{roïne} = /\text{ro-inə}/, \text{ not } /\text{rojnə}/$$

Old French diphthongs

Combinations of two vowel sounds in a single syllable are called diphthongs. Diphthongs are particularly characteristic of Old French, which had as many as sixteen distinct diphthongs and triphthongs in the early twelfth century. Modern standard French has no true diphthongs or triphthongs. The process of leveling that reduced the many Old French diphthongs to the monophthongs of modern French was already under way in the twelfth century; consequently, the assignment of values to individual diphthongs is a difficult task, particularly as the rate of leveling differed markedly from region to region, being generally more rapid in the west (Norman, Anglo-Norman) and much slower in the central and eastern zones (including Picard and Francien).

In the early twelfth century—the period, for example, of the Oxford version of the *Song of Roland* and the Anglo-Norman *Voyage of St. Brendan*—Old French diphthongs were stressed on the first element. These are called **descending diphthongs**: *íe, úe, ái, éi, ói, úi, áĩ, éĩ, áu, éu, íu, óu, éau*, and *íeu*. By the late twelfth century, the stress had shifted to the second element in several diphthongs (and the triphthongs *eau* and *ieu*). These **ascending diphthongs** are *ié, iẽ, oí > oé, oú, eáu*, and *iéu*. By this time, certain early diphthongs had already been completely leveled:

$$ai \ (> \ /e/ \ \text{or} \ /\varepsilon/)$$
$$ue, eu \ (> \ /\text{ø}/)$$

Although *ou* could still represent the ascending diphthong /oú/, it was more usually a spelling convention to represent /u/. Thus, in most Old French texts, *ai, ue, eu,* and *ou* are vowel digraphs but do not represent diphthongs. (See Phonology 10.)

Modern French has retained most of these traditional notations but none of the diphthongs, a fact that creates special problems in the pronunciation of Old French for those familiar with the modern language. In particular, one should note that:

ai was pronounced in early twelfth century Francien as in the English *by* but by the late twelfth century as in French *fait*;

ei was pronounced as in the English *hay*;

oi was pronounced in twelfth century Francien as in the English *boy* and then by the turn of the thirteenth century as in the English *sway*;

au was pronounced throughout the Old French period as in the English *cow*.

Modifications due to flexional *-s*

The only true inflexional ending in Old French is *-s*, which, as we have seen, can be added as a sign of the plural or of many nominative singulars. The addition of this *-s* caused phonological modifications to certain preceding consonants.

    1. The labials *p, b, f, v,* and supported *-m*, as well as the velar stops *c* and *g*, were completely absorbed by the *-s*:

OBL. SG.	NOM. SG.
le drap	li dras
le gab	li gas
la nef	la nés
le verm	li vers
le coc	li cos
le sanc	li sans

2.   Unsupported *m* was only partially assimilated:

le nom   li nons

3.   The dentals *t*, *d*, and supported *-n* combined with *-s* to produce the affricate /ts/, written *-z*:

le sergent   li sergenz
l'an   li anz (< ÁNNUS)
le jor   li jorz (< DǏŬRNUS)
la nuit   la nuiz

4.   The palatals /λ/ and /ɲ/ likewise combined with *-s* to produce /ts/, written *-z*:

le fil   li fiz (< FÍLǏUS 'son')
le poing   li poinz

5.   Palatal *l* (spelled *-il*) preceded by a vowel other than *i* became *-lz*, then *-uz*:

le travail   li travauz
le conseil   li conseuz

6.   Words whose radical ended in *-l* underwent various changes, depending upon the letter preceding the *-l*:

(a)   *-el + s* regularly gave *-eaus* in Francien, but one also frequently encounters the Picard *-iaus*:

le chastel   li chasteaus, li chastiaus
l'ostel   li osteaus, li ostiaus
bel   beaus, biaus

(b)   *-al* and *-ol + s* gave *-aus* and *-ous* respectively:

le cheval   li chevaus
le col   li cous

(c)   *-il + s* gave *-is*:

le fil   li fis (< FÍLUS 'thread')

(d) *-ul* + *s* gave *-us*:

nul   nus

Remarks

1. With most words the final consonant or group is apparent from the oblique singular form. With others, the final consonant was lost around the beginning of the twelfth century in the written forms of the oblique singular, leaving as its only trace the inflected *-z* of the NS:

OBL. SG.	EARLY OLD FRENCH FORM	NOM. SG.
le degré	degret	li degrez
l'an	ann (< ÁNNUM)	li anz
l'escu	escut (< SCŪTUM)	li escuz
nu	nut (< NŪDUM)	nuz

2. Conversely, one frequently encounters etymological letters that disappeared in pronunciation before *-s*:

| deus filz | (1:15) | /fitz/ |
| nuls | (17:26) | /nys/ |

3. In the thirteenth century, and already sporadically by the late twelfth century, the affricate /ts/ was reduced to /s/, and there resulted a general confusion in endings. The scribe of *Aucassin* never employs the final *-z*. Additionally, *-x* was frequently used as an abbreviation for *-us* and came to replace both *-s* and *-z* after *-u*:

bienz	(18:16)
drois	(21:38a)
autex	(22:8a)
biax	(20:3)

chapter 4

Reading and Textual Analysis, Selection 3a

In Reading Selection 3a, a maid-in-waiting suggests to the wife of the second knight that there is a way out of the trap that the lady unwittingly laid for herself with her ill-conceived words: the maid will take one of the twin daughters and place her before the door of a church, where someone will find her and take her in. In addition to extricating the evil-tongued lady from her predicament, Selection 3 also prepares the denouement of the lay: in traditional folktale fashion, the clothes in which the infant is wrapped and the ring that is tied to her arm will permit an identification many years hence.

Meschine (4:99) is frequently translated too simply as "girl" or "servant." Although it does occasionally have these meanings in Old French, it often refers to a young girl of noble birth sent (usually after the age of seven) to be raised and properly educated in the home of a nearby noble, sometimes on an exchange basis. There she learned such skills as sewing, embroidery, weaving, conversation—and even reading—until she reached the marriageable age of thirteen or fourteen.

4:95	Celes qui en la chambre estoient
4:96	La confortoient et disoient
4:97	Qu'eles nu soferroient pas;
4:98	D'enfant ocirre n'est pas gas.
4:99	La dame avoit une meschine,
4:100	Qui molt estoit de grant orinne;

4:101	Lonc tens l'ot gardee et norrie
4:102	Et molt amee et molt chierie.
4:103	Cele oï la dame plorer,
4:104	Durement plaindre et dolouser;
4:105	Angoisseusement li pesa.
4:106	A li vint si la conforta:
4:107	"Dame," fet ele, "ne vaut rien.
4:108	Lessiez cest duel, si ferez bien!
4:109	L'un des enfanz me bailliez ça!
4:110	Je vos en delivrerai ja,
4:111	Si que honnie n'en seroiz,
4:112	Ne que jamés ne la verroiz.
4:113	En un mostier la geterai;
4:114	Tot sain et tot sauf la lerai.
4:115	Aucun preudons la trovera,
4:116	Se Deu plet, qui la norrira."
4:117	La dame oï ce qu'el dit.
4:118	Grant joie en ot, molt li promit:
4:119	Se cel servise li faisoit,
4:120	Bon guerredon de li avroit.
4:121	En un chief d'un molt bel chainsil
4:122	Envelopent l'enfant gentil
4:123	Dedesus d'un paille roé:
4:124	Son sire li ot aporté
4:125	De Costentinoble ou il fu;
4:126	Onques si bon n'orent veü.
4:127	Et d'une piece d'un sien laz
4:128	Un gros anel li lie au braz.
4:129	De fin or i avoit une once;
4:130	El ceston ot une jargonce;
4:131	La verge entor estoit letree.
4:132	La ou la meschine ert trovee,
4:133	Bien sachent tuit veraiement
4:134	Qu'ele est nee de haute gent.

4:98   *D'enfant ocirre / D'ocirre enfant* (see 10.38.2).
4:114 *lerai*: fut. 1 of *laissier*.
4:115 *aucun* (NS): the correct form would be *aucuns*, with nom. *-s*.
4:124 *Son sire* (NS): the correct form would be *Ses sire* (see 6.19).
       li ot: dir. obj. pron. *le* omitted before ind. obj. *li* (see 7.26).
4:133 *tuit*: NP of *tot* (see 12.50).

10. Noun Inflections: Class III Nouns

All nouns of this class show a distinct form in the nominative singular—the result, in most nouns, of an accent shift in the Latin etymon (see Phonology 4). Many names designating animate beings and a few designating rivers belong to this class. Most Class III nouns are masculine, but there are a few feminine nouns as well. One can distinguish four types:

10.1. Type A (masculine). This type comprises names of agents formed by adding -*(i)ere* (for the NS) or -*eor* (for other cases) to the stem of a verb. Thus, from the verb *chanter* 'to sing,' stem *chant-*, the noun *chantere*, *chanteor* 'singer' can be formed.

NS   li chantere
OS   le chanteor
NP   li chanteor
OP   les chanteors

There are several hundred nouns of this type, so only a representative listing can be given here:

buvere, buveor 'drinker'
chaciere, chaceor 'hunter'
jugiere, jugeor 'judge'
lechiere, lecheor 'lecher, lover'
peschiere, pescheor 'sinner'
robere, robeor 'robber'
trouvere, trouveor 'lyric poet'

10.2. Type B (masculine). This type comprises names of persons and proper names (largely of Germanic origin) having a unique strong nominative singular and the suffix -*on* for other cases:

NS   li ber
OS   le baron
NP   li baron
OP   les barons

Some of the most common nouns of this common type are:

*ber, baron 'baron'
bris, bricon 'idiot, fool, rogue'

compaing, compaignon 'companion'
cuistre, cuistron 'cad'
*fel, felon 'felon'
*garz, garçon 'boy'
glot, gloton 'glutton, wretch, slob'
lerre, larron 'thief'

Proper names of this type include *Aymes, Aymon; Charles, Charlon; Guenes, Ganelon; Gui, Guion; Hues, Huon; Marsilie, Marsilion; Naimes, Naimon; Otes, Oton.*

10.3. Type C (feminine). Type C feminine nouns have unique nominative singular forms and the suffix *-ain* for other cases:

NS	la none	Marie
OS	la nonain	Mariain
NP	les nonains	
OP	les nonains	

The most common words of this type are:

ante, antain 'aunt'
niece, nieçain 'niece'
none, nonain 'nun'
pute, putain 'prostitute'
taie, taiain/taien 'grandmother'

Proper names of this type include *Aude, Audain; Berte, Bertain; Blere, Blerain; Eve, Evain; Marie, Mariain; Morgue, Morgain; Yde, Ydain.*

10.4. Type D: isolated nouns (all masculine except *suer, seror*):

NS	li hom, li hons, li huem	li sire
OS	l'home	le seigneur
NP	li home	li seigneur
OP	les homes	les seigneurs
NS	li enfes	la suer
OS	l'enfant	la seror
NP	li enfant	les serors
OP	les enfanz	les serors

Common words of this type include:

li abes, l'abé 'abbot'
li ancestre, l'ancessor 'ancestor'
*li cuens, le conte 'count'
li emperere, l'empereor 'emperor'
*li enfes, l'enfant 'child'
*li hom, l'home 'man'
li niés, le nevo/nevou/neveu 'nephew'
*li pastre, le pastor 'shepherd'
*li prestre, le prevoire/provoire 'priest'
*li preudom, le preudome 'gentleman'
*li sire, le seignor/seigneur 'lord, husband'
*la suer, la seror 'sister'
*li traïtre, le traïtor 'traitor'
*li viscuens, le visconte 'viscount'

11. Breakdown of the Declension System

The breakdown of the declension system in Class III nouns follows two
forms: (a) the addition or elimination of the masculine nominative singular -s (*cil preudons* 2:32; *ses sires* 2:43) and (b) the elimination of vocalic
alternation by using one form exclusively for all cases:

(a) NS li sires
     OS le seigneur
     NP li seigneur
     OP les seigneurs

(b) NS la suer   li garçons
     OS la suer   le garçon
     NP les suers   li garçon
     OP les suers   les garçons

Some words, for all practical purposes, had developed two inflections
by the thirteenth century:

NS li prestre(s)   li provoire(s)
OS le prestre   or   le provoire
NS li prestre   li provoire
OS les prestres   les provoires

NS	li sires		⎧	li seigneurs
OS	le sire	or	⎨	le seigneur
NP	li sire		⎬	li seigneur
OP	les sires		⎩	les seigneurs

The oblique forms replaced the nominative forms altogether by the Middle French period. Some early examples of the use of the oblique for the nominative can be found in "Le Fresne," in both nouns and adjectives:

> Et le pere li a donnee (15:510)
> And the father gave her to him

> Son pere n'i volt plus atendre (14:497)
> Her father did not wish to delay any longer

12. Invariable Nouns

Any noun whose oblique singular form ends in -s or -z (=/ts/) is invariable. Most are derived from Latin second declension neuters.

MASCULINE NOUNS

NS	li vis	li braz
OS	le vis	le braz
NP	li vis	li braz
OP	les vis	les braz

The following are the most common masculine invariable nouns:

*bois 'woods'
borjois 'city dweller'
*braz 'arm'
*cors 'body'
dos 'back'
fonz 'spring'
los 'praise'
*os 'bone'
*païs 'country'
palais 'palace'

*pas 'step'
*piz 'breast'
*pris 'price, esteem, value, worth'
respons 'reply'
sens 'sense'
solaz 'comfort'
*tens 'time, weather'
*uis 'door'
*vis 'face, opinion'

Most proper names, of both cities and people, were indeclinable or soon became so: *Ais* (*Aix*), *Angiés* (*Angers*), *Paris*, *Poitiés* (*Poitiers*), *Reims* (*Rheims*), *Alexis*, *Erec*, *Enide*, *Soredamors*, *Rollant* (although the form *Rolanz* also occurs).

FEMININE NOUNS:

NS	la foiz
OS	la foiz
NP	les foiz
OP	les foiz

The following are the most common feminine invariable nouns:

*croiz 'cross'
*empereriz 'empress'
*foiz 'time, occasion'
pais, pes 'peace'
soriz 'mouse'
voiz 'voice'

By the end of the twelfth century the number of invariable nouns, both masculine and feminine, had greatly increased. This development accentuated the trend toward S/V/C word order, in which the place of the noun rather than its inflection determined its function.

12.1. Invariable plurals in -e. Old French has a limited number of feminine nouns whose plurals end in *-e*. They are derived from Latin neuter plurals.

SINGULAR	PLURAL
une peire 'pair'	trois peire
une charre 'cartload'	cinquante charre
une doie 'width of a finger'	dous doie

13. Indefinites: The *Un* Group

The indefinites are a loose collection of adjectives, pronouns, and adverbs used when the referent is unspecified. We shall introduce them throughout the grammar as they occur. The first we shall consider are *un*, *aucun*, and *chascun*, which are all declined like the article *un* (see 1.3).

(a)   *un* 'one, some,' in addition to functioning as an article and as the numeral "one," is also an indefinite pronoun, normally accompanied in this usage by the definite article:

> *l'un* li trametra a lever (1:17)
> he will send him (the) one to raise
>
> deus filles oi, *l'une* en celai (14:476)
> I had two daughters, I hid the one

It is often opposed to *autre* 'the one(s) . . . the other(s), some . . . others':

> li un i unt saché e li altre buté (17:3)
> some pulled and the others pushed

(b)   *aucun, alcun*, as an adjective, means "some":

> *Aucun* preudons la trovera (4:115)
> Some good man will find her

As a pronoun, it means "someone":

> Cuida qu'*aucuns* les eüst pris (6:185)
> He thought that someone had stolen them

(c)   *chascun* 'each (one)' can be an adjective or pronoun:

> En *chascun* fonz font fere .ii. escris (8, 219)
> On each (barrel-)bottom they had two marks inscribed
>
> En sa destre main tint *chascuns* s'espee nue (18:2)
> In his right hand each held his naked sword(blade)

Chascun also occurs in the plural, where it may be translated "every, everyone":

> Sachiés qu'ainsinc faire le doivent
> *Chascun amant*, au mains li sage (*Rose*, 8097)
> Know that every lover, at least the wise ones,
> Should do it thusly
>
> Que que *chascuns* dïent (T-L)
> In spite of what everyone says

The adjective form *chasque*, which first appeared in the twelfth century, remained rare in Old French.

Phonology 4

After its introduction into Gaul, Latin rapidly became the sole legal, official, educational, and commercial language. Only in the hinterlands did the native Celtic language retain any currency, and then only until the early fifth century A.D. at the latest.

The Latin spoken throughout the Roman Empire was considerably different from the official written language, so much so that scholars have designated it Vulgar Latin, after the *vulgaris* (common people) who spoke it. Its vocabulary was similar to that of the classical language, but it included many diminutive forms and slang expressions, and it often replaced the synthetic forms of classical syntax with analytical expressions employing prepositions.

There were also important phonological differences between classical and Vulgar Latin. The principal change, which carried all others in its wake, was the shift from a pitch (or musical) accent to a stress (or tonic) accent. Classical Latin vowels were either long or short, with a long vowel or diphthong sounded approximately twice as long as a short vowel. The accent in Vulgar Latin was generally on the same syllable as in classical Latin, but it was of a different type. Instead of being held for a longer time and pronounced at a different pitch, it was pronounced more forcefully—as is the accent in a modern English word.

The different nature of the accent in Vulgar Latin had a profound influence on the vowel and syllable it struck and on neighboring vowels. Therefore, when one studies the development of any word, it is essential to know the accented syllable, and in order to determine its position one must understand the basics of syllabification.

Syllabification

In classical Latin, Vulgar Latin, and Old French, each word has as many syllables as it has separate vowels and diphthongs. Single consonants and mutes + *l, r* (e.g., *pl, cl, tl; pr, cr, tr*) are placed at the beginning of syllables; double consonants (*tt, ss,* etc.) and all other consonant groups are regularly split. Thus, the Latin words ĔAM (e-am), MĬSSŬS (mis-sus), PATREM (pa-trem), and POENA (poe-na) all have two syllables; DĔLĔŌ (de-le-o), SĬSTĔRE (sis-te-re), CAELĔSTĬS (cae-les-tis), and VOLŬCRĬS (vo-lu-cris) all have three.

A syllable is **long by nature** when it contains a long vowel or a diphthong. Thus, the initial syllable of FLŌREM, POENA, and TĒLA is long. It is **long by position**, and the vowel is "checked" whenever the syllable ends with a consonant. For example, the first *i* of MĬTTĔRE, ASTRĬNGIT, and CĬRCŬLŬM is checked and the syllable is long.

The last syllable of a word is the **ultima**, the next-to-last syllable is the **penult**, and the one before that is the **antepenult**.

Accent

Accents were not written in Latin, Vulgar Latin, or Old French, but the rules of Latin prosody and the subsequent phonological development of words reveal the existence and locations of word accents in Latin. Latin monosyllables were accented on their only syllable: MĚL, RĚM, PÓST. Words of two syllables were accented on the penult: FLŌREM, PĬLŬM, SÁEPES. A word of more than two syllables was accented on the penult if it was long—that is, if it had a long vowel or a diphthong (long by nature) or if it had a short vowel followed by a consonant within the syllable (long by position). Otherwise, the accent fell on the antepenult:

MARÍTUM, NEPÓTEM   — long penult vowel
ALÁUDA   — penult diphthong
ANĔLLŬM, ORNAMĚNTŬM   — short penult vowel, long syllable
TĚPĬDŬM, SŎMNĬŬM, ĚBŬLŬM — short penult vowel, short syllable

In words of four or more syllables, a secondary accent generally fell two syllables before the primary tonic accent. The syllable between these two accents is called **intertonic**: SÀCRAMĚNTUM, DÒRMĬTÓRĬŬM, SĬMŬLÁRE.

The first basic rule of phonology is that the syllable that received the principal accent in a Latin or Vulgar Latin word was always preserved in Old French. Early Old French was characterized by a strong tonic word accent, due perhaps to Germanic influence on the spoken Latin of Roman Gaul. Three important results of this strong stress accent were the creation of the numerous diphthongs of Old French, the introduction of *yod* in place of *e* or *i* in hiatus, and the frequent loss of syllables immediately preceding or following the accented syllable. Loss of the unaccented penult vowel and of all final vowels except *a* (> *e*) had a profound influence on the accentual system of Old French.

Accents in most Old French words fell on the final syllable, unless that syllable contained a weak e /ə/, in which case the accent was moved forward one syllable. Monosyllabic words, except enclitics and proclitics (e.g., articles, object pronouns) were stressed. Words accented on the final syllable are called **oxytones**:

preudons   – ´–

folement   – – –´

empereor   – – – –´

angoisseusement   – – – – –´

Words accented on the next-to-last syllable are **paroxytones**:

fame   –´ –

parole   – –´ –

aventure   – – –´ –

Words ending in e + consonant in Old French pose some problems of analysis. Clearly, when the accent is added by the editor of a text, the word is oxytonic:

mandét   – –´

jamés   – –´

Other words that are regularly oxytonic are those ending in -ez (*lessiez*, 4:108), -er (*plorer*, 4:103), and adverbial -ment (*durement*, 4:104).

Primarily paroxytonic words end in -es (*celes*, 4:95), in unstressed (feminine) -e (*ocirre*, 4:98; *paille*, 4:123), or in the verbal flexions -e (third person singl.) or -ent (third pl.) (*lie*, 4:128; *estoient*, 4:95; *sachent*, 4:133; *envelopent*, 4:122).

Words ending in -et are particularly troublesome in early texts, for editors generally do not distinguish between tonic and nontonic -et: *citet* = *cité*, but *il parolet* = *il parole*.

In the course of the Middle Ages, the strong stress accent of early Old French was gradually replaced by the phrase and sentence stresses that characterize modern French. In the Old French of the late twelfth and early thirteenth centuries, we can already perceive the beginnings of this shift in the development of enclitic and proclitic words, that is, words that have no proper accent of their own and therefore gravitate to the strongest word around them to form a word group:

ENCLISIS

au (a + le), *du* (de + le)

PROCLISIS

l'   (lonc tens l'ot gardee, 4:101)
d'   (d'enfant ocirre n'est pas gas, 4:98)
s'   (la fame au chevalier s'en rist, 2:25)
c'   (c'onques ne fu, 2:38)

In this period, unstressed monosyllabic articles and pronouns were the only words affected.

Nouns

Classical Latin was a **synthetic** language, in which the endings of words indicated their functions within the sentence; word order was relatively unimportant. A shift toward a more **analytic** language, with an increasingly stable word order and more prepositions and particles, was evident already in early spoken Latin. The loss of final -M (Phonology 5) and the reduction of unaccented final vowels (Phonology 6) destroyed the complex Latin six-case declension system. In Gaul only two cases remained: the **nominative**, which took over the functions of the old nominative and vocative, and the **oblique**, which replaced the Latin accusative, genitive, dative, and ablative.

Old French nouns were derived from the Vulgar Latin nominative and oblique cases. In words of Classes I or II, the number of syllables in the etymon and the accent remain constant:

NS FÉMĬNA   > /fém'na/   > feme (fame)   NS MÚRUS > murs
OS FÉMĬNAM > /fém'na/   > feme   OS MÚRUM > mur
NP *FÉMĬNAS > /*fém'nas/ > femes   NP MÚRI   > mur
OP FÉMĬNAS > /fém'nas/ > femes   OP MÚROS > murs

These words were derived largely from the Latin first and second declensions.

In words of Class III, the number of syllables varies and the accent shifts:

NS	BÁRO	>	ber
OS	BARÓNEM	>	baron
NP	*BARÓNI	>	baron
OP	BARÓNES	>	barons

Two Class III nouns, *hom* and *cuens*, resulted not from a shift of accent but from the loss of the unaccented penult syllable, producing a consonant cluster requiring a helping vowel:

NS HÓMO	> on (om, hom, etc.)	CÓMES	> cuens
OS HÓMĬNEM (> óm'ne)	> ome (omme, homme, etc.)	CÓMĬTEM	> conte
NP *HÓMĬNI	> ome	*CÓMĬTI	> conte
OP HÓMĬNES	> omes	CÓMĬTES	> contes

Class III words were derived largely from Latin third declension nouns, as were most Old French Class Ia and IIa nouns:

NS	FLÓS	>	/*flóris/ >	flors	PÁTER	>	pere
OS	FLÓREM	>	/flóre/ >	flor	PÁTREM	>	pere
NP	FLÓRĒS	>	/flóres/ >	flors	*PÁTRI	>	pere
OP	FLÓRES	>	/flóres/ >	flors	PÁTRES	>	peres

*The nominative plural ending -ES was transformed by analogy with the more common second declension (-I) ending throughout this class. Nominative singular FLOS was replaced in late Latin with the regularized /*flóris/.

chapter 5

Reading and Textual Analysis, Selection 3b

In Reading Selection 3b, the maid-in-waiting carries out the plan that she had proposed in the previous reading selection. She sets out upon a *grant chemin*, literally a "large road." This phrase corresponds precisely to the English "highway," a major thoroughfare connecting two villages or towns. The principal or "main" street of a town is called in Old French the *grant rue* (modern Fr. *grand'rue*). British English preserves this form in the archaic appellation "High Street." Similarly, the Old French *grant autel* is the English "high altar."

5:135	La damoisele prist l'enfant;
5:136	De la chambre s'en ist atant.
5:137	La nuit quant tout fu aseri,
5:138	Fors de la vile s'en issi;
5:139	En un grant chemin est entree,
5:140	Qui a la forest l'a menee.
5:141	Parmi le bois sa voie tint;
5:142	O tout l'enfant outre s'en vint,
5:143	Onques du grant chemin n'issi.
5:144	Bien loing sor destre avoit oï
5:145	Chiens abaier et cos chanter:
5:146	Ilec porra vile trouver.
5:147	Cele part vet a grant esploit

5:148	O la noise des chiens ooit,
5:149	En une vile riche et bele
5:150	Est entree la damoisele.
5:151	En la vile ot une abaïe
5:152	Durement riche et bien garnie;
5:153	Mien escïent, nonains i ot
5:154	Et l'abaesse ques gardot.
5:155	La meschine vit le mostier,
5:156	Les tors, le mur et le clochier:
5:157	Hastivement est la venue.
5:158	Devant l'uis s'est aresteüe.
5:159	L'enfant mist jus qu'ele porta;
5:160	Molt bonement s'agenoilla.
5:161	Ele encomence sa raison:
5:162	"Deus," fet ele, "par ton saint non,
5:163	Sire, s'i te vient a plesir,
5:164	Cest enfant garde de perir!"
5:165	Quant sa priere avoit finee,
5:166	Ariere soi s'est regardee,
5:167	Un fresne voit, lé et branchu
5:168	Et molt espés et bien foillu;
5:169	En quatre fors estoit quarrez;
5:170	Por ombre estoit illec plantez.
5:171	Entre ses braz a pris l'enfant,
5:172	Desi qu'au fresne vint errant,
5:173	Desus le mist, puis le lessa;
5:174	A Dieu du ciel le commanda.

5:142   *o tout*: reinforced preposition, "with." Occasionally written as one word, *otot* or *atot*.

5:151   *ot*: reduced form of the impersonal verb *il i a* (see 8.31.1).

5:152   *durement*: adverb, "very." See 19.82 and note to 2:62.

5:154   *ques*: enclitic, *qui + les* (see 13.51).
        gardot: see note to *mandot*, 1:14.

---

14. Nouns: Case Usage

Old French has preserved, for most masculine nouns and for feminine nouns of Classes Ia and III, a two-case inflection system (see 2.5.3, 3.6–7, and 4.10).

14.1. Nominative case. The nominative case is used most frequently to express the grammatical subject of a sentence:

> *Li riches*   *hom*   sist   au mengier (1:19)
> The wealthy (powerful) man sat down to eat
>
> *Ses   sires*   l'avoit regardee (2:43)
> Her husband had looked at her

It is also employed for the person or object addressed:

> *"Deus,"* fet ele (5:162)
> "God," said she
>
> *"Sire,"* font il (10:339)
> "My lord," said they

Note that with proper names the oblique form is often used for the nominative:

> Et *Erec* un autre apela (11, 244)
> And Erec called for another (squire)
>
> *Tristran* avoc s'amie dort (13, 17)
> Tristan is sleeping with his lady love

The nominative is also used for words qualifying or in apposition to nouns in the nominative case:

> Dui chevalier; *voisin* estoient (1:4)
> Two knights (lived); (they) neighbors were
> (There lived) two knights; (they) were neighbors
>
> *Aucasins* avoit a non li damoisiax (20:20)
> Aucassin had for name the youth
> The youth was named Aucassin

14.2. Oblique case. The oblique case has numerous functions:
  (a) Direct object of a transitive verb:

> La damoisele prist *l'enfant* (5:135)
> The young lady took the child
>
> La meschine vit *le mostier*,
> *Les tors, le mur* et *le clochier* (5:155–56)
> The girl saw the church,
> The towers, the (town) wall, and the bell tower

  (b) Words qualifying or in apposition to nouns in the oblique case:

> Mes a l'entree avoit portiers
> *trestoz armez deus chevaliers* (*Charrete*, 1087–88)

But at the entry there were gatesmen,
fully armed, two knights.

(c)   Indirect object, usually referring to persons in the singular:

Sa dame conte qu'ele a fait (6:176)
(To) her lady (she) relates what she has done

Se *Deu* plet (4:116)
If (to) God it is pleasing
If it pleases God

Que pur Dieu le donons *le prestre* (19, 16)
That for (the love of) God we give it (to) the priest

(d)   A genitive, to indicate possession or relationship (see 12.47.1):

Por l'amor *Dieu* (19, 27)
For the love of God

La vache *le prestre* s'abesse
Por ce que voloit pasturer (19, 46–47)
The priest's cow lowered its head
Because it wished to graze

(e)   Object of all prepositions:

De la chambre s'en ist atant (5:136)
From the room (she) went out at
once

Devant l'uis s'est aresteüe (5:158)
Before the door (she) stopped

(f)   Adverbial expressions of time, space, manner, direction, value, or attitude:

Lonc tens l'ot gardee et norrie (4:101)
(For) a long time (she) kept and nourished her

Issi fu celee *grant piece* (7:232)
Thus (she) was kept hidden (for) a long while

Cele part vet a grant esploit (5:147)
(In) this direction (she) went rapidly

Et dit, *oiant toute la gent* (2:30)
And (she) said, (within) hearing (of) all the household

Related to this usage are the numerous adverbial complements of the type *mien escïent, vostre veiant, son vueil, vostre merci*:

Mien escïent, nonains i ot (5:153)
My wisdom nuns there were
I believe there were nuns there

(g) Object of the presentative particles *voi ci, ez, ez vos, il i a, veïssiez, oïssiez*:

> Atant es vos *le mesagier* (1:20)
> Thereupon behold the messenger!
> At that moment the messenger entered!

> En la vile ot *une abaïe* (5:151)
> In the town there was an abbey

> Mult veïssiez par les mustiers
> Aler e venir *chevaliers* (9, 125–126)
> Many you would see through the churches
> To go and come knights
> You would see many knights
> Coming and going through the churches

15.   Breakdown of the Case System

By the second half of the twelfth century, the oblique case is frequently found in place of the nominative for proper names, first in direct address, then in other instances. The disintegration seems to have begun in the west, in England and Normandy, and then to have spread gradually to the center, with the case system being maintained the longest in the north (Picardy).

In some few words (*fils* 'son,' *sire* 'sir,' *prestre* 'priest,' *Charles*) frequently employed in direct address, the nominative case predominated; however, in most words, the nominative was supplanted by the oblique:

> Riche homme furent et mananz
> Et chevaliers preuz et vaillanz (1:5–6)
> Powerful men (they) were and well-to-do,
> And (they were) bold and valiant knights

This example significantly contrasts proper case usage for the principal nouns and adjectives (*riche homme*, NP) with incorrect usage in the rest of the sentence due to the fact that the second noun follows the verb and also to hesitation in using participles and adjectives predicatively.

> "Amis, or as tu fet savoir,"
> Fet li provoires (19,30–31)
> "My friend, now you've acted wisely,"
> Said the priest

Here, *amis* is used properly as a nominative in direct address. *Li provoires*, however, is a false nominative, being formed from the oblique Class III form *le provoire*.

16. The Verb System

Old French verbs are inflected for person, number, tense, and mood. The passive voice is distinguished from the active by the use of several different periphrases, to be discussed in 8.30.

There are three persons in the singular and plural. There are five synthetic tenses: present, imperfect, preterite, future, and conditional (or hypothetical future); and four compound tenses (formed with a conjugated auxiliary verb, usually *avoir*, plus the past participle): present perfect, past perfect (or pluperfect), future perfect, and conditional perfect. The present tense normally indicates present action; for the "historical" present, see 8.32. The imperfect tense indicates habitual or repeated action in the past and states of being in the past. The preterite tense indicates simple past action, completed. The future tense indicates future action. The hypothetical future (or conditional) tense indicates contingent, potential, or unrealizable action.

The indicative mood is employed for declarative statements. The subjunctive mood indicates uncertainty and, in subordinate clauses, volition or expectation. The imperative mood expresses commands.

The verbs inflected in these various categories can be either **weak** or **strong**. Weak verbs have only two stems and show no stem changes within a tense; strong verbs have two or more stems and show vocalic alternation in the stem in the present or preterite tenses or in both. No verb has vocalic alternation in the imperfect, future, or conditional.

16.1. Verb stems. Weak verbs have two stems, one for the present, imperfect, and preterite; a second for the future and *-roie* forms. Stem 1 is found by removing the characteristic infinitive marker *-er*, *-ir*, or *-re*: *parl er, nor ir, cor re*. Stem 2 is usually the full infinitive (less the final *-e* in *-re* verbs).

Strong verbs have as many as five stems: two each for the present and preterite, and a fifth for the future and conditional. (The imperfect stem is derived from the present.) Not all verbs will be strong in both the present and preterite; some may be strong only in the present (common with strong *-er* verbs), some only in the preterite.

17. Weak Verbs

Class I: Infinitives in *-er*, e.g., *conter, mander, esgarder, parler*. This is the most common verb class.

Class Ia: Infinitives in *-ier*, e.g., *mengier, mercier, lessier, otroiier*. This class, which is well represented in Old French, is absorbed into Class I in a later period. Verbs of Class Ia are conjugated like those of Class I except for the presence of the diphthong *-ie-* instead of *-e-* in the infinitive, the past participle, the second person plural of the present indicative, present subjunctive, and imperative, and the third person plural of the preterite.

Class II: Infinitives in *-ir*, most forms with the infix *-iss*, e.g., *norir* 'to nourish,' *choisir* 'to choose,' *obeïr* 'to obey.' This class is small in Old French but expands in subsequent periods with the addition of many verbs from Class II strong.

Class III: Infinitives in *-ir* without infix, e.g., *partir* 'to leave, depart,' *sentir* 'to feel'; and in *-re*, e.g., *corre* 'to run.' There are very few weak verbs of this type; most verbs with infinitives in *-ir* and *-re* are strong.

17.1. Verb endings. For Classes I and Ia, the endings for the present indicative are:

> —, -es, -e, -ons, -ez (-iez), -ent

For those same classes, the present subjunctive endings are:

> —, -s, -t, -ons, -ez (-iez), -ent

For Class III, the endings for the present indicative are the same as those for the present subjunctive of Class I verbs:

> —, -s, -t, -ons, -ez, -ent

whereas Class III present subjunctive has the same endings as Class I present indicative:

> —, -es, -e, -ons (-iens), -ez (-iez), -ent

The imperfect and *-roie* form (conditional) use the same endings for all classes:

> -oie, -oies, -oit, -iiens (-ïons), -iiez (-ïez), -oient

as do the future:

> -ai, -as, -a, -ons, -oiz (-ez), -ont

preterite:

> -i, -s, —, -mes, -stes, -rent

and imperfect subjunctive:

> -sse, -sses, -st, -ssons (-ssiens), -ssoiz (-ssez, -ssiez), -ssent

17.2.   Verb inflection: weak verbs (two stems):

Stem 1

PRESENT INDICATIVE

	Class I	*Class Ia*	*Class II*	*Class III*
inf.	durer	laissier	norir	corre
Sg. 1	dur	lais	nor is	cor
2	dur es	laiss es	nor is	cor s
3	dur e	laiss e	nor it	cor t
Pl. 1	dur ons	laiss ons	nor iss ons	cor ons
2	dur ez	laiss iez	nor iss ez	cor ez
3	dur ent	laiss ent	nor iss ent	cor ent

PRESENT SUBJUNCTIVE

Sg. 1	dur	lais	nor iss e	cor e
2	dur s	lais (+s)	nor iss es	cor es
3	dur t	lais t	nor iss e	cor e
Pl. 1	dur ons	laiss ons	nor iss ons	cor ons
2	dur ez	laiss iez	nor iss ez	cor ez
3	dur ent	laiss ent	nor iss ent	cor ent

IMPERFECT INDICATIVE

Sg. 1	dur oie	laiss oie	nor iss oie	cor oie
2	dur oies	laiss oies	nor iss oies	cor oies
3	dur oit	laiss oit	nor iss oit	cor oit
Pl. 1	dur iiens	laiss iiens	nor iss iiens	cor iiens
	(dur ïons)	(laiss ïons)	(nor iss ïons)	(cor ïons)
2	dur iiez	laiss iiez	nor iss iiez	cor iiez
3	dur oient	laiss oient	nor iss oient	cor oient

IMPERFECT SUBJUNCTIVE

Sg. 1	dur asse	laiss asse	nor isse	cor usse
2	dur asses	laiss asses	nor isses	cor usses
3	dur ast	laiss ast	nor ist	cor ust

Pl. 1	dur issons	laiss issons	nor issons	cor ussons
	-issiens	-issiens	-issiens	-ussiens
2	dur issoiz	laiss issoiz	nor issoiz	cor ussoiz
	-issez, -issiez	-issez, -issiez	-issez, issiez	-ussez,-ussiez
3	dur assent	laiss assent	nor issent	cor ussent

PRETERITE

Sg. 1	dur ai	laiss ai	nor i	cor ui
2	dur as	laiss as	nor is	cor us
3	dur a	laiss a	nor i	cor u
Pl. 1	dur ames	laiss ames	nor imes	cor umes
2	dur astes	laiss astes	nor istes	cor ustes
3	dur erent	laiss ierent	nor irent	cor urent

IMPERATIVE

Sg. 2	dur e	laiss e	nor is	cor
Pl. 1	dur ons	laiss ons	nor iss ons	cor ons
2	dur ez	laiss iez	nor iss ez	cor ez

PRESENT PARTICIPLE

	dur ant	laiss ant	nor iss ant	cor ant

PAST PARTICIPLE

	dur é	laiss ié	nor i	cor u

Stem 2

FUTURE*

Sg. 1	durer ai	lair ai	norir ai	corr ai
2	durer as	lair as	norir as	corr as
3	durer a	lair a	norir a	corr a
Pl. 1	durer ons	lair ons	norir ons	corr ons
2	durer oiz	lair oiz	norir oiz	corr oiz
	-ez	-ez	-ez	-ez
3	durer ont	lair ont	norir ont	corr ont

-ROIE FORM (CONDITIONAL)*

	Class I	*Class Ia*	*Class II*	*Class III*
Sg. 1	durer oie	lair oie	norir oie	corr oie
2	durer oies	lair oies	norir oies	corr oies
3	durer oit	lair oit	norir oit	corr oit
Pl. 1	durer iiens	lair iiens	norir iiens	corr iiens
	-ïons	-ïons	-ïons	-ïons
2	durer iiez	lair iiez	norir iiez	corr iiez
	-ïez	-ïez	-ïez	-ïez
3	durer oient	lair oient	norir oient	corr oient

*For special second stems, see 10.39.

Phonology 5

Vowels in Vulgar Latin

Unchecked by any artificial restraints, the language of the common Roman citizen of the fifth century A.D. scarcely resembled the Latin of the Golden Age. When in Vulgar Latin the accent shifted from pitch to stress, the long vowels became close, the short vowels became open, the classical diphthongs *ae* and *oe* were reduced to open and close *e* respectively, and short *i* and short *u* in all positions became *e* and *o*. The changes in the vowel system of Vulgar Latin can be represented schematically as follows:

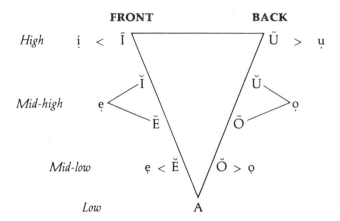

DIPHTHONGS

AE > ę
OE > ẹ
AU stayed

Thus: MĬNŬS > /mę́nǫs/, SŬB > /sǫ́b/, LÁETŬS > /lę́tǫs/, PÓENA > /pę́na/.

The intensified tonic stress emphasized the syllable upon which it fell to the detriment of those around it. For the development of Old French, this had several significant effects:

(1)   An unaccented penult syllable was lost, unless it was in hiatus and had become *yod* (see 3 below):

SÉMĬTAM > /sę́n'ta/; CÁLĂMŬM > /cál'mo/; PLÁNGĔRE > /pláng're/

(2)   All intertonic vowels except -A- (which > -*e*-) dropped:

LĪBĔRÁRE > /lib'ráre/; SÀNĬTÁTEM > /san'táte/

But, SÀCRAMÉNTUM > /sàcrəménto/

(3)   An unaccented *e* or *i* in hiatus before a following vowel lost its quality as a pure vowel to become the palatalized fricative *yod*, classified either as a semiconsonant or semivowel. It is the initial sound of the English words *yacht* or *yes*. *Yod* is represented by /j/.

(A hiatus existed in Latin whenever two vowels were side by side in a word in **separate** syllables without an intervening consonant. Thus, VĪNĔAM and RÁBĬAM each had three distinct syllables in Latin: VI-NE-AM, RA-BI-AM, and the Ĕ of VĪNĔAM and Ĭ of RÁBĬAM are said to be **in hiatus**. In Vulgar Latin these words were reduced to two syllables and pronounced /vin-ja/ and /rab-ja/.

(Note: Vowels in hiatus [e.g., IA, EA, IO] must not be confused with diphthongs [principally AE, OE, AU in Latin], in which both vowels are in the **same** syllable and form a single sound.)

Consonants in Vulgar Latin

Among the consonants, the following major changes took place before or during this period:

(1)   final -M and -N were lost, except for a few monosyllables: NĬDŬM > /nído/, VĪVŬM > /vívo/, RĔM > /rę́n/, NÓN > /nón/;
(2)   all Latin H's were lost: HÓMĬNĔM > /óm'ne/, PREHÉNDĔRE > /pre'énd're/;

(3) N was lost before S (pronounced /z/), while P and R assimilated before S to *ss* (pronounced /s/): MĒNSAM > /mẹza/; but ĬPSŬM > /ẹso/, DŌRSŬM > /dọso/;

(4) P assimilated to a following T: RŬPTAM > /rọtta/;

(5) initial S + consonant developed an initial glide *e* (<*i*): SPĔCŬLŬM > /espẹclo/, STĀTŬM > /estáto/;

(6) D and G before *yod* were effaced by palatalization: DĬŬRNŬM > /jórno/, ĔLĬGĬŬM > /elẹjo/;

(7) C and G before E, I palatalized to /ts/ and /dj/ respectively, after passing through an initial stage /kj/ and /gj/, although their spelling generally was not affected: CĒRAM > /kjẹra/ > /tsẹra/, GĔNTEM > /gjẹnte/ > /djént/; LĬCĒRE > /lekjére/ > /letsére/; REGĪNAM > /redjína/ (for the subsequent development of initial C, G, see Phonology 11; for intervocalic C, G, see Phonology 12);

(8) X (=/ks/) + consonant simplified to *s* + consonant in the prefix EX- and the complex group XT: ĒXTRA > /ẹstra/, JŬXTA > /jósta/; if EX- preceded a vowel, the two elements assimilated to *ss* /s/: EXÁMEN > /esáme/.

The gradual reduction of single consonants and consonantal groups by assimilation—a process that had begun by the Late Latin period—will be considered in Phonology 12 through 14.

Old French verb tenses and endings

Many of the French verb tenses came directly into Old French from Vulgar Latin, with appropriate phonological modifications: present indicative, present subjunctive, imperfect indicative, preterite, imperative, and present and past participles. The development of the present indicative of Class I verbs is typical:

infinitive	DURĀRE	>	durer
Sg. 1	DŪRO	>	dur
2	DŪRAS	>	dures
3	DŪRAT	>	dure
Pl. 1	DURĀMUS > *durúmus	>	durons
2	DŪRĀTIS	>	durez
3	DŪRANT	>	durent

The development of accented A > *e* and the eventual loss of final unaccented vowels except *a* > *e* will be studied in Phonology Sections 6 and 7, in which the regularity of this development will be made clear.

The only present tense ending that did not develop consistently was that for the first person plural (-ÁMUS), which should have given -*ains* (see Phonology 8). The ending -*ons* is not fully explained but is generally attributed to analogy with the first plural SÚMUS > *sons* of the copulative verb *estre* 'to be.' For this person there are a number of common variant endings: -*on, -om, -um, -omes, -umes*. Etymologically expected -*iens* is found after some palatalized stems.

The development of intervocalic *u*, *v* (pronounced /*w*/) into the bilabial fricative /β/ (see Phonology 12) intersected the development of intervocalic *b* > /β/. A number of Latin tenses that depended on the distinct pronunciation of *b* and *v* therefore fell together and were lost during the Vulgar Latin period:

(1) The Latin future DURABIT became confused with the perfect DURAVIT. The latter survived as the Old French preterite, whereas the former was replaced by a paraphrase conjoining the infinitive and the verb "to have": DURARE HABEO 'I have to endure' > *durerai* 'I shall endure.'

(2) The Latin imperfect subjunctive (DURAREM, DURARES), perfect subjunctive (DURAVERIM, DURAVERIS), and future perfect indicative (DURAVERO, DURAVERIS) all fell together and were replaced on the one hand by the former Latin pluperfect subjunctive, which became the Old French imperfect subjunctive (DURAVISSEM > *durasse*), and on the other hand by the new -*roie* form, which (like the future) was created from a Vulgar Latin paraphrase with "to have."

chapter 6

Reading and Textual Analysis, Selection 4a

In Reading Selection 4, the young girl who will become the protagonist of the story grows up to become the most beautiful and well-mannered adolescent in all of Brittany. This section bridges the two principal episodes of "Fresne": the circumstances surrounding the birth of the child and the eventual discovery of her true identity.

6:175	La damoisele ariere vait;
6:176	Sa dame conte qu'ele a fait.
6:177	En l'abaïe ot un portier,
6:178	Ovrir soloit l'uis du mostier
6:179	Defors par ou la gent venoient
6:180	Qui le servise oïr voloient.
6:181	Icele nuit par tens leva,
6:182	Chandoilles, lampes aluma,
6:183	Les sains sonna, les huis ovri.
6:184	Sor le fresne les dras choisi:
6:185	Cuida qu'aucuns les eüst pris
6:186	En larrecin et illec mis;
6:187	D'autre chose n'ot il regart.
6:188	Plus tost que pot vint cele part,
6:189	Tasta, si a l'enfant trové.
6:190	Il en a Dieu molt mercïé,
6:191	Et puis l'a pris, pas ne l'i lait.

6:192   A son ostel o tout s'en vait.
6:193   Une fille ot qui veve estoit,
6:194   Son sire ert mort, enfant avoit
6:195   Petit em berz et alaitant.
6:196   Li preudons l'apela avant:
6:197   "Fille," dist il, "levez, levez!
6:198   Feu et chandoille m'alumez!
6:199   Un enfant ai ci aporté;
6:200   Ça fors el fresne l'ai trové.
6:201   De vostre lait le m'aletiez;
6:202   Eschaufez le et sel baigniez!"
6:203   Cele fet son commandement:
6:204   Le feu alume et l'enfant prent,
6:205   Eschaufé l'a et puis baingnié,
6:206   Puis l'a de son let aletié.
6:207   Entor son braz trueve l'anel;
6:208   Le paille virent riche et bel.
6:209   Bien connurent a escïent
6:210   Qu'ele ert nee de haute gent.

6:176   *sa dame*: ind. obj., see 5.14.2.
6:179   For the use of the plural verb after *gent*, see 2.5.2 and note to 2:49.
6:198   For the weak pronoun *m(e)* before an imperative, see 17.72.1.

---

18.   The Noun Group: Word Order

Nouns in Old French rarely stand alone (for exceptions, see 2.4.3). Most commonly, they are in closely knit word groups known as **noun syntagms,** associated with other words that determine, modify, or qualify them. With the exceptions of the relative constructions studied in Section 6.21.2 and the possessive constructions considered in 12.47, nominal determiners, modifiers, and qualifiers regularly precede the noun in Old French.

Sections 1.3 and 2.4 presented the most common noun determiners: the articles, both indefinite and definite. The other principal noun determiners are the weak possessive adjectives, the demonstrative adjectives, and certain indefinite and interrogative adjectives. Two nominal determiners cannot occur in the same noun syntagm, but they can be used in conjunction with nominal modifiers and qualifiers.

The principal nominal modifiers are descriptive adjectives, relative clauses, and possessive constructions without pronouns. The nominal qualifiers are the strong possessives and the indefinite qualifiers.

19. Noun Determiners: The Weak Possessives (Forms)

Old French has two series of possessives: **unstressed** and **stressed**. The former function exclusively as adjectives and are incompatible with the articles and other nominal determiners. The latter function as either adjectives or pronouns and are compatible with the nominal modifiers and determiners (their forms will be listed in 18.81.1).

The forms of the weak possessives are:

	FIRST PERSON SINGULAR		SECOND PERSON SINGULAR		THIRD PERSON SINGULAR	
	my		*your*		*his/her/its*	
	masculine	*feminine*	*masculine*	*feminine*	*masculine*	*feminine*
NS	mes	ma	tes	ta	ses	sa
OS	mon	ma	ton	ta	son	sa
NP	mi	mes	ti	tes	si	ses
OP	mes	mes	tes	tes	ses	ses

	FIRST PERSON PLURAL		SECOND PERSON PLURAL		THIRD PERSON PLURAL	
	our		*your*		*their*	
	masculine	*feminine*	*masculine*	*feminine*	*masculine and feminine*	
NS	nostres	nostre	vostres	vostre	lor	(leur)
OS	nostre	nostre	vostre	vostre	lor	(leur)
NP	nostre	noz	vostre	voz	lor	(leur)
OP	noz	noz	voz	voz	lor	(leur)

Note: The feminine singular forms *ma*, *ta*, and *sa* regularly elide before words beginning with a vowel or an unsounded (non-Germanic) *h* (see 1.3.1):

> m'ante qui me norri   (13:440)
> My aunt who (me) raised
> My aunt who raised me
>
> s'amor   (9:285)
> her love

19.1. Agreement. In English, possessives agree regularly with the person or object possessing: "his book," "her hat," "its motor." In Old French, as in modern French, possessives (like all other nominal determiners and modifiers) agree in gender, number, and case with the object or person determined by them. Thus, *sa mere* might represent "his mother" or "her mother," depending on the context:

sa fame	(1:15)	his wife
son sire	(4:124)	her husband
son bon voisin	(1:14)	his good neighbor
son let	(6:206)	her milk

20. Noun Determiners: Demonstrative Adjectives (Forms)

In Old French the demonstrative adjectives function very much like articles, accompanying and particularizing the noun. There are two series: *cist* and *cil.*

CIST:

		masculine	*feminine*
	NS	cist	ceste
	OS	cest	ceste
stressed	OS	cestui	cesti
	NP	cist	cestes, cez, ces
	OP	cez	cestes, cez, ces

CIL:

		masculine	*feminine*
	NS	cil	cele
	OS	cel	cele
stressed	OS	celui	celi
	NP	cil	celes
	OP	cels, ceus (ces)	celes (ces)

Note: All forms can be reinforced by initial *i-*: *icist, icele* (see Section 20.3).

20.1. Usages. The forms in the preceding table were originally distinguished by a "near/far" differentiation. The *cist* forms, used primarily in dialogue, referred to the world of the speaker and the person spoken to (which is temporally and physically "near"); whereas the *cil* forms, which predominate in narrative, referred to the world of the person spoken about (temporally and physically "distant").

By the time of Marie de France, however, this original distinction had become blurred by a new distinction, that between pronoun and adjective. From the early twelfth century, there was a clear tendency to prefer certain forms of the *cist* series as adjectives and certain forms of the *cil* series as pronouns, although some of the latter forms lingered on as adjectives for a long while. Most affected were the plurals, where *cez/ces* (< *cist* series) almost totally displaced *cels, celes,* and *cestes* as adjectives. In the twelfth century, *cestui* and *celui* were rare as adjectives, but they are found more frequently in the thirteenth and fourteenth centuries. Toward the end of the Old French period, *ce* appears as an OS adjective, replacing both *cel* and *cest.*

In "Le Fresne" we find the *cil* forms used both as adjectives (*cele parole,* 2:50; *cil preudons,* 2:32) and as pronouns (*cele fet son commandement,* 6:203; *cil qui le mesage ot porté,* 2:57), whereas the *cist* forms were already almost exclusively adjectival (*ceste dame,* 2:47; *cest enfant,* 5:164; but *cest et un anel,* 13:443). There are also two examples of *ce* as an adjective: *ce mariage* (10:351) and *ce plet* (13:464).

20.2. Functions. *Cist* and *cil* have two principal uses—to evoke something that has been previously mentioned and to point out or present something that has not yet been brought up:

Lessiez *cest* duel (4:108)
Stop this grieving (i.e., the grief already referred to in lines 4:103–04)

Se *cel* servise li faisoit (4:119)
If this service (for) her (she) did
If she did her this service (i.e., the service proposed in lines 4:109–16)

    . . . me merveil
Ou *cil* preudons prist *cest* conseil (2:31–32)
    . . . I wonder
Where that gentleman got this idea

Although the "gentleman" has previously appeared, the nature of the advice is only explained in the following lines:

> Qui a mandé a mon seignor
> Sa honte et sa grant desonor
> Que sa fame a eüz deus fiz (2:33–35)
> Who informed my husband
> Of his shame and great dishonor:
> That his wife has borne two sons

Cil is often found in traditional descriptions of objects or beings regularly evoked in such situations. In this so-called **emphatic** mode, the demonstrative has essentially the value of a definite article:

> Cuntre soleil reluisent *cil* adub,
> Osbercs e helmes i getent grant flambur,
> E *cil* escuz, ki ben sunt peinz a flurs,
> E *cil* espiez, *cil* orét gunfanun. (6, 118–21)

> The equipment shines in the sun,
> Hauberks and helmets blaze forth great flashes,
> The shields, too, which are beautifully painted with flowers,
> The spears, and the golden ensigns.

20.3. Stressed forms. Early Old French created analogical stressed forms of the demonstrative on the model of *ici* 'here'; thus, all the forms in Section 20 may be found with prefixed *i-*: *icist*, *icest*, *iceste(s)*, *icil*, *icel*, *icele(s)*. Such forms are infrequent and appear archaic even in twelfth-century texts; however, for purposes of meter count, they are maintained quite late in some dialects.

By the late thirteenth century, the adverbs *ci* 'here' and *la* 'there' were beginning to be attached to the demonstrative or to the word modified, to restore the deictic force of the demonstrative, partially eroded by its functional overlap with the definite article.

21. Noun Modifiers

Descriptive adjectives, relative clauses, and possessive constructions modify the nouns with which they form noun syntagms. In general, they make the noun they modify more particular, precise, or concrete. Thus, "white horse" or "horse that gallops across the meadow" or "William's horse" are all more specific than "horse."

21.1. Descriptive adjectives. Adjectives in Old French agree with the noun or pronoun they modify in gender, number, and case. Unlike modern French adjectives, they normally precede the noun:

grant joie (4:118) 'great joy'
un gros anel (4:128) 'a huge ring'
merveilleus duel (10:365) 'unheard-of grief'
de haute gent (4:134) 'of high lineage'

For the sake of style, meter, or emphasis, the adjective is frequently placed after the noun or pronoun it modifies:

l'enfant gentil (4:122) 'the noble child'
une vile riche et bele (5:149) 'a wealthy and beautiful town'

When an adjective is used predicatively, it is regularly placed after the verb:

> Ses sires est liez et joianz (1:12)
> Her husband is happy and joyful

> Totes les fames qui l'oïrent
> Povres et riches (2:55–56)
> All the women who heard it,
> Poor and rich (alike)

21.2. Relative constructions. Relative constructions regularly follow the noun or pronoun modified. They are generally introduced in Old French by the relative pronouns *qui*, *que* (*quoi* in a stressed position), *ou*, or *cui*:

> Celes *qui en la chambre estoient* / La confortoient (4:95–96)
> Those who in the room were / her comforted
> Those who were in the room comforted her

> Selonc   le conte   *que je sai* (1:2)
> According to the tale that I know

> (Le lit) *Ou l'espousee dut couchier* (12:398)
> (the bed) In which the bride was about to lie down

In Old French the relative does not always follow its antecedent directly:

> *La fame* au chevalier s'en rist,
> *Qui joste lui au mengier sist* (2:25–26)
> The wife of the knight laughed,
> Who beside him at meal sat
> The knight's wife, who sat beside him at the meal, laughed.

> *La Virge* la me raporta
>   *Qu'a Dieu est mere.* (21, 241–42)
> The Virgin it to me brought back
>   Who to God is Mother
> The Virgin, who is God's mother,
>   Brought it back to me.

When the antecedent is undetermined, the unstressed neuter pronoun *ce* 'what, that' is sometimes used:

> La dame oï *ce* qu'el dit. (4:117)
> The lady heard what she said.

More frequently, Old French, like modern English, omits the unexpressed antecedent altogether:

> Nos savon bien ʌ qu'il i afiert (2:37)
> We know well what it means
>
> Dolenz en fu,   ne sot ʌ que fere (2:60)
> He was stricken by it and did not know what to do
>
> Sa dame conte ʌ qu'ele a fait (6:176)
> (To) her lady (she) tells what she did

21.3. Possessive constructions without pronouns. In earliest Old French, the noun used genitively to indicate possession regularly preceded the noun possessed:

> Pro *Deo* amur (1, 1)
> For God's love
>
> Or seras mes *Looÿs* provendier. (*Couronnement*, 1103)
> Henceforth you will be Louis' almsman.

This order survives archaically in standard Old French when the possessor is *Dieu* 'God,' *autrui* 'other, another,' or *cui* 'whose':

> *L'autrui joie* prise petit (10, 178)
> For another's joy he cares little

Even the possessor introduced by the preposition *de* could precede, particularly in epic style:

> Por Deu me done *d'Espaigne* toz les porz (*Charroi*, 491)
> By God, to me give of Spain all the passes
> By God, give me all the Spanish passes.

In most Old French texts, however, the possessor generally follows the possessed (see 12.47).

22. The Indefinites *Chose, Rien*

The Class I feminine noun *chose* is used in Old French with the indefinite meaning "something, thing." It is generally preceded by another indefinite—*une, autre, plusor, nule, aucune:*

D'autre chose n'ot il regart (6:187)
He had no regard for anything else
D'une chose se porpensa (8:271)
He reflected upon one thing

The Class IIa feminine noun *rien* 'thing, creature, being, person' is also used as an indefinite ("anything" or, after negative, "nothing"):

Ja Dix ne me doinst *riens* que je li demant (20:27a)
May God never give me anything I ask of him

Phonology 6

In a period well before Old French, the spoken Latin of Gaul was developing in a manner very similar to that of the spoken Latin of other parts of the Roman Empire. Therefore, most of the sound changes outlined in the preceding chapter occurred in the other Romance languages. Only between the Germanic invasions of the fourth and fifth centuries and the establishment of a relatively stable monarchy and economy in the early twelfth century did the Old French language take shape.

Since the first century A.D. there had existed an unofficial and uneasy truce between the Germanic and Latin peoples, under which the Germanic tribes stayed north of the Danube and east of the Rhine. Some Germanic settlements in Roman territory were permitted, and German mercenaries were even engaged to fill the Roman legions defending this long frontier. In the late fourth century, on the heels of Hunnish incursions in eastern Europe, the Germanic tribes began a steady push westward. The Visigoths (West Goths), who had settled south of the Danube as Roman *foederati*, revolted against Rome and, under their leader Alaric, plundered the eastern provinces. In August 410 Alaric's Visigoths occupied Rome itself, the first time that the city had been overrun by a foreign enemy in eight hundred years. After Alaric's death later that same year, the Visigoths pushed across southern Gaul, where in 419 they were granted a permanent homeland with Toulouse as its capital. They remained in Gaul until their defeat in 507 by the Franks at Vouillé (Vienne). The Vandals had crossed the Rhine frontier into Gaul in 406–07 and subsequently made their way to Spain (409) and across to Africa by 429 (see endpapers).

The Franks had been allowed to settle south of the Rhine in what is today northern Belgium by the mid-fourth century. In the fifth century they became independent and reached the Somme by 455. In 486, under their young leader Clovis, the Franks eliminated the last vestiges of Roman rule at the battle of Soissons. Place names indicate that Frankish settlement was heavy and widespread as far south as the Loire. In Picardy and northern France almost all place names are of Germanic origin, as are about half those in the Ile-de-France.

In 496 Clovis converted to the Catholic faith of Rome, and Latin was therefore adopted as the language of religion. It was also retained as the language of administration and trade. The native language of the Franks, however, left many traces in the vocabulary and sound system of the Latin spoken in Gaul. Many medieval terms relating to daily life—the household, food, dress, administration, battle, and the organization of feudal society—were of Frankish origin. Since the Renaissance, however, about half have been lost.

Two important sounds are definitely attributable to Frankish influence:
(a) the retention of aspirate *h* (Vulgar Latin, it will be recalled, eliminated all *h*'s of Latin origin);
(b) the introduction of bilabial *w*, which in Francien became *gu* /gw/, simplified to /g/ by the late twelfth century.

The Germanic expiratory accent intensified the effects of the shift in Vulgar Latin from a pitch to a stress accent. The importance accorded the tonic syllable overshadowed all others. Subsequent to the changes outlined in Phonology 5 (development of *yod*, loss of unaccented penult and intertonic vowels), the following changes occurred during the Gallo-Roman period:

(1) All final vowels except -A (which > -*e*) were lost, unless required as supporting vowels after certain consonant combinations (see Phonology 14):

*SANTÁTE > santé, NÁVEM > nef, FÁCTUM > fait
(A > *e*) SÉNTAM > sente, MÚLAM > mule, PÓRTAM > porte

supporting vowels: *CÁLMO > chaume, SÍMĬŬM > singe

(2) Any unstressed vowels that remained, generally only in the initial syllable, tended to close. Note that orthography was generally not affected except in the case of A closing to /e/ when in hiatus or when free and preceded by C > *ch*:

MATÚRŬ > madúro > meür
CABÁLLŬM > caballo > cheval

Note also that closed *o* could be spelled *ou* in unaccented as well as in accented position:

DŎLÓRĔM > /dolóre/ > doulour

As a result of the wholesale loss of unaccented syllables, Old French became a language in which all words were accented on the final syllable unless that syllable was -*e*, in which case the accent was always on the next-to-last (penultimate) syllable.

Development of accented vowels

During the formative period of Old French the strong Germanic stress greatly intensified the tonic stress already found in Vulgar Latin, affecting nearly every accented vowel and creating the numerous diphthongs and triphthongs that characterize Old French (see Phonology 3).

In studying an accented vowel, one should consider three influences in the following order:

(1)   whether it is **checked** or **free**;

(2)   whether it is influenced by a palatal;

(3)   whether it is influenced by a nasal.

Checked vowels are those followed by double consonants or any consonant groups except (usually) plosive + *l* or *r*. The accented vowels in the following words are checked: TÉRRA, MÍTTĔRE, HÁRPA. Note that many vowels that were not checked in the original Latin etymon became checked by the Gallo-Roman period through loss of the unaccented penult syllable (see above). Thus, by the Gallo-Roman era, the accented vowels in FÉMĬNAM > /fẹm'na/, ŎCŬLŬM > /ọc'lo/, and MÁNĬCAM > /mán'ca/ were all checked. Note, however, that this secondary check occurred after the diphthongization of accented short Ĕ > *ie* and accented short Ŏ > *uo* (see Phonology 7).

All vowels that are not checked are **free** and, with the exceptions of Ī and Ū, will generally diphthongize in Old French. They will be considered in Phonology Sections 7 and 8.

Checked vowels

Accented checked vowels were shortened and tended to close: ÁRBŎREM > /árb're/, ȚÁBŬLAM > /táb'la/ > table, FÉRRŬM > /fér/, TÉSTAM > /téste/, ÍLLAM > /élla/ > ele, ARÍSTAM > /arésta/ > areste, VÍLLAM > /víle/, NÚLLŬM > /núl/, FÚSTEM > /fust/.

This closing affects orthography only when checked *ọ* closes to /u/, which was often written *ou*. This *ou* is a digraph or false diphthong, created because the symbol *u* was already reserved for the sound /y/ (mod. French *mur*). The same *ou* was used to represent unaccented closed *ọ* > /u/ in initial syllables:

> accented, checked: CŬRTŬM > court, *BŎRBA > bourbe
>
> unaccented: PŎRCÉLLŬM > pourceau, JŎCÁRE > jouer

Accented vowels checked by *l* + consonant underwent a special development, since *l* regularly vocalized (i.e., became the vowel *u*) before a consonant, producing a diphthong in combination with the preceding vowel. $a + l +$ consonant gave the diphthong *au*, which in Old French was pronounced like the *-ow* of the English *cow*:

TÁLPAM > taupe   *ÁLBA > aube

$ę + l +$ consonant gave the Old French diphthong *eu*:

ĬLLOS > /éllọs/ > eus   *FĬLTRŬ > /féltrọ/ > feutre

$ę + l +$ consonant in the suffix -ĔLLUM, -ĔLLUS resulted in the Old French triphthong *-eau(s)* (pronounced /eao/):

BĔLLŬM > beau   MARTĔLLŬM > marteau

Both $ọ$ and $ǫ + l +$ consonant resulted in the early Old French diphthong *ou*, which in the course of the thirteenth century was reduced to the monophthong /u/ (still written *ou*; see Phonology 3):

*CŎLĂPU > /cǫl'po/ > coup   ŬLTRA > /óltra/ > outre

chapter 7

Reading and Textual Analysis, Selection 4b

The foundling is adopted by an abbess and given the name "Fresne" in memory of the ash tree in which she was discovered.

The successive stages in the growth of a child as understood in the Middle Ages are outlined in this section. The first six years of life were those of "infancy," when the child was ruled primarily by instinct; "childhood" began at about seven years of age, *"des qu'ele pot reson entendre"* 'after she reaches the age of reason.' At the age of thirteen or fourteen, a girl was considered eligible to marry and a young nobleman became a squire (*esquier* or *valet*) and began learning the skills of knighthood. In his early teens a townsman would be apprenticed to a master craftsman to learn a trade. A young man generally married after age twenty.

7:211	El demain emprés le servise,
7:212	Quant l'abaesse ist de l'eglise,
7:213	Li portiers vet a li parler.
7:214	S'aventure li velt conter
7:215	De l'enfant comment le trova.
7:216	L'abaesse li commanda
7:217	Que devant li soit aportez
7:218	Tout ainsi comme il fu trovez.
7:219	A sa meson vait li portiers;
7:220	L'enfant aporte volentiers,

7:221   Si l'a a la dame mostré;
7:222   Et ele l'a molt esgardé
7:223   Et dit que norrir le fera
7:224   Et por sa niece la tendra.
7:225   Au portier a molt defendu
7:226   Qu'il ne deïst comment il fu.
7:227   Ele meïsme l'a levee.
7:228   Por ce qu'el fresne fu trovee,
7:229   Le Fresne li mistrent a non
7:230   Et le Fresne l'apele l'on.
7:231   La dame la tint por sa niece;
7:232   Issi fu celee grant piece.
7:233   Dedenz le clos de l'abaïe
7:234   Fu la damoisele norrie.
7:235   Quant ele avoit passé set anz,
7:236   De son aé fu bele et granz.
7:237   Des qu'ele pot reson entendre
7:238   L'abaesse l'a fet aprendre,
7:239   Car molt l'amoit et chierissoit,
7:240   Et molt richement la vestoit.
7:241   Quant ele vint en tel aé
7:242   Que nature forme biauté,
7:243   En Bretaingne n'avoit si bele
7:244   Ne si cortoise damoisele:
7:245   Franche estoit et de bone escole
7:246   Et en semblant et em parole.
7:247   Nus ne la vit qui ne l'amast
7:248   Et merveille ne la proisast.
7:249   Li riche homme veoir l'aloient;
7:250   A l'abaesse demandoient
7:251   Sa bele niece lor mostrast
7:252   Et que sofrist qu'a eus parlast.

7:217   Understood subject is *li enfes* 'the child.'
7:227   See note to 1:17.
7:239   *l(e)* is the dir. obj. of *amoit* and *chierissoit*. When two verbs have the same obj. pron.,
        it is regularly omitted before the second verb (see 7.26).
7:250   The conj. *que* may be omitted in OF; but cf. 7:252, where a second clause is
        coordinated with the first and introduced by an expressed *que*. See 21.91.1.
7:252   "The abbess" is the subject of *sofrist*, whereas "her niece" is the subject of *parlast*.

23. Pronouns: Generalities

Pronouns replace nouns whenever the use of the noun would be awkward or grammatically impossible. Pronouns in Old French can be of the following types:
1. Personal pronouns
2. Demonstrative pronouns
3. Interrogative pronouns
4. Relative pronouns
5. Indefinite pronouns

24. Personal Pronouns

Personal pronouns designate persons or objects according to the function they have in the sentence: first person for the speaker, second person for the person addressed, third person for the person or object in question. They may be either singular or plural, masculine or feminine, nominative or oblique. They agree in person, gender, and case with the noun they replace.

A particularly important distinction in the Old French personal pronoun series is that between the **stressed** and the **unstressed** forms. **Unstressed pronouns** are used in close conjunction with a verb, either immediately preceding or following it, when there is no reason to give the object/person any autonomy from the verbal syntagm. They may neither begin sentences nor be coordinated. **Stressed pronouns** are used more flexibly, whenever the syntax requires a certain autonomy of the pronoun. They are thus used as objects of prepositions, for emphasis as subjects or objects, or in coordination.

Subject pronouns have only a single form for both stressed and unstressed usage (see Section 24.1).

The stressed oblique pronouns are *moi, toi, soi, lui* (m.), *li* (f.), *eus,* and *eles.* The unstressed oblique pronouns are *me, te, se, le, la, li* (m. and f.), and *les, lor* as well as the pronominal adverbs *i* and *en* (see the tables in 8.29).

24.1. Subject forms. In early Old French the combination of verb-stem + ending was sufficient in itself to indicate tense, mood, number, and person. A glance at the table in 5.17.1 will show that there is rarely cause for confusion. Only after the period of Old French will the final consonants weaken in pronunciation, creating potential as well as real confusion and necessitating extensive use of subject pronouns to clarify grammatical relations.

Thus, in Old French, the subject pronoun is autonomous and its use indicates, ideally, a certain expressivity or insistence. It is therefore properly *stressed*: it may be coordinated and need not immediately precede or follow the verb, as it must in modern French:

> Et *il* et *elle* en sont honniz (2:36)
> And he and she by it are shamed
> And he and she are shamed on account of it

In the course of the twelfth and thirteenth centuries, however, the change from word stress to group or sentence stress (see p. 44) robbed the subject pronouns of their autonomy, and they became more and more *unstressed* extensions of the verbal inflection, marking the person and number of the verb.

Subject pronouns take the following forms:

SINGULAR	PLURAL
1 je*	nos, nous, nus
2 tu	vos, vous, vus
3 il (m.)	il
ele, el (f.)	eles

Masculine and feminine forms are distinguished only in the third persons singular and plural.

*Other frequently encountered forms of the first person singular subject pronoun are *jo, jou, jeu, ju, jeo, ge,* and strongly stressed *gié* (see Phonology Sections 18 and 22).

24.2. Unstressed object forms.   Unstressed object forms serve as direct and indirect objects. Only the third person, singular and plural, has distinct forms for the two functions:

> S'aventure *li* velt conter (ind. obj.)
> De l'enfant comment *le* trova. (dir. obj.) (7:214–15)
> The story to her wished (he) to tell
> Of the child how he her found.
> He wished to tell her the story
> Of the child—how he found her.

Unstressed object pronouns take the following forms:

		SINGULAR	PLURAL
1		me	nos, nous
2		te	vos, vous
3	(dir. obj.)	le (m.)	les (m. and f.)
		la (f.)	
	(ind. obj.)	li	lor, leur, lur (m. and f.)

When two object pronouns are used together, the direct object always precedes the indirect object:

> De vostre lait *le m'*aletiez (6:201)
> With your milk nourish it for me

> Si *la vos* donron (10:350)
> We shall give her to you

Before *li* and *lor*, however, the direct object pronouns *le*, *la*, and *les* are often omitted (see Section 26).

For the weak reflexive pronoun *se*, see 8.29.2.

24.3. Special unstressed object forms in postposition. Whenever a verb begins a sentence—in imperatives, certain interrogatives, and interpolations, where there is no expressed subject (see 1.2.1)—any unstressed elements in the verb group must be postpositioned to avoid beginning a sentence with an unstressed form (see 1.2.2). The singulars *me*, *te*, and *se* have special forms to be used in postposition—*moi*, *toi*, and *soi*:

> Dites *moi* vostre volenté! (13:468)
> Tell me your desire! (wish, will)
> Garde *toi* des souduians (23:26)
> Watch out for the soldiers

Le, la, les, li, lor, nous, and *vous* remain unchanged in postposition:

> "Alum *nus* en," fait il (19:45)
> "Let's go," said he

> Eschaufez *le* et sel baigniez! (6:202)
> Warm it and bathe it!

For the enclitic form *sel*, see 13.51.

25. Omission of the Postpositioned Subject Pronoun

Inversion of the subject (see 1.2.2) is often obscured in Old French by the fact that this subject is consistently omitted when it is a pronoun:

> Icele nuit par tens leva (il) (6:181)
> That night early got up (he)
> He got up that morning before dawn

> L'enfant aporte (il) (7:220)
> The child brought (he)
> He brought the child

Upon first reading a passage in Old French, one might think that the subject is expressed or omitted capriciously, but a proper understanding of the inversion principle will help to clarify a large number of constructions:

> Du lay du Fresne vos dirai (1:1–2)
> Selonc le conte que je sai.
> Of the lay of Fresne you shall tell (I)
> Following the account that I know.
> I shall tell you of the lay of Fresne
> Following the account that I know.

Here the initial subject pronoun *je* is omitted since the complement (*Du lai du Fresne*) precedes the verb; however, since there is no inversion in subordinate clauses after relatives, the second *je* is stated. A similar case occurs in 6:209–10.

26. Omission of the Object Pronoun

In two specific but frequently encountered cases the third person direct object pronouns *la*, *le*, and *les* may also be omitted:

(a) when they are used in conjunction with an indirect object pronoun also of the third person (*li*, *lor*):

> L'abaesse ⌃ li a mostree (8:262)
> The abbess (her) to him showed
> The abbess showed her to him

> Se dui homes ne ⌃ li ont fait (2:42)
> If two men have not engendered (them) in her

> Son sire ⌃ li ot aporté (4:124)
> Her husband had brought (it) to her

Cil qui primes ⌃ li envoia (9:310)
He who first sent (her=Fresne) to her

(b) when two verbs have the same pronoun object, it is generally omitted before the second verb:

Car molt l'amoit et ⌃ chierissoit   (7:239)
For very much her (the child) she loved and cherished
For she loved and cherished her dearly

Cil a le bien qui Dieu le done,
Non cil qui le muce et ⌃ enfuet.   (19, 66–67)
He gains wealth who gives it to God,
Not he who hides and buries it.

This omission occurs even if the second verb would require a pronoun of a different form:

Nus ne le puet conforter
Ne nul bon consel ⌃ doner. (15.7, 4–5)
No one could comfort him
Nor give (to him) any good advice.

Si la rebeise et ⌃ fet grant joie   (*Erec*, 6465)
He kisses her again and makes (her) very happy.

For omission of the relative pronoun, see 11.46.

27. The Indefinite Pronoun *On*

Old French has a special third person singular pronoun used to refer to an undetermined person or persons. It was created from the pronominalization of the NS of the noun *ome* 'man' (see 4.10.4). It is spelled variously *on, hon, om, hom, an,* or *en,* and it is frequently preceded by the definite article: *l'on, l'hom, l'en.* It can be translated as "one," but it usually implies plurality and is better rendered by "they" or a passive construction:

Le Fresne l' apele *l'on* (7:230)
The Ash tree her calls one
They named her "Ash tree" (or) She was called "Ash tree"

Bon gré l'en devroit *l'en* savoir. (8:274)
Good will him for it should one know.
They should be well disposed toward him because of it.

28.   Compound Tenses

28.1.   Aspect.   From the beginning, Old French distinguished two series of verbal forms for all tenses and modes: the simple (synthetic) tenses and the compound tenses. The synthetic tenses were outlined in 5.17.1 for the regular verbs and in 3.9 for the principal auxiliaries, *avoir* and *estre*. The compound forms will be outlined in the following section.

The difference between the simple and compound tenses was originally one of **aspect**. The simple tenses described action in progress (in the past, present, or future) whereas the compound tenses described completed action:

> Quant ele *avoit passé* set anz,
> De son aé *fu* bele et granz.
> Des qu'ele *pot* reson entendre
> L'abaesse l'*a fet* aprendre,
> Car molt l'*amoit* et *chierissoit*. (7:235–39)

The imperfects in line 7:239 stress the continuing past action of endearment, which was "in progress" in the past. The preterites of lines 7:236–37 likewise stress the durative aspect—her beauty is more than passing, and she embodies and retains the ability to *reson entendre* by virtue of her increasing maturity. In contrast, the present perfect of line 7:238 and the past perfect of line 7:235 stress completion—the abbess had her educated; she reached the age of seven.

28.2.   Formation.   Compound tenses are formed in Old French by a conjugated form of the auxiliary + the past participle. In theory there can be a compound tense corresponding to every synthetic tense in each mode, but in practice the following are most frequently encountered:

Present perfect indicative (present tense of auxiliary):

> Ele l'*a* molt *esgardé* (7:222)
> She it has intently looked at
> She looked intently at it (the child of line 7:220)

Pluperfect indicative (imperfect tense of the auxiliary):

> Ele *avoit passé* set anz (7:235)
> She had passed seven years (of age)

Literary past perfect or *passé antérieur* (preterite of auxiliary):

> Cil qui le mesage *ot porté* (2:57)
> He who the message had carried
> He who had taken the message

Present perfect subjunctive (Present tense of auxiliary, subjunctive mode):

> Miex vaut que nous *aions perdu*
> .xxx. ou .xx. de nos prisons
> Que ce qu'a lui nos combatons. (23, 126–28)
> It is better that we lose
> 30 or 20 of our prisoners
> than fight with him.

Pluperfect subjunctive (imperfect tense of auxiliary, subjunctive mode):

> Cuida qu'aucuns les *eüst pris/* En larrecin (6:185–86)
> (He) thought that someone them had taken/ in theft
> He thought that someone had stolen them

28.3. With the auxiliary *estre*.   *Estre* is used as an auxiliary verb
   (a)   with a restricted number of verbs of motion (e.g., *aler* 'to go,' *venir* 'to come,' *arriver* 'to reach shore,' *repairier* 'to return,' *entrer* 'to enter'):

> En un grant chemin *est entree* (5:139)
> Onto a highway (she) entered

   (b)   to express the passive voice:

> Que devant li *soit aportez*
> Tout ainsi comme il *fu trovez* (7:217–18)
> That before her (the infant) be brought
> Just as it was found

> Ore *est* sa voisine *vengiee* (3:68)
> Now is her neighbor avenged

   (c)   with all pronominal verbs (whether or not the reflexive pronoun is actually expressed):

> Ariere soi *s'est regardee* (5:166)
> Behind herself (she) looked
> She looked behind herself

Phonology 7

Free vowels

Free vowels are **oral** unless they are followed immediately by the nasal consonants *n* or *m* or the palatal *yod*. Nasal and palatalized vowels will be studied in Phonology 8.

Accented free oral vowels regularly lengthened and diphthongized under stress. A mental comparison of the pure vowels of modern French with the generally diphthongized vowels of contemporary English, which like early Old French has a strong tonic stress, will clarify the process.

First affected were tonic short Ĕ and Ŏ, which became *ie* and *uo* respectively. This diphthongization occurred even before the loss of the unaccented penult, so that a secondary check would not affect it:

Ĕ > ę̆ > ie   MĔL > /*mę́l/ > miel
              PĔTRAM > /pę́dra/ > pierre
              TĔPĬDŬM > /tę́pędo/ > tiede
Ŏ > ǫ̆ > uo   CŎR > /cǫ́r/ > cuor
              SŎROR > /sǫ́ror/ > suor

Next affected were tonic long Ē and Ō, which became *ei* and *ou*:

Ē > ę > ei   TĒLAM > /tę́la/ > teile
              HABĒRE > /aßę́re/ > aveir
Ō > ǫ > ou   FLŌREM > /flǫ́re/ > flour
              SŌLUM > /*sǫ́lo/ > soul

For the subsequent differentiation of these diphthongs, see Phonology 10.

Perhaps the most characteristic phonological trait of Old French is the evolution of accented free A to *e*. Although its history is unclear, it too probably lengthened and diphthongized before raising:

A > ae > e   MĀREM > /*máere/ > mer
              PRĀTŬM > /*práedo/ > pré

The high vowels Ī and Ū did not diphthongize in any position in French, but the pronunciation of *u* shifted from velar /u/ to palatal /y/. This change remains unexplained, but it is often attributed to the influence of the Gallic (Celtic) substratum:

ÍRAM > ire	LÍBRAM > livre	SPÍNAM > espine
MÚRUM > mur	PLÚS > plus	NÚLLUM > nul

Pronouns

The phonological history of Old French pronouns is complex, affected by factors such as analogy, sentence position, stress, case, and dialect. Stressed forms generally functioned autonomously within the sentence and received individual accents; unstressed forms were allied so closely with noun or verb groups that they received no accent of their own. Since vowels under stress develop differently from unaccented vowels, the same Latin pronoun could produce distinct stressed and unstressed forms in Old French.

Object pronouns

LATIN ETYMON	STRESSED	UNSTRESSED
MĒ	mei, moi	me
TĒ	tei, toi	te
SĒ	sei, soi	se
ĬLLĪ + CUI/HUIC > (el)lui	lui	
ĬLLAE + CUI/HUIC > (el)lei	li	
(IL)LUM		le
(IL)LAM		la
(IL)LOS, (IL)LAS		les
ĬLLOS	els, eus	
ĬLLAS	eles	

Subject pronouns and articles

The Latin demonstrative ILLE, when stressed, became the third person subject pronouns; when unstressed, it developed into the Old French definite articles:

LATIN ETYMON	STRESSED	UNSTRESSED
ĬLUM	il	le
ĬLLAM	ele	la
ĬLLĪ	il	li
ĬLLOS		les
ĬLLAS	eles	les

The maintenance of *i* in the pronominal (stressed) form *il* is attributed to analogy with the subject relative pronoun *qui* and the raising effect of the final -*i* in NP ĬLLĪ.

Only the first person singular subject pronoun has both a stressed and an unstressed form: *gié* versus *jo, je, ge, jeu*. Both series are from the Latin EGO, with the *e* lengthening and diphthongizing in the stressed form.

Possessive pronouns and possessive adjectives

When stressed, Latin possessive adjectives became the Old French strong possessives, which functioned either as adjectives or as pronouns (see 18.81). When unstressed, they became the Old French weak possessives, which functioned only as adjectives:

LATIN ETYMON	STRESSED	UNSTRESSED
masculine		
MEUS		mes
MEUM	mien	mon
MEI		mi
MEOS		mes
TUUM	tuen	ton
SUUM	suen	son
feminine		
MEA		ma
MEAM	moie	ma
MEAE		mes
MEAS		mes
TUAM	toue	ta
SUAM	soue	sa

These adjectives constitute an excellent study in analogical reformation. First, the oblique forms *mien, tuen, suen, moie, toue, soue* were used to create complete paradigms:

li miens	la moie
le mien	la moie
li mien	les moies
les miens	les moies

Next, the *mien* form was generalized for the masculine: *li tiens* for *li tuens*, *le sien* for *le suen*, etc. Finally, the feminine was reformed on the masculine model: *la mienne* for *la moie*, *la tienne* for *la toue*, etc.

The plural possessives are from NOSTER, NOSTRUM and *VOSTER, *VOSTRUM (by analogy from VESTER, VESTRUM). The third plural *lour, leur* is a rare survival of a Latin genitive plural, (IL)LORUM.

chapter 8

Reading and Textual Analysis, Selection 5a

Reading Selection 5 introduces the noble youth who will become a protagonist in the second part and whose love for Fresne will lead to her eventual recognition and to reconciliation with her family. In the manuscript of "Fresne" that we have chosen as the basis for our text (B.N. f. fr. 1104) his name is given as "Bruron," whereas in manuscript H he is named "Guron."

The existence of more than one manuscript for a given work leads inevitably to variant readings. Usually the differences are minor and can be explained away as "scribal errors" or as permissible variant spellings:

tendra (8:266)	v.	tandra
aparcevroit (8:269)	v.	apercevroit
velt (8:275)	v.	volt

In other instances, however, the differences are of more significance and require editorial choices or intervention.

In line 260 our manuscript has *repera* whereas manuscript H gives *retorna*; since the words are equivalent in meaning, we have retained the reading in our manuscript. Similarly, in line 263 our scribe wrote present tense *voit* where the scribe of H chose the preterite *vit*. This tense shift gives relief to Bruron's action and seems preferable to the traditional reading.

Examples of errors by our scribe can be found in lines 268, where he wrote *Car il i reperoit* (which fails to introduce the conditional of the following line), and 279, in which he used *Molt* instead of *Mes*, perhaps owing to inattention or haste. All changes to the base manuscript are listed in the Textual Emendations section, pp. 294–96.

The most significant variants in this selection are to be found in lines 272–74, which in manuscript H read:

> L'abaïe croistre voldra,
> De sa terre tant i donra,
> Dont a toz jors l'amendera . . .

The reading of our base manuscript employs the rhetorical figure *reduplicatio* (repetition) and also has the merit of avoiding four straight lines on the same rhyme.

The theme of "love from afar" for a beautiful maiden or renowned knight whose beauty or deeds have only been recounted (see lines 8:257–58) is among the most popular themes in Old French lyric poetry and romance.

8:253	A Dol avoit un bon seignor,
8:254	Ainz puis, ço cuit, n'i ot meillor.
8:255	Ici vos nomerai son non:
8:256	El païs l'apelent Bruron.
8:257	De la pucele oï parler,
8:258	Si l'acommença a amer.
8:259	A un tornoiement ala;
8:260	Par l'abaïe repera.
8:261	La damoisele a demandee;
8:262	L'abaesse li a mostree.
8:263	Molt la voit bele et ensaingnie,
8:264	Sage, cortoise et afaitie.
8:265	Se il nen a l'amor de li,
8:266	Molt se tendra a malbailli.
8:267	Esgarez est, ne set comment,
8:268	Car se il reperoit sovent
8:269	L'abaesse s'aparcevroit;
8:270	Jamés des eulz ne la verroit.
8:271	D'une chose se porpensa:
8:272	Que il du sien tant li donra.
8:273	Tant i donra terre et avoir,
8:274	Bon gré l'en devroit l'en savoir;
8:275	Car il i velt avoir retor
8:276	Et le repere et le sejor.
8:277	Por avoir la fraternité
8:278	I a del sien grantment donné,

8:279   Mes i avoit autre achoison
8:280   Que de reçoivre le pardon.
8:281   Soventes foiz i repera,
8:282   A la damoisele parla;
8:283   Tant li parla, tant li promist,
8:284   Qu'ele otroia ce qu'il li dist.

8:262   The past participle *mostree* agrees with the omitted fem. dir. obj. pron. *la*.

8:274   The first occurrence of *l'en* is as a proclitic combining the ind. obj. pron. *li* 'to him'
         and *en* 'for it'; the second *l'en* = *l'on*, the impersonal subj. pron. See 7.27 and
         11.42.3.

---

29. Personal Pronouns

29.1. Stressed object forms. In 7.24.2 we presented the unstressed
object pronoun forms, which function as both direct and indirect objects
in close association with the matrix verb. Stressed object pronouns are
required whenever the pronoun is syntactically independent of the verb.
They are most commonly employed as objects of prepositions, but they
are also used to avoid beginning statements with weak forms, for stylistic
effect, and with infinitives and gerundives.

Stressed object pronouns take the following forms:

SINGULAR	PLURAL
1 moi	nos, nous
2 toi	vos, vous
3 lui (m.)	els, eus (m.)
li (f.)	eles (f.)

There are a number of these strong forms that function as objects of
prepositions in Reading Selections 5a and 5b:

l'amor de li	(8:265)
de moi	(9:288)
entor li	(9:293)
o lui	(9:301)

For stressed object forms used with ordinal numbers, see 16.67.2.

29.2. Reflexive object forms. With many Old French verbs, the object of the action of the verb is identical with the subject of the verb. In these cases, the action is said to "reflect" upon the subject, and this reflexivity is expressed by means of a special pronoun, identical in person and number with the subject. Such reflexive pronouns may be either weak (W) or strong (S) in Old French:

SINGULAR	PLURAL
1 me (W) moi (S)	nos, nous (W or S)
2 te (W) toi (S)	vos, vous (W or S)
3 se (W) soi (S)	se (W) soi (S)

These may be translated as "myself, yourself, himself," and so forth:

as sainz de l'iglise *se* comande erramment (19:14)
to the saints of the church he commends himself at once

More frequently, however, they are best left untranslated in English:

molt *me* merveil (2:31)
I am most/quite surprised

D'une chose *se* porpensa (8:271)
(Of) one thing he determined

Ensemble o lui *s'*en est alee (9:301)
Together with him (she) went away

The personal pronouns *li, lui, els,* and *eles* are often used for the reflexive *soi*:

Mais *lui* meïsme ne volt mettre en ubli.   (6, 365)
But he does not wish to forget (prayers for) himself.

Adont se loga li hoos en une grande pree . . . pour *euls* aisier   (27, 76–78)
Then the army camped in a large meadow . . . to rest themselves

Conversely, the reflexive form *soi* may replace *li, lui, eus,* or *eles* as the object of a preposition:

Le coffre fist o *soi* porter   (9:313)
She had the chest brought with her

30. Active and Passive Verbs

The subject of an active verb accomplishes the action of that verb or is in the state indicated by the verb: *a un tornoiement ala* (8:259). The subject of a passive verb is itself the object of the action of that verb. Old French most frequently expressed the passive with the auxiliary *estre* + past participle:

> Tout ainsi comme il *fu trovez*.   (7:218)
> Just as it was found.

Sometimes, however, the auxiliary *avoir* was used with or without a reflexive pronoun:

> Parfitement *s'ad* a Deu *cumandét*   (3, 58)
> He commended himself sincerely to God
>
> A icel mot l'un a l'altre *ad clinét*   (*Roland*, 2008)
> After he said this, they bowed to each other

Alternatively, a pronominal verb was employed:

> Molt *se tendra* a malbailli   (8:266)
> He will consider himself most unfortunate
>
> Ariere chiet, si *se pasma*   (13:456)
> She fell backwards and fainted

31. *Il i a* and the Impersonal Verbs

31.1. Il i a. Impersonal verbs are those that express an action whose subject is not specified—verbs expressing existence, modes of action, necessity, or atmospheric phenomena. By far the most commonly employed impersonal construction in Old French is *il i a* 'there is, there are.' It is formed from the verb *avoir* (see 3.9) and can be conjugated through all tenses and moods. Like other impersonal verbs, however, it exists only in the third person singular, and its subject pronoun, *il*, is considered neuter rather than masculine. This subject pronoun, as well as the neuter *i*, is frequently omitted:

> A Dol *avoit* un bon seignor
> Ainz puis, ço cuit, n'*i ot* meillor   (8:253–54)
> At Dol there was a good lord
> Never afterwards, I believe, was there a better (one)

Avoit in 8:253 should not be confused with *avoit* 'he/she had' from *avoir*. In 8:254 the inclusion of *i* makes the construction more easily recognizable. Another example of this impersonal verb occurs in this lesson's reading at line 279:

> Mes *i avoit* autre achoison   (8:279)
> But there was (an)other reason

Not all occurrences of *i* + *avoir* are impersonal, however:

> Car il *i* velt *avoir* retor   (8:275)
> For he to there wishes to have return
> For he wishes to be able to return there

31.2. Other common impersonal verbs and expressions in Old French:

> chaloir (il chaut)—expresses appropriateness, suitability, interest
> coster (il coste)—expresses suffering, pain, displeasure
> covenir (il covient)—expresses necessity
> estovoir (il estuet)—expresses necessity
> faillir (il faut)—expresses lack or necessity
> loisir (il loist)—expresses permission
> seoir (il siet)—expresses pleasure

> ajorner (il ajorne)—day breaks
> anuitier (il anuite)—night falls
> avesprer (il avespre)—evening falls
> neiger (il neige)—it snows
> plovoir (il pleut)—it is raining

> avoir mestier (a)—to serve, be of use to
> estre bel (a)—to be agreeable to, to please
> estre tart (a)—to be eager
> estre (a)vis (a)—to be of the opinion, to think, to seem

Mais ore en *coveneit* un sul a mort livrer (18:59)
But now it was necessary to hand over a single (person) to death

The subject of an impersonal verb could be expressed by a direct or an indirect object or pronoun:

> Molt *est la reïne tart* (12, 112)
> The queen is very eager
>
> Morir *le covint* (*Yvain*, 4701)
> He had to die
>
> *leur couvint* le nef desloier (24, 52–53)
> they had to untie the ship
>
> *Tei cuvenist* helme e brunie a porter (3, 181)
> You must wear helmet and burney

Early Old French mainly used the direct object pronoun, but after the beginning of the thirteenth century the indirect object forms became more common, until they supplanted the direct object forms altogether during the late Middle French period. Note that a certain determination can be made only of the third person forms *le, la, les, li,* and *lor* since other forms (*me, te, moi, toi, lui, nous, vous*) could be either direct objects or indirect objects.

Note also that, to express necessity, *estovoir* was usually employed in the twelfth century and *covenir* in the thirteenth century. By the end of the fourteenth century, they had both been supplanted by *faillir/falloir,* which has continued into modern French.

31.3.   Verbs used both personally and impersonally:

Et ceste parolle n'est pas assez *pesee* avant que dicte   (30, 121–22)
And this word was not sufficiently weighed before spoken

Molt li *pesa*   (3:70)
It grieved her deeply

Cele *fet* son commandement   (6:203)
She does as he asks

Qui mieus de lui *fet a loer*   (3:90)
Who is more worthy than he to be praised

Ne *n'avendra* cele aventure   (2:39)
Nor will this (event) come to pass

Tut lur *est avenu* selunc lur volenté   (16:9)
It all came to pass for them as planned

Il vos *sist*   (12, 136)
It pleases you

Qui joste lui au mengier *sist*   (2:26)
Who was seated beside him at table

Note particularly that the verb *faillir* was generally used personally in Old French with the meanings "to fail, to let down, to lack, to be missing," whereas in modern French *falloir* can only be used impersonally:

Certes, jamés ne vos *faudrai*   (9:297)
Indeed, I'll never fail you (i.e., cause you to want for anything)

Puis parlerent a lor pleisir
De quanque lor vint a pleisir;
Ne matiere ne lor *failloit*   (12, 153–55)
Then they spoke as much as they liked
Of anything that pleased them;
Nor did they lack for subject matter

32. The Indicative Mood: Tense Usage in Narration

The indicative is used to relate that which has happened, is happening, or will happen. It is the privileged mood of narration. In modern languages, a writer regularly chooses a single tense as the principal vehicle for a narrative: generally past or "historical" present. Old French, however, readily and sometimes unpredictably mixes the past and present in a single narration. Furthermore, there are several pasts to choose from: preterite, imperfect, and present perfect.

Normal chronological past action is expressed in Old French by the synthetic preterite:

> Soventes foiz i repera,/A la damoisele parla   (8:281–82)
> He often returned there/(And) spoke with the girl

Completed action, however, presupposes a preceding completion. The compound tenses, which were used to view an action in its state of completion (see 7.28.1), therefore came to express actions that were past chronologically as well as logically. Thus, the same action can be referred to in the preterite:

> Le chevalier (qui) l'enmena   (9:315)
> The knight (who) led her

and in the present perfect:

> En son chastel l'en a menee   (9:302)
> Into his castle he has led her

The historical present, which expressively transfers a chronological past into the narrative present, is very common in Old French:

> A sa meson *vait* li portiers
> L'enfant *aporte* volentiers   (7:219–20)
> To his house went (lit.: goes) the doorkeeper
> The child (he) carried (lit.: carries) willingly

The reading selection in this chapter displays a mixture of preterites (258–60, 271–73, 281–84), present perfects (261–62, 278), historical presents (263–65, 275), and imperfects (253, 279).

32.1. Preterite versus present perfect.

The principal narrative tense of "Fresne" (and indeed of all selections included in this volume) is the past, generally conveyed by the preterite:

> De la pucele *oï* parler,
> Si l'*acommença* a amer.
> A un tornoiement *ala*;
> Par l'abaïe *repera*.   (8:257–60)

> He heard tell of the maiden,
> And he began to love her.
> He went to a tournament;
> He returned by way of the convent.

It alternates with the present perfect, which can indicate the present result of a past action:

> Por avoir la fraternité
> I *a* del sien grantment *donné.*   (8:277–78)
> In order to meet with her
> He gave (the convent) a great deal of his wealth.

In other words, the present enjoyment of Fresne's company is the direct result of the action of giving lands to the abbey.

In many instances, however, the relationship of past to present is tenuous at best:

> La damoisele *a demandee;*
> L'abaesse li *a mostree.*   (8:261–62)
> He asked (to see) the young girl;
> The abbess showed her to him.

The preterite is used to evoke the permanent qualities of individuals:

> Riche homme *furent* et mananz   (1:5)
> They were powerful and well-to-do men

32.2.   Preterite versus historical present.   The historical present is used to give relief and special expressivity to the action. When the Lord of Dol first sees Fresne, the narrative shifts expressively to the present:

La damoisele *a demandee;*	(past)
L'abaesse li *a mostree.*	(past)
Molt la *voit* bele et ensaingnie. . . .	(pres.)
Se il nen *a* l'amor de li,	(pres.)
Molt *se tendra* a malbailli.	(fut.)
Esgarez *est*, ne *set* comment. . . .	(pres.)
(8:261–67)	

He asked (to see) the young girl;
The abbess showed her to him.
He finds her to be very beautiful and well-educated. . . .
If he does not win her love,
He will consider himself most unfortunate.
He is confused, he doesn't know how. . . .

The historical present often indicates a shift to direct discourse:

> Deus filles ot. Molt li pesa,
> Molt durement en fu dolente;
> A soi mesmes *se demente*:
> "Lasse," fet ele, "que ferai?"   (3:70–73)
> She bore two daughters. It grieved her deeply,
> She was extremely upset;
> To herself she laments:
> "Alas," says she, "what shall I do?"

> Molt bonement s'agenoilla.
> Ele *encomence* sa raison:
> "Deus," fet ele, "par ton saint non"   (5:160–62)
> She knelt down very tenderly.
> She begins to speak:
> "Lord God," says she, "by your holy name"

It is also used in moments of high tension in the story, such as the presentation of the infant to the abbess at the beginning of Reading Selection 4b.

Not all tense shifts are meaningful, however. This is especially evident when the poet shifts from past to present within the same sentence:

Le feu *alume* et l'enfant *prent*.	(pres.)
Eschaufé l'a et puis *baingnié*. . . .	(pres. perf.)
Entor son braz *trueve* l'anel;	(pres.)
Le paille *virent* riche et bel.	(pret.)
(6:204–08)	

> She lights the fire and takes the child,
> She warmed it and then bathed it. . . .
> Around its arm she finds the ring;
> They saw that the cloth was expensive and
> fine.

32.3. Preterite versus imperfect.   Whereas the preterite designates past action as completed, with no ties to the present, the imperfect expresses past actions or states that are durative, indefinite, repetitive, or somehow understood as not perfected. It designates states of being:

> A Dol *avoit* un bon seignor (8:253)
> In Dol there was a good lord

The imperfect eventually came to rival the preterite for evoking the permanent qualities of individuals:

Ele *ert* fainte et orgueilleuse   (2:27)
She was deceitful and proud

Li quens Garins de Biaucaire *estoit* vix et frales, si avoit son tans trespassé. Il n'avoit nul oir, ne fil ne fille, fors un seul vallet. Cil *estoit* tex con je vos dirai. Aucasins avoit a non li damoisiax. Biax *estoit* et gens et grans et bien taillés de ganbes et de piés et de cors et de bras. Il *avoit* les caviax blons et menus recercelés et les ex vairs et rians et le face clere et traitice et le nés haut et bien assis. Et si *estoit* enteciés de bones teces qu'en lui n'en *avoit* nule mauvaise se bone non. (20:17–23)

It marked duration:

> Molt *l'amoit* et *chierissoit* (7:239)
> (The abbess) loved and cherished her (over many years)

and repeated or habitual action in the past:

> Ovrir *soloit* l'uis du mostier (6:178)
> He was accustomed to (He regularly) open(ed) the church door

Phonology 8

Nasalization

Throughout the Old French period vowels and diphthongs were progressively nasalized before *m*, *n*, and palatal /ɲ/ (spelled "gn" or "ng"). Checked and free, accented and unaccented vowels were affected. Nasalization began with the vowels /a/ and /e/ and the diphthongs /ai/ and /ei/ in the tenth and eleventh centuries, then spread to /o/, /oi/ and other diphthongs after the shift of stress in the late twelfth century (see Phonology 3). /i/ and /u/ were only incompletely nasalized in Old French. It is perhaps more correct to speak of "nasalized" vowels in Old French than of "nasal" vowels, for the nasalizing consonant was never completely assimilated by the vowel during the Old French period:

ÁNNUM	> an	/ãn/
FÉMINAM	> feme	/fẽmə/
MÀNDUCÁRE	> mangier	/mãɲier/
GÉNTEM	> gent	/ǰẽnt/

SAPÓNEM	> savon	/savõn/
BÒNITÁTEM	> bonté	/bõnte/
*PÓMA	> pome	/põmə/

Only Ē and Ĕ diphthongized in regular fashion before a nasal:

| PLĒNAM | > pleine | /plējnə/ |
| RĔM | > rien | /rjen/ |

Note that *ie* did not nasalize to /jē/ until late in the thirteenth century, near the end of the Old French period.

Accented free A followed by a nasal diphthongized to /ãj/, unless preceded by a palatal:

	PÁNEM	> pain	/pãjn/
	MÁNUM	> main	/mãjn/
but	CÁNEM	> chien	/tʃien/

Both Ŏ and Ō nasalized in the course of the twelfth century to /õ/. Ī /i/ and Ū /y/ did not nasalize until the end of the Old French period, and then only to /ĩ/ and /ỹ/. They were not lowered to the modern nasal phonemes /ẽ/ and /œ̃/ until the sixteenth century.

The process of nasalization peaked in Middle French, at which point a reaction resulted in the denasalization of many vowels. Consequently, modern French pronunciation habits will frequently lead one astray in Old French.

Development of *yod*

The effects of the palatal fricative *yod* on vowels were more pervasive and are less easily classified than those of nasalization. *Yod* might have several origins, both Latin and Gallo-Roman:

(a) Latin initial or intervocalic I: IÁM > /jám/, MÁIOR > /májor/
(b) Vulgar Latin intervocalic *di* and *gi*: RÁDĬUM > /rájo/, EXÁGĬUM > /eksájo/
(c) Vulgar Latin *e, i* in hiatus: VĪNĔAM > /vínja/, TĪBĬAM > /tíbja/ (see Phonology 5)
(d) Gallo-Roman *c, g* before *t, d, l, r*: NŎCTEM > /nójte/ > *nuit*, FRĪG(Ĭ)DUM > /fréjdo/ > *freit*, FÁC(Ĕ)RE > /fájre/ > *faire*
(e) Gallo-Roman intervocalic *c, g* before *a, ę, i*: PACÁRE > /pajáre/ > *paiier*, NEGÁRE > /nejáre/ > *neiier*, FLAGĔLLŬM > /flajéllo/ > *flaiel*

Note also that initial and supported Latin C (/k/) before *a* > /tʃ/ and before *e* or *i* > /ts/, while Latin G (/g/) before *a, e, i* > /dʒ/, and that these palatalized consonants could in turn affect the development of the following vowel.

Influence of *yod* on accented vowels

The presence of *yod* in a word could influence vowels both preceding and following it. *Yod* often checked the normal diphthongization of a preceding accented vowel, combining with it to form an Old French diphthong:

Á > a + yod > ai	FÁCĔRE > faire
Ē > ẹ + yod > ei	FĒRIĀM > feire
Ō > ọ + yod > oi	RAṢŌRIUM > rasoir
Ū > ụ + yod > ui	FRŪCTUM > fruit

Normal diphthongization initially occurred with Ĕ and Ŏ, but in each case the resulting triphthong was reduced:

Ĕ > é + yod > /iej/ > i	LĔCTUM > /liejto/ > lit
Ŏ > ǫ́ + yod > /uoj/ > ui	NŎCTEM > /nuojtə/ > nuit

Ŏ, Ō + palatal *l* also diphthongized:

Ŏ + palatal l > /uojʎ/ > ueill	FŎLĬUM > /fuójʎo/ > fueil
Ō + palatal l > /ojʎ/ > ouill	FENŪCŬLŬM > /fenǫ́clo/ > fenouil

A preceding palatal influenced the following sounds:

palatal + Ā > ie	CÁNEM > chien
palatal + Ē > /iej/ > i	PLACĒRE > /*pladzére/ > plaisieir
	> plaisir

An A preceded and followed by a palatal > *i*:

yod + A + yod > /iaj/ > i	CÁCAT > /*kiaje/ > chie
	IÁCET > /*dʒiájset/ > gist

The Latin -ÁRIŬM (-ÁRĬAM)   ending, used to designate an agent, developed into *-ier* (*-iere*):

> POMÁRIŬM > pomier
> CABALLÁRIŬM > chevalier
> LUMINÁRIA > /lụm'nárja/ > lumiere

The Latin diphthong AU

Whereas the diphthongs AE and OE became *ę* and *ę* respectively in Vulgar Latin, the diphthong AU only became *o* around the mid-sixth century, after initial C > *ch* (see Phonology 11):

> ÁURUM > *aoro > or
> *HÁUNITHA > *haonta > honte
> CÁUSAM > *chaosa > chose

chapter 9

Reading and Textual Analysis, Selection 5b

At the beginning of Chapter 8 we discussed some of the choices facing the editor of an Old French text. In approaching a text, some editors may be excessively conservative and reproduce every letter of the manuscript exactly as written, without correcting scribal errors, resolving standard abbreviations, or supplying punctuation and diacritics. Others can be quite liberal, rewriting the text to make it conform to the dialect in which it was supposedly composed and to the original form as the editor perceives it. Words or lines may be restored or omitted based on internal evidence or evidence derived from other manuscripts.

In editing "Fresne" for this volume, I have chosen a middle road: I reproduce the base manuscript whenever it is not obviously in error, and I resolve abbreviations and supply punctuation and diacritical marks such as accents and diareses. In the present chapter, for instance, I omit two lines that are found in other editions of this *lai* immediately after my line 310:

> Plus de aveir ne receut od li;
> Come sa niece la nuri.

Comparison of manuscript readings may well suggest that Marie de France did indeed write these lines, but they are in no way necessary to the comprehension of the passage, they are repetitive (see 7:224; 7:231), and they interrupt the syntax (*les* of line 311 refers back to *paille* and *anel* of 309). I have therefore chosen to follow the scribe of my base manuscript, B.N. 1104, in omitting them—though he may not have omitted them for any good reason.

A practical guide to editing Old French texts, prefaced by a historical overview of the various approaches favored by editors in different periods, can be found in Alfred Foulet and Mary Blakely Speer, *On Editing Old French Texts*.

9:285	Quant asseür fu de s'amor,
9:286	Si la mist a reson un jor:
9:287	"Dame," fet il, "or est ainsi,
9:288	De moi avez fet vostre ami.
9:289	Venez vos en du tout o moi.
9:290	Savoir pöez, ce cuit et croi,
9:291	Se vostre ante s'aparcevoit
9:292	Que durement l'em peseroit.
9:293	S'entor li estes enceintie,
9:294	Durement en ert coroucie.
9:295	Se mon conseil croire volez,
9:296	Ensemble o moi vos en venrez.
9:297	Certes, jamés ne vos faudrai,
9:298	Richement vos conseillerai."
9:299	Cele qui durement l'amot
9:300	Li otroia quanque li plot.
9:301	Ensemble o lui s'en est alee;
9:302	En son chastel l'en a menee.
9:303	Son paille emporte et son anel:
9:304	De ce li puet estre molt bel.
9:305	L'abaesse li ot rendu
9:306	Et dit comment ert avenu,
9:307	Quant primes li fu envoiee:
9:308	Desus le fresne fu cochiee;
9:309	Le paille et l'anel li bailla
9:310	Cil qui primes li envoia.
9:311	La meschine bien les garda;
9:312	En un coffre les enferma.
9:313	Le coffre fist o soi porter,
9:314	Nu volt lessier ne oublier.
9:315	Le chevalier qui l'enmena
9:316	Molt la chieri et molt l'ama;
9:317	Tuit si homme et si serjant,

9:318   N'i ot un seul, petit ne grant,
9:319   Por sa franchise ne l'amast,
9:320   Ne la servist et l'anorast.

9:299   *amot*: see note to *mandot*, 1:14.
9:305   The dir. obj. *le*, referring to the cloth, is omitted before the ind. obj. *li*. See note
          to 4:124.
9:307–08 The past participles agree with the unexpressed subject *ele* (= Fresne).
9:310   See note to 9:305.
9:315   *Le chevalier* is for NS *Li chevaliers*.

---

33. Demonstrative Pronouns

33.1. Syntax of *cel*. Demonstrative pronouns have the same forms as
the demonstrative adjectives *cel* and *cest* (see 6.20). By the late twelfth
century, however, *cest* had come to be specialized as an adjective and was
rarely used as a pronoun. *Cel*, on the other hand, is found in our texts
equally as a pronoun and as an adjective. This differentiation in usage
arose from the essential distinction between the two forms: *cest* indicates
that which is near in time, space, or psychological interest, whereas *cel*
applies to more distant concepts or objects. Only in very rare instances,
where the pronominalized item is immediately at hand and is the primary
subject of conversation, can *cest* be found as a pronoun:

> *Cest* et un anel me baillierent (13:443)
> This (cloth) and a ring (they) gave me

The demonstrative pronoun is most frequently employed to indicate
the subject in the narration of past events:

> *Cil* et *celes* qui la veoient (11:390)
> Those, both male and female, who saw her

In many cases it is a simple substitute for the strong-form subject
pronoun and is best translated as "he, she, they":

> *Cele* qui durement l'amot (9:299)
> She who strongly (i.e., dearly) loved him

> *Cil* qui primes li envoia (9:310)
> He who first sent (Fresne) to her

33.2. The neuter demonstrative pronoun *ce*. The neuter demonstrative pronoun *ce* (*ço*) may be used as a subject, as an object, or in combination with *que* to introduce direct relative or prepositional clauses:

SUBJECT

*c'*est veritez (3:75) 'it's true'

OBJECT

ce cuit et croi (9:290) 'I believe and trust this'

As a subject or object, *ce* generally refers back to the preceding sentence, clause, or concept:

> Son paille emporte et son anel:
> De *ce* li puet estre molt bel. (9:303–04)
> She carries her cloth and her ring:
> For this she can be most glad.

TO INTRODUCE CLAUSES

> *Ço'*st granz merveile *que* li mens quors tant duret. (3, 215)
> This is a great wonder, that my heart still beats.
>
> Ele otroia *ce qu'*il li dist (8:284)
> She granted that which he asked (lit.: told) her
>
> Et molt la tenoit en destroit,
> San ce qu'ele nu deservoit. (2:63–64)
> And he guarded her very closely, without her deserving it.

34. Strong Present Tenses

Verbs whose stems have more than one form in their present indicative and present subjunctive tenses are said to have "strong presents." Most variation in form is due to **vocalic alternation**, which means that the **stem vowel** throughout the singular and in the third person plural is different from that in the first and second persons plural. This difference resulted from regular phonological developments that are explained in the phonology section at the end of this chapter. In six verbs only there is

syllabic alternation, in which the first person singular and the first and second persons plural forms have one less syllable than the other forms. Syllabic alternation, too, is explained in the phonology section.

Verbs showing vocalic alternation in the present tenses can be divided into two types:

(I) those in which the first, second, and third persons singular and the third person plural share a single stem;

(II) and those in which, additionally, the first person singular has its own unique development, attributable to the effects of palatalization.

34.1. Vocalic alternation, Type I. The endings are the same as those for Classes I, Ia, and III weak verbs (see 5.17.1):

PRESENT INDICATIVE

	Class I amer	*Class Ia* proisier	*Class III* criembre, cremir
Sg. 1	aim	pris	criem
2	aim es	pris es	crien s
3	aim e	pris e	crien t
Pl. 1	am ons	prois ons	crem ons
2	am ez	prois iez	crem ez
3	aim ent	pris ent	criem ent

PRESENT SUBJUNCTIVE

Sg. 1	aim	pris	criem e
2	ain z	pris	criem es
3	ain t	pris t	criem e
Pl. 1	am ons	prois ons	crem ons
2	am ez	prois iez	crem ez
3	aim ent	pris ent	criem ent

For modifications to stem consonants based on verbal endings, see Phonology 3.

34.2. Vocalic alternation, Type II. Many Class III verbs (infinitives in *-ir*, *-oir*, *-re*) have unique forms in the first person singular indicative owing to palatalization (see Phonology 15):

PRESENT INDICATIVE

	boillir	coillir	doloir	pooir	joindre
Sg. 1	boil	cueil	dueil, doil	puis	joing
2	bous	cueuz	dueus	puez	joinz
3	bout	cueut	dueut	puet	joint
Pl. 1	boillons, bolons	coillons	dolons	poons	joignons
2	boilliez, bolez	coilliez	dolez	poez	joigniez
3	boillent, bolent	cueillent	duelent	pueent	joignent

PRESENT SUBJUNCTIVE

The palatalized first person form is generally taken for the stem throughout the present subjunctive:

Sg. 1	boill e	cueill e	dueill e	puiss e	joign e
2	boill es	cueill es	dueill es	puiss es	joign es
3	boill e	cueill e	dueill e	puiss e	joign e
Pl. 1	boill iens	cueill iens	dueill iens	puiss iens	joign iens
2	boill iez	cueill iez	dueill iez	puiss iez	joign iez
3	boill ent	cueill ent	dueill ent	puiss ent	joign ent

But a number of these verbs can maintain stem alternation in the present subjunctive, creating alternate forms in the first and second persons plural:

Sg. 1	cueill e	dueill e
2	cueill es	dueill es
3	cueill e	dueill e
Pl. 1	coill iens	doill iens
2	coill iez	doill iez
3	cueill ent	dueill ent

In the first person plural the ending *-iens* is regular after the palatalized stem. By analogy, however, the ending *-ons* is frequently extended to these verbs; for example:

nous cueilliens; nous cueillons; nous coilliens; nous coillons
nous puissiens; nous puissons
nous joigniens; nous joignons

34.3. Syllabic alternation. Six common verbs show alternating forms
in the present tense due to syllabic rather than vocalic alternation—that
is, the shift of accent from the stem to the ending causes the first and
second persons plural to have one less syllable than the other persons.
The verbs so affected are *aidier* 'to aid,' *araisnier* 'to speak to, to address,'
deraisnier 'to argue,' *disner* 'to dine,' *mangier* 'to eat,' and *parler* 'to speak':

PRESENT INDICATIVE

Sg. 1	aiu	araison	deraison	desjun	manju	parol
2	aiues	araisones	deraisones	desjunes	manjues	paroles
3	aiue	araisone	deraisone	desjune	manjue	parole
Pl. 1	aidons	araisnons	deraisnons	disnons	manjons	parlons
2	aidiez	araisniez	deraisniez	disnez	mangiez	parlez
3	aiuent	araisonent	deraisonent	desjunent	manjuent	parolent

PRESENT SUBJUNCTIVE

Sg. 1	aiu	araison	deraison	desjun	manju	parol
2	aiuz	araisons	deraisons	desjuns	manjuz	parous
3	aiut	araisont	deraisont	desjunt	manjut	parout
Pl. 1	aidons	araisnons	deraisnons	disnons	manjons	parlons
2	aidiez	araisniez	deraisniez	disnez	mangiez	parlez
3	aiudent	araisonent	deraisonent	desjunent	manjuent	parolent

35. Prepositions

With the loss of the Latin case system, prepositions assumed a much
more important role in the syntax of Vulgar Latin and Old French.
Because Old French appropriated many Latin prepositions and formed
numerous new prepositions, it could express subtle syntactical relationships with considerable facility.

In theory, prepositions and adverbs fulfill different functions. A **preposition** relates a nominal element (noun, pronoun, adjective, infinitive,
present participle, gerund, or adverb) to some other element in the
sentence, usually a verb or noun, when a direct relationship between
these elements is not possible. An **adverb** modifies the meaning of an

entire sentence or of a sentence element other than a noun, such as an adjective, a verb, or another adverb. In Old French, however, there is frequently no clear morphological distinction between prepositions and adverbs, and much of the color and richness of Old French syntax is due to the imaginative and varied ways in which they can be employed. For example, in "Fresne" 5:173 *desus* is an adverb:

> au fresne vint errant,
> *Desus* le mist
> to the ash tree (she) came running,
> on it (she) put it (i.e., the infant)

But in line 9:308 it functions as a preposition:

> *Desus* le fresne fu cochiee
> On the ash tree (she) was laid

Similarly, *entor* is an adverb in line 4:131:

> La verge *entor* estoit letree
> The band around (the ring) was (engraved with) letters

and a preposition in line 6:207:

> *Entor* son braz trueve l'anel
> Around her arm (she) found the ring

35.1. Prepositions versus adverbs. The following are some of the more common words that may be either prepositions or adverbs in Old French:

*ainz 'rather, but, before'
*aprés 'after, afterward'
*ariere 'behind'
*avant 'before'
*avuec, aveuc, avec 'with'
*com, com(e) 'with'
*contre, encontre 'against; toward, facing'
*devant 'before'
deriere 'behind'
endroit 'about, as regards'
*enz, denz 'within'
environ 'around, about, near'
*entor 'around'
*fors, hors 'out, outside, except'
*joste 'beside'

lez 'next to'
*pres 'near, nearby'
*puis 'since'
*sus 'above, over, on, upon'
*sous, soz 'beneath, below, under'
tres 'beside, through'

Words preceded by an asterisk are all found in the reading selections in this volume.

35.2. Exclusive prepositions. The following words function almost exclusively as prepositions:

*a, ad (most common preposition in Old French; numerous meanings)
*de (second most common preposition; numerous meanings)
*en 'in, into, onto'
*entre 'between, among'
*o, o tot (a tot) 'with'
*par 'through, by, by means of'
*por 'because of, for the sake of, in order to'
*sans 'without'
*sor 'on, above, against'
*tresque, jusque 'up to'
*vers 'toward, against'

Note: this is not a complete listing of all prepositions in Old French, only of those that are most common or are found in the reading selections in this volume.

35.3. Formation of prepositions. In addition to accommodating many Latin prepositions (*a, contre, entre, o, par, selon, tres*), Old French created a rich series of prepositions by appropriating Latin nouns (*fors, chez, lez*), adjectives (*lonc, proche, sauf*), past participles and gerunds (*pres, pendant, suivant*), and adverbs (*soz, puis, ainz*) and by combining the simple prepositions listed in the preceding sections. The most common compound prepositions were those formed by adding *de* to the base form: e.g., *deenz, dedenz, defors, delez, desor, desus, devers, desoz, dejoste*. These in turn could be recompounded: e.g., *dedevant, dedesus*. *De* followed certain prepositions: e.g., *fors de, pres de*. Forms beginning with *de-* could be further varied by adding *par*: e.g., *par delez, par dejoste, par desus, par desoz, par devers, par devant*. Other combinations were equally possible: *parmi, envers*. Two prepositions in particular had multiple variants, all with little or no change in meaning: *tresque, dusque, desque, entresque, jusque, trusque* (all + *a: tresqu'a,* etc.) and *desque, deci, decique, desique* (all + *a, de, en*).

35.4. Types of prepositions. For convenience, we shall list the prepositions found in "Fresne" in two series: those that have multiple functions, to whose syntax we shall devote separate sections (14:59 and 15:60), and those with simple functions.

Multiple function prepositions: *a, de, en, o, par, por.*

Simple function prepositions: *selonc* 2 'according to'; *devant* 21, 158, 217 'before'; *joste* 26 'next to'; *desqu'a* 69 'up, to'; *desi qu'a* 172 'from here to'; *vers* 93, 376, 474 'toward'; *fors de* 138 'outside'; *parmi* 141 'through the midst of'; *entor* 207, 293, 387 'around'; *emprés, aprés* 211, 328 'after'; *dedenz* 233 'within'; *ensemble o* 296, 301 'with, together with'; *desus* 308 'on'; *pres de* 339 'near.'

36. Prepositional Phrases: Word Order

When the prepositional phrase complements a noun or pronoun, it generally follows that noun or pronoun:

> l'uis *du mostier* (6:178)
> The door of the church
>
> Petit *em berz* (6:195)
> Small in (the) cradle

When the prepositional phrase is a verbal complement, however, it regularly precedes that verb, especially in verse:

> *Ensemble o moi* vos en venrez (9:296)
> Together with me you will come away
>
> *En son chastel* l'en a menee (9:302)
> To his castle he brought her

This construction is equally prevalent in dependent clauses:

> La fame . . .
> Qui *joste lui* au mengier sist (2:25–26)
> The woman . . .
> Who was seated beside him at table
>
>   . . . cele aventure
> Qu'*a une seule porteüre*
> Une fame deus enfanz ait (2:39–41)
>   . . . this marvel
> That one woman would have
> Two children at one delivery

Phonology 9

Vocalic alternation

In all Latin conjugations except the third, the accent shifted from the stem to the ending for the first and second persons plural. This pattern was generalized in Vulgar Latin and is found in all Old French verbs:

Sg. 1	dur	< DÚRO	cor	< córro	< CÚRRO
2	dures	< DÚRAS	cors	< córres	< CÚRRIS
3	dure	< DÚRAT	cort	< córret	< CÚRRIT
Pl. 1	durons	< *DURÚMUS	corons	< *corrómos	< CÚRRIMUS
2	durez	< DURÁTIS	corez	< corrétes	< CÚRRITIS
3	durent	< DÚRANT	corent	< córront	< CÚRRUNT

This accent shift had no effect on the conjugation of most Old French verbs, but in well over a hundred verbs of Classes I, Ia, and III it resulted in a double stem.

Alternation was possible in any verb with a radical containing a free vowel whose development was affected by changes in stress (see Phonology Sections 7 and 8). In those persons in which the accent strikes the stem vowel, that vowel when free will tend to diphthongize; otherwise the stem vowel will remain. Consider the verb *amer* 'to love':

		PRESENT INDICATIVE		**PRESENT SUBJUNCTIVE**	
Sg. 1	aim	< ÁMO	aim	< ÁMEM
2	aimes	< ÁMAS	ains	< ÁMES
3	aime	< ÁMAT	aint	< ÁMET
Pl. 1	amons	< *AMÚMUS	amons	< *AMÚMUS
2	amez	< AMÁTIS	amez	< AMÉTIS
3	aiment	< ÁMANT	aiment	< ÁMENT

In this case, accented free A followed by the nasal M diphthongized to *āi*; unaccented A remained. Other verbs of this type include: *clamer/claime* and *manoir/maint*. Similarly:

Sg. 1	lef	< LÁVO	lef	< LÁVEM
2	leves	< LÁVAS	les	< LÁVES
3	leve	< LÁVAT	let	< LÁVET

Pl. 1	lavons	< *LAVÚMUS	lavons	< *LAVÚMUS
2	lavez	< LAVÁTIS	lavez	< LAVÉTIS
3	levent	< LÁVANT	levent	< LÁVENT

Here, accented free A > *e*; unaccented A remains. Other verbs of this type include *comparer/compere, parer/pere, hair/het, paroir/pert*, and *savoir/set*.

The following table lists other frequently encountered modifications. The heading gives the unstressed vowel followed by the stressed vowel. For the verbs, the infinitive is given as an example of the unstressed form; the third singular present indicative illustrates the stressed form. For those few verbs with stressed infinitives, the first person plural is added.

e/a
acheter/achate; traveillier/travaille.
e/ei > oi
adeser/adoise; *(a)percevoir/(a)perçoit; boivre/boit/bevons; celer/çoile; *concevoir/conçoit; conreer/conroie; croire/croit/creons; *decevoir/de-çoit; devoir/doit; esfreer/esfroie; errer/erroie; esperer/espoire; peser/poise; *recevoir/reçoit; sevrer/soivre; veoir/voit. *Infinitives preceded by an asterisk are also found with a stressed vowel:* aperçoivre, conçoivre, *etc.*
e/ēi (+ nasal)
mener/meine; pener/peine.
e/ie
achever/achieve; assegier/assiege; cheoir/chiet; crever/crieve; depecier/depiece; ferir/fiert; geler/giele; grever/grieve; lever/lieve; querre/quiert; seoir/siet.
e/iē (+ nasal)
criembre/crient/cremons; tenir/tient; venir/vient.
e/i
concheer/conchie; gesir/gist.
ei > oi/i
empoirier/empire; loiier/lie; noier/nie; oissir/ist; otroiier/otrie; ploiier/plie; proiier/prie; proisier/prise. *These verbs later adopted stressed infinitives:* empirier, issir, lier, nier.
o > ou/o > ou > eu
aorer (aourer)/aore (aeure); avoer (avouer)/avoe (aveue); cousdre/keust; demourer/demeure; espouser/espeuse; labourer/labeure; onourer/oneure; plourer/pleure; savourer/saveure.
o > ou/ue
couillir/cueilt; couvrir/cuevre; doloir/dueut; enfouïr/enfuet; estovoir/estuet; morir/muert; moudre/mueut; movoir/muet; ouvrir/uevre; plovoir/pluet; pooir/puet; prouver/prueve; rover/rueve; soloir/suelt; soufrir/suefre; trouver/trueve; voloir/vuelt (vueut).

oi/ui
apoiier/apuie; aproismier/apruisme; enoiier/enuie.

Note that in some verbs vocalic alternation exists without affecting the spelling: *apeler/apele, metre/met* (which alternate weak with stressed *e*), *aprochier/aproche* (closed /o/ with open /ɔ/).

Syllabic alternation

Syllabic alternation, like vocalic alternation, had its origin in the Latin accent shift. In this case, the unaccented intertonic vowel dropped out altogether before the stress:

Sg. 1	parol	<	*paráulo
2	paroles	<	*paráulas
3	parole	<	*paráulat
Pl. 1	parlons	<	*par(au)lúmus
2	parlez	<	*par(au)látis
3	parolent	<	*paráulant

Both syllabic and vocalic alternation were lost for most verbs during the Middle French period as a result of a process known as **leveling** or **regularization**. Some very common verbs, however, maintained alternation into modern French and are now classified as **irregular verbs**.

chapter 10

Reading and Textual Analysis, Selection 6

With this selection we arrive at a major turning point in our story. The hero, who has lived with Fresne for a long while, cannot marry her, for her background is unknown and any children he might have by her would therefore be ineligible to inherit his lands.

The question of a peaceful succession was of critical importance throughout the Middle Ages. Largely through the influence of the Christian church, the earlier Roman and Germanic concepts of elected kingship were replaced after Merovingian times by the notion of kingship "by the grace of God." In the earliest periods the kings, who could be selected from any of the noble families, ruled by popular consent (*voluntas populi*) and could be deposed if necessary. In Gaul, in the seventh and eighth centuries, power gradually became concentrated in the hands of a single noble family, or dynasty: first the Merovingians (pre-751), then the Carolingians (751–987), and finally the Capetians (post-987). The kings now appealed to God as the ultimate source of their power, rather than to the people. To preserve power within the family, the notion of primogeniture—by which the eldest son inherited the father's crown—was gradually formulated. This principle was clearly established by the early twelfth century, as is clear in a work such as the *Couronnement de Louis*, an Old French epic poem of the 1130s. In the *Couronnement*, the loyal vassal William of Orange comes to the rescue of the ignoble but nonetheless legitimate eldest son of Charlemagne, Louis. William stands by Louis and ensures his coronation in spite of Louis's obvious incapacity for leadership. William's role is, indeed, that of peacemaker. The existence of a legitimate male heir, however unworthy, was perceived as a sine qua non for securing peace upon the death of a king. In France until the time of Philippe-Auguste, the heir had to be crowned during the lifetime of his ruling father in order to ensure the rights of primogeniture. Louis VIII was the first king to be crowned after the death of his father (1223). In this reading selection the feudal knights urge their leader to make a proper marriage so as to provide an heir and, by implication, a peaceful succession.

10:321	Longuement a o lui esté,
10:322	Tant que li chevalier fiefé
10:323	A molt grant mal li atornerent.
10:324	Sovente foiz a lui parlerent,
10:325	C'une gentil fame espousast
10:326	Et de cele se delivrast.
10:327	Lié seroient, s'il avoit oir
10:328	Qui aprés lui peüst avoir
10:329	Sa terre et son grant heritage;
10:330	Trop i avroient grant dommage
10:331	Se il lessoit por sa soignant
10:332	Que d'espouse n'eüst enfant;
10:333	Jamés por seignor nu tendront
10:334	Ne volentiers nu serviront
10:335	Se il ne fet lor volonté.
10:336	Li chevaliers a creanté
10:337	Qu'a lor conseil fame prendra;
10:338	Or esgardent ou ce sera.
10:339	"Sire," font il, "ci pres de nos
10:340	A un preudom; per est a vos.
10:341	Une fille a, si n'a plus d'oir;
10:342	Molt poez terre o li avoir.
10:343	La Coudre a non la damoisele,
10:344	En tout cest païs n'a tant bele.
10:345	Por le Fresne que vos perdroiz
10:346	En eschange la Coudre avroiz.
10:347	En la coudre a noiz et deduiz;
10:348	Le fresne n'a onques nus fruiz.
10:349	La pucele porchaceron:
10:350	Se Deu plet, si la vos donron."
10:351	Ce mariage ont porchacié
10:352	Et de totes pars otroié.

10:353   Ha las! comme est mesavenu
10:354   Que li preudom n'orent seü
10:355   La verité des damoiseles,
10:356   Qui estoient serors jumeles.
10:357   Le Fresne cele fu celee,
10:358   L'autre a ses amis espousee.
10:359   Quant ele sot que il le prist,
10:360   Onques poior semblant nen fist.
10:361   Son seignor sert molt noblement
10:362   Et ennore toute sa gent.
10:363   Li chevalier de la meson
10:364   Et li vilain et li garçon
10:365   Merveilleus duel por li fesoient,
10:366   Por ce que perdre la devoient.

10:323   Dir. obj. pron. *le* omitted before ind. obj. See note to 4:124.
10:340   *A*: reduced form of *il i a* (see 8.31.1).
10:343   An example of C/V/S word order.
10:348   *Le Fresne* is NS. Most proper names became indeclinable very early; see 4.12.
10:350   *Deu*: ind. obj.; see 5.14.2.
10:351   An early appearance of the adj. *ce*; see 6.20.1.
10:357   "The former (i.e., Coudre) was kept hidden from Fresne."
10:366   *devoient* 'were about to.' See 21.92 and note to 2:54.

---

37. Infinitives: Forms

As a result of the instability of certain conjugation patterns in Vulgar Latin, Old French verbs frequently had more than one infinitive. The verbs most commonly affected were those ending in -*ir*, -*oir*, and -*re*. (For infinitives of weak verbs, see 5.17.)

The following verbs had infinitives in -*ir* and -*re*:

asaillir/asaudre	to assail, to assault, to attack
beneïr/beneïstre	to bless
bolir/boudre	to boil
coillir, cueillir/cueldre	to gather, to collect
corir/corre	to run
cremir/criembre, criendre	to fear
issir/istre	to exit, to leave

luisir/luire	to shine
nuisir/nuire	to harm
plaisir/plaire	to please
querir/querre	to seek
sevir, sivir/sivre, siure	to follow
taisir/taire	to quiet, to be silent
tolir/toldre, toudre	to take away, to remove

The following had infinitives in *-oir* and *-re*:

(a)percevoir/(a)perçoivre	to perceive
ardoir/ardre	to burn
concevoir/conçoivre	to conceive
decevoir/deçoivre	to deceive
manoir/maindre	to live (in a place)
recevoir/reçoivre	to receive
remanoir/remaindre	to remain
semonoir/semondre	to summon
soloir/soldre, soudre	to be wont, to be accustomed

The following had palatalized as well as nonpalatalized infinitives:

bolir/boillir	to boil
faloir/faillir	to fail
salir/saillir	to go out, to sally forth

Other verbs, without changing conjugations, developed various spellings for their infinitives. These changes sometimes involved nothing more than the phonetic evolution of *-ei-* to *-oi-* in the central and eastern dialects or the vocalization of *l* + consonant, both of which occurred in the course of the Old French period:

> creire/croire; creistre/croistre; leisir/loisir.
> cueldre/cueudre; moldre/moudre; toldre/toudre.

In other verbs, it represented the hesitation between palatalized and nonpalatalized infinitives:

> bolir/boillir; faloir/faillir; salir/saillir.

It could also be the end product of individual phonological developments too diverse to discuss in detail in this context, as in:

cheoir/chaoir; cosdre/coudre; criembre/craindre; eissir/issir; foïr/fuïr; gesir/gisir; laier/laissier; raembre/raeindre; veintre/vaincre.

38. Infinitives: Syntax

Although the infinitive is, strictly speaking, a verbal element, it functions as a substantive much more frequently in Old French than in the modern language. As a substantive it can take an article or other nominal determiner and act as subject, apostrophe, or object. It regularly takes the nominative -s and is declined like a Class II noun (3.6.2):

Tant i donra terre et *avoir* (8:273)
He will give (the abbey) so much land and goods

Si defenderont il mix lor cors et lor *avoirs* (20:25b)
Thus they'll defend better themselves (lit. their bodies) and their
   possessions

ele est reperie a son *estre* (19, 53)
she has returned to her home

Encontrez les aveient el cloistre *al repairier* (17:20)
They had met them in the cloister at their return

38.1. Infinitives used as subjects. An infinitive used as the subject would usually be in the nominative case:

Ja *li corners* ne nos avreit mester (6, 52)
Sounding the horn would be of no use to us now

When the infinitive is the logical subject of the sentence, it is often preceded by *de* (*del, du*) and has no nominative marker:

*D'*enfant *ocirre* n'est pas gas. (4: 98)
(Normal word order: *D'ocirre* enfant n'est pas gas.)
To kill a child is no light matter.

Il n'est corteisie ne san
de plet d'oiseuse *maintenir.* (*Yvain,* 98–99)
(Normal word order: *De maintenir* plet d'oiseuse. . . .)
It is not courteous or wise
to speak of idle things.

Dex! je ne sai que doie faire,
Ou *de l'ocire* ou *du retraire*. (13, 169–70)
God! I don't know what I should do,
Whether to kill him or to withdraw it.

38.2. Infinitives used as objects.   When the infinitive functions as an object, it may be used directly after the verb that governs it, or it may be introduced by *a*, *de*, or any of a variety of other prepositions. In early Old French one finds mostly the pure infinitive. In the course of the twelfth century, the infinitive with *a* became popular, then both the pure infinitive and the infinitive with *a* lost ground to the infinitive with *de*.

The infinitive is used directly, without an introductory preposition, as the object of modal auxiliary verbs: *voloir*, *devoir*, *pooir*, *soloir*, *savoir*, *oser*, *querre*, *estovoir*, *covenir*:

Se mon conseil *croire volez* (9:295)
If you wish to believe my advice

Molt *poez* terre o li *avoir* (10:342)
You can have much land with her (i.e., upon marrying her)

Ovrir soloit l'uis du mostier (6:178)
He regularly opened the door of the church

It is likewise used directly after the causative auxiliaries *faire* and *laissier*:

A un mostier la *fis geter* (14:477)
I had her placed in a church

"Dame," fet il, "*laissiez ester!*" (2:45)
"Milady," said he, "let it be!" ("Stop!")

It is used directly as a complement of destination or purpose after *aler*, *venir*, and other similar verbs:

Li portiers *vet* a li *parler* (7:213)
The gateman goes to speak with her

As an object, the infinitive may be introduced by *a* and, more rarely, by *de*, which ideally indicate a relationship of direction. In fact, however, the *a* is usually untranslatable and serves only to link the infinitive to what precedes it:

Si la commande *a despoillier* (12:416)
And she ordered her to undress

Cil qui *a norrir* m'envoiererent (13:444)
Those who sent me away to be raised

Apresté *de* grant mal *comencier* (16:27)
(Normal word order: apresté *de comencier* grant mal)
Ready to undertake great wickedness

As a circumstantial complement, the infinitive may be introduced by a number of prepositions to distinguish a variety of subtle relationships: *a* (purpose, manner, means, cause), *aprés* (temporal), *de* (cause, means, circumstances), *por* (reason, consequence, cause, concession), *sanz* (exclusion), *sor* (used in threats with the meaning "under penalty of"):

L'un li trametra *a lever* (1:17)
He will send him one (of the twins) to raise

Alez la sus el quer *a* voz vespres *chanter* (17:40)
Go up there to the choir (in order) to sing your vespers

Por avoir la fraternité (8:277)
So as to be able to meet with her

Li chevaliers . . .
L'a resgardé *sans dire* mot (5, 102–03)
The knight . . .
Looked at him without saying a word

For the infinitive used as an imperative, see 17.72.

38.3. Objects of infinitives. An infinitive in Old French may have as its object a noun or a pronoun in the oblique case. It generally precedes the matrix verb, especially if the latter is a modal auxiliary. The pronoun object is regularly unstressed:

Ja tant ne *les porroiz destraindre* (12, 292)
Never will you be able to twist them enough

Il *se vindrent* touz *assembler* devant nous (26, 107)
They all came to assemble themselves before us

Por ce que *perdre la devoient* (10:366)
Because they were about to lose her

If, however, the infinitive is itself introduced by a preposition, the stressed object pronoun form is used:

Corage avoie *d'eus ocire* (13, 177)
I had intended to kill them

De toy ferir
J'ai grant talent et grant envie. (23, 70–71)
I have a strong desire and strong urge
To kill you.

De li servir se presenterent (10, 343)
They volunteered to serve her

39.   The Future and the -*roie* Form (Conditional or Hypothetical Future)

In 5.16–17 we noted that all verbs have a special stem for the future and -*roie* forms. For most verbs, this stem is the full infinitive (less the final unaccented -*e* in Class III verbs):

> servir ont (10:334)
> porchacer on (10:349)
> prendr a (10:337)
> perdr oiz (10:345)

For verbs with alternate infinitives (see Section 37), the stem for the future and -*roie* form is generally that of the -*re* infinitive:

> ardoir/ardre : ardrai
> coillir/cueudre : cueudrai
> manoir/maindre : maindrai
> plaisir/plaire : plairai
> querir/querre : querrai
> soloir/soudre : soudrai
> tolir/toudre : toudrai

Many -*oir* and a few -*ir* verbs drop their characteristic vowel before these endings:

> avoir : av'r : avrai, aurai, arai
> devoir : dev'r : devrai
> estovoir : estov'r : estovra
> ferir : fer'r : ferrai
> morir : mor'r : morrai
> movoir : mov'r : movrai, mourai, morrai
> ovrir : ovr'r : ovrai
> paroir : par'r : parrai
> plovoir : plov'r : plovra, plora
> savoir : sav'r : savrai, saurai, sarai
> sivir : siv'r : sivra, siura

If there is no consonant immediately preceding the vowel, the final -r is doubled:

> cheoir : che'rr : cherrai
> haïr : ha'rr : harrai
> joïr : jo'rr : jorrai
> oïr : o'rr : orrai
> pooir : po'rr : porrai
> seoir : se'rr : serrai
> veoir : ve'rr : verrai

When the vowel loss brings together *l'r*, a *-d-* is intercalated and the *-l-* is regularly velarized to *-u-* (see Phonology 14):

> chaloir : chal'r : chaudra
> doloir : dol'r : doudrai
> valoir : val'r : vaudrai
> voloir : vol'r : voudrai

When the vowel loss brings together *n'r*, a *d* is likewise intercalated:

> tenir : ten'r : tendrai
> venir : ven'r : vendrai

Boillir, faillir, and *saillir* follow the same pattern and, additionally, lose their palatal element:

> boillir : bol'r : boudrai
> faillir : fal'r : faudrai
> saillir : sal'r : saudrai

Infinitives in *-oi(v)re* take their vowel from the first person plural present indicative:

> boivre : nous bevons : bevrai
> croire : nous creons : crerrai
> reçoivre : nous recevons : recevrai

The following verbs develop an unaccented -e- helping vowel:

> covrir : covr'r : covrera/coverra
> ofrir : ofr'r : ofrera/oferra
> ovrir : ovr'r : ovrera/overra
> sofrir : sofr'r : sofrera/soferra

A few verbs have special developments:

> aler : irai
> doner : donrai/dorrai
> estre : serai (*also*: estrai, er, ier)
> faire : ferai
> issir : istrai
> laissier : lerrai/lairai
> mener : menrai/merrai

40.   The Future

40.1.   Function.   Old French had two futures that were marked mor-phologically, the future indicative and the hypothetical future (*-roie* form), as well as several syntactic paraphrases that could indicate future action.

The future indicative situates an event after the time of narrative. If the narrative is in the present, it is translated by the future in English:

> La pucele *porchaceron*:
> Se Deu plet, si la vos *donron*. (10:349–50)
> We *shall seek* the girl:
> If it please God, we *shall give* her to you.

If the narrative time is past, it is better translated by the modern English conditional:

> Li chevaliers a creanté
> Qu'a lor conseil fame *prendra*. (10:336–37)
> The knight has promised
> That he *would take* a wife in accord with their advice.

In the second person, the future may be used as an imperative:

> "Nel ferez!" (17:35)
> "You'll not do it!"

40.2. Use of -roie form. The *-roie* form introduces an action that is likely to come to pass in the present or future. It may be used for either possible (potential) or impossible action, and it is particularly common in the apodosis of hypothetical statements introduced by *se* 'if':

Mout i *ariés* peu conquis, car tos les jors du siecle en *seroit* vo arme en infer, qu'en paradis n'*enterriés* vos ja. (22:5)
You would have gained very little, since your soul would be in Hell for eternity, for you would never enter Paradise.

Lié *seroient*, s'il avoit oir (10:327)
They *would be* happy if he had an heir

40.3. Periphrases to mark the future. The auxiliaries *devoir*, *pooir*, and *voloir* and the expressions *estre a* and *estre pres de* are occasionally used to mark simple futurity in the sense of "to be about to" (see also 21.92):

> Merveilleus duel por li fesoient,
> Por ce que perdre la *devoient*. (10:365–66)
> They grieved greatly for her,
> For they were about to lose her.

Imminence, rather than obligation, is implied here:

> Chaoir *voloit* del destrier arabi,
> Qant .j. borgois en ses bras le saisi. (*Raoul*, 3527–28)
> He was about to fall from his Arabian steed,
> When a townsman took him in his arms.

> Il savoit bien que *ert a* estre (Béroul, 325)
> He foresaw the future (lit: what was to be)

41. Hypothetical Statements

41.1. Introduced by *se*. There are several methods of producing hypothetical or conditional statements in Old French. The most common by far is the use of *se* to introduce the subordinate statement:

> *Se* il nen a l'amor de li,
> Molt se tendra a malbailli. (8:265–66)
> If he does not receive her love,
> He will consider himself most unfortunate.

The use of the present in the protasis (**If-clause**), followed by the future, imperative, or present in the apodosis (**Result-** or **Main-clause**), indicates the indubitability of the statement: if he does not receive her love he will most assuredly be unfortunate. When there is some uncertainty concerning the relationship between the two clauses—that is, when the eventuality is doubtful or problematic—there are two ways of expressing the statement:

(A)   The use of the imperfect subjunctive in both clauses:

Ne nos ne l'avïens veü,
Que fame deus enfanz *eüst*,
Se deus hommes ne *conneüst*. (3:82–84)
Nor had we seen it (happen) that a woman would have two children if she had not known two men.

Au parlemant molt volentiers
S'an *alast s'il fust* anuitié. (12, 228–29)
He would willingly go to speak (with her)
If it were dark.

(B)   The use of the imperfect indicative in the protasis and the *-roie* form in the apodosis:

Trop i *avroient* grant dommage
Se il *lessoit* por sa soignant
Que d'espouse n'eüst enfant. (10:330–32)
They would be very badly served if he were not to have legitimate children because of his mistress.

Type A was especially popular in poetry. It was totally atemporal in its statement of a hypothesis, which could be past, present, or future. Only the context will permit one to choose between:

that a woman have two children if she has not known two men;
that a woman would have two children if she had not known two men;
that a woman have two children if she doesn't know two men.

Type B situates the hypothesis temporally in the problematical present or future.

For a hypothesis bearing on the past, in addition to Type A above, Old French uses the pluperfect subjunctive in either the apodosis or the protasis, or in both:

Se il *fust* vif, jo l'*oüsse amenet*. (*Roland*, 691)
Had he survived, I would have brought him.

41.2. Without *se*. Old French has several methods of introducing hypothetical statements other than with *se*. These constructions, because of their relative infrequency, are apt to give trouble and should be considered here:

(a)   The subjunctive used in parataxis, rather than in subordination:

> Et je fusse morz grant piece a
> Ne fust li rois (*Charrete*, 4019–20)
> And I would have been dead long ago
> Were it not for the king

(b)   The subjunctive preceded by *mais* or *mais que*, meaning "provided that," "unless":

> Je n'i quier entrer, *mais que* j'aie Nicolete (22:7a)
> I don't care to enter (heaven) unless I have Nicolete.
> (i.e.: If I don't have Nicolette, I don't care to enter there.)

(c)   Use of the conjunctions *quant, que, si que,* and especially *por ce que, por tant que,* and *por que*:

Ja Dix ne me doinst riens que je li demant, *quant* ere cevaliers,
ne monte a ceval . . . (20:27a)
May God never give me anything I ask of Him if I were to become a
  knight, or mount a horse . . .

(d)   By using the undetermined relative *qui* followed by the present, future, or *-roie* form:

> *Qui* sor autrui mesdit et ment
> Ne set mie qu'a l'ueil li pent (3:87–88)
> If one slanders and lies about another
> He cannot see beyond the nose on his face
> (lit.: he doesn't know what is hanging before his eye)

Phonology 10

The diphthongization of vowels during the Gallo-Roman and early Old French periods (see Phonology 7) continued into the Old French period proper, for the tonic stress was still strongly felt. During the eleventh and early twelfth centuries, the early diphthongs *uo, ei,* and *ou* were further differentiated, becoming *ue, oi,* and *eu* respectively, as the following examples show:

| | **VULGAR** | **EARLY** | |
| **LATIN** | **LATIN** | **OLD FRENCH** | **OLD FRENCH** |

Ŏ > ǫ > uo > ue

| CŎR | > | /cǫr/ | > | cuor | > | cuer |
| SŎROR | > | /sǫror/ | > | suor | > | suer |

Ē > ẹ > ei > oi

| TĒLAM | > | /tẹ́la/ | > | teile | > | toile |
| HABĒRE | > | /aβẹ́re/ | > | aveir | > | avoir |

Ō > ọ > ou > eu

| FLŌREM | > | /flọ́re/ | > | flour | > | fleur |
| SŌLUM | > | /sọ́lo/ | > | soul | > | seul |

In Francien and the northwestern dialect region, the development of *ei* > *oi* was checked by the presence of a nasal:

| PŎENAM | > | /pẹ́na/ | > | peine | > | peine |

In the course of the twelfth century, both *ue* and *eu* were monophthongized to /ø/ (written *eu, ueu, el, oe, oeu*, or *ue*), as was the earlier diphthong *ai* to /e/.

Development of Old French Conjugations

Latin had four conjugations, distinguished by the vowel preceding the final -RE of the present infinitive: A in the first conjugation, Ē in the second, Ĕ in the third, and Ī in the fourth.

Old French Classes I and Ia (infinitives in -*er* and -*ier*). When, during the very early Old French period, unstressed A > *e* /ə/ and stressed A > *e* /e/, Latin first conjugation -ARE verbs became Old French Class I verbs with an infinitive in -*er*. Verbs whose radical ended with a palatal or palatalized consonant during this period became Class Ia verbs with infinitives in -*ier*, since free accented A preceded by a palatal > *ie* (Phonology 8). Verbs in this subclass differ from Class I verbs in only four instances: their infinitives (e.g., *laissier*), past participles (*laissié*), second plural present indicatives (*laissiez*), and third plural preterites (*laissierent*).

Old French Class II (infinitives in -ir). Old French Class II verbs developed out of Latin inchoative verbs with an -SC- infix. In Latin these verbs came from any conjugation and took the infix to express the notion of beginning an action or changing state. But in Gaul during the Vulgar Latin and Gallo-Roman periods, this infix became almost exclusively associated with verbs of the Latin fourth conjugation (-ĪRE), spreading to many verbs that did not take it in Latin and losing any notion of inchoativeness. The infix was palatalized to -iss- and is found in the present indicative plural and throughout the present subjunctive, imperfect indicative, imperative, and present participle.

Old French Class III (infinitives in -ir, -eir, -re). Old French Class III was a catchall conjugation for Latin second, third, and fourth conjugation verbs that did not fall into Classes I or II. When phonological development in the Gallo-Roman period obliterated the distinction between unstressed Ē, Ĕ, and Ĭ (Phonology 8), the conjugation patterns of verbs of these three conjugations became meaningless, and they tended to fall together. Already in Old French it was a "dead" conjugation, unable to take in any new verbs that might be created, and as a result it was subject to much analogical reformation. One of the principal results was the existence of alternate infinitives, some on the normal stress patterns, others reformed by analogy.

Thus, confusion between Ē and Ĕ resulted in such double infinitives as TACĒRE > taisir, TÁCĔRE > taire; PLACĒRE > plaisir, PLÁCĔRE > plaire (stressed Ē preceded by palatal > i—see Phonology 8).

When the stressed future endings (originally from the verb HABEO, HABERE) were added to an infinitive, the final vowel of the infinitive might then be treated as intertonic and drop if not originally an A. Thus, ARDERE + HABEO > ardoir + ai > ardrai, and EXIRE + HABES > eissir + as > istras. These future forms without characteristic vowels gave rise to new infinitive forms, which led to the series of doublets ardoir/ardre, manoir/maindre, recevoir/reçoivre, and so on.

chapter 11

Reading and Textual Analysis, Selection 7A

The last third of the lay of "Fresne" centers on the wedding day and the recognition of the eponymous heroine as the rejected and long-lost daughter of the Lord of Brittany.

Throughout the medieval period there was an ongoing struggle between church and state for temporal supremacy, of which the most notable manifestation was the Investiture Controversy. At least from the time of Charlemagne, kings and lay magnates controlled appointments to church offices, particularly in Germanic territories and Britain. After offering homage to the lay overlord, the churchman was granted his position, titles, lands, and income by an act known as investiture (from VESTĪRE 'to put in possession'). This practice led to numerous abuses, especially simony, and to the frequent subordination of spiritual concerns to secular interests. In the late eleventh century the papacy, under the strong leadership of Gregory VII (1073–85) and Urban II (1088–99), asserted its right to make ecclesiastical appointments. Throughout the twelfth century there were concessions on each side. In England particularly, capable kings like William I and Henry I were able to challenge papal interference successfully. The resolution of this controversy, confirmed in Magna Carta (1215), foreshadowed the separation of church and state that has so profoundly affected the course of Western civilization. Lines 369–70 of this selection suggest that the archbishopric of Dol was filled by the Lord of Dol rather than by ecclesiastical authorities.

11:367	Au jor des noces qu'il ot pris,
11:368	Li sire i vint et ses amis;
11:369	Li arcevesques i estoit,
11:370	Cil de Dol qui de lui tenoit.
11:371	S'espouse li ont amenee;
11:372	Sa mere est o li alee:
11:373	De la meschine avoit peor,
11:374	O cui li sire ot tele amor,
11:375	Que a sa fille mal tenist
11:376	Vers son seignor, s'ele poïst.
11:377	De sa meson la getera;
11:378	A son gendre conseillera
11:379	Qu'a un preudome la marit,
11:380	Si s'en delivrera, ce dit.
11:381	Les noces tindrent richement;
11:382	Molt i ot esbanoiement.
11:383	La damoisele es chambres fu.
11:384	Onques de qanque a veü
11:385	Ne fist semblant qu'a li pesast
11:386	Sol tant qu'ele s'en coroçast.
11:387	Entor la dame bonement
11:388	Servoit molt afetiement.
11:389	A grant merveille le tenoient
11:390	Cil et celes qui la veoient.
11:391	Sa mere l'a molt esgardee,
11:392	En son cuer proisiee et amee.
11:393	Pensa et dist s'ele seüst
11:394	La maniere et que el fust,
11:395	Ja por sa fille nel perdist
11:396	Ne son seignor ne li tolist.

11:368 *ses amis*: OP for NP.
11:369 *li arcevesques*: m. NS *-s* by analogy. See 3.7.2 and 3.8.
11:383 *la demoiselle*: i.e., Fresne.
11:395 *perdre* 'to destroy.'

42. The Pronominal Adverbs *I* and *En*

These forms are always unstressed and therefore cannot begin a sentence or word group, nor can they immediately precede an infinitive. In all of these cases they are postpositioned (see 1.2.2).

42.1.   *I*:

(a)   True to its etymology (< IBI), *i* functions primarily as an adverb of place, "there":

> Li sire *i* vint et ses amis (11:368)
> The lord and his friends came there

> Un couvertor *i* ont jeté (12:406)
> (They) have thrown a coverlet there (i.e., over the bed)

(b)   An important extension of this meaning involves its use in the verbal expression *i avoir*: *i a*, *i ot* 'there is, there are':

> Molt *i ot* esbanoiement (11:382)
> There was great rejoicing/partying

> Mes *i avoit* autre achoison (8:279)
> But there was another reason

(Review Section 8.31.1.)

(c)   *I* is frequently the equivalent of a pronoun preceded by the preposition *a*. Note that in Old French, as opposed to modern French, both *i* and *en* may refer to persons as well as to objects:

> Ce poise moi qu'il *i* va ne qu'il *i* vient ne qu'il *i* parole (21:6)
> It disturbs me that he visits her (lit: that he goes to
>   her and comes to her) and speaks to her

> Se vos *i* parlés (22:12a)
> If you speak to her

42.2.   *En*:

(a)   *En* functions as an adverb of place ("from there"), particularly with verbs of motion:

> Venez vos *en* du tout o moi (9:289)
> Come away from there (completely) with me

In most instances it is redundant and is better left untranslated:

> De la chambre s'*en* ist atant (5:136)
> From the room (she) left at once
> She left the room at once

(b) *En* is frequently the equivalent of a personal pronoun preceded by the preposition *de*. It can mean "of it, about it, of me/him/her/them, about me/him/her/them." Like *i*, *en* may refer to persons as well as to objects:

> Si s'*en* delivrera (11:380)
> Thus (she) will rid herself of her
>
> Por la joie que il *en* ot (1:13)
> Because of the joy he felt (lit: had) about it
>
> Et cil *en* est si adolés! (5, 119)
> And he is so sad about me!

(c) *En* is used to replace the noun in counting:

> Or *en* ai deus (3:85)
> Now I have two (of them)
>
> Deus filles oi, l'une *en* celai (14:476)
> I had two daughters, one of them I hid

42.3. Possible confusions. The pronominal adverb *i* should not be confused with the rarely used pronoun *i* (= *il* before consonants):

> Sire, s'*i* te vient a plesir (5:163)
> Sir, if it please you

The pronominal adverb *en* should not be confused with the multipurpose preposition *en* (see 15.60.4) or with the rare pronoun *en* (= *on*):

> De tel homme puet *en* parler (3:89)
> Of such a man can one speak

(See 7.27.)

43. Relative and Interrogative Pronouns: Forms

In Old French, relative and interrogative pronouns share the same forms and have nearly identical declensions. There is no distinction for gender and number; forms are specialized, however, by applying either to persons or to things, and neuter forms occur only with singular verbs.

43.1. Relatives (who, whom, whose, which, that, what):

SG./PL.	PERSONS	THINGS	NEUTER USES
Nom.	qui	qui	que
Obl. direct	que	que	que
Obl. direct (stressed)	cui	quoi	quoi
Obl. indirect	cui		

43.2. Interrogatives (who? whom? whose? which? what?):

SG./PL.	PERSONS	THINGS	NEUTER USES
Nom.	qui	qui	que, quoi
Obl. direct	—	que	que
Obl. direct (stressed)	cui	quoi	quoi
Obl. indirect	cui		

Cui and *quoi* occur only as stressed forms; *que* and *qui* may be either stressed or unstressed. The interrogative usage of *qui, cui, que, quoi* will be considered in 13.52. Other relatives and interrogatives—*o* (*ou*), *ont, dont, d'ou, d'ont, quanz, quels, li quels,* and the compounds *qui que, que que,* and *cui que*—will be discussed in 20.88.1–3.

44. Relative Pronouns: Functions

As we saw in Section 6.21.2, relative constructions function primarily as nominal modifiers. They may also take pronouns for their antecedents and, in rare cases, may be used without any antecedents, expressed or implied. On word order in sentences with relative clauses, see 6.21.2.

44.1. *Qui.* *Qui* is used exclusively as a subject in the nominative case; it may refer to persons or things in the singular or plural:

> Cil de Dol *qui* de lui tenoit (11:370)
> He of Dol who was invested by him

> Cil et celes *qui* la veoient (11:390)
> Those, both male and female, who saw her

La gent *qui* en la meson erent (2:49)
The people who were in the house

Totes les fames *qui* l'oïrent (2:55)
All the women who heard her/it

Used without an antecedent, *qui* generally refers to a singular person in the indefinite sense "he/she, who, whoever":

Qui sor autrui mesdit et ment
Ne set mie (3:87–88)
Whoever slanders and lies about another
Does not know

Qui dunc veïst le sanc od le cervel chaïr . . .
De roses e de lilies li peüst sovenir. (19:46–48)
Whoever saw the blood spill forth with the brains
Would be reminded of roses and lilies.

Qui may also be used without an antecedent in the sense "if one, even if one" or to introduce an exclamation: "You should have . . . ."

Qui le veïst dedenz le fanc entrer . . .
A grant merveille le peüst resgarder. (8, 247–49)
If one were to see him enter the mud . . .
He would look on it with wonder.

Qui ore eüst du bacon
Te taiien, bien venist a point. (22, 148–49)
If we now had some of your granny's bacon,
It would be just what we need.

Ki puis veïst Rollant e Oliver
De lur espees e ferir e capler! (*Roland*, 1680–81)
You should have seen then Roland and Oliver
striking and slashing with their swords!

44.2. *Cui.* *Cui* is an oblique case relative pronoun, used with persons or with objects that are in some way personified. It may function as the indirect object, the direct object, the object of a preposition, a nominal determiner, or a possessive. It soon became confused with *qui* following the passage of its initial /kw/ sound to /k/.

INDIRECT OBJECT:

Al martyr saint Denis, *qui* (= *cui*) dulce France apent (19:13)
To the martyr St. Denis to whom sweet France belongs (or, is devoted)

DIRECT OBJECT:

> Ne fust la poor
> Del traïtor
> *Cui* je redotteroie. (16b, 15–17)
> Were it not for fear
> Of the traitor
> Whom I would dread.

OBJECT OF PREPOSITION:

> O *cui* li sire ot tele amor (11:374)
> For (lit.: with) whom the lord had such love

NOUN DETERMINER:

> Li cancelers, *cui* li mesters an eret,
> Cil list le cartre. (3, 146)
> The chancelor, whose duty it was,
> (This man) read the charter.

> . . . se ce est voirs que cil morz soit,
> Por la *cui* vie ele vivoit. (*Charrete*, 4175–76)
> . . . if this were true that the one
> For whom she lived was dead.

POSSESSIVE:

When preceded by the definite article, *cui* expresses the possessive case of the relative pronoun "whose":

> La Virge la me raporta
> Qu'a Dieu est mere,
> *La qui* (= *cui*) bonté est pure et clere (21, 241–43)
> The Virgin brought it back to me,
> Who is God's mother,
> Whose goodness is plain and evident

44.3.   *Que.* (a) The most frequent use of the relative pronoun *que* is as an unstressed object pronoun referring to persons or things in the singular or plural:

> Por le Fresne *que* vos perdroiz (10:345)
> For Fresne whom you will lose

> Por la joie *que* il en ot (1:13)
> On account of the joy which he had from it

> Au jor des noces *qu*'il ot pris   (11:367)
> On the wedding day that he had set

Used as an object without specified antecedent, *que* means "what":

Ne sot *que* fere (2:60)
He didn't know what to do

. . . s'ele seüst
La maniere et *que* el fust (11:393–94)
. . . if she knew
The whole story and what she was

With a temporal or spatial antecedent, *que* may translate as "in which" or "where":

Quant ele vint en tel aé
Que nature forme biauté (7:241–42)
When she reached that age
In which Nature creates beauty

Il n'a païs ne marce ne rené . . .
Que jou nen aie aprés l'enfant esté (*Huon. Bord.*, 8594–96)
There is no country, march, or kingdom . . .
Where I have not gone to seek the child.

(b) *Que* is used as a subject, especially after the neuter antecedent *ce*:

Or dites *ce que* vos plaira (*Villehardouin* 4.16)
Now say what you please

Trestot me plest *ce que* li siet (*Yvain*, 4594)
Everything that pleases her suits me

44.4. *Quoi.*   *Quoi* is a stressed relative pronoun that is most frequently employed as the object of a preposition whose antecedent is a thing or the neuter *ce*:

li cevaus *sor quoi* il sist rades et corans (15.10, 4)
the fiery and swift horse on which he was seated

il a ung tres mauvés desboit pour cause du fust *en quoy* il est (29, 57–58)
it has a very unpleasant aftertaste because of the barrel it's in

The antecedent is frequently not expressed:

se je li pooie dire, *par quoi* il ne s'aperceuscent (23:13a)
if I could tell her (in such a way) by which (=that) they not notice

45. The Ubiquitous Relative *Que*

Que can be used for any other relative, even as a subject and after prepositions. It is also a multipurpose conjunction (see 21.91.1).

Subject: In addition to its proper use as a neuter subject (13.52C), *que* substitutes for *qui* subject in many northern and western dialects, including Anglo-Norman:

> Treske al tref l'unt amené,
> *Que* mut fu beaus e bien asis. (10, 1–2)
> They led him right up to the tent,
> Which was very beautiful and well placed.

> Celui *que* tant la peot amer. (10, 53)
> He who might love her so much.

Object: It frequently replaces *cui* and *quoi*:

> N'avront garde que sor aus veingne
> Force de *que* maus lor aveingne. (*Cligés*, 1943–44)
> They will be unable to prevent the force from which
> Evil might come to them from overtaking them.

46. Omission of the Relative Pronoun

Old French frequently omitted the relative pronoun *qui* or *que*, especially in negative sentences after *cele, celui, un sul,* or *nul*:

> *N'i ad celoi* ⌄ a l'altre ne parolt (6, 113)
> There was not a one (who) did not say to the
> other

> Qant il oient ⌄ Tristran s'en vet,
> *N'i a un sol* ⌄ grant duel ne fet. (*Béroul*, 2963–64)
> When they hear (that) Tristan is leaving,
> There was not a one (who) did not lament
> deeply.

The relative was also omitted after the indefinite pronoun *tel*:

> Plux seux liés, per saint Marcel,
> Ke *teils* ⌄ ait chaistel ou tour. (*Colin Muset*, 9, 23–24)
> I am happier, by St. Marcel,
> Than someone (who) has a castle or tower.

Both the relative and its antecedent may be omitted, as in the following instance, in which *que ce que* is reduced to *que*:

> De tot l'avoir du monde n'ai je plus vaillant *que* vos veés sor le cors
> de mi. (*Auc. et Nic.* 24, 57–59)
> Of all this world's wealth I have no more *than that which* you see me
> wearing.

Phonology 11

The development of consonants was dependent upon the position they had in the word. They might be **initial** (T in TERRAM), **interior** (T in NAUTAM), or **final** (T in REGIT). If interior, they could be **preceded by another consonant** (T in ALTUM), **intervocalic** (T in VITA), or **followed by another consonant** (T in PATREM). Consonants preceded by another consonant or by themselves (double or geminate consonants) are called **supported** (T in ALTUM and MITTERE).

Following the loss of unaccented penult, intertonic, and most final vowels (see Phonology 6), consonants sometimes assumed a different position in the word than in Latin. For example, the *T* in Latin MARĪTUM or NEPŌTEM is intervocalic, but with the loss of -M in Vulgar Latin and of final -O and -E in Gallo-Roman, T in both words became **secondarily final** in early Old French (*marit, nevout*). In Latin TĔPĬDŬM, P and D are both intervocalic, but after the loss of the unaccented penult Ĭ they were respectively followed and preceded by another consonant (/tiep'do/).

When, in Late Latin, E and I in hiatus partially consonantalized to *yod*, another new position for consonants developed: that of consonant + *yod*. The palatalizing influence of this *yod* on preceding consonants had a profound effect on the development of the French language.

For the classification of consonants by group, see Phonology 2.

Initial and supported consonants

Consonants that were initial or supported were in the strongest possible positions and were maintained without exception into Old French: TÉRRAM > *terre*, MĬTTĔRE > *metre*, FÓRTEM > *fort*, ÁLTUM > *(h)alt* > *haut*, RŬMPĔRE > *rompre*.

The development of *c, g* before the vowels *a, e, i* shows the effect of progressive palatalization. In Latin, C and G were both velar and were pronounced /k/ and /g/ before *e, i* as well as before *a, o, u*. Thus, the initial sounds of CICERO /kíkero/ and GENER were similar to those of CABALLUS, CONTRA, GALLIAM, and GUTTA.

Before the front vowels *e* and *i*, the articulation points of *c, g* moved forward by progressive stages (see Phonology 5) until, in twelfth century Gaul, they were pronounced /ts/ and /dʒ/ respectively. Their orthography, however, had not changed: CĔNTUM > *cent* (/tsẽnt/), GĔNĔRE > *gendre* (/dʒẽndrə/).

Before an *a,* initial and supported *c, g* palatalized in Northern Gaul to /tʃ/ and /dʒ/, which were generally transcribed *ch* and *j* respectively:

CÁRRUM > *char*, ÁRCA > *arche*, GÁMBA > *jambe*. This palatalization of *c*, *g* before *a* was confined to the region of Northern Gaul and, like the development of free accented A > E, is one of the distinguishing traits of Old French phonology.

Initial *yod* (from Latin DE, DI, GE, GI, and J) palatalized first to /dj/. By the twelfth century it was pronounced /dʒ/, and in the thirteenth century it opened to /ʒ/.

Intervocalic consonants

Consonants that were intervocalic or followed by another consonant were in the weakest positions and were generally modified or lost between Latin and Old French: VÍTAM > *vie*, PÁTREM > *pere*. The details of their development will be taken up in Phonology 12 and 13.

Consonants + *yod*

Single or multiple consonants followed by *yod* generally palatalized. This palatalization took place throughout the late Latin and Gallo-Roman periods and was far-reaching in its effects. It will be considered in Phonology 15.

Final consonants

Most Latin words ended in -M, -N, -R, -S (-X), or -T. -M and -N were lost in Vulgar Latin except in a few common monosyllables (RÉM > *rien*, NÓN > *non*). -R and -S were retained in French (CÓR > *cuer*, TRÁNS > *tres*). -T survived into Old French as *ṭ* (pronounced like the *th* of English *think*), only to be lost in the early twelfth century (DONAT > *doneṭ* > *done*).

When final unaccented vowels were lost in the Gallo-Roman and early Old French periods (see Phonology 6), many consonants became **secondarily final**. In the secondarily final position, consonants regularly unvoiced. The labials (-P, -B, -V, -F) all became unvoiced -*f* when preceded by a vowel:

CÁPUT > /cábo/ > chief
BRÉVEM > /bréve/ > brief
TRÁBE > tref

When supported, -P and -B remained (and were pronounced in Old French), whereas -V > -f:

CÁMPUM > /cámpo/ > champ
PLŬMBUM > /plómbo/ > plomb
NĔRVUM > /nérvo/ > nerf

The dentals -T, -D became unvoiced -t when supported; otherwise they were lost early in the twelfth century:

PŎRTUM > /pórto/ > port
GRÁNDEM > /gránde/ > grant
NEPŎTEM > /nebóde/ > nevout > neveu
MARÍTUM > /marído/ > marit > mari

Dental /z/ (spelled s) unvoiced to /s/:

*GRÍSI > /gríz ə/ > gris

The velars -C and -G became unvoiced -c when supported; otherwise C > yod and combined with the preceding vowel:

ÁRCUM > /árco/ > arc
LÓNGUM > /lóngo/ > lonc
PRĔÇO > /priéi/ > pri
AMÍCUM > /amígo/ > /*amii/ > ami

chapter 12

Reading and Textual Analysis, Selection 7b

This selection, like the preceding one, dwells on the selflessness and complete devotion of Fresne to her lover. Her willingness to sacrifice her own happiness leads to her eventual recognition and also makes her a fitting mate for the Lord of Dol. By sacrificing that which is dearest to her, the cloth given her by the abbess, she will win him who is dearest to her. Her story has been compared to that of patient Griselda, the wife who was deliberately put to harsh tests by her husband to determine the extent of her devotion. But that tale, in its retellings by Chaucer (Clerk's Tale) and Boccaccio (final tale of the *Decameron*), is much more developed psychologically: the happy denouement is the direct result of the deliberate choices made by the husband and wife. In "Fresne," on the other hand, there is no moment of decision or hesitation; Fresne is the incarnation of goodness and devotion, and her triumph is that of the simple justice of the fairy tale.

12:397	La nuit au lit apareillier,
12:398	Ou l'espousee dut couchier,
12:399	La damoisele i est alee;
12:400	De son mantel s'est desfublee.
12:401	Les chambellans i apela;
12:402	La maniere lor ensaingna
12:403	Comment son sire le vouloit,

12:404	Car meintes foiz veü l'avoit.
12:405	Quant le lit orent apresté,
12:406	Un couvertor i ont jeté.
12:407	Le drap estoit d'un viel bofu;
12:408	La damoisele l'a veü:
12:409	N'iert mie bien, ce li sembla;
12:410	En son corage l'em pesa.
12:411	Un coffre ouvri, le paille prist,
12:412	Sor le lit son seignor le mist.
12:413	Quant la chambre fu delivree,
12:414	La dame a sa fille amenee;
12:415	El la voloit fere couchier,
12:416	Si la commande a despoillier.
12:417	Le paille esgarde sor le lit,
12:418	Onques mes nul si bel ne vit
12:419	Fors seul celui qu'ele donna
12:420	O sa fille qu'ele cela.
12:421	Adont li remembra de li;
12:422	Toz li corages li fremi.
12:423	Le chambellenc apele a soi.
12:424	"Di va!" fet ele, "entent a moi:
12:425	Ou fu cis bons pailles trovez?"
12:426	"Dame," fet il, "bien le savrez:
12:427	La damoisele l'aporta,
12:428	Sor le couvertor le geta,
12:429	Qu'il ne li sembla mie bons.
12:430	Je cuit que li pailles est sons."

12:398 *dul*: see note to 2:54.

12:403 *son sire* for *ses sire* (cf. 14:497).

12:407 *le drap* for NS *li dras*.

12:419 *fors seul celui qu'ele* 'except that one alone which she.'

12:421 For the use of the ind. obj. as subj. of an impersonal verb, see 8.31.2.

12:430 The stressed forms *son* and *sons* for *sien(s)* are also found in the Anglo-Norman *Life of St. Alexis* (Aspland, 3): 3, 42; 3, 50.

---

47. Possessive Constructions

There are three common possessive constructions in Old French, of which only the last has survived into modern French: the genitive use of the oblique case, *a*, and *de*.

47.1. Genitive use of the oblique case. The possessor follows the object or person possessed without an intervening preposition:

> le lit son seignor (12:412)
> her husband's bed
>
> La mort le roi Artu (Aspland, 14)
> The death of King Arthur

This construction is used exclusively when the possessor is a singular person referred to by proper name or by title indicating family status (e.g., father, mother, son) or social position (e.g., king, count, knight). Note that in genitive constructions in which the possessor is *Dieu* 'God,' *cui* (see 11.44.2), *autrui* 'other, another,' or *nului* 'no other, no one,' or in certain archaic or fixed expressions, the possessor may precede:

> li Deu enemi (16:1)
> God's enemies
>
> L'autrui joie prise petit (10, 178)
> The joy of another he scarcely esteems

47.2. Possessor preceded by *a* (*au, aus*):

> La fame au chevalier (2:25)
> The knight's wife

This construction is likewise used only when the possessor is a person or a personification. Originally it was restricted to situations in which the possessor was not specified:

filz a baron 'a baron's son'
le file a un roi 'a king's daughter'

but as the example from 2:25 shows, its usage was extended.

47.3. Possessor preceded by *de* (*del, du, des*):

> le lay du Fresne (1:0)
> the lay of Fresne
>
> l'uis du mostier (6:178)
> the church('s) door

This construction was originally used in possessive constructions in which the determiner was an animal or inanimate object (ash tree, church), but it later came to be widely generalized and eventually supplanted the other two constructions completely save for a few frozen expressions: *Dieu merci, Hotel-Dieu.*

48. Old French Politeness

English no longer retains the distinction between a second person singular (*thee, thou*) and a second person plural (*you*). In Old French, however, the second singular forms such as *tu, te, ta, ton* were properly used when addressing one person, whereas the plural forms *vous, vostre,* and so on were for addressing more than one person.

Yet even in Old French a new opposition was being created, based not on number but on degrees of politeness. Between persons of the noble class the *vous* is almost obligatory. It is even used by the doorkeeper and his daughter in "Fresne," Reading Selection 4a (Chapter 6). Although they are perhaps not actually of the nobility, this use of the polite plural in addressing a single person is probably intended to reflect their nobility of spirit and purpose. But medieval politeness was not stilted or exaggerated, and the use of *tu* was not necessarily an expression of superiority or disdain. It was employed, for example, in addressing prayers to God:

> "Deus," fet ele, "par *ton* saint non,
> Sire, s'i *te* vient a plesir,
> Cest enfant *garde* de perir!" (5:162–64)
> "Lord God," says she, "by your holy name,
> Lord, if it please you,
> Preserve this infant from death!"

In "Fresne", the familiar form is used only once as a sign of class distinction, when the lady addresses a servant:

> Le chambellenc apele a soi.
> "*Di* va!" fet ele, "*entent* a moi:
> Ou fu cis bons pailles trovez?"
> "Dame," fet il, "bien le savrez. . . ." (12:423–26)
> She calls the chamberlain to her.
> "Say there," says she, "listen to me:
> Where was this fine cloth found?"
> "My lady," says he, "well shall you know. . . ."

The shift from *vous* to *tu* is skillfully managed in Reading Selection 7c to increase the pathos of the recognition scene.

Significantly, in Norman and Anglo-Norman texts, where the influence of English would be the strongest, the use of *tu* and *vous* is the most arbitrary.

49. Descriptive Adjectives: Inflection

Old French descriptive adjectives, which generally precede the noun they modify (see 6.21.1), agree with it in gender, number, and case. The

Old French adjective declension system is closely modeled on that of the noun (see 3.6–7 and 4.10–12).

There are three basic types of Old French descriptive adjectives:

I.   those in which the feminine form is marked by a final unaccented -e;
II. those in which the feminine forms differ from the masculine only in inflection, with no characteristic feminine marker;
III. comparatives with stem alternation.

49.1. Type I:

	CLASS I (FEMININE)	CLASS II (MASCULINE)
NS	bone	bons (buens)
OS	bone	bon (buen)
NP	bones	bon (buen)
OP	bones	bons (buens)

Class I feminine adjectives are declined like Class I feminine nouns (3.6.1), Class II masculine adjectives are declined like Class II masculine nouns (3.6.2). All past participles are declined on this model:

	CLASS I (FEMININE)	CLASS II (MASCULINE)
NS	entree	entrez
OS	entree	entré
NP	entrees	entré
OP	entrees	entrez

49.2. Type II.

Type II includes those adjectives in which the feminine declension is modeled on the masculine (Class Ia) and those in which the masculine declension resembles the feminine (Class IIa).

Many feminine adjectives derived from Latin Class II adjectives, which had the same forms for the masculine and feminine, have no distinct feminine markers in Old French. These are declined for the feminine like Class Ia feminine nouns (see 3.7.1), with a regular Class II masculine declension:

CLASS IA

	(feminine)	(masculine)
NS	granz	granz
OS	grant	grant
NP	granz	grant
OP	granz	granz

The NS of Class Ia adjectives frequently lacks the -s marker by analogy with Class I.

All present participles are declined on this model:

	(feminine)	(masculine)
NS	coranz	coranz
OS	corant	corant
NP	coranz	corant
OP	coranz	coranz

For phonological reasons, certain masculine adjectives end in un-stressed -e. These are declined like Class IIa masculine nouns and properly lack the NS -s marker. The feminine forms of such adjectives are declined like regular Class I feminines:

CLASS IIA

	(feminine)	(masculine)
NS	riche	riche
OS	riche	riche
NP	riches	riche
OP	riches	riches

The NS of Class IIa adjectives frequently has the -s marker by analogy with Class II.

The following are the most common adjectives of Class Ia:

*avenant 'attractive' naturel 'natural'
brief 'short' puissant 'powerful, mighty'
cruel 'cruel' *prod, preu 'bold, valiant'
fol 'foolish' *quel 'which'
fort 'strong' roial 'royal'
*gentil 'noble' soëf 'sweet, gentle'
*grant 'great, large' *tel 'such'
*grief 'grievous' tranchant 'sharp'
loial 'loyal' *vaillant 'valiant'
luisant 'bright' vert 'green'
*mortel 'mortal' *vil 'vile'

Adjectives preceded by an asterisk occur in the readings in this volume.

The following are common Class IIa adjectives:

aigre 'acid, bitter'	*povre 'poor'
amable 'amiable'	quite 'free of'
aspre 'rough'	*riche 'rich, powerful'
*autre 'other, another'	*sage 'wise, intelligent'
*destre 'right'	*senestre 'left'
foible 'feeble'	tendre 'tender'
	triste 'sad'

49.3. Indeclinable adjectives. Adjectives whose oblique masculine singular ends in -*s* or -*z* are indeclinable in the masculine. The feminine forms, however, end in -*e* and are declinable:

	(feminine)	*(masculine)*
NS	cortoise	cortois
OS	cortoise	cortois
NP	cortoises	cortois
OP	cortoises	cortois

The following are common indeclinable adjectives:

bas/basse 'low'
*cortois/cortoise 'courteous, well-mannered, noble'
*douz/douce 'sweet'
faitiz/faitice 'handsome, pretty'
faux/fausse 'false'
françois/françoise 'French'
frois/fresche 'cool, fresh'
*gros/grosse 'large'
joios/joiose 'joyous'
*mauvais/mauvaise 'bad'
ploros/plorose 'tearful'
precios/preciose 'precious'
*tierz/tierce 'third'

49.4. Type III. The comparatives of a number of common adjectives show stem alternation similar to that of Class III nouns (see 4.10):

	(feminine)	*(masculine)*
NS	mieudre	mieudre(s)
OS	meillor	meillor
NP	meillors	meillor
OP	meillors	meillors

There are very few adjectives of this type:

COMPARATIVES	POSITIVES
graindre, graignor 'larger'	grant 'large'
joindre (*or* genvre), joignor 'younger'	juene 'young'
maire, maior 'greater'	grant 'great'
mendre, menor 'lesser'	petit 'small'
*mieudre, meillor 'better'	buen, bon 'good'
noaudre, noaillor 'worse'	mal 'bad'
*pire, peior 'worse'	mal 'bad'

One Class III masculine noun is frequently used as an adjective and is therefore declined on this model:

	(feminine)	*(masculine)*
NS	felenesse (felone)	fel
OS	felenesse	felon
NP	felenesses	felon
OP	felenesses	felons

Finally, the indefinite *plusor*, used only in the plural, is Type III:

NP	plusor
OP	plusors

(See 19.86.)

The most common method of making comparisons in Old French, however, is by preceding the adjective with an adverb: *assez, aussi, bien, molt, tres, si,* and especially *plus* and *moins.*

> *Molt* espés et *bien* foillu (5:168)
> Very thick and quite leafy
>
> ainc *plus* bele ne veïstes (21:18)
> never have you seen a more beautiful (girl)

For more on comparisons, see 19.83–84.

50. *Tot* 'all'

The common adjective *tot* has an irregular declension:

	MASCULINE	FEMININE
NS	toz	tote
OS	tot	tote
NP	tuit	totes
OP	toz	totes

By the thirteenth century, NS *toz* (> *tous*) and NP *tuit* are often replaced by *tout*. *Tot* is also used frequently as an adverb of degree (see 19.82) and as an indefinite pronoun (see 19.86).

Phonology 12

Intervocalic consonants

Consonants that were intervocalic or followed by another consonant in Latin or Vulgar Latin were already weakening by the beginning of the Gallo-Roman period, possibly under the influence of the Celtic substratum. In Vulgar Latin, intervocalic unvoiced consonants had become voiced:

P > b   RÍPAM > /ríba/
T > d   VÍTAM > /vída/
K > g   BÁCAM > /baga/
F > v   *REFÚSÁRE > /revuzare/
S > z   RÓSAM > /roza/

At the same time, voiced plosives were becoming fricatives:

B > β   *NÚBAM > /núβa/
D > δ   NÚDAM > /núδa/
G > γ   *AGÚSTUM > /aγósto/
V > β   VÍVAT > /víβat/

This progressive weakening continued throughout the Gallo-Roman period. Intervocalic dentals all dropped completely:

T > d > — VĪTAM > /vída/ > /víða/ > vie
D > ð > — NŪDAM > /núða/ > nue

The fricatives F and V, velar K and G, and bilabial β were lost in the vicinity of the velar vowels O, U:

F > v > — *REFŪSÁRE > /rèvuzáre/ > reüser
V > β > — PAVÓNEM > /paβóne/ > paon
G > γ > — *AGŪSTU > /aγósto/ > aoust
K > g > — SECŪRUM > /segúro/ > seür
                CARRŪCAM > /carrúga/ > charrue
B > β > — *NŪBAM > /núβa/ > nue

The labials P, B, V, F were shifted to V if not in the presence of O, U:

P > b > v RĪPAM > /ríba/ > rive
B > β > v FABAM > /faβa/ > feve
F > v > v *STÉF(A)NU > /Estievene/ > Estievne, Estienne
V > β > v VĪVAT > /víβat/ > vivet, vive

The velars C, G, J all palatalized before A, E, I:

K > g > i (if + a) BÁCAM > /bága/ > baie
G > γ > i FLAGĒLLUM > /flaγéllo/ > flaiel
K > dz > is (if + e or i) PLACĒRE > /pladzére/ > plaisir
                *VECĪNU > /vedzíno/ > veisin, voisin

The vibrants R, L, the nasals M, N, and the fricative Z (< S) were unaffected by this trend.

Adjectives

Old French Type I adjectives all came from Latin three-termination adjectives of the type BONUS (m.), BONAM (f.), BONUM (n.). The neuter was lost, but the masculine and feminine developed regularly, with the exception of the addition of flexional -s to the feminine nominative plural by analogy with all other feminine plurals. As with nouns, the Latin six-case declension system was simplified to two cases only, the nominative and the oblique:

	MASCULINE			FEMININE		
NS	BÓNUS	>	bons	BÓNA	>	bone
OS	BÓNUM	>	bon	BÓNAM	>	bone
NP	BÓNI	>	bon	*BÓNAS	>	bones
OP	BÓNOS	>	bons	BÓNAS	>	bones

Old French Type II adjectives came from Latin two-termination adjectives of the type GRANDIS (m., f.), GRANDE (n.), in which the masculine and feminine were undistinguished in Latin. The masculine nominative plural lost flexional -s by analogy with all other nominative plurals:

	MASCULINE			FEMININE		
NS	GRÁNDIS	>	granz	GRÁNDIS	>	granz
OS	GRÁNDEM	>	grant	GRÁNDEM	>	grant
NP	*GRÁNDI	>	grant	GRÁNDES	>	granz
OP	GRÁNDES	>	granz	GRÁNDES	>	granz

Note that the modifications due to flexional -s are the same for adjectives as those outlined for nouns in Phonology 3. Thus, $d + s > z$. For secondarily final supported $d > t$, see Phonology 11.

The fate of a consonant therefore depended on its position within a word, which explains the differences observed in the stem consonants of many Type I adjectives. In the feminine, a single stem consonant was always intervocalic; in the masculine, it was either secondarily final or followed by flexional -s.

Following the rules explained in previous phonology sections, the development of labial radicals, such as that in VIVUS, VIVA, becomes clear:

	FEMININE			MASCULINE				
NS	VÍVA	>	vive	VÍVUS	>	/vívos/	>	vis
OS	VÍVAM	>	vive	VÍVUM	>	/vívo/	>	vif
NP	*VÍVAS	>	vives	VÍVI	>	/víve/	>	vif
OP	VÍVAS	>	vives	VÍVOS	>	/vívos/	>	vis

Intervocalic V > β > v before A, E, I (Phonology 12): VĪVA > vive
Secondarily final labial + flexional s is lost (Phonology 3): VĪVUS > vis
Secondarily final V > f (Phonology 11): VĪVUM > vif
Other labial radicals follow this pattern: e.g., baillif/baillive, chauf/chauve.

Dental radicals with supported D, T had a similar development:

	FEMININE			MASCULINE		
NS	FRÍGIDA	>	froide	FRÍGIDUS	>	froiz
OS	FRÍGIDAM	>	froide	FRÍGIDUM	>	froit
NP	*FRÍGIDAS	>	froides	FRÍGIDI	>	froit
OP	FRÍGIDAS	>	froides	FRÍGIDOS	>	froiz

d supported (by yod) remains before a: FRÍGIDA > /fréida/ > froide.
Secondarily final dental + flexional -s > -z: FRÍGIDUS > /froid's/ > froiz.
Secondarily final d, t supported > -t: FRÍGIDUM > /froid/ > froit.
Others of this type include roit/roide, vuit/vuide.

The dentals s and z show the following alternations:

MASCULINE	FEMININE		
-s	-ss-	las/lasse	(both unvoiced, < LASSUS/LASSA)
-s	-s-	gris/grise	(m. unvoiced, f. voiced, < GRISUS/GRISA)
-z	-ce	tierz/tierce	(both unvoiced, < TERTIUS/TERTIA)

Velar radicals with supported *c*, *g* developed along parallel lines:

	MASCULINE			**FEMININE**		
NS	SĬCCUS	>	ses	SĬCCA	>	seche
OS	SĬCCUM	>	sec	SĬÇCAM	>	seche
NP	SĬCCI	>	sec	*SĬCCAS	>	seches
OP	SĬCCOS	>	ses	SĬCCAS	>	seches
NS	LÁRGUS	>	lars	LÁRGA	>	large
OS	LÁRGUM	>	larc	LÁRGAM	>	large
NP	LÁRGI	>	larc	*LÁRGAS	>	larges
OP	LÁRGOS	>	lars	LÁRGAS	>	larges

Others include *frois/fresche, anglois/anglesche, lonc/longe, blanc/blanche*.

chapter 13

Reading and Textual Analysis, Selection 7c

Although there is no direct connection between "Fresne" and the Griselda legend, there is a close relationship between our lay and a series of popular ballads, particularly in Scottish, about "Fair Annie." In these songs, a young maiden is stolen from her parents. She is purchased from the robbers by a young man and bears him seven sons, but he then decides to marry another. Before the marriage ceremony is completed, however, the bride recognizes Annie as her lost sister. Annie takes her sister's place and becomes the rightful bride of her former lover. It is possible that both versions go back to a Breton original, alluded to by Marie in her opening and closing lines. The ballads are much more sparing in details, particularly in the recognition scene. In the ballads the heroine is stolen away at a later age; the bride overhears her laments at the loss of her lover, asks her about her parents, and then recognizes her as her long-lost sister. In Marie's work, the role and character of Fresne are greatly amplified and the recognition scene is carefully prepared from the beginning. The emphasis is no longer on deeply felt sorrow, as in "Fair Annie," but on selfless devotion.

The use of a ring or an article of clothing (here, a blanket) to confirm identity is commonplace in medieval French literature.

13:431   La dame l'avoit apelee,
13:432   Et cele est devant li alee;
13:433   De son mantel se desfubla,

13:434	Et la mere l'aresona:
13:435	"Bele amie, nel me celez!
13:436	Ou fu cis bons pailles trovez?
13:437	Dont vos vint il? qui l'achata?
13:438	Car me dites quil vos donna!"
13:439	La meschine li respondi:
13:440	"Dame, m'ante qui me norri,
13:441	L'abaesse quil me bailla
13:442	A garder le me commanda.
13:443	Cest et un anel me baillierent
13:444	Cil qui a norrir m'envoierent."
13.445	"Bele, puis ge veoir l'anel?"
13:446	"Oïl, dame, ce m'est molt bel."
13:447	L'anel li a donc aporté
13:448	Et ele l'a molt esgardé;
13:449	Ele l'a bien reconneü
13:450	Et le paille qu'ele ot veü.
13:451	Ne doute rien, bien set et croit
13:452	Que le Fresne sa fille estoit.
13:453	Oiant toz dit, nu cele mie:
13:454	"Tu es ma fille, bele amie!"
13:455	De la pitié que ele en a
13:456	Ariere chiet, si se pasma.
13:457	Quant de pasmoisons se levoit,
13:458	Por son seignor tost enveoit,
13:459	Et il i vient toz esfreez.
13:460	Quant il en la chambre est entrez,
13:461	La dame li chaï as piez;
13:462	Estroitement li a baisiez:
13:463	Pardon li quiert de son mesfet.
13:464	Il ne sot noient de ce plet.
13:465	"Dame," fet il, "que dites vos?
13:466	Ja n'a se bien non entre nos.
13:467	Quanque vos plet, soit pardonné!
13:468	Dites moi vostre volenté!"
13:469	"Sire, quant pardonné l'avez,
13:470	Jel vos dirai, si m'escoutez."

13:438 *Car*: to reinforce the imperative (see 17.72).
13:452 *le Fresne*: see note to 10:348.
13:455 *ele* 'the mother.'

51. Elided and Enclitic Forms

In Sections 1.3 and 7.24 we saw that a number of Old French words—mainly articles and pronouns—were syntactically unstressed and, therefore, could not stand alone, be coordinated, or begin sentences. The vowels in these words often became so effaced that the word combined by elision or enclisis with the word immediately preceding or following it. Combination by **elision** was common between articles, unstressed possessive pronouns, and following nouns beginning with a vowel or a nonaspirate *h*:

l'anel (13:445) 'the ring'
m'ante (13:440) 'my aunt'

Elision also occurred between reflexive pronouns, unstressed object pronouns, the negative *ne*, and following verbs:

> s'est desfublee (12:400)
> (she) took off (her cloak)
>
> la dame l'avoit apelee (13:431)
> the lady had called her
>
> si m'escoutez (13:470)
> listen to me
>
> Ja n'a se bien non entre nos (13:466)
> There is nothing but good between us

All modern editors indicate elision with an apostrophe. In most cases, the use of such elisions has continued into modern French.

Enclisis is the loss of the unstressed vowel in a monosyllable, resulting in its combination with a preceding word ending in a vowel. Enclitic forms were common in twelfth-century Old French, but most of them disappeared in succeeding centuries. The most common enclitic forms were those combining an oblique definite article (other than feminine *la*) with the prepositons *a*, *de*, or *en* (listed in 1.3.2). The enclitic forms *au*, *as/ aus* (> *aux*), *du*, and *des* persist in modern French. The following are other commonly encountered enclitic forms, many of which occur in our text:

je	+	le	jel (13:470), gel, jeu, ju
je	+	les	jes, ges
ne	+	le	nel (13:435), nu (13:453)
ne	+	les	nes (16:30)

qui	+	le	quil (13:438)
qui	+	les	quis (17:22)
que	+	le	quel (4, 50)
que	+	les	ques (5:154)
si	+	le	sil (18:52), sel (6:202)
si	+	les	sis (4, 132), ses (8, 88)
se	+	le	sel (8, 169)
se	+	les	ses (16:53)

The following enclitic forms are rare in Old French texts but are listed here for the sake of completeness. None occur in the reading selections in this volume, although most can be found in C. W. Aspland's *Medieval French Reader*:

non	+	se	nos	quei	+	me	queim
je	+	me	jem	quei	+	te	queit
jo	+	te	jot	qui	+	me	quim
jo	+	le	jol	qui	+	se	quis
jo	+	les	jos	qui	+	en	quin
tu	+	le	tul	si	+	me	sim
tu	+	me	tum	si	+	se	sis
lui	+	en	luin	si	+	en	sin
ne	+	me	nem	si	+	est	sist
ne	+	te	net				
ne	+	se	nes	ço	+	est	çost

Many editors, including Aspland, indicate enclisis by a raised dot: *ne·s* (3, 35), *je·l* (5, 44), *ne·l* (11, 140), *se·s* (11, 252).

52.   Interrogative Pronouns: *Qui, Cui, Que, Quoi*

This section treats the most frequently encountered Old French interrogatives. Others will be discussed in 20.88.

A. *Qui* refers to an animate being used as a subject: "who?"

> *Qui* l'achata? (13:437)
> Who bought it?
>
> E certement me di *qui* es (4, 51)
> And tell me with certainty who you are

B. *Cui* is used to refer to persons in the oblique case, whether alone or following a preposition:

> "O filz, *cui* erent mes granz ereditez?" (3, 171)
> "O son, to whom will go my great wealth?"
>
> Savez de *cui* je vos voel dire? (*Yvain*, 2401)
> Do you know about whom I wish to speak to you?

It was frequently confused with *qui*:

> E Oliver, en *qui* il tant se fiet (*Roland*, 586)
> And Olivier, on whom he relies so much
>
> De ço *qui* calt? (6, 116)
> Of that to whom concerns?
> But what is the use?

C. *Que* functions generally as a neuter:

> "*Que* dites vos?" (13:465)
> "What are you saying?"
>
> "*Que* ferai?" (3:73)
> "What shall I do?"

D. *Quoi* (*coi*) is the stressed form of *que*. It is usually found after prepositions but may be used alone for special emphasis:

> Por *coi* plorez an tel meniere?
> De *coi* avez ire ne duel? (11, 136–37)
> Why are you crying so?
> What has caused you such anger and grief?
>
> Hostes, et que ferai je donques?
> —*Coi*, sires? Ce vos dirai gié. (*Perceval*, 7752–53)
> Sir host, what shall I do then?
> —What, sir? I shall tell you.

53. Types of Adverbs

If the verb is the heart of an Old French sentence, then surely the adverb is its soul. Adverbs in Old French are many and varied, and their classification is sometimes troublesome and arbitrary. They range from the etymologically simple through the reduplicated, and there are almost always three or four adverbs to convey each concept. It would be impossible in a grammar such as this to distinguish between such forms as *sus*, *desus*, and *dedessus*, all of which mean "above, over, on"; or between *lez*, *delez*, *joste*, *dejoste*, *pres*, and *emprés*, all of which mean "beside, near." Serious lexicological study of adverbs and prepositions of this type is yet to be undertaken.

In addition to using pure adverbs, Old French employs many adjectives as adverbs and adverbializes a great number of prepositional phrases. In this and following chapters we shall study the formation and recognition of adverbs—adverbs of manner, degree, time, place, and negation. As might be expected, there will be some overlapping among these various categories.

53.1. Simple adverbs. Derived from Latin nouns, adjectives, and adverbs, these adverbs are etymologically simple and have no characteristic adverb "marker":

Manner: *bien* 'well,' *com* 'as,' *si* 'so.'
Degree: *molt* 'much, very,' *plus* 'more,' *tres* 'very,' *par* 'very much,' *tant* 'so much,' *trop* 'very, too much,' *pres* 'nearly.'
Time: *hui* 'today,' *ore* 'now,' *ja* 'already,' *lors* 'then,' *puis* 'next, then,' *tost* 'at once,' *ier* 'yesterday.'
Place: *ci* 'here,' *la* 'there,' *enz* 'within,' *fors/hors* 'outside,' *sus* 'on, above,' *jus* 'below,' *soz* 'under,' *pres* 'near,' *loing* 'far,' *ici* 'here,' *iluec* 'there.'
Negation: *non* 'no,' *ne* 'not.'

53.2. Compound adverbs. Compound adverbs are formed by combining two simple adverbs or a preposition and an adverb: *pres de* 'almost,' *non mie* 'not at all,' *onques mes* 'never again,' *deça* 'near.'

Many of the combinations fused into single adverbs by the twelfth century. Editors, however, will occasionally separate the two elements that are here combined: *amont* 'up,' *aval* 'down,' *atant* 'thereupon,' *adont* 'then,' *aprés* 'after,' *avant* 'before,' *asez* 'enough,' *ausi* 'thus,' *autant* 'as much,' *autretant* 'as much,' *autretel* 'likewise,' *autrier* 'yesterday, the other day,' *çaienz* 'in here,' *demain* 'tomorrow,' *dedenz* 'within,' *defors* 'outside,' *dessus* 'above,' *devant* 'before, in front of,' *delez* 'beside,' *jadis* 'once,' *maintenant* 'now,' *pieça* 'a short while ago, just recently,' *mar* 'in an evil hour = unfortunately,' *buer* 'in a good hour = fortunately.'

There are also recompounded adverbs: *de çaienz*, *ça defors*, *de dedenz*, *de laienz*, among others. In addition, adverbial phrases can be condensed into a single word: *isnelepas* 'quick the step = quickly,' *doresanavant* 'from now on.'

53.3. Adjectives used as adverbs. A number of common adjectives were frequently used as adverbs: *bel, chier, cler, droit, fort, haut, petit, soëf, seul, tot, voir*:

> "Oïl, dame, ce m'est molt *bel*" (13:446)
> "Yes, milady, this pleases me very much"
>
> *Dreit* devers le chardin (16:45)
> Right toward the garden
>
> Naie *voir* (23:5a)
> No indeed
>
> Ausi rent ele *petit* lait (19, 17)
> And she (the cow) gives only a little milk

Adjectives used as adverbs might agree with the adjective or participle they modified. This agreement is usual in the case of *tot*:

> Il avoit les caviax blons et *menus* recercelés (20:22a)
> He had blond and tightly curled hair
>
> et les flors des margerites qu'ele ronpoit as ortex de ses piés . . .
> estoient *droites* noires avers ses piés et ses gambes (15, 12.21–23)
> and the daisies she broke with the toes of her feet . . . were quite
> black in comparison with her feet and legs

For adverbs formed by adding *-ment* to the feminine singular of adjectives, see 14.56-57.

54. Adverbs of Negation

The two most frequently encountered adverbs of negation are the stressed form *non* and the unstressed *nen, ne, n'*.

54.1. *Non*. *Non* implies total negation. It may stand alone:

> Mengüe il pain?/—*Non*, mais bonne char. (22, 49–50)
> Does it eat bread?/—No, just good meat.
>
> Ne dirras mes ne o ne *nun* (7, 71)
> You will no longer (be able to) say yes or no
>
> Dunc l'en unt al mustier, u voille u *nun*, mené (17:1)
> Then they brought him, whether he wished it or not, to the church

It may be used in combination with auxiliary verbs, especially *estre*, *avoir*, and *faire*:

> —S'estes ore seur vos gaveles.
> —*Non* sui, voir. (*Saint Nicolas*, 766–67)
> —Now you are pretending to be rich.
> —In truth, I am not

> —Sire, por coi m'avez traïe?
> —Ge *non* ai, voir, la moie amie. (*Eneas*, 1749–50)
> —Milord, why have you betrayed me?
> —I have not, in truth, my friend.

> "Avoi!" dist Renart, "*non* ferons." (20, 16)
> "Look here!" said Renart, "we won't do it."

It can be a total negation in the very common restrictive expression *se* ... *non*:

> Ja n'a *se* bien *non* entre nos (13:466)
> Never is there if good not between us
> There is never anything but good between us

> puis que vos ariiés jut en lit a home, *s*'el mien *non* (23:4a)
> after you will have slept in a man's bed if in mine not
> after you will have slept in a man's bed other than my own

> Ja n'i avra riens *se* bien *non* (20, 83)
> There will never be anything but good
> (i.e., Nothing but good will come of it)

(See also 21.91.4.)

It can be a negative prefix before a noun, an infinitive, a participle, or an adjective:

> *nun* savant (17:24) 'unwise, foolish'

It may be reinforced with nouns and adverbs:

> Li mostre a l'uel, *non mie* au doi (12, 195)
> (It) to him (she) shows with the eye, not a bit with the finger
> She indicates it to him with a glance, not by pointing

or with the pronoun *il*: *nenil*. This form is the usual one for replying negatively to a question:

> Vestirai je me bele cote?
> —*Nennil*, Perrote, *nenil* nient. (22, 266-67)
> Shall I wear my beautiful gown?
> —No, Perrote, definitely not.

Ne porrai je dont faire
Chose qui te viengne a talent?
—Sire, sachiés certainement
Que *nenil.* (22, 373–76)
Can I not do something
That would please you?
—Sir, know for certain
That you cannot.

54.2. *Nen.* This unstressed form occurs primarily before vowels in order to preserve an extra syllable in versification:

> Se il *nen* a l'amor de li (8:265)
> if he does not have her love
>
> C'onques ne fu ne ja *nen* iert (2:38)
> Never was it nor ever will it be

54.3. *Ne, n'.* *Ne* is the main negative particle in Old French and is sufficient by itself to negate a principal or dependent clause:

> *nel* me celez! (13:435) (*nel* = enclitic *ne* + *le*)
> don't hide it from me!
>
> Nus ne la vit qui *ne* l'amast
> Et merveille *ne* la proisast. (7:247–48)
> No one saw her who did not love her
> And esteem her greatly.

It is used in combination with indefinite articles, both positive (*aucun* 'any, anyone'; *rien* 'some, something') and negative (*nul* 'no one, none'; *nesun* 'no one, not any'; *noient* 'nothing'):

> *Ne* doute *rien* (13:451)
> She does not doubt anything
> She doubts nothing
>
> *Nus ne* la vit qui ne l'amast (7:247)
> No one saw her who did not love her
>
> Il *ne* sot *noient* de ce plet (13:464)
> He knew nothing about this situation

Ne is frequently reinforced with nouns and adverbs. Combined with nouns such as *mie* 'crumb,' *pas* 'step,' *goute* 'drop,' and *point* 'dot,' *ne* forms a total negation in which the original noun generally loses its nominal quality:

Eles *nu* soferroient *pas* (4:97)
They will not put up with it (at all)

Cil *n'*i entrerent *pas* (17:19)
These did not enter there

*N'*iert *mie* bien (12:409)
It wasn't (at all) good

Car *n'*i avoit *point* de faintise (5, 169)
For there was no pretence

As these examples show, usual Old French syntax places *ne* before, and the nominal or adverbial particle after, the verb form negated; however, for stylistic or metrical reasons, especially in verse, both may precede:

pas ne l'i lait (6:191)
he does not leave it there (at all)

Of the nouns used with *ne*, *point* retained its nominal quality the longest. It may be preceded by *un* 'a' or followed by *de* to introduce what in modern syntax would be the direct object of the principal verb:

ne faire *point de* quanque faire doie (21:4)
nor to do anything (at all) of what he should do

Ne is used in combination with the adverbial particles *mais* (*me*), *ja*, *plus*, *onques*, and *gaires* to form restrictive or partial negations—"no more, no other, no longer, not much":

en paradis *n'*enterriés vos *ja* (22:5)
you'll never enter paradise

Onques si bon *n'*orent veü (4:126)
Never had they seen such good (cloth)

Ainz (= ainc) puis *n'*i ot meillor (8:254)
Never afterward was there (a) better (lord)

Note: for the confusion *ainz/ainc* see 16.71.2.

The particle *mais* (*mes*) is often used in combination with *onques* or *ja* to mark continuity:

Onques mes nul si bel *ne* vit (12:418)
Never before had she seen such (a) beautiful (cloth)

ja mais ne resurdra! (19:45)
never again will he arise!
(never more)

During this period the terms *ja* and *mais* fuse into a single concept: "never." Some editors choose to maintain them as two separate words; others combine them. (See Section 53.2.)

55. Negative Indefinites: *Nesun, Noient, Nul, Rien*

Certain negatives function as indefinite pronouns and adjectives when the referent is unspecified. *Nesun, negun, neün, nun* 'not one, not any, none' are declined like the article *un* (1.3) and are generally associated with the negative particle *ne*:

> *Ne* criement *negun* asalt (*Eneas*, 442)
> They do not fear any assault

> Ne li lessa l'evesque seignorie *nesune* (21, 260)
> Not to him left the bishop power not any
> The bishop did not leave him any power

Noient, nïent, neant 'nothing' or, after a negative, 'anything':

> Por *neant* en parlez (8, 238)
> You're speaking for nothing
> (i.e., You're wasting your breath)

> Il ne sot *noient* de ce plet (13:464)
> He didn't know anything about this matter

Nul 'no one, none, not any, no,' or, after a negative, 'any,' can function as a pronoun or as an adjective:

> *Nus* ne la vit qui ne l'amast (7:247)
> No one saw her who did not love her

> Il n'avoit *nul* oir (20:18)
> He had no heir

> Le Fresne n'a onques *nus* fruiz (10:348)
> The Ash never bears any fruit

Rien + negative = "nothing":

> Ne doute *rien* (13:451)
> She doubts nothing
> (i.e., She has no doubts)

For the more common positive use of *rien* in Old French, see 6.22.

Phonology 13

In Latin, a consonant might be followed by another consonant (R of DORSUM), or it might come to be followed by a consonant after the loss of a penult or intertonic vowel in Vulgar Latin (M in FEMINA > *fem'na*, B of ARBOREM > *arb're*). The last consonant of a group was in a strong position and was generally maintained; the first and middle consonants of a group were in weak positions and were often modified. In many Vulgar Latin words, consonants were already being assimilated to following consonants. Where they had been distinctly pronounced in the classical language, their points of articulation began to come together in Vulgar Latin:

NS	>	s	MÉNSAM	>	mesa
PS	>	ss	CÁPSAM	>	cassa
RS	>	ss	DǪRSUM	>	dǫsso
PT	>	tt	RÚPTAM	>	rǫtta

Developments in the Gallo-Roman period accentuated this process of assimilation. In this phonology lesson we shall consider groups of three consonants and simple groups of two consonants. In Phonology 14 we shall take up consonants + R and L, and in Phonology 15 we shall treat consonants + *yod*.

Groups of three consonants

In most groups of three consonants, the middle consonant was a plosive: K, G; T, D; P, B, V, F. This middle plosive was retained if the final consonant of the group was an L or an R:

ÁRBŎREM	>	/árb're/	>	arbre
PÉRDĔRE	>	/pérd're/	>	perdre
CĬRCŬLŬM	>	/cérc'lo/	>	cercle
ĬNFLÁRE	>	/enflàre/	>	enfler
CǪNTRA			>	contre
ŬNGŬLAM	>	/ǫngl'a/	>	ongle

The middle plosive was lost otherwise:

PǪRCUS	>	/pǫrc's/	>	pors
PÉRTICĂ	>	/pért'ca/	>	perche
PÉRDIT	>	/pérd't/	>	pert
RŬMPIT	>	/rómp't/	>	ront
CǪRPUS	>	/cǫrp's/	>	cors
*HǪSPĬTÁLE	>	/òsp'tále/	>	ostel
GÁLBĬNŬM	>	/dʒálb'no/	>	jalne, jaune

An important exception to this general rule is -SCL- > -sl-:

MÁSCŬLUM   >   /másc'lo/   >   masle
MĬSCŬLÁRE   >   /mèsc'láre/   >   mesler

When the first consonant of a three-consonant group was T, D, P, B, or V, it was assimilated to the following consonant:

MÍTTĔRE   >   /métt're/   >   metre
ŎBSTÁRE   >   /ostáre/   >   oster

Groups of two consonants

The labials P, B, and V were lost very early before any consonant other than *r* and *l*:

TÉPĬDŬM   >   /tjéb'do/   >   tiede
DŬBĬTÁRE   >   /dòb'táre/   >   douter
NÀVĬGÁRE   >   /nàv'gáre/   >   nagier

Similarly, the dentals T and D were lost:

PLÁTĂNŲM   >   /plát'no/   >   plane
*PÀRTĬÇÉLLA   >   /pàrt'célla/   >   parcelle
ADVENÍRE   >   >   avenir

The velars K and G became *yod* before most consonants:

FÁCTUM   >   /fájto/   >   fait
RĬGĬDŬM   >   /réj'do/   >   reit (roit)
LÉGIT   >   /ljéj't/   >   lit

The labial M assimilated to *n* before the dentals T and D:

SĔMĬTAM   >   /sém'ta/   >   sente
ĬMPŬTÁRE   >   /emp'táre/   >   enter

A development peculiar to French is the reverse assimilation of M'N to
m or *mm*:

FÉMĬNAM	>	/fém'na/	>	fame, femme
HÓMĬNĔM	>	/óm'ne/	>	ome, homme
TÉRMĬNŬM	>	/térm'no/	>	terme
SÓMNUM			>	somme

Throughout the Vulgar Latin and Gallo-Roman periods, R, L, M, N,
and S were maintained before consonants. With the exception of *r*,
however, they too began to be effaced in the Old French period. In the
course of the twelfth century, the liquid *l* vocalized to *u* before following
consonants:

*ÁLBA			>	aube
*FÍLTRU	>	/féltrə/	>	feutre
ÍLLOS	>	/él's/	>	eus (eux)

S + consonant was gradually effaced in the course of the Old French
period. It was maintained longest before /p/, /t/, and /k/ (see Phonology
1). This pattern is revealed in English borrowings around the time of the
Norman Conquest of 1066. On the one hand, there is no /s/ sound in
English *blame, male, hideous* (Old French *blasme, masle, hisdeus*); on the other
hand, we maintain it in *beast, espouse, esquire* (Old French *beste, espouser,
escuier*).

R + consonant was maintained into modern French:

FĬRMÁRE	>	/fermáre/	>	fermer
SERVÍRE			>	servir

chapter 14

Reading and Textual Analysis, Selection 7d

The recognition of Fresne as the abandoned daughter of the Lord of Brittany is confirmed by her mother's confession. Her father's open and generous acceptance of her, as well as his refusal to blame his wife further, aptly reciprocates the generosity and love shown throughout the *lai* by Fresne herself.

14:471	"Jadis, par ma grant vilenie,
14:472	De ma voisine dis folie,
14:473	De ses deus enfanz mesparlai.
14:474	Vers moi meïsmes mesdit ai.
14:475	Veritez est je ençaintai;
14:476	Deus filles oi, l'une en celai.
14:477	A un mostier la fis geter
14:478	Et vostre paille o li porter,
14:479	Et l'anel que vos me donastes
14:480	Quant vos primes o moi parlastes.
14:481	Ne vos puet mie estre celé:
14:482	L'anel et le paille ai trové;
14:483	Nostre fille ai ci conneüe
14:484	Que par mon pechié ai perdue,
14:485	Et ja est ce la damoisele
14:486	Qui tant est preuz et sage et bele,
14:487	Que li chevaliers a amee

14:488   Qui sa seror a espousee."
14:489   Li sires dit: "De ce sui liez;
14:490   Onques mes ne fui si haitiez.
14:491   Quant no fille ravon trovee,
14:492   Grant joie nos a Deus donnee,
14:493   Ainz que li pechiez fust doublez.
14:494   Fille," fet il, "avant venez!"
14:495   La meschine molt s'esjoï
14:496   De l'aventure qu'ele oï.
14:497   Son pere n'i volt plus atendre;
14:498   Il meïsmes va por son gendre,
14:499   Et l'arcevesque i amena.
14:500   Cele aventure li conta.

14:475   For the omission of the relative *que*, see 11.46.
14:489   *li sires*: NS -*s* by analogy, see 3.8.
14:491   *no*: this Picard poss. adj. form is used frequently in other dialects for metrical
         reasons (see Phonology 22). *ravon trovee* 'we have found once again' (cf. *refont*,
         15:515).
14:497   *Son pere = Ses pere* (cf. 12:403).
14:499   *l'arcevesque* (OS).

---

56. Recognition of Adverbs

Most of the simple and compound adverbs listed in 13.53 have no
characteristic adverb marker. There are, however, three important adverbial markers in Old French: -*tre*, -*ment*, -*s*.

56.1. Adverbial -*tre(s)*. A series of adverbs end in -*tre(s)*: *soventre, soentre*
'next,' *endementres* 'meanwhile, while,' *nuitantre* 'nightly, by night.'

56.2. Adverbial -*s*. Many simple Old French adverbs ended in -*s* (*plus,
tres, lors, puis, sus, jus*) or -*z* (< T'S) (*soz, enz*). This ending was extended by
analogy to many other adverbs: *primes, soventes, volentiers, meismes, encores,
merveilles* and others. Note that forms with and without the -*s* marker
occur, often in the same text:

> je *meïsmes* me jujai (3:79)
> I (myself) judged myself
>
> Ele *meïsme* l'a levee (7:227)
> She herself raised her

56.3. Adverbial *-ment.* Although many common adjectives could become adverbs without undergoing any modification (see 13.53.3), most adjectives and participles used as adverbs were marked by the addition of *-ment* (< MENTE 'in a ———— spirit,' 'in a ———— manner') to their feminine singular forms: *noblement, richement, veraiement, sifaitement.* This suffix could also be added to nouns and adverbs: *vassalment, premierement, comment, ensement.*

57. Modifications Due to the Addition of Adverbial *-ment*

As we saw in 12.49, the two types of Old French adjectives from which adverbs can be derived are distinguished by their feminine singular forms: Type I adjectives have a feminine singular that ends in *-e*, whereas Type II adjectives end in consonants.

57.1. Type I adjectives. Addition of *-ment* to Type I adjectives entails no modifications: *hastivement, veraiement, bonement, durement.*

57.2. Type II adjectives. Addition of *-ment* to Type II adjectives involves the following modifications:

-t and *f* are assimilated:	fort + ment > forment
	grief + ment > griément
-nt > *n* > *m*:	grant + ment > granment > gramment
	avenant + ment > avenanment > avenamment
	vaillant + ment > vaillanment > vaillamment
-l vocalizes to *u*:	loial + ment > loiaument
	cruel + ment > crueument
but *-l* is lost after *i*:	gentil + ment > gentiment
	sotil + ment > sotiment

Note that unmodified forms are occasionally encountered: *grantment* (8:278).

58. Adverbial Doublets

In addition to modified (*gramment*), partially modified (*granment*, 19:22), and completely unmodified (*grantment*, 8:278) forms of the same adverb, morphological development also created a number of adverbial doublets.

In the Middle French period, most of the Type II adjectives were reformed on the Type I model:

grant (FS)	>	grande
fort (FS)	>	forte
cruel (FS)	>	cruele

As a result, new and corresponding adverbial forms were developed: *grandement, fortement, cruelement*. These existed concurrently with the traditional forms before replacing them altogether by the late Middle French period. Other types of adverbial doublets likewise evolved, for example:

(a) by addition of *de*: *lez/delez, sus/desus*.

(b) by addition of *-e*: *or/ore, arrier/arriere*.

(c) by addition of *-s*: *meïsme/meïsmes, mervoille/mervoilles*.

By a combination of processes, several adverbs developed multiple forms, such as: *luec/iluec, illec, illueque, illuecques* 'there'; *dementre, dementres, dementiers, endementres, endementiers* 'while.'

Spelling variants are, of course, common, even in the same text: *ainsi* (15:504), *einsint* (15:507).

59. Multiple Function Prepositions

In 9.35.4 we divided Old French prepositions into two types: those with simple functions (and, thus, generally with only a single translation) and those with multiple functions. In the present section we shall consider three of the most common multiple function prepositions: *a, de,* and *o*.

59.1. A (ad).   The preposition *a* regularly combines by enclisis:

$$a + le = al, au$$
$$a + les = as, aus$$

Note that *a* does not combine with the feminine article *la*.

By far the most common preposition in Old French, *a* serves a variety of purposes that are virtually impossible to summarize. It most often corresponds to English "to," implying direction toward, as opposed to *de* 'from.' It usually introduces verbal complements but may also introduce substantival, adjectival, or even adverbial complements.

A indicates the object (direct or indirect) of the action (real or implied) of the verb, meaning "to, toward, at, in, into, before, with":

A un mostier la fis geter (14:477)
Into a church I had her placed (lit.: thrown)

Si l'a *a* la dame mostré (7:221)
And (he) showed it (i.e., the child) to the lady

Ne set mie qu'*a* l'ueil li pent (3:88)
(He) doesn't know what is hanging before his eye.

A indicates possession, association, accompaniment, or a characteristic trait:

li fil *a* l'aversier (18:51)
the devil's son

les ustilz *as* ovriers (16:51)
the workers' tools

Ysolt *as* Blanches Mains (Thomas, *Tristan*, Sneyd 197)
Isolde of the White Hands

(See also 12.47.2.)

A establishes time:

L'arcevesques aveit *a* cel'ure mangié (16:16)
The archbishop had at (by) that time eaten

la nuit *a* l'avesprer (18:47)
during the night at (the hour of) vespers

Encontrez les aveient el cloistre *al* repairier (17:20)
(They) had met them in the cloister upon (their) return

A indicates means, manner, or cause, in the sense of "by, with, by means of, in, on, in accord with, according to":

A eschieles i ad les chevaliers muntez (16:50)
By (means of) ladders the knights climbed up

si se met ens *a* piés et *a* mains. (24, 97–98)
and he went in on hands and feet.

a lor conseil fame prendra (10:337)
(he) will take a wife in accord with their advice

A is required after many verbs to introduce a following infinitive (see 10.38). In this function it is untranslatable in English:

Si l'acommena *a* amer (8:258)
And he began to love her

Cil qui *a* norrir m'envoierent (13:444)
Those who sent me to be raised

A is used in combination with many verbs to form idiomatic expressions:

> Le Fresne li mistrent *a* non (7:229)
> Fresne to her (they) put to name
> They named her Fresne
>
> Si la mist *a* reson un jor (9:286)
> Thus her (he) put to speech one day
> Thus he spoke to her one day
>
> Molt se tendra *a* malbailli (8:266)
> (He) will consider himself very unfortunate

A is also used to create many adverbial expressions:

> *a* grant esploit (5:147)   quickly
> *a* escïent (6:209)   clearly, evidently

59.2. *De.* The preposition *de* regularly combines by enclisis with the definite article, yielding the following forms:

> de + le = del, dou, du
> de + les = des

Note that *de* does not combine with the feminine article *la*.

In opposition to *a*, *de* indicates separation or movement (real or perceived) away from a place or a person, in space or in time. It translates generally as "from":

> *De* Costentinoble ou il fu (4:125)
> From Constantinople where he had been
>
> l'abaesse ist *de* l'eglise (7:212)
> the abbess left (from) the church
>
> Bon guerredon *de* li avroit (4:120)
> A good reward from her (she) would have

De can also indicate a relationship between two persons or objects, a relationship of possession, attribution, or qualification:

> Dedenz le clos *de* l'abaïe (7:233)
> Within the enclosure of the abbey
>
> *De* ma voisine dis folie (14:472)
> About my neighbor (I) spoke folly

De biauté semble roïne (15:520)
In beauty (she) seems a queen

(Ele) est . . . entecie *de* toutes bones teces (20:32b)
(She) is . . . marked with all good qualities

In this usage it is frequently untranslatable in English:

A molt esté *de* bone fame (2:48)
(she) has been a very good woman (wife)

Franche estoit et *de* bone escole (7:245)
She was noble and well schooled

De introduces circumstantial complements of means, manner, and cause:

furent *de* Deu haï (16:2)
(they) were hated by God

mort *de* justise (16:20)
death by justice (i.e., in the name of justice)

Puis l'a *de* son let aletié (6:206)
Then she nursed it with her milk

De deus enfanz est enceintiee (3:67)
With two children (she) is pregnant

ja mais ne le verra *de* ses ex (21:8b)
never more will (he) see her with his eyes

De ce sui liez (14:489)
About this I am happy

La meschine molt s'esjoï
De l'aventure qu'ele oï (14:495–96)
The girl was very happy
Because of what she had heard

Like *a*, *de* is required after certain verbs to introduce a following infinitive. It is not translated:

Tost furent apresté *de* grant mal comencier (16:27)
(They) were prepared at once to start great trouble

E *del* ferir se sunt durement esforcié (19:37)
And to strike him (they) strove mightily

De also introduces infinitives used as subjects:

Mort *de* fuïr est coardie (*Piramus*, 762)
To flee death is cowardice

It enters into the composition of certain adverbial expressions:

> Del martire suffrir sui *del tut* aprestez (18:42)
> To suffer martyrdom (I) am completely ready/prepared
>
> Ensement cum la mort atendist *de sun gré* (17:2)
> As if he awaited death willingly

It is used to form comparisons (see also 19.83.2):

> Qui mieus *de* lui fet a loer (3:90)
> Who more than he is worthy of praise
> Who is more worthy of praise than he

59.3.   *O* (od).   *O* indicates spatial proximity or accompaniment and is generally translated "with":

> Quant vos primes *o* moi parlastes (14:480)
> When you first spoke with me

It may also indicate a physical characteristic:

> s'amie *o* le cler vis (20:7)
> his ladylove with the radiant (unblemished?) face

It can identify manner or means, the "instrument with which":

> Le cervel *od* l'espee hors del chief li geta (19:43)
> He thrust his brains out of his head with his sword

Frequently, *o* is preceded by the adverb *ensemble* to underscore the notion of proximity:

> *Ensemble o* lui s'en est alee (9:301)
> Together with him she went off

O combines with *tot/tout* either for reinforcement as a preposition or for adverbial usage:

> *O tout* l'enfant outre s'en vint (5:142)
> With the child she came out (on the other side of the woods)
>
> A son ostel *o tout* s'en vait (6:192)
> To his lodging he comes together (with the child)

The preposition *o* (< APUD) should not be confused with the adverb *o* 'where' < UBI or with the conjunction *o* 'either, or' < AUT.

Phonology 14

Single consonant + *r* or *l*

Before R and L, most consonants developed as if they were intervocalic (cf. Phonology 12). The labials P, B, and V all passed to *v* before *r*:

CÁPRAM	>	/kjéβra/	>	chievre
*LÁBRA			>	levre
VĪVĔRE	>	/vív'rǝ/	>	vivre

Before L, the labials P and B both resulted in *bl*. It is conjectured that they did not develop, as expected, to *vl* because that combination did not exist in Latin:

DŬPLŬM	>	/dóplo/	>	double
TÁBŬLAM	>	/táb'la/	>	table

The dentals T and D were assimilated to a following R or L, generally giving *rr* or *ll* (later vocalized to *ul*):

LATRÓNEM	>	/ladrónǝ/	>	larron
CLÁUDĔRE	>	/cláud'rǝ/	>	clorre, clore
SPÁTŬLAM	>	/espát'la/	>	espalle, espaule
MÓDŬLŬM	>	/mód'lo/	>	molle, moule

The velars K and G became *yod*:

FÁCĔRE	>	/fác're/	>	faire
FLAGRÁRE			>	flairier
MÁCŬLAM	>	/mác'la/	>	maille
VĬGĬLÁRE	>	/vèg'lárǝ/	>	veillier

Consonant clusters ending in *r* or *l*

The loss of the unaccented penult often produced consonant clusters that were not viable in Gallo-Roman. In these cases, an epenthetic plosive developed between the two consonants corresponding in point of articulation and voicing to the first consonant:

M'L	>	mbl	SĬMŬLÁRE	>	/sèm'lárə/	> sembler
M'R	>	mbr	NŬMĔRŬM	>	/nóm'ro/	> nombre
N'R	>	ndr	CĬNĔREM	>	/cén'rə/	> cendre
S'R	>	str	ANTECĔSSORE	>	/ant'sés'r/	> ancestre
S'R	>	str	*ĔSSĔRE	>	/éss'rə/	> estre
L'R	>	ldr, udr	MÓLĔRE	>	/mọl'rə/	> moldre, moudre

A number of Latin second, third, and fourth conjugation verbs were affected by this sound change and produced the Old French Class III verbs (see Phonology 10).

When clusters of two dissimilar consonants were present in the initial affected Latin syllable, the second consonant assimilated in point of articulation to the others:

LV'R	>	ldr, udr	SỌLVĔRE	>	/sọlv'rə/	> soldre, soudre
LG'R	>	ldr, udr	FŬLGŬREM	>	/fọlg'rə/	> foldre, foudre
RG'R	>	rdr	TĔRGĔRE	>	/térg'rə/	> terdre
NG'R	>	indr	TÁNGĔRE	>	/táng'rə/	> taindre
SC'R	>	istr	PÁSCĔRE	>	/pásc'rə/	> paistre

For all other groups of three consonants ending in R or L, see Phonology 13.

Supporting vowel

After certain consonant groups, an off-glide *e* /ə/ was developed to facilitate articulation. This final "helping vowel" is found:

(1) after primary consonant groups whose last element is a liquid or nasal, except RR, LL, RM, RN:

PÁTREM	>	/péðre/	>	pere
DŬPLŬM	>	/dóblo/	>	double
*HĔLMU	>	/hélmo/	>	helme (heaume)
but				
CÁRRUM	>	/cárro/	>	char
CÓLLUM	>	/cọllo/	>	col

(2) after a labial plus *yod*:

RŬBĔŬM	>	/róbjo/	>	rouge
SĪMĬŬM	>	/símjo/	>	singe

(3) after most secondary consonant groups (formed after the unaccented Latin penult or final vowel was dropped):

LĔPŎREM	>	/lép'rə/	>	lievre
*TRĔMŬLO	>	/trém'lo/	>	tremble
ĬNTĔR	>	/ént'r/	>	entre
ĬNSĬMUL	>	/ensém'l/	>	ensemble
but				
CÁLĬDŬM	>	/cál'do/	>	chalt, chaut
NĬTĬDŬM	>	/net'do/	>	net

chapter 15

Reading and Textual Analysis, Selection 8

Selection 8 concludes the story of Fresne. Following her recognition as the legitimate daughter of the Lord of Brittany, Fresne is able at last to marry her lover without jeopardizing his succession.

Institutional marriage in the Christian Middle Ages traditionally consisted of three stages: betrothal, public celebration, and consummation. The betrothal, or espousal, was a publicly recognized contract of future marriage, usually signed by the contractants before ecclesiastical or lay witnesses. After espousal (< SPONSALIS), the wife-to-be was referred to as spouse (*espouse*: 11:371) or even wife (*dame*: 11:387), for the marriage was considered ratified (RATUM). The second stage, the marriage ceremony proper, occurred in Reading Selection 7a; but before the final step—the conjugal act—can be completed, Fresne's true identity is discovered. Although Pope Alexander III (1159–81) had declared that nonconsummated marriages between baptized parties were real sacraments, he recognized that they were sometimes dissoluble. The ease with which the Archbishop of Dol annuls Coudre's marriage in the present selection corresponds, undoubtedly, to the established practice of the day. This evidence from literary history contrasts with the statement in the *New Catholic Encyclopedia* (1967) that "Extant documents establish no certain proof of actual dispensations of nonconsummated marriage prior to Martin V (1417–31)" (9: 287).

15:501   Li chevaliers qant il le sot,
15:502   Onques mes si grant joie n'ot.

15:503	Li arcevesque a conseillié
15:504	C'or soit ainsi la nuit lessié;
15:505	El demain les departira,
15:506	Lui et cele espousera.
15:507	Einsint l'ont fet et devisé.
15:508	El demain furent dessevré;
15:509	Aprés a s'amie espousee,
15:510	Et le pere li a donnee,
15:511	Qui molt ot vers li bon corage;
15:512	Par mi li part son heritage.
15:513	Il et la mere as noces furent
15:514	O lor fille, si comme il durent.
15:515	Granz noces refont derechief;
15:516	A un riche homme seroit grief
15:517	D'esligier ce qu'il despendirent
15:518	Au grant couvine que il firent.
15:519	Por la joie de la meschine,
15:520	Que de biauté semble roïne,
15:521	Qu'il ont sifaitement trovee,
15:522	Ont molt grant joie demenee.
15:523	Quant en lor païs s'en alerent,
15:524	La Coudre, lor fille, emmenerent.
15:525	Molt richement en lor contree
15:526	Fu puis la pucele donnee.
15:527	Quant l'aventure fu seüe
15:528	Comment ele estoit avenue,
15:529	Le lay du Fresne en ont trové;
15:530	Por la dame l'ont si nomé.

15:506 *Lui et cele*: Bruron and Fresne.
15:510 *le pere* for *li pere* (see 4.11). The dir. obj. pron. *la* is omitted before the ind. obj.; nonetheless, the past participle agrees (see 22.95).
15:512 "On her account he divided his legacy in half."
15:528 *ele = l'aventure.*

---

60. Multiple Function Prepositions

60.1. *Par.* *Par* indicates localization or movement through time or space; it is translated as "by." In a static sense, it may indicate a specific moment in time or a specific part of a place, person, or thing:

Icele nuit *par tens* leva (6:181)
That night he arose early

Par l'acor del mantel l'aveit Reinalz saisi (18:15)
Renald had grabbed him by the edge (?) of his cloak

et cil departiroient les fiez et les honors *par* les hommes (25, 24–25)
and they would divide the fiefs and offices among the men

In an active sense, it indicates movement through space or time:

Jo vus metrai laienz *par un altre sentier* (16:42)
I'll put (get) you in there by another path

Par toute Bretaingne seüe (2:52)
Known throughout all Brittany

La sus amunt pargetent tel luiserne
Par la noit la mer en est plus bele. (*Roland*, 2634–35)
They cast such a glow from on high
(That) the sea is made more beautiful through the night.

Par identifies adverbial expressions of manner, means, or cause:

Jadis *par* ma grant vilenie (14:471)
Formerly, by my great wickedness

qui del pain li gaegnast *par* honor (22:2c)
who would win (earn) her bread honorably

As an extension of the preceding usage, *par* is used to introduce an agent in oaths and after verbs in the passive:

"Deus," fet ele, "*par ton saint non*" (5:162)
"God," said she, "by your holy name"

cels qui sunt *par vus* suspendu e lacié (18:38)
those who have been tied up and hanged by you

Par also reinforces a number of other prepositions (*par desus, par devers, par ou*; see 9.35.3). Particularly common is the expression *par mi* 'through the middle.' In 15:512 the expression is used in its original sense, with *mi* still functioning as a substantive:

Par mi li part son heritage
Down the middle he divided his inheritance for her
(i.e., he gave her half of all he owned)

Very early the combination fused into a single preposition, meaning simply "through":

Parmi l'encloistre ariere s'en erent returné (19:52)
They went back through the cloister

60.2. *Por/pur.* *Por* indicates primarily the purpose or cause of an action. It can translate as "in order to, for":

> Il meïsmes va *por son gendre* (14:498)
> He himself goes for (to find) his son-in-law
>
> . . . des proueces qu'il fist
> *por s'amie* (20:6–7)
> . . . the bold deeds that he did
> for his ladylove

It can also mean "because of, for the sake of, on account of, for":

> *Por la joie* de la meschine (15:519)
> On account of the joy (that they had upon finding) the girl
>
> N'i ot un seul . . .
> *Por sa franchise* ne l'amast (9:318–19)
> There was not a one . . .
> Who did not love her because of her goodness

Por introduces the idea of a substitution or exchange—"as, for":

> La dame la tint *por sa niece* (7:231)
> The lady treated her as her niece
>
> *Por le Fresne* que vos perdroiz (10:345)
> (In exchange) for Fresne whom you will lose

Por + an infinitive or present participle may simply indicate the purpose of the action of the main verb:

> *Por* moi *desfendre* de honnir
> L'un des enfanz m'estuet murdrir. (3:91–92)
> In order not to shame myself,
> I must kill one of the infants.

If, however, the verb in the principal clause is negated, *por* generally means "for fear of, even if (someone) were to":

Ja *pur murir* le camp ne guerpirunt (6, 219)
Never, for fear of dying, will they abandon the field
Even if they faced certain death, they would never abandon the field

Ne vos leroie *por les membres perdant* (*Prise*, 1427)
Never, for fear of losing my limbs, will I leave you
Even if I were to lose my limbs, I would never leave you

60.3. Confusion of *por* and *par*. Since *por* and *par* both had causative meanings and commonly had similar abbreviations in manuscripts, they were easily confused. Most frequently, one finds *por* where *par* would be anticipated:

> *Por cel apostre* qu'en quiert en Noiron pré (*Charroi*, 279;
> MS A1)
> In the name of that pope one seeks in Nero's meadow
>
> *Por matinet*, à l'aube, se sunt anchemiñé (*Floovant*, 2356)
> In the early morning, at dawn, they rode off

The preposition *par* should not be confused with the adverb *par* (see 19.82):

> Molt par est bone se puis n'est enpirie (8, 152)
> It is very very good if it is not devalued later

60.4. En. The preposition *en* combines by enclisis with the articles *le* and *les*, as follows:

$$en + le = el, ou$$
$$en + les = es$$

En localizes a complement within a place, state, or time period. It usually translates as "in":

> *El* demain les departira (15:505)
> On the morrow (he) will separate them
>
> *En* l'an meïsmes enceinta (3:66)
> In that very year (she) became pregnant
>
> La damoisele *es* chambres fu (11:383)
> The young girl was in the room(s) (the suite)
>
> *En* une vile riche et bele (5:149)
> Into a splendid and beautiful town
>
> La gent qui *en* la meson erent (2:49)
> The people who were in the house

It may also be used figuratively to indicate a state:

> Or sunt chaü *en* dolenté (19:55)
> Now they have fallen in grief

En can indicate manner, means, or the attribute of a substantive:

> Et *en* semblant et *em* parole (7:246)
> Both in looks and in words

En quatre fors estoit quarrez (5:169)
It was quartered in four forks

Cuida qu'aucuns les eüst pris
En larrecin (6:185–86)
He thought that someone had taken them
In theft (had stolen them)

En eschange la Coudre avroiz (10:346)
In exchange you will have Coudre

It may introduce both infinitives and the *-ant* form:

en plus *demorer* ne poons nos riens gaengnier (*Mort Artu*, 21, 9–10)
in remaining longer we can gain nothing

La voiz oï tot *an dormant* (11, 130)
He heard the voice while sleeping

It combines with certain verbs to form idiomatic expresssions:

Et molt la *tenoit en destroit* (2:63)
And he kept very close watch over her (tortured her?)

The preposition *en* must not be confused with the adverb *en*, used in verbs of motion:

Ensemble o lui s'*en* est alee (9:301)
Together with him she went away

en lor païs s'*en* alerent (15:523)
into their land they went (returned)

nor with the pronominal adverb *en*, meaning "of it, of them, for it, about it/them":

Le lay du Fresne *en* ont trové (15:529)
The lay of Fresne has been composed about it (i.e., about the *aventure*)

61. Indefinites: The *Tant* Group

These are all declined like Type I adjectives and may function as adjectives, pronouns, or adverbs:

	MASCULINE	FEMININE
NS	tanz	tante
OS	tant	tante
NP	tant	tantes
OP	tanz	tantes

Tant means "so large, so many, so much":

> Nicolete ma tresdouce amie que j'aim *tant* (22:7a)
> Nicolette my sweetest friend whom I love so much
>
> *tanz* bienz t'ai fait (18:16)
> I have done so many good (deeds) for you
>
> *Tantes* dolurs ad pur tei andurede[s] (3, 167)
> She has endured so many sufferings on your account

For the adverbial use of *tant*, see 19.82.

Quant means "how(ever) many, how(ever) much":

> Ne vus sai dire quels ne *quanz* (9, 184)
> I cannot tell you which or how many
>
> La reïne Semiramis,
> *Quant* ele ot unkes plus aveir . . .
> N'esligasent le destre pan. (10, 3–4, 7)
> Queen Semiramis,
> However much wealth she had . . .
> Could not have paid for the right (tent) flap.

For *quant* relative and interrogative, see 20.88.2.

Auquant, alquant means "some, several, certain ones." It is usually plural and is often found with the definite article.

> Contre els unt les uis clos des moines *li alquant* (17:21)
> Some of the monks closed the doors against them

It may be used in place of *li un/li autre* (see Section 63 below):

> *li auquant* dient qu'ele est fuïe fors de la terre
> et *li auquant* dient que li quens . . . l'a faite mordrir. (21:35b–c)
> some say that she has fled the land, and others
> that the count . . . has had her killed.

62. Indefinites: The *Tel* Group

All are declined like Type II adjectives (see 12.49.2):

	MASCULINE	FEMININE
NS	tels, teus	tel
OS	tel	tel
NP	tel	tels, teus
OP	tels, teus	tels, teus

(I)tel 'such a one, such' is used as an adjective or a pronoun:

> je l'envoierai en tel tere (21:8b)
> I'll send her to such a land

> C'en paradis ne vont fors *tex* (= *tels*) gens con je vous dirai (22:7b)
> For to heaven only go such people as I'll tell you

> *Tiex* (= *tels*) en parla qui puis en ot grant honte (8, 202)
> Such a one spoke who afterwards was greatly shamed for it

As an adjective before numbers, it means "about, some":

> Jeo quid k'il en i ot *teus cent* (Marie, "Lanval," 420)
> I believe there were some hundred of them

> I aveit *iteus deus milliers* (Marie, "Chaitivel," 136)
> There were about two thousand

Autel 'similar, like, the same' is often reinforced with *tot*:

> fet *tot autel*
> con s'il fust devant un autel (12, 405–06)
> he acted just the same
> as if he were before an altar

Autretel is an alternate form of *autel*:

> Vos qui avez fet *autretel* (12, 239)
> You who have done the same

63. Indefinites: Various

The following indefinites do not fit well into any individual categories:
Autre 'other, another' is a pronoun or adjective. It may be preceded by
an article, a demonstrative adjective, or a possessive adjective, and it is
declined like a Class II adjective (see 12.49.2):

> ele s'en voloit aler en *autre* païs (23:1)
> she wanted to go into another land

> L'*autre* a ses amis espousee (10:358)
> Her lover married the other (girl)

> la u je fiere cevalier ni *autres* mi (20:27b)
> there where I might strike a knight, or another me

Autre is often opposed to *un* in the sense of "some . . . others." The
expressions *li alquant* (see Section 61) and *tels i ot qui* have similar meanings:

Tels i ot qui se traistrent ariere de l'assaut et les
vaissials en quoi il estoient; et *tels i ot qui* remestrent
a ancre si pres de la ville que il getoient a pierrieres
et a mangonials *li un as autres*. (25, 50–52)
Some withdrew from the assault along with the ships they were
in; and others remained anchored so near the town that they
catapulted stones upon one another.

Autrui is a stressed oblique singular form of *autre*. It is most commonly
used as a direct object or an object of a preposition, but it can also serve as
an indirect object or possessive:

> Qui *sor autrui* mesdit et ment (3:87)
> (She) who slanders and lies about another
>
> L'*autrui joie* prise petit (10, 178)
> The joy of another he esteems very little
>
> Por moi fu dit, non *por autrui* (11, 142)
> For me was it said, not for another

El 'something else' or, after a negative, 'anything else' is used only as a
pronoun:

> que feroient [il] *el* (8, 126)
> what else could [they] do?
>
> Se pur mei nun, pur *el* n'i est (4, 168)
> If not for me, then not for anything else

(See also Section 64 below.)

Maint 'many, many a' can be an adjective or a pronoun:

> Car *meintes* foiz veü l'avoit (12:404)
> For she had observed it many times
>
> En sa conpaigne avoit il *maint* princier (8, 2)
> In his company there was many a prince

Meïsme(s), *meesmes* means "same, very, self":

> Ceo m'est avis, *meïsmes* l'an (10, 140)
> I believe, that very year
>
> En l'an *meïsmes* enceinta (3:66)
> That same year she became pregnant
>
> Les uis ad il *meesmes* overt e desbarez (17:31)
> He himself opened and unbarred the doors

64.   Four Functions of the Form *El*

The form *el* has four uses, which must be carefully distinguished. They are listed in order of decreasing frequency:

(a)   A contracted form of *en* (preposition) + *le* (article) (see 1.3.2):

Por ce qu'*el* fresne fu trovee (7:228)
Because in the ash tree (she) was found

El demain les departira (15:505)
On the morrow (he) will separate them (i.e., annul their marriage)

(b)   An alternate form of the third singular feminine subject pronoun (see 7.24.1):

El la voloit fere couchier (12:415)
She wished to have her go to bed

(c)   A neuter indefinite pronoun meaning "something else" (after a negative, "anything else"):

"Estes vos dame qui pleurt ses vevetez?"
"Nenil voir, niés, einçois pense por *el*." (8, 35–36)
"Are you a woman crying over her widowhood?"
"Indeed not, nephew; on the contrary, I'm downcast because of
    something else."

(d)   In certain dialects, a neuter pronoun used impersonally in place of *il*:

Peser m'en deit, e si fet *el* (*Troie*, 20263)
It should grieve me, and it does.

Phonology 15

Consonants + *yod*

One of the most important phonological developments during the Vulgar Latin period was the consonantalization of Latin E and I in hiatus to *yod* (see Phonology Sections 5 and 8). Few consonants escaped the influence of this *yod*.

C + *yod* supported and intervocalic was palatalized to /tj/. By the twelfth century it had shifted forward to /ts/, and it was pronounced /s/ in the thirteenth century. It is generally spelled *c* or *ss* when intervocalic and *z* when final, but numerous exceptions exist.

SUPPORTED

ARCĬŌNEM	>	/arkjóne/	>	/artsón/	>	arçon
LÁNCĔAM	>	/lánkja/	>	/lántsə/	>	lance

INTERVOCALIC

FÁCĬAT	>	/fáttjat/	>	/fátsə/	>	fasse, face
VĪNÁCĔAM	>	/vináttja/	>	/vinátsə/	>	vinasse

G and D were effaced very early by the palatalizing effect of a following *yod* (see Phonology 5). In initial and supported positions, they became
/dʒ/ in the twelfth century and opened to /ʒ/ by the thirteenth century.
They were usually written *j* or *ge*:

DIŬRNUM	>	/djórno/	>	/dʒórn/	>	jour
HÓRDĔUM	>	/órdjo/	>	/órdʒə/	>	orge
GEÓRGĬUS	>	/djórdjos/	>	/dʒórdʒəs/	>	Georges

Intervocalic G and D + *yod* likewise palatalized in Vulgar Latin but
then opened to /j/, which combined with preceding vowels to form
diphthongs in Old French (see Phonology 8):

RÁDIŬM	>	/rádjo/			>	rai
*GÁUDĬA	>	/gaúdja/			>	joie
CORRĪGĬA	>	/korrégja/			>	courroie

T + *yod* supported was palatalized to /tsj/. By the twelfth century it
was pronounced /ts/, and it opened in the thirteenth century to /s/. It
was generally spelled *c* or *ss*:

*FÓRTĬA	>	/fórtja/	>	/fórtsjə/	>	force
CANTĬŌNEM	>	/kantjóne/	>	/tʃantsjónə/	>	chanson
*MÁTTĔA	>	/mátja/	>	/mátsjə/	>	masse

Intervocalic T + *yod* likewise palatalized to /tsj/, but then it voiced to
/dʒ/ before becoming /iz/ (written *is*):

PŌTĬŌNEM	>	/potsjóne/	>	/pojdʒónə/	>	poison
PALÁTĬUM	>	/palátsjo/	>	/palájdʒə/	>	palais

S + *yod* metathesized to *is*:

BASĬÁRE	>	/basjáre/	>	baisier
NAÚSĔAM	>	/naúsja/	>	noise

The groups -SCI-, -STI-, -SSI-, -X-, and -SC- before E, I all became -*iss*- intervocalic and -*is* final:

*PĬSCĬÓNE	>	/pestjóne/	>	peisson, poisson
MESSĬÓNEM	>	/messjóne/	>	meisson, moisson
ANGÚSTĬAM	>	/angóstja/	>	angoisse
*ÚSTĬUM	>	/ústjo/	>	uis (huis)
EXĪRE	>	/eksíre/	>	eissir
ÁXEM	>	/ákse/	>	ais
NASCÉNTEM	>	/nastjénte/	>	naissant

R + *yod* metathesized to *ir*:

ÁRĔAM	>	/árja/	>	aire
CÓRĬUM	>	/córjo/	>	cuir

N + *yod* and NG before E, I palatalized to /ɲ/, spelled -*ign*- interior and -*ing* final. After the nasalization of diphthongs, final -*ing* dentalized to -*n*:

LĬNĔAM	>	/línja/	>	ligne
*MONTÁNĔAM	>	/montánja/	>	montaigne (montagne)
BÁLNĔUM	>	/*bánjo/	>	baing (> bain)
LÓNGE	>	/lóndje/	>	loing (> loin)

L + *yod* became /λ/, spelled -*ill* intervocalic and -*il* final:

FĪLIAM	>	/fílja/	>	fille
TALĬÁRE	>	/taljáre/	>	taillier
MĬLĬUM	>	/míljo/	>	mil
MÁLLĔUM	>	/máljo/	>	mail

The labials P, B, V were absorbed by a following *yod*, which became /dʒ/ (spelled *g*) after voiced *b, v* and /tʃ/ (spelled *ch*) after unvoiced *p*:

RÁBĬAM	>	/rábja/	>	/rábdʒə/	>	rage
CÁVĔAM	>	/cáβja/	>	/cádʒə/	>	cage
SÁPĬAT	>	/sápjat/	>	/saptʃə/	>	sache

The labial M was assimilated to *n* before *yod*, which became /ɲ/; the combination was written *ng*:

SĬ́MĬŬM	>	/símjo/	>	/sindʒə/	>	singe
SŎ́MNĬŬM	>	/sǫ́mjo/	>	/sǫ̃ndʒə/	>	songe

chapter 16

Reading and Textual Analysis, Selection 9

The reading selections in Chapters 16 through 19 are taken from the *Life of Saint Thomas Becket* by Guernes de Pont-Sainte-Maxence.

Thomas Becket, Archbishop of Canterbury, was murdered in his cathedral on 29 December 1170 by knights from the household of King Henry II Plantagenet. Early in his career, the handsome, vigorous, and energetic Thomas had been an ally and confidant of Henry. After Henry was crowned in 1154, he appointed the young cleric to be his chancellor. Following in the footsteps of his predecessors William I and Henry I (see Chapter 11), Henry II was determined to consolidate his power by obtaining the submission of the nobles and high clergy. When the important archbishopric of Canterbury came open in 1161, Henry saw an opportunity to place the see under his immediate influence. In spite of Thomas' own protestations and the opposition of the monks and bishops, Henry appointed his chancellor Archbishop of Canterbury in 1162. No sooner was Thomas installed, however, than he proved a disappointment to Henry. He obstinately resisted all royal encroachments on ecclesiastical liberties and repudiated the Constitutions of Clarendon whereby Henry, in 1164, asserted customary royal privileges over ecclesiastical matters. His pugnacious defense of the Church earned Thomas six years of exile in France.

Matters came to a head in June 1170 when Henry, in defiance of the archbishop's prerogatives, had his son "the Young King" crowned as his successor. Pope Alexander upheld Thomas' rights and suspended the participating bishops. Henry relented, and there was a reconciliation in

July. Thomas returned in triumph to England on 1 December. He excommunicated the bishops of York, London, and Salisbury, who had assisted
in the coronation of the Young King. Angered by this affront, Henry
suggested that he would be well rid of his enemy. Four members of his
entourage—Renald Fils-Ours, William de Tracy, Hugh de Moreville, and
Richard the Breton—took him at his word, crossed the Channel, and rode
to Canterbury, after having been joined by Randel del Broc and several of
his men.

The reading selection begins with their passage to England and arrival
at Canterbury.

16:1	Mais cil quatre felun e li Deu enemi
16:2	(Pur lur malvaise vie furent de Deu haï):
16:3	Hue de Morevile, Willaumes de Traci,
16:4	E Reinalz li fiz Urs e li quarz altresi,
16:5	Ço fu Richarz li Brez, sunt de la curt parti . . .
16:6	Li dui des quatre sunt a Dovre mer passé,
16:7	Dui a Wingelesé. Ne furent desturbé
16:8	Pur nef ne pur passage, pur vent ne pur oré;
16:9	Tut lur est avenu selunc lur volenté.
16:10	A Saltewode sunt venu e asemblé . . . .
16:11	Venu sunt al quint jur de la Nativité
16:12	A Cantorbire cil, quant gent orent digné,
16:13	En l'endemain que furent Innocent decolé . . .
16:14	En la curt l'arcevesque vindrent li enragié,
16:15	Tut dreit devant la sale sunt descendu a pié.
16:16	L'arcevesques aveit a cel'ure mangié;
16:17	En la chambre seeit od sun privé clergié.
16:18	Nis li sergant s'esteient des tables ja drecié.
16:19	Fait li dunc sainz Thomas: "Tuz nus estuet murir;
16:20	Ne pur mort de justise ne me verrez flechir,
16:21	E pur l'amur de Deu voil la mort sustenir;
16:22	Ne il ne sunt pas mielz apresté del ferir
16:23	Que mis curages est del martire suffrir."
16:24	Endementres s'armerent la fors li chevalier,
16:25	E osterent les cotes, ceinstrent les branz d'acier;
16:26	Car tut vindrent armé, chascuns sur sun destrier;
16:27	Tost furent apresté de grant mal comencier.
16:28	Asez fu qui l'ala l'arcevesque nuncier.
16:29	"Sire," funt li li moine, "alez en cel mustier.
16:30	Il chantent ore vespres; nes deüssiez laissier.

16:31	Cil chevalier vus volent e prendre e detrenchier."
16:32	"Ne me verrez" fait il, "pur ço rien esmaier.
16:33	Ci atendrai tut ço que Deus m'i volt jugier."
16:34	Quant se furent armé li quatre bacheler,
16:35	Vunt as uis de la sale; mais n'i porent entrer,
16:36	Car um les out ainz fait aprés els bien barrer.
16:37	Dunc comencent as uis durement a buter,
16:38	Car il voleient prendre le saint e decolper.
16:39	Quant ne porent les uis par force depecier,
16:40	Roberz del Broc, qui sout le mal mult enginnier:
16:41	"Or me siwez," fait il, "seignur franc chevalier;
16:42	Jo vus metrai laienz par un altre sentier."
16:43	Par devers la quisine sunt entré el vergier.
16:44	A l'uis de la chambre out un oriol fermé,
16:45	Dreit devers le chardin, qu'i out maint jor esté.
16:46	Pur refaire erent dunc abatu li degré,
16:47	E li carpentier erent a lur disner alé.
16:48	A cel oriol sunt li chevalier turné.
16:49	Par iloec est es chambres Roberz del Broc entrez;
16:50	A eschieles i ad les chevaliers muntez.
16:51	Les ustilz as ovriers qui firent les degrez,
16:52	Besagues e cuignies, en unt od els portez
16:53	Pur depecier les uis, ses trovassent fermez.

16:10 After arriving in England, the four traitors met at Saltwood with Randel del Broc, recently excommunicated by Thomas, who would accompany them to Canterbury.

16:11 I.e., 29 December.

16:18 The knights accused Thomas of plotting against Henry II and summoned him to appear at court. He staunchly refused, placing duty to God and Church above that due Henry. They threatened him as they left, and Thomas spoke the following words to a confidant.

16:19 *li*: Johan of Salisbury, friend and adviser to Thomas.

16:28 *l'arcevesque*: ind. obj., see 5.14.2.

16:40 Robert del Broc, the brother of Randel, was likewise excommunicated.

---

65. Numerals: Transcription

In manuscripts numerals might be spelled out in full, but they were more likely to be written as roman numerals. Editors of Old French texts vary in their methods of handling numerals. In the past, most editors wrote out any forms found in roman numerals, basing their transcriptions on forms found in full elsewhere within the text or creating forms in conformity with the major dialectal peculiarities of the text. It is difficult, however, to determine proper forms for all numerals not written in full, so editors today often leave roman numerals or compromise by transcribing only those written out elsewhere in the text.

66. Cardinal Numbers

66.1. Forms. Cardinal numbers, whether used as numerals or as pronouns or adjectives, are generally indeclinable:

> cil quatre felon (16:1)
> these four felons

The first three cardinal numbers, however, are regularly declined if used as masculine adjectives or pronouns.

One: The declension is identical to that of the article *un, une* (see 1.3).
Two: NP   dui
        OP   dous, deus
Three: NP   troi
          OP   trois

Feminine forms are the same as masculine OP, although on occasion masculine NP forms are used as feminines. As in modern French, ten (*dis*) is used as a base to form seventeen, eighteen, and nineteen: *dis et set, dis et uit, dis et nuef*. Twenty (*vint*) and one hundred (*cent*) and their multiples are used as bases to form higher numbers:

vint et trois 'twenty-three'
vint et doze 'thirty-two'
douze vins vessiaus (Joinville, 182) '240 ships'
de sis a huit vingtz 'between 120 and 160'
quatre cenz milie atendent l'ajurnee (*Rol.*, 715) '400,000 await the dawn'
treis cenz milie cumbaturs '300,000 fighting men'
doze cent chevaliers '1,200 knights'
plus de cinc cens gens 'more than five hundred men'

The system of multiplying by twenty was introduced during the Gallo-Roman period and probably represents Celtic influence. When multiplied

as bases, *vingt* and *cent* generally became *vinz/vins* and *cenz/cens*. *Milie* (<
MILLIA) was properly the plural of *mil*, but they were already confused in
the earliest texts. Neither took an *-s* when multiplied.

Collective forms of numerals were made by adding *-aine*: *une centaine, une
disaine, une dozaine*. An exception is "a thousand": *un millier*.

66.2. Usage. The cardinal numbers *un, dous, trois* are declined only
when used as adjectives or pronouns, in which case they agree with the
noun they modify or replace.

A number referring to a fraction of a whole is preceded by the definite
article:

> *Li dui* des quatre (16:6)
> Two of the four
>
> *Li dis* devant la tor assaillent . . .
> *Li dis* remainnent an l'estor (*Cligés*, 1952, 1955)
> Ten (of the twenty men) assaulted the tower . . .
> (The other) ten remained in the press

Approximation is indicated by *tel, itel*:

> A icest mot *tels* .c. milie s'en vunt (6, 221)
> When they heard this, about a hundred thousand left
>
> *Teus* mil maisons i ot e plus (*Troie*, 3019)
> There were some thousand and more houses

67. Ordinal Numbers

67.1. Forms. Ordinal numbers are declined like Type I adjectives (see
12.49.1):

	FEMININE	MASCULINE
NS	la premiere	li premiers
OS	la premiere	le premier
NP	les premieres	li premier
OP	les premieres	les premiers

Others follow the same paradigm—*la seconde, li seconz; la tierce, li tierz; la
quarte, li quarz; la quinte, li quinz; la siste, li siste;* and so forth.

The basic forms of the ordinal numbers from first to tenth were as
follows:

first	premier	sixth	siste
second	secont	seventh	setme
third	tierz	eighth	uitme
fourth	quart	ninth	neufme
fifth	quint	tenth	disme

Ordinal numbers above "tenth" consisted of the cardinal numbers + the ending *-isme* (or its dialectal variant *-iesme*). Analogical forms for first through tenth were created by the use of this same ending: *troisime, troisisme, troisiesme, quatrisme, quatriesme.* Other ordinals were generated by the addition of the ending *-ain: premerain, quartain, quintain, disain, vintain.* There were, then, a multitude of forms for the ordinal numbers, especially when one takes into account spelling and dialectal variants.

67.2. Usage. Ordinals are used for days of the month and successive kings, nobles, or prelates of the same name:

> al *quint* jur de la Nativité (16:11)
> on the fifth day of the feast of the Nativity
>
> Charles *Quint*
> Charles the Fifth

Ordinals may indicate portions of the whole, with or without the word *part*:

> il ne li estoit pas demouré *la tierce partie* de ses gens (26, 31)
> he did not have left a third of his men
>
> Et en Espaigne en ai tant conquesté
> Que je ne sai ou *le disme* poser. (*Couronnement*, 2239–40)
> And in Spain I've won so much
> That I do not know where to put the tenth (part) of it.

An important construction in Old French combines the stressed object pronoun and an ordinal number: *lui troisime* 'he and two others,' *moi quart* 'three others and myself':

> *li disime* de chevaliers (24, 108)
> he the tenth of knights
> he and nine other knights
>
> E si y alai *moy disieme* de chevaliers, et *moy tiers* de banieres. (Joinville, 112)
> And I went there with nine other knights and two other bannerets.

68. Dates and Time

Dates and time in the Middle Ages were based on the Church's calendar and hours.

Dates were numbered in relation to the principal feasts and liturgical seasons: Easter (the Sunday following the vernal equinox), Ascension (40 days after Easter), Pentecost (50 days after Easter), Saint John the Baptist (24 June), Christmas (25 Dec.):

al quint jur de la Nativité (16:11)
on the fifth day of the feast of Christmas (i.e., 29 Dec.)

En l'endemain que furent Innocent decolé (16:13)
On the day following the feast of the (slaying of the) Holy Innocents

le vendredi devant la Trinité (26, 37–38)
Friday before Trinity Sunday

Times of day were based on the canonical hours, laid down in the early Middle Ages by the Rule of St. Benedict:

matins 'matins'	the first canonical hour; varies from midnight to dawn
laudes 'laud'	varies from about 3 a.m. to dawn
prime 'the first hour'	sunrise, about 6 a.m.
terce 'the third hour'	mid-morning, about 9 a.m.
seste 'the sixth hour'	about midday, 12 p.m. (rare)
midi 'midday'	about midday, noon
none 'the ninth hour'	mid-afternoon, about 3 p.m.
vespre 'vesper'	nightfall, about 6 p.m.
complie 'compline'	about 9 p.m.
mienuit, minuit 'midnight'	midnight

The prayers of matins and laud were often combined and sung at dawn.

These hours, generally calculated on sun time, varied considerably with the seasons. Mechanical clocks were not developed until the thirteenth century and were rare until the late fourteenth century, when they began to appear on public buildings. Most people in medieval France and England estimated time from the position of the sun or from the striking of the bells to signal the hours for work and prayer at the local monastery. In summer, the time between daylight hours such as *terce* and *none* would be longer than in winter, whereas the time between *vespre* and *complie* would be longer in winter.

Ensi dura cil assals mult durs et mult fors et mult fiers trosque vers *hore de none* (25, 45–46)
Thus this mighty, powerful, and bold assault lasted until near mid-afternoon

Aprés *vespres* androit *conplie* (*Charrete*, 2014)
After vespers, about compline

Vinc ci entre *nune* e *midi* (4, 220)
I came here between mid-afternoon and noon

This last citation indicates a distinction between *none* and *midi*, but in some localities the two were synonymous, as English "noon" attests. The hours varied from region to region and from season to season, so it is impossible to equate them with clock hours until the fifteenth century.

The time could be rendered slightly more precise by indicating whether it was nearer to nightfall (*bas, basse*) or to noon (*haut, haute*) within the given hour:

Et *vespres* iere ja *bas* (25, 104)
And it was already late evening

Jusqu'a po sera *none basse* (*Yvain*, 5884)
Soon it will be late mid-afternoon

De *halt vespre* s'ala colchier (*Eneas*, 8914)
Shortly after vesper (i.e., in early evening) he went to bed

jusques a *basses vespres* (27, 76)
until late evening (i.e., nightfall)

69. Weights and Measures

The system of weights and measures in medieval France, like the language itself, was far from fixed. It was for the most part inherited from the Roman system, but it varied considerably from region to region and from town to town, in spite of Charlemagne's unflagging efforts throughout his reign to impose a set of standards.

69.1. Weights. In the twelfth and thirteenth centuries the principal weights, used mostly for determining the values of precious metals and coins, were as follows:

1 livre	=	2 mars (16 onces)
1 marc	=	8 onces
1 once	=	8 gros

$$1 \text{ sol} \quad = \quad 4 \text{ gros (12 deniers)}$$
$$1 \text{ gros} \quad = \quad 3 \text{ deniers}$$
$$1 \text{ denier} \quad = \quad 24 \text{ grains}$$

(The *livre*, however, could also be divided into 12 *onces*, each approximately 30 grams.)

The most widely used coin was the silver *denier*, which was the twelfth part of a *sol*:

.iij. mars d'argent a mis desus l'autel (8, 83)
he placed 3 marks of silver upon the altar

Por *un denier* .ij. granz pains i preïsmes (8, 150)
For one denier we took 2 large (loaves of) bread

U altrement ne valt .iiii. *deners* (6, 190)
Or otherwise he's not worth 4 pennies

69.2. Liquids and solids. Both liquid and solid volume measures were based on the *muid*, established by Charlemagne:

$$1 \text{ tonel} \quad = \quad 6 \text{ muiz}$$
$$1 \text{ muid} \quad = \quad 12 \text{ sestiers or 12 mines}$$
$$3 \text{ muiz} \quad = \quad 1 \text{ tonne}$$

These measures afford a good example of medieval imprecision, for the official *muid* might have been 12 *sestiers*, but it was 36 at St. Denis, 24 at Clermont, and 11 at Corbie.

Less frequently, one finds measurements based on the *pinte* (just under a modern liter):

$$1 \text{ quarte} \quad = \quad 2 \text{ pintes}$$
$$1 \text{ pinte} \quad = \quad 2 \text{ chopines}$$
$$8 \text{ pintes} \quad = \quad 1 \text{ sestier}$$

Plus a paroles an plain pot
De vin qu'an un *mui* de cervoise. (*Yvain*, 592–93)
There are more words in a full jug
Of wine than in a *muid* of beer.

A ces qu'an avoient mestier
Dona deniers plus d'un *setier* (*Erec*, 6483–84)
To those in need
He gave more deniers than (there were in) a *sestier*

69.3. Distance. Distance measures were based on the foot (*pié*), which was the equivalent of 12 *pouz*. Also common was the *toise* (about 2 meters). Longer distances were usually measured in leagues (*lieues*), which generally ranged from 4 to 5 kilometers. Cloth was often measured in *aunes* (slightly less than 2 meters).

> Il n'orent mie .*iiij. liues* alé
> Qu'an mi la voie ont un vilain trové. (8, 114–15)
> They had not gone 4 leagues
> When they encountered a peasant in the road.

> Il nen i ad ne veie ne senter,
> Ne voide tere, ne *alne* ne plein *pied*,
> Que il n'i ait o Franceis o paien. (*Roland*, 2399–401)
> There was no road or path,
> No open ground, no yard, no foot of land
> Not covered with a Frenchman or a pagan.

> *Toise* ot de lonc, si fu demi *pié* lée
> Et plus tranchans que n'est faus acerée (*Gaydon*, 1058–59)
> (The sword) was a *toise* long and a half foot wide
> And sharper than a steel scythe.

Since the official measures were so imprecise, it is not surprising that we find a variety of colorfully expressed unofficial measurements, akin to the modern American "as long as three football fields":

> Et li empereres Morchofles li traitres estoit molt pres d'iluec,
> *a mains de le getee d'un cailleu* (24, 112–14)
> And the Emperor Morchofles the traitor was very near there,
> less than a stone's throw away

> A nostre main destre, *bien le tret a une grant arbalestree*,
> ariva la galie la ou l'enseigne saint Denis estoit. (26, 110–11)
> To our right, the distance of a crossbow shot away,
> landed the galley on which the banner of St. Denis was (carried).

70. Adverbs of Time

70.1. Present time. Adverbs of time situate an event in relation to the speaker's present or the present of the narrative. Present time is indicated by *or* 'now,' *(h)ui* 'today,' *oan* 'this year':

> Il chantent *ore* vespres (16:30)
> They are now singing vespers

Immediate past action is expressed by *lors* 'then,' *(h)ier* 'yesterday,' *l'autrier* 'the day before yesterday, the other day.' Action in the more distant past is referred to by *ja, jadis* 'formerly, in the past,' *pieç'a* 'long ago,' *antan* 'last year.' Future action is recorded by *main, demain* 'tomorrow,' *a piece* 'in a moment,' *tantost* 'shortly,' *tost* 'soon':

> *Tost* furent apresté de grant mal comencier (16:27)
> Soon they were ready to begin (doing) great evil

70.2. Succession of events. Adverbs of time are used in narrative to indicate the succession of events. Present time is indicated by *maintenant* 'now,' simultaneity by *endementres* and its variants (see 14.58):

> *Endementres* s'armerent la fors li chevalier (16:24)
> Meanwhile the knights armed themselves outside there

Anteriority is expressed by *ainz, ainçois, avant, devant*:

> Car um les out *ainz* fait aprés els bien barrer (16:36)
> For one them had previously had after them well barred
> For previously they had had the doors well barred after themselves

> Riche erent *ainz, or* sunt chaü en dolenté (19:55)
> Formerly they were powerful men, now they have fallen on hard times

For the use of *dont, donc, lors, atant, adont, puis,* and *aprés* as **punctuation adverbs**, see 20.87.

70.3. Temporal conjunctions with *que*. *Que* combines with a number of adverbs and prepositions to form a rich series of compound conjunctions used to indicate the temporal relationship between two clauses. A subordinate clause whose action is simultaneous to that of the main verb is introduced by *que que, endementiers que, entrues que, tandis que* 'while':

> Maistre Eduvard le tint, *que qu*'il l'unt desachié (19:6)
> Master Edward held him while they tore him away

> *Que que* il iert en cel martire,
> Si oit tel chose qui l'esmaie (20, 182–83)
> While he was in this torment,
> He heard something that upset him

A subordinate clause whose action precedes that of the main verb may be introduced by *puis que, aprés que, des que, tantost que, errant que, maintenant que*, among others:

> Certes jamés ne m'ameront
> *Des que* ceste parole orront. (3:77–78)
> Indeed they'll never love me
> After they will have heard this report.

Et *puis que* vos ariiés jut en lit a home, s'el mien non (23:4a)
And after you will have slept in another man's bed

A subordinate clause whose action follows that of the main verb may be introduced by *ainz que, ainçois que, devant (ço) que*:

> Quant no fille ravon trovee,
> Grant joie nos a Deus donnee,
> *Ainz que* li pechiez fust doublez. (14:491–93)
> God has given us great joy,
> Since we have found our daughter
> Before the sin was doubled.

> "Si sera," dist Renart, "*ainzcois*
> *Que* vii. anz soient trespassé." (20, 152–53)
> "Yes it will be," said Renart, "before
> Seven years have passed."

To indicate how long the action of the principal clause lasted, the subordinate clause is introduced by *tant que, jusqu'a, de ci que, tresqu'a*, and the like:

> Longuement a o lui esté,
> *Tant que* li chevalier fiefé
> A molt grant mal li atornerent. (10:321–23)
> She remained a long while with him,
> Until the knights in his service
> Grew very upset with him.

> et ceminerent *jusques a* basses vespres. (27, 75–76)
> and they rode until nightfall.

71. *Ja, Ainz*

These two adverbs of time have special uses that may confuse the student.

71.1. *Ja.* *Ja* may refer to the past, present, or future:

Past: *Ja·t* portai en men ventre (3, 223)
           Formerly I carried you in my womb
Present: Cum avïez la face clere. . . . Cum l'avez *ja* teinte e müee! (7, 288)
           How bright your face was [then]. . . . How dark and changed
           it is now!
Future: Je vos en delivrerai *ja* (4:110)
           I shall free you of it at once

From its temporal meaning, *ja* comes to indicate affirmation, in a positive or negative sense:

Positive: *ja* est ce la damoisele (14:485)
           indeed this is the maiden
Negative   (often with *mais*; see 13.54.3):
           *Ja n'*a se bien non entre nos (13:466)
           Indeed there is nothing but good between us

           ja mais ne resurdra! (19:45)
           never again will he arise!

71.2. *Ainz.* *Ainz*, from its temporal meaning "before," comes to indicate preference or opposition ("rather, to the contrary"):

Aucassins n'en fu mie liés, *ains* traist au visconte de la vile (21:36a)
Aucassin was not happy at all, (so) instead he went to the viscount
     of the town

tant n'atenderoie je mie; *ains* m'esquelderoie. . . . (23:5a)
I'll not wait so long; on the contrary, I'll throw myself. . . .

Ainçois is synonymous with *ainz*, whereas *ainc* is synonymous with *onc*, *onques* and means "never" (see 13.54.3):

           ainc plus bele ne veïstes (21:18)
           you never saw more beautiful

Their phonological similarity, however, led to frequent confusion even in Old French:

           Ainz (=*ainc*) puis, ço cuit, n'i ot meillor (8:254)
           Never afterwards, I believe, was there (a) better (lord)

Phonology 16

Anglo-Norman

The *Life of St. Thomas Becket* was copied down in Anglo-Norman, the dialect of Old French spoken and written in England after the Norman Conquest of 1066. It was in this dialect that the works of Marie de France were preserved, that Thomas of England wrote his *Tristan et Iseut*, and that the most famous version of the *Song of Roland* (Oxford MS, Digby 23) was set down. Numerous didactic, religious, theatrical, and historical works were also written in Anglo-Norman.

Thousands of French settlers streamed into England after the battle of Hastings, and French was the language not only of literature and the court but also of commerce, law, and education. With the loss of Normandy and Anjou to Philippe-Auguste in the early thirteenth century, French lost some of its prestige in England, but it remained the language of the court until Henry IV (1399–1413), the first king whose native tongue was English. King Edward III, whose victory in the battle of Crécy in 1346 signaled the end of French chivalric dominance, could not even put together a formal sentence in English.

The first French grammars we have were composed in the fourteenth century to teach the English how to write and speak the language properly. Their very appearance was a clear indication of the decline of French in England.

Because of its relative isolation and the marked influence of English speech habits, Anglo-Norman was a rapidly evolving idiom, and it is not possible to give a detailed analysis of it here. This is available elsewhere, particularly in the remarkable study by Mildred K. Pope, *From Latin to Modern French with Especial Consideration of Anglo-Norman.*

The following orthographic peculiarities will help one readily identify an Anglo-Norman text:

u for Francien *ou, o*
ei, e, ai for Francien *oi*
aun, aust for Francien *an, ast*
k for *qu* or *c*
w, gw for *gu*
iw for *iu, iv*

Literary texts exhibiting these features will almost invariably be Anglo-Norman. Since most of these traits are shared with other dialects, as is shown by the tables in Phonology Sections 19 and 23, identification of nonliterary texts cannot be confirmed on this basis alone.

The presence of many of the above traits in this chapter's reading selection gives evidence that it was copied in England:

u for *o*: felun, pur, lur, sunt, desturbé
ei for *oi*: dreit, aveit, seeit, s'esteient
use of *w*: Willaumes, siwez

Phonology 17 lists the principal phonological features of Anglo-Norman, and Phonology 18 considers the major morphological differences.

chapter 17

Reading and Textual Analysis, Selection 10a

The martyrdom of Thomas Becket in his own cathedral on 29 December 1170 made a powerful impression on his contemporaries. A number of people who had known him personally set down their memories of his life and character in Latin or Old French. By far the most important French biography was written by Guernes de Pont-Sainte-Maxence between 1172 and 1174. Guernes was a native of a small town north of Paris and began his work almost immediately upon hearing of Thomas' death. Not satisfied with his initial attempt, however, he traveled to Canterbury to get firsthand information, and the work we have today is the fruit of this effort at research:

> Primes traitai d'oïe, e suvent menti.
> A Cantorbire alai, la verité oï;
> Des amis saint Thomas la verité cuilli,
> E de ces ki l'aveient des enfance servi. (146–49)

> At first I wrote from hearsay, and often erred.
> I went to Canterbury and heard the truth;
> From St. Thomas' friends I gathered the truth,
> And from those who had been in his service since childhood.

This version of the poem has been edited by Emmanuel Walberg and appears in the collection *Les Classiques Français du Moyen Âge*, published by the Librairie Champion in Paris.

The reading selection for this chapter shows Thomas' strength and

courage in the face of those who would kill him. Although his friends and
fellow monks carry him forcibly into the cathedral for protection, Thomas refuses to accept sanctuary there and unbars the doors himself.

17:1	Dunc l'en unt al mustier u voille u nun mené,
17:2	Ensement cum la mort atendist de sun gré.
17:3	Li un i unt saché e li altre buté,
17:4	Tant qu'il sunt le grant pas dedenz l'encloistre entré.
17:5	Mais il se sunt dous feiz enz el cloistre aresté.
17:6	Car si tost cum li sainz peut la terre atuchier
17:7	E il peut a la terre ses dous piez afichier,
17:8	Tuz les empainst de sei, comença a plaidier:
17:9	"Que me volez," fait il, "detraire e desachier?
17:10	Laissiez mei!" Dunc l'unt pris e porté al mustier.
17:11	Quant l'orent al mustier li moine einsi porté,
17:12	Dunc sunt li chevalier dedenz l'encloistre entré,
17:13	Lur espees es poinz e des haubercs armé,
17:14	E uns Hue Mauclerc (einsi l'a um numé;
17:15	Clers ert Robert del Broc, mult plains d'iniquité).
17:16	Avant vindrent li quatre pur le mal comencier,
17:17	Mais de loinz les siwirent quatre altre chevalier.
17:18	Cil Hue alad od els e entra el mustier.
17:19	Cil n'i entrerent pas, car li fil l'aversier
17:20	Encontrez les aveient el cloistre al repairier.
17:21	Les uis unt contre els clos des moines li alquant.
17:22	"Ovrez," fait sainz Thomas, quis ala atendant;
17:23	"Par sainte obedïence," fait il, "le vus comant.
17:24	Lur voil lur laissiez faire, ciu sunt e nun savant.
17:25	Tant cum tendrez les uis, n'irai un pas avant.
17:26	Nuls hum ne deit chastel ne fermeté ne tur
17:27	Faire de la maisun Deu, le verai seignur.
17:28	Mais nus clerc, qui en sumes ministre e servitur,
17:29	En devrïum adés estre defendeür,
17:30	Faire del cors escu contre le malfaitur."
17:31	Les uis ad il meesmes overt e desbarez,
17:32	Buta le pueple ariere, qui i ert asemblez
17:33	Pur veer l'aventure. Fait lur il: "Que cremez?"
17:34	Funt li il: "Veez ci les chevaliers armez."
17:35	"J'irai," fait il, "a els." Funt li il: "Nel ferez!"
17:36	Tresque sur les degrez del nort l'unt fait aler;
17:37	A guarant as cors sainz le voleient mener.

17:38   "Seignur," fait il as moines, "car me laissiez ester.
17:39   Vus n'avez ci que faire; Deu en laissiez penser.
17:40   Alez la sus el quer a voz vespres chanter."

17:1-2   Thomas preferred to await death in his own chambers, but his men hurried him into the cathedral, where, they believed, his enemies would not dare to shed his blood.
17:21   Subj. is *li alquant des moines*.
17:38   *car*: reinforces the imperative: see 17.72 and note to 13:438.

---

72. The Imperative

Forms for the imperative mood of weak verbs are listed in Section 5.17.2. The imperative of most other verbs is the strong (accented) stem with no ending in the singular and the present indicative forms in the plural:

	amer	*venir*	*croire*	*dire*	*faire*	*aidier*
Sg. 2	aim	vien	croi	di	fai	aiu
Pl. 1	amons	venons	creons	dimes	faimes	aidons
2	amez	venez	creez	dites	faites	aidiez

The imperative is used to express a direct command, a wish, a request, or a suggestion:

"Mais les miens en *laissiez* aler." (18:43)
"But let my people go."

"*Alum* nus en," fait il. (19:45)
"Let's go," said he.

The imperative is often introduced by *car*, which has the effect of emphasizing it and may be translated "please" or "do now":

"car me laissiez ester." (17:38)
"please let me be."

Car proiiés Dieu, vo sovrain pere (5, 84)
Do now pray to God, your sovereign Father

Note the contrast between lines 17:10 and 17:38. In both instances Thomas is addressing his own monks, but in the former he is angry and frustrated, whereas in the latter he is at peace with himself and in complete control of the situation. The same verb is used in both cases; the change of emotion is underscored by *car*.

The infinitive may also be used as an imperative, either negatively:

> Ne *dire* a nul ce que tu sez (13, 73)
> Don't tell anyone what you know

> "Deus pere, n'en *laiser* hunir France!" (6, 320)
> "God our Father, do not let France be dishonored in this way!"

> Ne t'*esmoier*! (23, 78)
> Don't be dismayed!

or positively, preceded by *or* + *de* + *le* (see 20.87.3):

> *or du* bien *faire*! (24, 119–20)
> now let's fight valiantly!

72.1. Use of object pronouns with the imperative. If the imperative begins a sentence, it is followed by the strong forms of the first and second person pronouns but by the weak forms of the third person pronouns:

> "Eschaufez *le* et sel baigniez!" (6:202)
> "Warm it and bathe it!"

> "Laissiez *mei*!" (17:10)
> "Let me be!"

When the imperative does not begin the line or clause, there is no cause for inversion and the direct or indirect object precedes in the weak form:

> De vostre lait *le m'*aletiez (6:201)
> Nourish it with your milk (for me)

> Feu et chandoille *m'*alumez! (6:198)
> Light me a fire and taper!

> Ben *le me* garde si cume tel felon! (6, 129)
> Guard him well, as befits the felon he is!

73. Old French Preterites

The preterite (or perfect) is used principally to indicate a completed past event; it may also refer to states in the past. It vies with the present perfect as the principal tense of historical narration (see 8.32.1). Preterites are classified as **strong** or **weak** depending upon the presence of vocalic alternation in the stem.

Weak preterites are accented throughout on the first vowel of the ending and have no vocalic alternation. They can be classified into three principal types and two subtypes according to the characteristic accented vowel. All preterites, weak and strong, share the same personal endings: *-i, -s, —* or *-t, -mes, -stes, -rent.*

73.1. Type I weak (IW). Characteristic Vowel: *a*.

		chanter
Sg.	1	chantai
	2	chantas
	3	chanta(t)
Pl.	1	chantames
	2	chantastes
	3	chanterent

All verbs with an infinitive ending in *-er* are of this type. *Ester, arester, rester* may be of this type but are usually IVS. The characteristic *-a-* becomes *-e-* in the third person plural only. The third person singular ending *-t* can be found in many early texts, particularly in the Anglo-Norman dialect region.

73.2. Type Ia weak (IaW). Characteristic vowel: *a*.

		baillier
Sg.	1	baillai
	2	baillas
	3	bailla(t)
Pl.	1	baillames
	2	baillastes
	3	baillierent

All verbs in *-ier* are of this type, which differs from Type I only in having a palatalized ending in the third person plural: *-ierent* versus *-erent.* This subclass was well represented throughout the Old French period.

73.3. Type II weak (IIW). Characteristic vowel: *i*.

ferir

Sg. 1   feri
    2   feris
    3   feri(t)
Pl. 1   ferimes
    2   feristes
    3   ferirent

All verbs ending in -*ir* are of this type except *venir* and *tenir* (IS), *morir* (also IIIW), *gesir* (IIIaS), and verbs like *nuisir/nuire* and *plaisir/plaire*, which have infinitives in both -*ir* and -*re* (see 10.37).

The first person singular ending -*i* merged in Type II verbs with the preceding tonic *i*. The third person singular ending -*t* was preserved in the strong preterites but effaced for phonological reasons in the weak preterites; however, in the thirteenth century it was restored to Type II and Type III weak preterites by analogy with the strong preterites.

73.4. Type IIa weak (IIaW). Characteristic vowel: *i*.

vendre

Sg. 1   vendi
    2   vendis
    3   vendié(t)
Pl. 1   vendimes
    2   vendistes
    3   vendierent

This subclass differed from Type II only in the third persons. It was represented by only about twenty-five verbs whose infinitives ended in a consonant (usually *d*, *t*) + *re*, and it was generally absorbed into Type II by the early thirteenth century. Thus:

Sg. 1   vendi
    2   vendis
    3   vendi(t)
Pl. 1   vendimes
    2   vendistes
    3   vendirent

Verbs of this subclass include:

(a) in *-dre*: *aerdre* (also IIS), *atendre, cosdre, defendre, descendre, entendre, espandre, fendre, fondre, mordre, pendre, perdre, rendre, respondre, tendre, toldre/tolir, tordre* (also IIS), *vendre*;

(b) in *-tre*: *batre, benoïstre, iraistre* (pret. 1: *irasqui*), *naistre* (pret. 1: *nasqui*), *veintre/vaincre* (pret. 1: *venqui*);

(c) other: *criembre* (also IIW or IIS), *rompre, sivre/siure* (among other infinitive forms; pret. 1: *sivi*), *luire* (also IIS), and *vivre* (pret. 1: *vesqui*).

73.5. Type III weak (IIIW). Characteristic Vowel: *u*.

		paroistre
Sg.	1	parui
	2	parus
	3	paru(t)
Pl.	1	parumes
	2	parustes
	3	parurent

The most important verb of this type is the auxiliary *estre*:

Sg.	1	fui
	2	fus
	3	fu(t)
Pl.	1	fumes
	2	fustes
	3	furent

Only the following verbs qualify: *chaloir* (also IIS), *corre/corir* (also IVS), *criembre* (also IIW or IIS), *doloir, escorre, moldre/moudre, morir* (also IIW), *paroir/ paroistre, secorre* (also IVS), *soldre/soloir* (also IIS), and *valoir*.

74. Adverbs of Manner

These, the most common adverbs, can qualify verbs, adjectives, adverbs, or entire sentences:

> *Bien* crei que sainz Thomas. . . . (18:22)
> I really believe that St. Thomas. . . .

Onques mes *si* grant joie n'ot (15:502)
Never before had he been so happy

s'i hurteroie *si* durement me teste que. . . . (23:5b)
and I'll dash my head so hard against it that. . . .

"*Certes*, vos le savrez!" (18:18)
"Indeed, you'll know it."

74.1. Si and its derivatives.   These translate as "thus, so, in this manner":

E uns Hue Mauclerc (*einsi* l'a um numé) (17:14)
And a certain Hugh Mauclerc (thus was he named)

la meschine . . .
Qu'il ont *sifaitement* trovee (15:519, 521)
the girl. . .
Whom they have thus found

For special uses of *si*, see 20.87.1.

74.2. *Com(e), coment.*   These adverbs translate as "how":

S'aventure li velt conter
De l'enfant *comment* le trova (7:214–15)
He wanted to tell her his story
How he found the child

Com is also used frequently to introduce an exclamation:

comme est mesavenu (10:353)
how unfortunate

For *com* conjunction, see 21.91.2.

75.   Distinctions among Adverbs

Often there is only a subjective distinction among adverbs of manner and those of degree or even of time. Adverbs of manner such as *si, ausi, bien, com, durement* are used in comparisons as adverbs of degree (see 19.83). To indicate swiftness, delay, or duration, Old French has a number of adverbs that express both manner and time: *briément, viste, tost, errant,* and *erramment* may mean "quickly" or "soon, at once," depending on the context. In 5:172 *errant* is an adverb of manner:

Desi qu'au fresne vint errant
He came running (i.e., quickly) to the ash tree

In 19:14 *erramment* is an adverb of time:

as sainz de l'iglise se comande erramment
to the saints of the Church he commends (his soul) at once

76. Adverbs of Place

The most common simple adverbs of place are *ça, ci* 'here,' *la* 'there,' *enz* 'in, inside,' *fors* 'out, outside,' *lez* 'beside,' *sus, sor* 'above, on,' *jus, soz* 'below, under.' Numerous doublets, triplets, and spelling variants occur (see 9.35 and 14.58.)

The distinction of proximity versus distance is translated by the adverbs *ci* 'here' and *la* 'there':

Senpres est *ci* et senpres *la* (*Béroul,* 3433)
Sometimes he's here and sometimes there

Ço dist Rollant: "*Ci* recevrums martyrie." (6, 232)
Thus said Roland: "Here we shall die."

A la Croiz Roge, as chemins fors,
La on enfuet sovent les cors. (13, 75–76)
At the Red Cross, at the crossroads,
There one often buries bodies.

Ça is used for *ci* in direct discourse with verbs of movement:

"*Ça* en vendrez!" (18:20)
"You'll come here!"

When no near-far opposition is implied, *la* is predominant:

La l'unt trait e mené (18:36)
They pulled and took him there

The distinction of interiority versus exteriority is expressed by the adverbs *enz* 'within' and *fors* 'outside.' The former is frequently combined with *en*:

il se sunt *enz el* (*el* = en + le) cloistre aresté (17:5)
they stopped within the cloister

Adverbs of exteriority-interiority are frequently found in combination with adverbs of proximity-distance:

Ça fors el fresne l'ai trové (6:200)
I found her out here in the ash tree

Endementres s'armerent *la fors* li chevalier (16:24)
Meanwhile the knights armed themselves outside there

Jo vus metrai *laienz* par un altre sentier (16:42)
I'll put you in there by another path (way)

Adverbs indicating movement of position forward or backward are
avant, *devant* 'forward, ahead, in front of':

Avant vindrent li quatre (17:16)
The four came forward

and *arier(e)(s)*, *derier(e)(s)*, *detriers* 'back, backward, behind':

Buta le pueple *ariere* (17:32)
He shoved the people back

Other common adverbs of place are *ici*, *pres* (corresponding to *ci*); *iluec*,
loing (corresponding to *la*); *joste*, *tres*, *detrés* (corresponding to *lez*).

Phonology 17

Anglo-Norman phonology and orthography

This section describes the main phonological and orthographical differences between Anglo-Norman and Francien. The development of sounds
not specifically mentioned here was generally the same in both dialects.

A. Initial Ō and accented free or checked, oral or nasal Ō > /u/
(spelled *u*, later *ou*):

ETYMON		EARLY OF		ANGLO-NORMAN	FRANCIEN
DŌNÁRE	>	doner	>	duner	doner
*TÓTTUM	>	tot	>	tut	tout
(IL)LÓRUM	>	lor	>	lur	lour > leur
*CÓRTEM	>	cort	>	curt	court

B. The diphthong *ei* (< Ē) was retained in early Anglo-Norman. It was
leveled subsequently to /e/, whereas in Francien and in the north and
east it > *oi*:

D(I)RÉCTUM	>	dreit	>	dreit, dret	droit
FĪDEM	>	fei	>	fei, fe	foi
CRÉDERE	>	creire	>	creire, crere	croire

C. The diphthongs *ai* and *ie* (oral and nasal) were also leveled to /e/:

FÁCTUM	> fait	> fet	fait, fet
BÉNE	> bien	> ben	bien
CÁELUM	> ciel	> cel	ciel

Since the diphthongs *ei*, *ai*, and *ie* were all leveled to /e/, the symbols representing them became interchangeable among themselves as well as with *e*, *ea*, and *eo* (from English influence). Thus, one might find the single word *fait* spelled *fait, fet, feit, feat.*

D. *eu* and usually *ue* and *ueu* were leveled to /ø/, which might be spelled *eu, ue, oe* or *oeu*: *peut* (17:6), *Deu* (17:27), *pueple* (17:32), *quer* (17:40), *iloec* (16:49).

E. Similar confusions in spelling resulted from the reduction of /y/, /u/, /ui/, /iu/, and sometimes /yi/, /ue/, and /ueu/ to /u/. For this sound, spellings varied from *u* to *o, ou, u, oi, ui, ue,* and *uo*: *dous* (17:5), *mustier* (17:11), *voille* (17:1), *uis* (17:25).

F. *A* velarized before a nasal consonant or before *st* and was spelled *au*:

*AB-ÁNTE	> avant	> avaunt	(avant)
BRÁNCAM	> branche	> braunche	(branche)
CASTÉLLUM	> castel	> chaustel	(chasteau)
*TASTÁRE	> taster	> tauster	(taster)

G. Nasal /ē/ was maintained as distinct from nasal /ã/, whereas in Francien they had fallen together by the early twelfth century. Thus, *prent* (< PREHÉNDET) rhymes with *avant* (< *AB-ÁNTE) in Francien but not in Anglo-Norman.

H. The strong presence of the Middle English tonic accent caused most vowels in hiatus and unstressed /ə/ to be lost: *asmer* (= *aasmer*), *runz* (= *roonz*), *lel* (= *leel*), *fru* (= *feru*), *fra* (= *fera*), *espé* or *spé* (= *espee*). Conversely, some words acquired an extra *e* as a result of either "hypercorrection" or Germanic influence: *povere* (= *povre*), *despenderai* (= *despendrai*), *perdereient* (= *perdraient*).

I. Unstressed pretonic and posttonic *e* was raised to *i*: *iglise* (18:57).

J. Among the consonants, the most salient trait of Anglo-Norman phonology was the retention of /δ/ and /θ/. These sounds came from *t*, *d* intervocalic or before *r*, *l*, *u*; from *t*, *d* final; or from *s* before *n*, *l*. These phonemes were spelled *d* or *t*, and modern editors frequently put a subscript (.) under them to indicate their pronunciation as in English *then* or *thin*:

VĪTAM	>	/víða/	>	vide	vie
PÁTER	>	/péθre/	>	pedre	pere
ÁD	>	/áð/	>	ad	a
PÓRTET	>	/pórteθ/	>	portet	porte
ÁSĬNUM	>	/as'ne/	>	adne	asne, ane

They are particularly prevalent in early texts like the *Song of Roland* or the *Voyage of St. Brendan*:

Puis o*d* les ewes lava*t* les prez del sanc (6, 88)
Then with streams of water he washed the blood from the meadows

Sur la roche u sunt venu*d* (4, 11)
Upon the rock where they came

Faldra*t* ma morz n'ivern n'esté*t*? (4, 32)
Will my death not occur in winter or summer?

But they are still frequent in some texts as late as the *Life of St. Thomas*:

Cil Hue ala*d* o*d* els e entra el mustier (17:18)
This Hugh went with them and entered the church

K. The shift of /ts/ to /s/, which in Francien appears not to have occurred until the late twelfth or early thirteenth century, took place much earlier in Anglo-Norman. The scribe of the *Life of St. Thomas* distinguishes them well but does slip occasionally: *voz* (17:40), *bienz* (18:16). As a result of this shift, the symbols *s*, *z*, *ss*, *sc*, *c*, and *x* are virtually interchangeable in later Anglo-Norman texts.

L. Palatal *l* and *n* tended to depalatalize, since English did not have these sounds: *seinur* (3, 4 for *seignur*), *esluiner* (3, 30 for *esluigner*), *peril* rhyming with *mil* (4, 258).

M. Initial Germanic *w-* was retained: Willaumes de Traci (16:3).

Old French weak preterites

Weak preterites came principally from Latin first and fourth conjugations, in which the accent remained upon the ending throughout:

CANTÁVI	FERÍVI
CANTAVÍSTI	FERIVÍSTI
CANTÁVIT	FERÍVIT
CANTÁVIMUS	FERIVÍMUS
CANTAVÍSTIS	FERIVÍSTIS
CANTAVÉRUNT	FERIVÉRUNT

In Gallo-Roman these endings were reduced to the following:

*cantai	*ferii
*cantasti	*feristi
*cantat	*ferit
*cantamus	*ferimus
*cantastis	*feristis
*cantarunt	*ferirunt

The reduction of the final unaccented vowel to /ə/ in Old French led to the paradigms listed in Section 73 of this chapter.

Type Ia weak (IaW) verbs resulted from the development of free accented A (preceded by a palatal in the third person plural ending) into -ie- (see Phonology Sections 8 and 10).

Type IIa weak (IIaW) represents a Vulgar Latin creation from Latin reduplicated perfects of the type VENDĪDI > VENDĔDI, PERDĪDI > PERDĔDI:

*VENDĔDI	>	*vendiei	>	vendi
*VENDĔDISTI	>	*vendieist	>	vendis
*VENDĔDIT	>	*vendieit	>	vendié(t)
*VENDĔDIMUS	>	*vendieimes	>	vendimes
*VENDĔDISTIS	>	*vendieistes	>	vendistes
*VENDĔDIRUNT	>	*vendieirent	>	vendierent

In Gaul, -ĔI- was reduced to -i- after passing through a stage as the triphthong *-iei- (see Phonology 8). Nonetheless, a distinction was retained in these verbs in the third persons singular and plural until the thirteenth century.

chapter 18

Reading and Textual Analysis, Selection 10b

In the reading selection for this chapter, what has heretofore remained implicit is made manifest: the passion of the martyr Thomas Becket is to be compared to that of Christ himself. The image of the shepherd to whom Thomas is likened in line 45 is traceable to the parable of the shepherd (Luke 15.4–7) who leaves behind the rest of his flock to seek the one lost sheep. Christ is compared to this good shepherd in John 10.1–18, and verse 11 is particularly recalled. "I am the good shepherd; the good shepherd is one who lays down his life for his sheep." Thomas' concern that those around him be spared though he himself goes willingly to die recalls the arrest of Jesus in the garden of Gethsemene:

> [Jesus] asked them a second time, "Who are you looking for?" They said, "Jesus the Nazerene." "I have told you that I am he," replied Jesus. "If I am the one you are looking for, let these others go." (John 18.7–9)

18:1	La maisnie al Satan est el mustier venue.
18:2	En sa destre main tint chascuns s'espee nue,
18:3	En l'autre les cuignies, e li quarz besague.
18:4	Un pilier ot iluec, la volte ad sustenue,
18:5	Qui del saint arcevesque lur toli la veüe.
18:6	D'une part del pilier en sunt li trei alé,
18:7	Le traïtur le rei unt quis e demandé;

18:8	Reinalz de l'altre part ad un moine encontré;
18:9	Demanda l'arcevesque. Dunc ad li sainz parlé:
18:10	"Reinalz, se tu me quiers," fait il, "ci m'as trové."
18:11	Le nun de traïtur sainz Thomas n'entendi,
18:12	Mais al nun d'arcevesque restut e atendi,
18:13	E encontre Reinalt del degré descendi.
18:14	"Reinalz, se tu me quiers, trové," fait il, "m'as ci."
18:15	Par l'acor del mantel l'aveit Reinalz saisi.
18:16	"Reinalz, tanz bienz t'ai fait," fait li buens ordenez;
18:17	"E que quiers tu sur mei en saint' iglise armez?"
18:18	Fait Reinalz li fiz Urs: "Certes, vus le savrez!"
18:19	Sachié l'aveit a sei, que tuz fu remüez:
18:20	"Traïtres le rei estes," fait li il; "ça vendrez!"
18:21	Car fors del saint mustier traïnier le quida.
18:22	Bien crei que sainz Thomas a cele feiz s'ira
18:23	De ço que cil Reinalz le detraist e buta;
18:24	Si ad enpaint Reinalt qu'ariere rehusa,
18:25	E l'acor del mantel hors des mains li sacha.
18:26	"Fui, malveis hum, d'ici!" fait li sainz corunez.
18:27	"Jo ne sui pas traïtres, n'en dei estre retez."
18:28	"Fuiez!" fait li Reinalz, quant se fu purpensez.
18:29	"Nel ferai," fait li sainz. "Ici me troverez,
18:30	E voz granz felonies ici acumplirez."
18:31	Devers l'ele del nort s'en est li bers alez,
18:32	E a un pilier s'est tenuz e acostez.
18:33	(Entre dous alteus est cil piliers maiserez;
18:34	A la mere Deu est cil de desuz sacrez,
18:35	El nun saint Beneeit est li altre ordenez.)
18:36	La l'unt trait e mené li ministre enragié.
18:37	"Asolez," funt il, "cels qui sunt escumengié,
18:38	E cels qui sunt par vus suspendu e lacié."
18:39	"N'en ferai," fait il, "plus que je n'ai comencié."
18:40	A oscire l'unt dunc ensemble manecié.
18:41	Fait il: "De voz manaces ne sui espöentez;
18:42	Del martire suffrir sui del tut aprestez.
18:43	Mais les miens en laissiez aler, nes adesez,
18:44	E faites de mei sul ço que faire en devez."
18:45	N'ad les suens li bons pastre a la mort oblïez.
18:46	Einsi avint de Deu quant il ala orer
18:47	Desur Munt Olivete la nuit a l'avesprer:
18:48	E cil li comencierent quil quistrent a crïer
18:49	"U est li Nazareus?" "Ci me pöez trover,"
18:50	Fist lur Deus; "mais les miens en laissiez tuz aler."
18:51	Dunc l'unt saisi as puinz li fil a l'aversier,

18:52	Sil comencent forment a traire e a sachier;
18:53	E sur le col Williaume le voldrent enchargier,
18:54	Car la hors le voleient u oscire u lïer.
18:55	Mais del pilier nel porent oster ne esluignier.
18:56	Car sainz Thomas s'esteit apuiez al piler
18:57	Qui suffri mort en cruiz pur s'iglise estorer;
18:58	Ne l'en pöeit nuls huem esluignier ne oster.
18:59	Mais ore en coveneit un sul a mort livrer,
18:60	Al piler del mustier, pur le pueple salver.

18:5   *qui*: antecedent is *pilier*.
18:31 *li bers*: i.e., Thomas.
18:57 *qui = de celui qui*. The antecedent rather than the relative pronoun is omitted (see 11.46).

---

77. Strong Preterites

Whereas weak preterites had the accent fall throughout the conjugation upon the ending, strong preterites had the accent shift to the stem in the first and third persons singular and the third person plural. The presence of the accent on the stem in these persons preserved the Latin stem vowel, while in the second person singular and the first and second persons plural it tended to weaken to -*e*-. There were four types of strong preterites, classified according to stem alternations.

77.1. Type I strong (IS). Alternation: *i/e*.

		veoir	*venir*	*tenir*
Sg.	1	vi	vin	tin
	2	veïs	venis	tenis
	3	vit	vint	tint
Pl.	1	veïmes	venimes	tenimes
	2	veïstes	venistes	tenistes
	3	virent	vindrent, vinrent	tindrent, tinrent

These are the only three verbs of this type. The first person singular ending -*i* merged with the preceding tonic *i* in *vi* and was lost after the consonant in *vin* and *tin*.

77.2.   Type II strong (IIS).   Alternation: *s/si*.

		dire	*faire*	*ardre*	*clore*
Sg.	1	dis	fis	ars	clos
	2	desis	fesis	arsis	closis
	3	dist	fist	arst	clost
Pl.	1	desimes	fesimes	arsimes	closimes
	2	desistes	fesistes	arsistes	closistes
	3	distrent	firent	arstrent	closdrent

This preterite is frequently referred to as the **-s- preterite**. The first person singular ending *-i* was lost after the stem *-s-* throughout this type. The third person plural developed three different endings: *-sdrent* for verbs in which the *-s-* was intervocalic in Latin and thus voiced (*closdrent, misdrent, prisdrent*); *-strent* for verbs in which the *-s-* was supported or geminate in Latin and therefore unvoiced (*distrent, arstrent, plainstrent*); *-rent* in *firent* only (*fistrent* is rare but possible). There was some confusion among the endings, and forms in *-strent* came to dominate: *mistrent, pristrent*.

77.3.   Principal verbs of Type IIS.   We list here the principal verbs of Type IIS; those that occur in the reading selections in this volume are marked with asterisks. The first column contains the infinitive and the principal English translation; the second column lists the first and second person singular forms to clarify the vocalic alternation.

CLASS A: *-SDRENT* ENDING IN THIRD PERSON PLURAL

*clore 'to close'	clos, closis
conclure 'to conclude'	conclus, conclusis (also IIIW)
despire 'to despise'	despis, despesis
frire 'to fry'	fris, fresis
*(re) manoir 'to live'	mes, masis (also class B: mains, mainsis)
*metre 'to put'	mis, mesis
*ocire 'to kill'	ocis, ocesis
*prendre 'to take'	pris, presis
*querre 'to seek'	quis, quesis
rere 'to cut, to shave'	res, rasis
*rire 'to laugh'	ris, resis
*(as)seoir 'to sit'	sis, sesis

CLASS B: *-STRENT* ENDING IN THIRD PERSON PLURAL

aerdre 'to seize'	aers, aersis (also IIaW)
*ardre 'to burn'	ars, arsis
ataindre 'to touch, to concern'	atains, atainsis
braire 'to shout, to make noise'	brais, braisis
*ceindre 'to strap on, to gird'	ceins, ceinsis
chaloir (impersonal) 'to matter'	chalst (also IIIW)
conduire 'to conduct'	conduis, conduisis
construire 'to build'	construis, construisis
*criembre 'to fear'	crens, crensis (also IIaW or IIIW)
cuire 'to cook'	cuis, cuisis or cuissis
destruire 'to destroy'	destruis, destruisis
*dire 'to say'	dis, desis
duire 'to lead'	duis, duisis or duissis
escorre, escodre 'to shake'	escos, escosis or escossis
escrivre 'to write'	escris, escresis
espardre 'to scatter'	espars, esparsis
esteindre 'to destroy'	esteins, esteinsis
estraindre 'to press'	estrains, estrainsis
feindre 'to pretend'	feins, feinsis
fraindre 'to break'	frains, frainsis
gesir 'to lie'	gis, gesis (also IVS)
joindre 'to join'	joins, joinsis
lire 'to read'	lis, lesis (also IVS)
luire 'to shine'	luis, luisis or luissis (also IIaW)
moldre 'to grind, to mill'	mols, molsis
mordre 'to bite'	mors, morsis
nuire, nuisir 'to harm'	nuis, nuisis (also IVS)
oindre 'to anoint'	oins, oinsis
peindre 'to paint'	peins, peinsis
*plaindre 'to lament'	plains, plainsis
poindre 'to prick, to spur'	poins, poinsis
pondre 'to lay' (e.g., an egg)	pos or posis, pons or ponsis (also IIaW)
raembre 'to redeem, to ransom'	raens, raensis
semondre 'to summon'	semons, semonsis
(a)soldre 'to pay for'	sols, solsis
sordre 'to gush forth'	sors, sorsis
terdre 'to wipe'	ters, tersis
tordre 'to twist'	tors, torsis (also IIaW)
*(de)traire 'to draw, to pull'	trais, traisis

78. Modifications to Type IIS Class A verbs

Faire, dire, lire, and all IIS verbs of Class A (those ending in *-sdrent* in the third person plural) frequently lost their characteristic *-s-* in the second person singular and the first and second persons plural, by analogy with Type I *veoir* (*vi, veïs*). Further, by analogy with *firent* and *virent,* their third plurals were modified. The modified forms generally replaced the older etymological forms by the thirteenth century:

		faire	*dire*	*prendre*	*querre*
Sg.	1	fis	dis	pris	quis
	2	feïs	deïs	preïs	queïs
	3	fist	dist	prist	quist
Pl.	1	feïmes	deïmes	preïmes	queïmes
	2	feïstes	deïstes	preïstes	queïstes
	3	firent	dirent	prirent	quirent

79. *Voloir*

The preterite of *voloir* can be a strong hybrid in *-i,* strong in *-s,* or weak in *-i*:

		hybrid in -i	*strong in -s (IIS)*	*weak in -i (IIW)*
Sg.	1	voil	vols/vous	voli/volsi
	2	volis	volsis	volis/volsis
	3	volt	volst	voli/volsi
Pl.	1	volimes	volsimes	volimes/volsimes
	2	volistes	volsistes	volistes/volsistes
	3	voldrent	volstrent	volirent/volsirent

During the Middle French period *voloir* became a Type IIIW verb under the influence of its past participle, *voulu.*

80. Strong Preterites, Types III and IV

Historically, these two types belong together. They have been separated here for pedagogical purposes only.

80.1.   Type III strong (IIIS).   Alternation: *o/e*.

	avoir	*pooir*	*savoir*
Sg. 1	oi	poi	soi
2	eüs	peüs	seüs
3	ot	pot	sot
Pl. 1	eümes	peümes	seümes
2	eüstes	peüstes	seüstes
3	orent	porent	sorent

The only other verbs of this type are:

paistre 'to feed an animal'	poi, peüs
plaire/plaisir 'to please'	ploi, pleüs
taire/taisir 'to be quiet'	toi, teüs

80.2.   Type IV strong (IVS).   Alternation: *u/e*.

	devoir	*croire*	*movoir*
Sg. 1	dui	crui	mui
2	deüs	creüs	meüs
3	dut	crut	mut
Pl. 1	deümes	creümes	meümes
2	deüstes	creüstes	meüstes
3	durent	crurent	murent

As with Type IIIS, forms in *-o-* exist for these verbs as well. The only other verbs of this type are:

boivre 'to drink'	bui, beüs
*conoistre 'to know'	conui, coneüs
*croistre 'to grow'	crui, creüs
*ester 'to stand'	estui, esteüs (also IW)
*estovoir 'to be necessary'	estut (impersonal)
*gesir 'to lie'	jui, geüs (also IIS)
loisir 'to be permitted'	lut (impersonal)
lire 'to read'	lui, leüs (also IIS)
movoir 'to move'	mui, meüs

nuisir, nuire 'to harm'   nui, neüs (also IIS)
plovoir 'to rain'   plut (impersonal)
ramentevoir 'to remember'   ramentui, ramenteüs
*reçoivre 'to receive'   reçui, receüs

Arester and *rester* are conjugated like *ester; apercevoir, concevoir,* and *decevoir* are conjugated like *reçoivre/recevoir.* Note that *estovoir, loisir,* and *plovoir* are impersonal and therefore have only third person singular forms (cf. *chaloir,* Type IIS, class B).

81. Noun Qualifiers: The Strong Possessives

81.1. Forms. As noted in 6.19, Old French has two series of possessives. We present here the strong possessives, which are much less common than the unstressed forms and which may function as adjectives or pronouns in Old French:

	FIRST PERSON SINGULAR (MY, MINE)		SECOND PERSON SINGULAR (YOUR, YOURS)		THIRD PERSON SINGULAR (HIS, HER, HERS, ITS)	
	masculine	*feminine*	*masculine*	*feminine*	*masculine*	*feminine*
NS	miens	meie, moie	tuens	toe, toue, teue	suens	soe, soue, seue
OS	mien	meie, moie	tuen	toe, toue, teue	suen	soe, soue, seue
NP	mien	moies	tuen	toues	suen	soues
OP	miens	moies	tuens	toues	suens	soues

	FIRST PERSON PLURAL (OUR, OURS)		SECOND PERSON PLURAL (YOUR, YOURS)		THIRD PERSON PLURAL (THEIR, THEIRS)	
	masculine	*feminine*	*masculine*	*feminine*	*masculine*	*feminine*
NS	nostre(s)	nostre	vostre(s)	vostre	lor	lor
OS	nostre	nostre	vostre	vostre	lor	lor
NP	nostre	nostres	vostre	vostres	lor	lor
OP	nostres	nostres	vostres	vostres	lor	lor

In the twelfth century, the additional stressed feminine forms *toie, soie* had already been created by analogy with *moie.* In the course of the thirteenth century, the singular forms, both masculine and feminine, were completely reformed by analogy with the masculine *mien*, and the paradigm was greatly simplified (see Phonology 7):

	FIRST PERSON SINGULAR		SECOND PERSON SINGULAR		THIRD PERSON SINGULAR	
	masculine	*feminine*	*masculine*	*feminine*	*masculine*	*feminine*
NS	miens	mienne	tiens	tienne	siens	sienne
OS	mien	mienne	tien	tienne	sien	sienne
NP	mien	miennes	tien	tiennes	sien	siennes
OP	miens	miennes	tiens	tiennes	siens	siennes

Additionally, there were important dialectal forms of the stressed possessives (see Phonology).

81.2. Functions.

(a) As adjectives, occasionally on their own, but usually accompanied by an article:

> *Mien* escïent (5:153)
> I believe; to my knowledge
>
> une piece d'un *sien* laz (4:127)
> a piece of one of her ribbons

(b) As pronouns, agreeing in number and gender with the nouns they replace and usually accompanied by a definite article:

> Mais *les miens* en laissiez aler (18:43)
> But let my (people) go
>
> N'ad *les suens* li bons pastre a la mort oblïez (18:45)
> The good shepherd at death has not forgotten his own

Phonology 18

Anglo-Norman morphology

The Anglo-Norman noun and adjective declension systems, because of their contact with English, were the most defective in Old French. Their disintegration, well under way by the twelfth century, was everywhere evident in the thirteenth century. This corruption is not pronounced, however, in the *Life of St. Thomas*, which was composed not by a native Anglo-Norman but by a man born in the Ile-de-France.

A. There were relatively few peculiarities among the pronouns. Anglo-Norman frequently used the stressed forms *jeo, gié,* and *jo* for the first person singular *je*: 18:27; 4, 67; 7, 14; 7, 174. One also finds *ceo* for *ce* (7, 12). The reduction of /yi/ to /u/ (Phonology 17) caused the confusion of *li* (m. and f. unstressed dative) and *lui* (m. stressed oblique):

> Cil *lui* (= *li*) respunt a voiz basse (4, 55)
> He answered him in a low voice

B. Among the possessive adjectives, one generally finds masculine nominative singular *mis, tis, sis* for Francien *mes, tes, ses* (see 6.19 for declensions):

> ... Que *mis* curages est del martire suffrir (16:23)
> ... Than is my heart to suffer martyrdom
>
> Remés i est *sis* uncles Marganices (6, 224)
> His uncle Marganice remains

C. In the feminine stressed possessives, the spellings *meie, tue,* and *sue* for Francien *moie, toue, soue* (see 18.81) reflect regular Anglo-Norman phonological development:

> La cause saint'iglise e *la sue* ensement (19:15)
> Both his cause and that of Holy Church

D. The Anglo-Norman verb system is characterized by its variety of forms and its instability. The most frequently encountered particularities are:

(1) Analogical /k/ (spelled *c, g, k*) in the first person singular: *erc* (3, 225), *prenc* (4, 96), *vinc* (4, 220).

(2) *-um, -om, -oun* (later *-ums, -oms, -omes, -umes*) for Francien *-ons* in the first person plural: *devrium* (17:29), *alum* (19:45), *demurum* (4, 7).

(3) The present subjunctive in *-ge*: *prengent* (4, 264), *tolget* (3, 275), *augiez* (7, 54).

(4) Use of western imperfect indicative endings *-oue, -out, -ouent* (later *-oe, -ot, -oent*) for Francien *-eie/-oie, -eit/-oit, -eient/-oient* in Class I (*-er*) verbs: *mandot* (1:14), *gardot* (5:154), *celoue* (4, 67), *coronouent* (4, 80), *amoent* (10, 318).

	FRANCIEN	ANGLO-NORMAN
Sg. 1	mandoie	mandoue/mandoe
2	mandoies	mandoues/mandoes
3	mandoit	mandout/mandot
Pl. 1	mandïiens	mandïiens, mandïons
2	mandïiez	mandïiez
3	mandoient	mandouent/mandoent

Old French strong preterites

Old French strong preterites came principally from Latin perfects in
-SI- (-X-) and -UI-. The accent shifted from the stem in the first and third
persons singular and the third person plural to the ending in the second
person singular and the first and second persons plural:

DÍXI	> dis	ÁRSI	> ars	HÁBUI	> *aui	> oi	
DIXÍSTI	> desis	ARSÍSTI	> arsis	HABUÍSTI	> *aust	> eüs	
DÍXIT	> dit	ÁRSIT	> arst	HÁBUIT	> *aut	> ot	
*DIXÍMUS	> desimes	*ARSÍMUS	> arsimes	*HABUÍMUS	> *aumus	> eümes	
DIXÍSTIS	> desistes	ARSÍSTES	> arsistes	HABUÍSTIS	> *austes	> eüstes	
*DÍXERUNT	> distrent	*ÁRSERUNT	> arstrent	*HÁBUERUNT	> *auerunt	> orent	

The preterites of *veoir* and *venir* in Type IS are the only remains of the
Latin -I- perfect. *Tenir* is a reformed -UI- perfect:

VÍDI	> vi	TÉNUI	> *teni	> tin	
VIDÍSTI	> veïs	TENUÍSTI	> *tenisti	> tenis	
VÍDIT	> vit	TÉNUIT	> *tenit	> tint	
*VIDÍMUS	> veïmes	*TENUÍMUS	> *tenimus	> tenimes	
VIDÍSTIS	> veïstes	TENUÍSTIS	> *tenistis	> tenistes	
*VÍDERUNT	> virent	*TÉNUERUNT	> *tenerunt	> tindrent	

All type IIIS verbs except *pooir* (< *POTÉRE, reformed from classical
POSSE) have -A- as their stem vowel in Latin: *avoir* (< HABÉRE), *paistre*
(< PÁSCĔRE), *plaire* (< PLÁCĔRE), *savoir* (< SAPÉRE), and *taire* (<
TÁCĔRE).

Type IVS verbs have -E- or -O- as stem vowel: *devoir* (< DEBÉRE),
croire (< CRÉDĔRE), *movoir* (< MOVÉRE), *conoistre* (< COGNÓSCĔRE).

Illustration 2

The murder of Saint Thomas Becket (from the Carrow Psalter, folio
15v, Walters Art Gallery, Baltimore)

chapter 19

Reading and Textual Analysis, Selection 10c

This reading selection describes the martyrdom of Thomas Becket (see the illumination from the Carrow Psalter). Christ's acceptance of death and his perfect composure in the face of it are paralleled by St. Thomas' passivity (19:36–40); and Thomas' dedication of himself to God (19:12) reflects and fulfills Christ's priestly prayer in the seventeenth chapter of John's Gospel.

19:1	E maistre Eduvard Grim l'aveit forment saisi,
19:2	Enbracié par desus quant l'orent envaï.
19:3	Contre els tuz le retint, de rien ne s'esbahi;
19:4	Ne pur les chevaliers ne l'aveit pas guerpi.
19:5	Clerc e moine e sergant s'en erent tuit fuï.
19:6	Maistre Eduvard le tint, que qu'il l'unt desachié.
19:7	"Que volez," fait il, "faire? Estes vus enragié?
19:8	Esguardez u vus estes e quel sunt li feirié.
19:9	Main sur vostre arcevesque metez a grant pechié!"
19:10	Mais pur feirié ne l'unt, ne pur mustier, laissié.
19:11	Or veit bien sainz Thomas sun martire en present.
19:12	Ses mains juint a sun vis, a Damnedeu se rent.
19:13	Al martyr saint Denis, qui dulce France apent,
19:14	E as sainz de l'iglise se comande erramment,
19:15	La cause saint' iglise e la sue ensement.
19:16	Vuillaumes vint avant, n'i volt Deu aürer.

19:17   Pur estre plus legiers n'i volt hauberc porter.
19:18   Le traïtur lu rei comence a demander.
19:19   Quant ne porent le saint hors del mustier geter,
19:20   Enz el chief de l'espee grant colp li vait duner,
19:21   Si que de la corune le cupel en porta
19:22   E la hure abati e granment entama.
19:23   Sur l'espaule senestre l'espee li cula,
19:24   Le mantel e les dras tresqu'al quir encisa,
19:25   E le braz Eduvard pres tut en dous colpa.
19:26   Dunc l'aveit a cel colp maistre Eduvarz guerpi.
19:27   "Ferez! ferez!" fait il. Mais idunc le feri
19:28   Danz Reinalz li fiz Urs, mais pas ne l'abati.
19:29   Idunc le referi Willaumes de Traci,
19:30   Que tut l'escervelad, e sainz Thomas chaï. . . .
19:31   Mais quant Richarz li Brez le vit si abatu
19:32   E sur le pavement gesir tut estendu,
19:33   Un poi en bescoz l'ad des autres colps feru,
19:34   Qu'a la pierre ad brisié en dous sun brant molu.
19:35   (Al Martir baise l'un la piece tut a nu.)
19:36   Que que li felun l'unt feru e detrenchié
19:37   E del ferir se sunt durement esforcié,
19:38   N'aveit brait ne groni ne crïé ne huchié,
19:39   Ne pié ne main n'aveit a sei trait ne sachié;
19:40   Car a Deu out del tut sun corage apuié. . . .
19:41   E cil Hue Malclerc, qui aprés els entra,
19:42   Sur le col saint Thomas mist sun pié e ficha;
19:43   Le cervel od l'espee hors del chief li geta
19:44   Desur le pavement, e a cels s'escria:
19:45   "Alum nus en," fait il; "ja mais ne resurdra!"
19:46   Qui dunc veïst le sanc od le cervel chaïr
19:47   E sur le pavement l'un od l'autre gesir,
19:48   De roses e de lilies li peüst sovenir:
19:49   Car dunc veïst le sanc el blanc cervel rovir,
19:50   Le cervel ensement el vermeil sanc blanchir.
19:51   Idunc s'en sunt parti li serf d'iniquité;
19:52   Parmi l'encloistre ariere s'en erent returné,
19:53   Les espees es poinz, e unt "Reaus!" crïé.
19:54   Ainz erent chevalier, or sunt vil e hüé;
19:55   Riche erent ainz, or sunt chaü en dolenté.

19:1   The cleric Edward Grim was the only person who did not abandon Thomas. He composed the principal Latin source for Guernes' poem.

19:13 *qui = cui.*
19:27 *il*: i.e., William of Tracy.
19:35 *un = on.* The piece of Richard's sword that broke off when it struck the paving
       was preserved and later revered as a relic.
19:38 Subj. of *n'aveit brait. . .* is Thomas.

---

82. Adverbs of Degree

The fullest degree, totality, or completeness is expressed by the adverbial usage of the adjective *tot* (see 12.50):

> Idunc le referi Willaumes de Traci,
> Que *tut* l'escervelad. . . . (19:29–30)
> Then William of Tracy struck him,
> Which completely spilled his brains. . . .
>
> sur le pavement gesir *tut* estendu (19:32)
> lying all stretched out on the stone floor

Guernes uses *del tut* in the same manner:

> Car a Deu out *del tut* son corage apuié (19:40)
> For he had completely placed his trust (lit. "heart") in God

The notion "much, very much, most" is conveyed by *molt* (*de*), *tres, tant,*
or *par,* alone or in combination:

> *mult* plains d'iniquité (17:15)
> very full of iniquity
>
> *Tant par* est douce (20:15)
> So very sweet is she
>
> *Tres* dous Diex (5, 130)
> Most sweet God

Old French *trop* generally means "very, much, very much" rather than
its modern meaning "too much":

> *Trop* i avroient grant dommage
> Se il lessoit por sa soignant
> Que d'espouse n'eüst enfant. (10:330–32)
> They would be very badly served
> Were he, on account of his mistress,
> Not to have a child by a (legitimate) wife.

In courtly style, adverbs of manner such as *durement, forment,* and *granment* can function as adverbs of degree:

Forment te vont maneçant (23:29)
They are threatening you greatly

Sa preude fame enhaï
Et *durement* la mescreï (2:61–62)
He hated his wife
And distrusted her very much

Note that whereas Marie and the author of *Aucassin and Nicolette* have a great affection for the "courtly" use of these adverbs, Guernes seems to prefer them with their etymological meanings:

E maistre Eduvard Grim l'aveit *forment* saisi (19:1)
And Master Edward Grim seized him tightly

del ferir se sunt *durement* esforcié (19:37)
they strove very hard to strike him

A sufficient degree is indicated by *asez* (*de*) or *auques* (*de*) 'enough, a little, some, somewhat':

Faisons de che que nous avons,
Ch'est *assés* pour le matinee. (22, 152–53)
Let's make do with what we have,
It's enough for the morning.

E Hüe point e broche e fiert,
Qu'il lur est *auques* esloinné. (7, 125–26)
And Hugh spurs and goads and whips (his horse),
Until he is somewhat distant from them.

Note, however, that *asez* more frequently means "very, much, very much, many":

Il les enveie pur Lanval,
Que *asez* ad dolur e mal. (10, 252–53)
He sends them for Lanval,
Who feels very much grief and pain.

Mes larges terres dunt jo aveie *asez* (3, 172)
My extensive lands of which I have many

Assez fu dite et conneüe (2:51)
(The news) was very much told and made known

A small or minimal degree is expressed by *poi, un poi, petit, un petit*:

Un poi en bescoz l'ad des autres colps feru (19:33)
He struck him with the other blows (which were) a little slanting

Mout i ariés *peu* conquis (22:5)
You would have gained very little

Important spelling variants of *poi* are *po, pou, peu, poc*.

Complete absence is indicated by adverbs of negation (13.54). Note that the nouns used to reinforce the negative *ne* (13.54.3) may be used alone as adverbs to indicate a small or minimal degree, best translated "ever" in English:

> Tut seie fel se jo *mie* l'otrei! (*Roland*, 3897)
> I'll be damned if ever I consent to it!
>
> Ne ja Dex n'ait de moi merci
> Se jel di *mie* por orguel. (*Charrete*, 1112–13)
> May God have no mercy on me
> If ever I said it out of pride.

83. Comparisons

Adverbs of degree are used to make implied or stated comparisons. Superiority is indicated by *plus* 'more,' inferiority by *moins* 'less,' and equality by *si, ausi, autresi, tant, autant, autretant*.

83.1. Implied comparisons:

> Pur estre *plus* legiers n'i volt hauberc porter (19:17)
> In order to be lighter, he did not wish to wear a halberk
>
> Mais quant Richarz li Brez le vit *si* abatu (19:31)
> But when Richard the Breton saw him so struck down

83.2. Stated comparisons.
In stated comparisons, the second term is introduced by *que* or (more rarely) *de* after *plus* or *moins* and by *com(e)* after expressions indicating equality:

Plus erent curteis e vaillant . . .
Que chevalier en altres regnes (9, 199, 201)
They were more courtly and brave . . .
Than knights in other kingdoms

Et qant il virent l'escu Lancelot, il ne furent mie *meins* liez *que* de l'autre
   don. (14, 125–26)
And when they saw Lancelot's shield, they were not less happy (with
   it) than with the other gift.

Mais j'ai trop *mains de* chaviaus
Devant que derriere (22, 206–07)
But I have much less hair
In front than behind

E sunt ensemble *plus de* cinquante milie (6, 229)
And together they are more than fifty thousand

Car *si* tost *cum* li sainz peut la terre atuchier (17:6)
For as soon as the saint could touch ground

Si l'encaeinent *altresi cum* un urs (6, 137)
And they chain him like a bear

83.3. Superlatives. Modern French forms its superlative by preposing an article to the comparative: *le plus, le moins.* In Old French this distinction is dependent upon the context, and the article is not used:

Ceo est la rien que *plus* desir (10, 51)
This is the thing that I most desire

"Seigneurs, vos estes li home el monde ou ge *plus* me fi" (14, 15–16)
"My lords, you are the men I trust most in the world"

The use of the *-isme* ending to indicate a superlative is relatively rare:

Ne s'en corucet giens cil *saintismes* hom (3, 38)
That most holy man did not get angry at all

et avoit li navies bien une *grandesme liwe* de front (24, 6–7)
and the fleet was a good league wide

The absolute superlative is most commonly indicated by adverbs such as *molt, tant, tres, trop, mais, asez,* all meaning "much, very much," particularly in combination with *par*:

ma *tresdouce* amie (20:31a)
my sweetest (dearest) friend

Tant par est douce (20:15)
She is so very sweet

Car *mut par* ert bon chevalier (7, 130)
For he was an exceptionally good knight

84. Special Comparative Forms

Although most comparatives and superlatives in Old French are indicated by adverbs, a limited number of frequently used adjectives have synthetic comparatives:

POSITIVES	COMPARATIVES
buens 'good'	mieudre, meillor 'better'
maus 'bad'	pire, peior, pis
	noaudre, noaillor, noauz 'worse'
granz 'large, tall'	graindre, graignor
	maire, maior 'greater'
petiz 'small, short'	mendre, menor 'smaller'

A Dol avoit un *bon* seignor,
Ainz puis, ço cuit, n'i ot *meillor*. (8:253–54)
At Dol there was a good lord,
I don't believe there's been a better one since (him).

In the earliest texts one finds a few other adjectives of this type, but they are extremely rare: *haus, halçor* 'higher'; *beaus, belisor* 'more beautiful'; *genz, gençor* 'fairer'; *forz, forçor* 'stronger'; *juene, joignor* 'younger.' Equally rare are the synthetic comparative forms in *-isme*. These were learned forms, usually found in religious contexts in imitation of Latin, and they were never popular: *grandisme, altisme, seintisme.*

85. Adverbial Expressions

In 13.53 we stated that adverbs were the "soul" of the Old French sentence. A particularly colorful characteristic of adverbial usage in Old French is the abundance of adverbial expressions. Most consist of a noun preceded by a preposition:

par force (16:39) 'forcibly'
a desmesure (12, 283) 'excessively, inordinately'
a poi, por poi + *ne* 'almost'
a grans painnes 'laboriously (with great effort)'
a grant esploit (5:147) 'rapidly'
a grant pechié (19:9) 'sinfully'
a escïent (6:209) 'certainly, deliberately'
a estros 'completely'
de totes pars (10:352) 'on all sides'
de sun gré (17:2) 'willingly'
en bescoz (19:33) 'obliquely, slantingly'

Others consist of undetermined nouns, nouns determined by an article, or nouns modified by an adjective:

merveille (7:248) 'amazingly, greatly'
le pas (10, 313) 'at a walk'
le grant pas (17:4) 'swiftly'
les grans galoz 'rapidly (at a fast gallop)'
chaut pas 'immediately'
toutes voies (5, 127) 'however, nevertheless'

Several of these expressions became fused in writing:

atant (1:20) 'thereupon'
amont (11, 110) 'up, above, upwards'
aval (20, 96) 'down, below, downwards'

The preceding lists are exemplary only. They emphasize the adverbial expressions found in our readings, and they represent only a small portion of the hundreds to be found in Old French texts.

86. Indefinite Qualifiers

A number of the adverbs of degree used in making stated or implied comparisons (see Section 83) also appear as indefinite pronouns. *Auques* 'some, a little, somewhat' is indeclinable:

> le chef cresp e *aukes* blunt (10, 301)
> hair curly and somewhat blondish

Molt 'many, much' is declined as a Type I adjective:

> *Molt* poez terre o li avoir (10:342)
> You can have much land with her
> She will bring you much land in dowry

> *Molt* ot de joie et de deduit (12, 373)
> There was much of both joy and pleasure

Poi, pou, peu 'little, a little' is indeclinable:

> si aroit il assés *peu* en li (20:32a)
> yet it would be rather little for her

> N'i ad guair(e)s fors sul *un po(i)* (4, 117)
> There was just a very little (distance left to go)

Plusor 'many' is used only in the plural. It may be an adjective as well as a pronoun, and it is declined as a Type III adjective:

> De *plusurs* choses a remembrer li prist (6, 360)
> He began to remember many things

> Et si fu de *plusors* blasmé (18, 66)
> And he was blamed by many

Li plusor 'the majority' is NP only:

> moult avoient *li pluseur* d'eus grant poor (14, 50–51)
> the majority of them were very afraid

Tot 'all, everything, everyone, every' (for declension, see 12.50) may be an adjective, a pronoun, or an adverb:

> Bien sachent *tuit* veraiement (4:133)
> Everyone knew truly (that she was of noble blood)
>
> Amor, qui *tout* vaint (20:24a)
> Love, which conquers all
>
> Si l'emple *tout* d'umilité (5, 138)
> And he fills him completely with humility

Phonology 19

Anglo-Norman is the westernmost dialect area of Old French. It is most closely akin to its parent dialect, Norman, but it also shares traits with other dialects. This phonology section considers the main traits that Anglo-Norman has in common with Norman and with the western (Anjou, Maine, Touraine, Brittany) and southern dialects (Berry, Orléanais). It also touches on certain traits that set these areas apart.

The following chart lists the main characteristics common to these dialects:

TRAITS	A-N	N	W	S
1. *a* > *ei* (rarely *ai*)		xx	x	
2. *o* > *ou, o, u*	xx	xx	xx	x
3. *ei* stays or > *e*	xx	xx	xx	xx
4. *ie* > *e*	xx		x	x
5. 1st pl. in *-om* (rarely *-on*), *-um, -un*	xx	xx	x	x
6. Class I imperf. in *-oue, -oe*	xx	x	xx	
7. *e* + nasal stays /ẽ/	xx	x	x	
8. accented *ẹ* + palatal > *ei, e, ie*	x	x	xx	x
9. accented *ǫ* + palatal > *oi, oui, eu*			xx	x

---

xx — Occurs in most texts.

x — Occurs in certain texts only or is scattered through a number of texts.

---

1. Free accented A gave *ei, ai* in many dialects. Some linguists see this as an early palatalization, others as a late palatalization, and still others as a "parasitic" *-i-*:

LATIN	EARLY OLD FRENCH	FRANCIEN	DIALECTS	ANGLO-NORMAN
PÁTREM	> *paedre	pere	peire	pere
TÁLEM	> ʻtael	tel	teil	tel
LEVÁRE	> *levaer	lever	leveir	lever

2. Accented Ō diphthongized to /ou/ in early Old French. In Francien and Picard it was differentiated to /ø/ (spelled *eu*), whereas in other dialects it tended to simplify to /u/. This sound was spelled *ou* or *o* in dialects other than Anglo-Norman, which spelled the sound *u*:

NEPÓTEM	> nevout	neveu	neveu, nevo	nevu
SENIÓREM	> seignour	seigneur	seigneur, seignor	seignur
ILLÓRUM	> lour	leur	lour, lor	lur

3. In all of the dialects considered in this section, *ei* was lowered to /e/ (spelled *ei, e*) rather than dissimilated to /oi/:

HABÉRE	> aveir	avoir	aveir, aver	aveir
D(I)RÉCTŬM	> dreit	droit	dreit, dret	dreit
FÍDEM	> fei	foi	fei, fe	fei

4. The reduction of the diphthong *ie* to *e* was the rule in Anglo-Norman. It was also common in Norman, the southern and western dialects, and Burgundian:

CABALLÁRIŬM	> chevalier	chevalier	chevaler	chevaler
*MANÁRĬA	> maniere	maniere	manere	manere
DENÁRIŬS	> deniers	deniers	deners	deners
BÉNE	> bien	bien	ben, bien	ben

5. The ending of the first person plural was spelled without an *-s* in the west and southwest (*-om, -on*) and in Anglo-Norman (*-um, -un*):

*PARLÚMUS	> parlons	parlons	parlon,	
			parlom	parlum
*DONÚMUS	> donons	donons	donon,	
			donom	donum

6. The imperfect endings *-oe, -oes, -o(u)t, -oent* for the first conjugation were continued much longer in Anglo-Norman and the western dialects than in the other dialects, which soon replaced them with the endings *-ois, -oit, -oient* by analogy with the other conjugations:

*PAROLÁBAM	> parloue	parloie	parloe	parloue
*DONÁBAT	> donot	donoit	donot	donot, donout

7. Anglo-Norman was not the only dialect to distinguish nasal /ẽ/ from nasal /ã/. It shared this trait with Norman, with the western dialects, and with Picard and Walloon to the north.

8. Accented open ẹ + palatal gave *ei, e, ie* instead of Francien *i*:

PRĔTĬŬS	> *prieis	pris	pres, preis	pris, preis
DĔCEM	> *dieis	dis	dez, deiz	dis, des
MĔDĬŬM	> *miei	mi	mey	mi, me

Note that this trait is also characteristic of Burgundian (see Phonology 23).

9. Accented open ø + palatal gave *oi, oui, eu* instead of Francien *ui* in the western and southern regions:

PŎDĬŬM	> *puoi	pui	peu, poi	pui
*PŎSSĬAT	> *puoisse	puisse	poisse	puisse
ŎCTO	> *uoit	uit, huit	oict	uit

Norman

Norman scribes frequently inserted an inorganic or "parasitic" *i*: *iceile, saichent, queil, abbei, leveir* for Francien *icele, sachent, quel, abbé, lever*.

Norman also shared a number of important characteristics with its neighbor to the northeast, Picard. These are summarized in Phonology 23.

Western dialects (Anjou, Maine, Touraine, Brittany)

In the western dialect region, the aforementioned traits prevailed and the Vulgar Latin diphthong *au* became /u/ rather than /ɔ/:

CÁUSAM	> chose	chose	chouse	chose

Final palatal *-z* and *-s* depalatalized:

*ÚSTĬŬM	> uis	huis, uis	us	huis, uis
*PERTÚSĬŬM	> pertuis	pertuis	pertus	pertuis

Present subjunctive forms in *-ge* were common (see Phonology 18): *prengent, demurgent, donge*.

Southern dialects (Berry, Orléanais)

The southern dialect region reveals in its spellings the influence of Occitan: *lh, hl* are used for palatal *l* (*ffilha, vilhe, lhi*); *nh, hn* for palatal *n* (*senhor, tesmohn*); *tz* for /ts/ (*totz*); *ff* for initial *f* (*ffilha, fforns, ffema*).

Phonologically, the southern dialects occasionally show final /a/ for northern weak final *e* (/ə/): *ffilha, ffema, cesta letra*.

Southwestern Dialects (Angoumois, Poitou, Saintonge, Aunis)

Latin accented A + L gave *-au* rather than Francien *-al, -el, -eu*: *mau, ostau, quas* for *mal, ostel, queus*

As in the southern dialects, Occitan influence is occasionally to be noted: *vila, de las, Segnhor, doñam, deviam*, etc.

Unaccented *a* in hiatus does not > *e*:

| fau, fahu | (=feü < *FATÚDUM) |
| maür | (=meür, mur < *MATÚRUM) |

chapter 20

Reading and Textual Analysis, Selection 11a

The reading selections for the final four chapters are from the late twelfth- or early thirteenth-century *chantefable, Aucassin and Nicolette.*

Aucassin and Nicolette is unique in Old French in its alternation of prose and verse. In the final lines of the work the anonymous artist who composed it coined a word to describe the process, combining the Old French words for "to sing" and "to narrate" into *cantefable* (Francien: *chantefable*):

Or a sa joie Aucassins	Now Aucassin is happy
Et Nicolete autresi:	And Nicolette likewise:
No cantefable prent fin,	Our *chantefable* is drawing to a close,
N'en sai plus dire.	I have nothing more to say.

There was no literary prose in Old French before the end of the twelfth century. The repetitive, highly oral style of *Aucassin* suggests that it may have been among the first prose works written in Old French, before satisfactory literary models had been established. Once attempted, the prose form developed quite rapidly, and by the mid-thirteenth century a number of significant prose works had been created, among them Ville-hardouin's *Chronicle of the Fourth Crusade*, the mystical *Perlesvaus* (*High Book of the Grail*), and the voluminous *Prose Lancelot* cycle. One reason cited for the emergence of prose is that, in the Aristotelian thirteenth century, works in verse came to be regarded as fictional, whereas works in prose seemed to assure the reader of a greater sense of reality. Prose, however, would not entirely supplant verse as the medium for narrative fiction until the fifteenth century.

In the reading passage for this chapter we meet the hero, Aucassin. He refuses to take up arms to help his father, Garin of Beaucaire, defend his lands against Count Bougar of Valence because his father will not allow him to marry the girl he loves, our heroine, Nicolette. His father's objection is that Nicolette—like Fresne—appears to come from an unknown and unverifiable background, and any children she would have could therefore not be legitimized (see Chapter 10).

20:1	Qui vauroit bons vers oïr
20:2	Del deport du viel antif
20:3	De deus biax enfans petis,
20:4	Nicholete et Aucassins,
20:5	Des grans paines qu'il soufri
20:6	Et des proueces qu'il fist
20:7	Por s'amie o le cler vis?
20:8	Dox est li cans, biax li dis,
20:9	Et cortois et bien asis:
20:10	Nus hom n'est si esbahis,
20:11	Tant dolans ni entrepris,
20:12	De grant mal amaladis,
20:13	Se il l'oit, ne soit garis
20:14	Et de joie resbaudis,
20:15	Tant par est douce.

20:16a	Or dient et content et fablent
20:16b	que li quens Bougars de Valence faisoit guere au conte Garin de Biaucaire si grande et si mervelleuse et si mortel
20:16c	qu'il ne fust uns seux jors ajornés qu'il ne fust as portes et as murs et as bares de le vile a cent cevaliers
20:16d	et a dis mile sergens a pié et a ceval, si li argoit sa terre et gastoit son païs et ocioit ses homes.
20:17	Li quens Garins de Biaucaire estoit vix et frales, si avoit son tans trespassé.
20:18	Il n'avoit nul oir, ne fil ne fille, fors un seul vallet.
20:19	Cil estoit tex con je vos dirai.
20:20	Aucasins avoit a non li damoisiax.
20:21	Biax estoit et gens et grans et bien tailliés de ganbes et de piés et de cors et de bras.

20:22a   Il avoit les caviax blons et menus recercelés et les ex vairs et rians

20:22b   et le face clere et traitice et le nés haut et bien assis.

20:23   Et si estoit enteciés de bones teces qu'en lui n'en avoit nule mauvaise se bone non.

20:24a   Mais si estoit soupris d'Amor, qui tout vaint, qu'il ne voloit estre cevalers, ne les armes prendre,

20:24b   n'aler au tornoi, ne fare point de quanque il deüst.

20:25a   Ses pere et se mere li disoient: "Fix, car pren tes armes, si monte el ceval, si deffent te terre et aïe tes homes:

20:25b   s'il te voient entr'ex, si defenderont il mix lor cors et lor avoirs et te tere et le miue."

20:26   "Pere," fait Aucassins, "qu'en parlés vos ore?

20:27a   Ja Dix ne me doinst riens que je li demant, quant ere cevaliers, ne monte a ceval, ne que voise a estor ne a bataille,

20:27b   la u je fiere cevalier ni autres mi, se vos ne me donés Nicholete me douce amie que je tant aim."

20:28   "Fix," fait li peres, "ce ne poroit estre.

20:29a   Nicolete laise ester, que ce est une caitive qui fu amenee d'estrange terre, si l'acata li visquens de ceste vile

20:29b   as Sarasins, si l'amena en ceste vile, si l'a levee et bautisie et faite sa fillole,

20:29c   si li donra un de ces jors un baceler qui du pain li gaaignera par honor: de ce n'as tu que faire.

20:30a   Et se tu fenme vix avoir, je te donrai le file a un roi u a un conte:

20:30b   il n'a si rice home en France, se tu vix sa fille avoir, que tu ne l'aies."

20:31a   "Avoi, peres!" fait Aucassins, "ou est ore si haute honers en terre, se Nicolete ma tresdouce amie l'avoit,

20:31b   qu'ele ne fust bien enploiie en li?

20:32a   S'ele estoit enpereris de Colstentinoble u d'Alemaigne, u roïne de France u d'Engletere, si aroit il assés peu en li,

20:32b   tant est france et cortoise et de bon aire et entecie de toutes bones teces."

20:1   *Qui* might also be construed as a relative with the hypothetical meaning "If anyone" (see 11.44.1). In that case, change the question mark to a comma at the end of line 7.

20:2   The exact meaning of *du viel antif* is a matter of conjecture. Some believe it refers to the author of either the *cantefable* or its ostensible source; others understand it as referring to the lost source itself; still others propose various emendations to the line, none of which has been generally accepted.

20:15   *douce*: syntactically, the antecedent should be the dir. obj. pron. *le* (*l'*) in line 13, for masc. *li cans* of line 8. The f. form has been explained as referring either to the unexpressed but understood *cantefable* or to Nicolette.

20:22a *menus*: adj. used as adv.; note that it agrees in number and gender with the adj. it modifies (see 13.53.3).

20:29a *que = car*: see 21.90 and 91.1. The usage is frequent in *Aucassin and Nicolette*.

20:31b *ele* refers to *haute honers*; *Nicolete* is the antecedent for *li*.

---

87. Old French Punctuation

Few Old French manuscripts have any indications regarding punctuation. The punctuation found in modern editions of medieval texts is inserted by editors to suggest a particular reading or interpretation. In composing works that would be read aloud, Old French authors frequently worked certain devices into the syntax or prosody to indicate phraseology. Foremost among these devices is the use of assonance or rhyme: all early Old French works are written in verse and, until the late twelfth-century works of the finest Old French poet, Chrétien de Troyes, almost all lines were end-stopped. With the end of the line came the end of the syntactical group. Rare indeed in Marie de France or Guernes de Pont-Sainte-Maxence is an enjambment of the type:

> En Bretaigne jadis manoient
> Dui chevalier (1:3–4)
> Formerly in Brittany there lived
> Two knights

Another common "punctuating device" is the use of certain adverbs that signal, as it were, the beginnings of phrases. The most important of these "punctuation adverbs" are *si, car, or, dont, donc, adont, atant*. Note the use of *car* and *si*, for example, in the following prose passage from *Aucassin and Nicolette*, which we reproduce without conventional punctuation:

> Nicolete laise ester *que* (= car) ce est une caitive qui fu amenee d'estrange terre *si* l'acata li visquens de ceste vile as Sarasins *si* l'amena en ceste vile *si* l'a levee et bautisie et faite sa fillole *si* li donra un de ces jors un baceler. . . . (20:29a–c)

This passage is, however, exceptional, and one must note that rhymes and punctuation adverbs mark half pauses (modern commas or semicolons) as well as full pauses (modern periods) and that their use is not consistent. We must recall once again that Old French is characterized by tendencies, not by rules.

87.1. *Si.* *Si* is properly an adverb of manner meaning "thus, so" (see 17.74.1), but it is also commonly used as a conjunction equivalent to *et* 'and.' Since its presence at the beginning of a clause requires postpositioning of the subject—a property of adverbs but not of conjunctions in Old French—it is perhaps best classified as a conjunctive adverb:

> A li vint *si* la conforta (4:106)
> She came to her and comforted her
>
> L'enfant aporte volentiers,
> *Si* l'a a la dame mostré (7:220–21)
> He willingly brings the child,
> And showed her to the lady

It may be used, as in the above cases, to link two independent and consecutive clauses. More frequently, it introduces and emphasizes the main clause after an initial dependent clause:

> Quant asseür fu de s'amor,
> *Si* la mist a reson un jor (9:285–86)
> When he was sure of her love,
> (Then) he spoke to her one day

After a negative clause, *si* may act as a temporal conjunctive adverb meaning "until":

> Ainz ne finerent, *si* vindrent a Nesene (8, 295)
> They did not stop until they reached Nesene

Si is used, particularly with the verb *faire*, to introduce a contradiction to a negative assertion:

> "Et tu ne me reconnissoies?"
> "*Si fis*, au chant et as brebis." (22, 116–17)
> "And didn't you recognize me?"
> "Indeed I did, by your song and your sheep."

Si is also found in the formulation of oaths:

> *Si* m'aït Dieus (2:31)
> So help me God!

87.2. *Car.* *Car* is essentially a coordinating conjunction indicating an explanation or motivation:

> Vunt as uis de la sale; mais n'i porent entrer,
> *Car* um les out ainz fait aprés els bien barrer.
> Dunc comencent as uis durement a buter,
> *Car* il voleient prendre le saint e decolper. (16:35–38)

They went to the doors of the room; but they could not enter there,
Because previously they had had them well barred after them.
Then they began to beat hard on the doors,
For they wanted to take the holy man and behead him.

Guernes and many other writers, however, found *car* to be a useful connective or sentence opener even when there was little implied explanation:

> *Car* si tost cum li sainz peut la terre atuchier (17:6)
> Now as soon as the holy man could touch ground
>
> *Car* tut vindrent armé, chascuns sur sun destrier (16:26)
> (Now? For? And? So?) they all came armed, each on his warhorse

Car is also found at the head of imperative sentences, as a demarcative adverb similar in function to modern French *or*:

> *Car* me dites quil vos dona! (13:438)
> Tell me who gave it to you!
>
> Fix, *car* pren tes armes (20:25a)
> Son, take up your arms

For *car* as a coordinating conjunction, see also 21.90.

87.3.   *Or*.   *Or*, in addition to its function as an adverb of time (16.70.1), is used like *car* to introduce an imperative:

> *Or* me siwez (16:41)
> Follow me

Or and *car* are best left untranslated in these cases, although on occasion they seem to attenuate the force of the request (implying "please") or to accentuate it (implying "do now").
Or de + article + infinitive likewise indicates an imperative:

> Seigneur, fet il, *or del monter*! (*Mort Artu*, 94:8–9)
> My lords, said he, mount (your horses)!

87.4.   *Donc, dont*.   *Donc* is an adverb of time meaning "then" (see 16.70). It is commonly used in narrative along with *lors, atant, adont, puis, après* (all meaning "then, next") to indicate the logical succession of events and thereby set off the discrete parts of the discourse. *Donc* is heavily relied upon by Guernes de Pont-Sainte-Maxence:

> *Dunc* l'en unt al mustier . . . mené (17:1)
> Then they took him to the church
>
> *Dunc* sunt li chevalier dedenz l'encloistre entré (17:12)
> Then the knights entered the cloister

Dont is properly an adverb of place (see Section 88), but owing to phonological similarities and the fact that Gothic script *t* and *c* are virtually identical, *dont* and *donc* became hopelessly confused in their syntax, and it is frequently impossible to determine which is intended.

87.5. Adont, atant. These two words are synonymous in meaning "then, thereupon," and both are used to begin syntactic groups:

> *Adont* li remembra de li (12:421)
> Then she remembered her
>
> *Atant* es vos le mesagier! (1:20)
> Then behold the messenger!

In the second example, *atant* is perhaps best left untranslated.

88. Relatives and Interrogatives

Old French had a number of relatives and interrogatives that were somewhat less commonly employed than those outlined in 11.43.

88.1. Relative and interrogative adverbs and pronouns: *dont, ou, ont, se.* *Dont* is an adverb of place that is frequently encountered as a relative or interrogative pronoun indicating origin—"whence, from where, from there":

> *Dont* vos vint il? (13:437)
> From where did it come to you? (i.e., Where did you get it?)

It easily took on the related meaning "therefore, for this reason":

> *Dont* se clama orphenine (21:22)
> For this reason she called herself an orphan
>
> vos n'en irés mie, car *dont* m'ariis vos mort (23:2)
> you'll not go away, for if you did you would kill me

Consequently, it came to be used as a relative pronoun:

> tant que je trovasse coutel *dont* je me peüsce ferir el cuer (23:4b)
> until I might find a knife by which I might strike myself in the heart

Occasionally it had a personal antecedent and meant "of whom, whose":

> Assez out en la curt *baruns*
> *Dunt* jo ne sai dire les nuns (9, 1–2)
> There were at court many lords
> Whose names I cannot tell (you)

O, ou is a relative or interrogative adverb of place meaning "where, in which." It may also have a person as an antecedent and mean "in whom, over whom":

> *ou* est ore si haute honers en terre? (20:31a)
> where is there so high an honor on earth?

> La *ou* la meschine ert trovee (4:132)
> There where the girl will be found

> Seigneurs, vos estes li home el monde *ou* ge plus me fi (14, 15–16)
> My lords, you are the men (in) whom I most trust in this world

Ont, unt (< UNDE) is often confused with *ou* (< UBI). It is used especially in Anglo-Norman and is generally preceded by the preposition *par*. It means "through which, where":

> As altres chambres out une chambre ajustee
> *Par unt* la veie esteit al cloistre plus privee. (*Vie de St. Thomas*, 5446–47)
> There was another room beside the others
> Through which the view of the cloister was more private.

> Sur la fenestre les ad mises
> Bien serreies e bien asises,
> *Par unt* li chevaliers passot
> Quant a la dame repeirot. (Marie, "Yonec," 291–94)
> On the window he placed (the iron spikes),
> Close together and firmly affixed,
> Through which the knight passed
> When he returned to the lady.

Se is occasionally found as an interrogative adverb introducing both direct and indirect questions:

> que cuideriés vous avoir gaegnié, *se* vous l'aviés asognentee ne mise
>   a vo lit? (22:4)
> what do you think you will have gained if (when) you made her
>   your mistress
> and put her in your bed?

> "Dame," fet il, "*s*'il vos remanbre
> del nain qui hier vos correça
> et vostre pucele bleça?" (*Erec*, 1110–12)
> "Lady," said he, "do you recall
> the dwarf who angered you yesterday
> and wounded your maid-in-waiting?"

... Où sunt il remenant?
S'il sont encore sain et delivre et vivant? (*Fierabras*, 4604–05)
... Where are they staying?
Are they still alive and safe and well?

For the use of *se* as a conjunction, see 21.91.4.

88.2.   Relative and interrogative adjectives and pronouns: *quant, quel*.
Quant is declined as a Type I adjective (see 12.49.1):

	FEMININE	MASCULINE	NEUTER
NS	quante	quanz, quans	quant
OS	quante	quant	quant
NP	quantes	quant	
OP	quantes	quanz, quans	

As an interrogative adjective or pronoun it means "how much, how many":

> Ne vus sai dire quels ne *quanz* (9, 184)
> I cannot tell you which or how many
>
> Sire, j'en vi je ne sai *kans* (22, 27)
> Sire, I don't know how many I saw

Quant is also found in Old French as a conjunction (see 21.91.3) and as an indefinite pronoun (see 15.61).
Quels is declined as a Type II adjective (see 12.49.2):

	FEMININE	MASCULINE	NEUTER
NS	quel(s), queus	quels, queus	quel
OS	quel	quel	quel
NP	quels, queus	quel	
OP	quels, queus	quels, queus	

As a relative or interrogative adjective or pronoun it means "which one, which, what":

> Esguardez u vus estes e *quel* sunt li feirié. (19:8)
> Take note of where you are and what the feast days are.

N'il ne lur dist, ne il nel demanderent,
Quels hom esteit ne de *quel* terre il eret. (3, 9–10)
He did not tell them, nor did they ask him,
What man he was nor from what land he came.

The analogical feminine form with *-e* also occurs:

Reste maintenant le tiers point ou nous avons a
declairer *quelle* obeissance doit estre gardee vers le prince (30, 1–2)
There remains now the third point in which we must
state what obedience is due the prince

Associated with the definite article first as an interrogative pronoun
and then as a relative, *li quels* was declined as a combination of *quel* and the
definite article. It was rare before the thirteenth century and does not
occur in any of our selections, but it became increasingly predominant in
the course of the later Old French and Middle French periods:

Je ne sai *li quex* plus me het,
Ou la Vie qui me desirre,
Ou Morz qui ne me vialt ocirre. (12, 18–20)
I know not which hates me more:
Life, who wants me,
Or Death, who refuses to take me.

car la bonne roine . . . m'escripsi deviers le roi David
    d'Escoce, *liquels* fu fils au roi Robert de Brus. . . . (27, 40–42)
for the good queen . . . wrote a letter of introduction for me
    to King David of Scotland, who was the son of King Robert
    Bruce. . . .

**88.3. Compound relatives and interrogatives: *Que que, qui que, cui
que, quanque, etc.*** Old French developed a series of compound indefinite relatives whose first element was a pronoun, adverb, or adjective
serving as an antecedent to the second element, which was generally *que*.
These compound relatives usually introduced a generalizing adjectival
clause with the verb in the subjunctive. In our texts we find *ce que, ço que,
qui que, quanque*. Many others existed in Old French (*quiconques, comment que,
ou que, don que, quel que, qui qui, cui que, que que*), but most have disappeared
from the modern language.

ne fare point de *quanque* il deüst (20:24b)
nor do anything that he should

Qui qu'en eüst joie, Aucassins n'en fu mie liés (21:36a)
Whoever (else) might be happy about it, Aucassin was not at all glad

"Jeo nel lerroie pur murir
Que jeo ne l'auge ja ferir,
Que ke m'en deie avenir." (7, 14–16)
"Even if I were to die, I would not
Refrain from going to strike him,
No matter what might be the consequences to me."

Quiconques a fame geüst (28, 114)
Whoever should lie with a woman

These led to a long series of conjunctions of the type *mais que, des que, ainz que, por ce que, puis que, san ce que, tant que* (see Chapter 21).

Phonology 20

Picard

The only surviving manuscript of *Aucassin and Nicolette* is in the Picard dialect of northern France. Picardy comprised the ancient counties of Eu, Clermont, Vermandois, Cambrai, Artois, Pontieu, Boulogne, Montreuil, and Hainaut, the lordships of Coucy and Guise, and the southern portion of the county of Flanders. Norman was spoken to the west, Flemish to the north, Walloon to the east, and Francien to the south. Picardy corresponded to no geographical or political area; it was a region set apart by its dialect and ethnicity.

It was a prosperous commercial region throughout most of the Middle Ages, the center of a thriving textile industry. Wool, imported from England, was manufactured into finished goods in the great cities of Lille, Amiens, Tournai, Abbeville, Douai, Arras, St. Quentin, St. Omer, Béthune, and Corbie. A wealthy middle class and a powerful nobility encouraged the arts and literature. Adam de le Halle wrote his *Jeu de la Feuillee* and *Robin et Marion* in the Picard dialect, Robert de Clari his *Conquest of Constantinople*, Gerbert de Montreuil his *Roman de la Violette*, and Jehan Froissart his *Chronicles*. Countless works composed elsewhere were copied by Picard scribes for their insatiable wealthy patrons, both noble and bourgeois.

Picard was perhaps the most idiosyncratic dialect of Old French, and it was recognized as "unusual" even in the medieval period. Conon de Béthune in his chanson "Mout me semont Amors ke je m'envoise" (Aspland, 16d) expresses his acute awareness that his speech is "provincial" (*mos d'Artois*) and says that the French at court have mocked it:

Ke mon langaige ont blasmé li François (16d, 5)
For the French (at court) have made fun of my speech

It would be impossible to list all the peculiarities of Picard here. The student interested in a more detailed analysis should consult the excellent volume by Charles T. Gossen, *Grammaire de l'ancien picard.*

A few dominant traits will enable one to identify a text written in this region:

C + A stays /k/ (> *ch* in Francien)
G + A stays /g/ (> *j* in Francien)
C + E, I > /tʃ/ (written *ch*, fronted to /ts/ in Francien)
-iau for Francien *-eau*
le for the feminine article *la*
me, te, se for Francien possessives *ma, ta, sa*

Most of these traits are illustrated in the present reading selection:

C + A stays: *cans* (20:8) for Francien *chanz* (< CANTUS); *teces* (20:32b) for Francien *teches* (< *TEKAN); *france* (20:32b) for Francien *franche* (< FRANKA)
G + A stays: *ganbes* (20:21) for Francien *jambe* (< GAMBA)
-iau for *-eau*: *biax* (20:3) for *beaus* (*-x* is an abbreviation for *-us* much favored by the scribe of *Aucassin and Nicolette*)
le for *la*: *le vile* (20:16c); *le file* (20:30a)
te, se for *ta, sa*: *te tere* (20:25b); *se mere* (20:25a)

Picard shared many important characteristics with its neighbors to the west (Norman and Anglo-Norman) and to the east (Walloon). Certain of its traits were even popular in Francien and other central dialects: *-iau* for *-eau*; *no, vo* for *notre, votre.* There is probably no text in Old French that is dialectally "pure," but a text with a preponderance of the above traits can be assigned to Picardy with relative certainty.

Phonology 21 considers the principal phonological characteristics of Picard; Phonology 22 outlines its morphological particularities. The final phonology section compares Picard with dialects to the south and east as well as with Norman and Anglo-Norman.

chapter 21

Reading and Textual Analysis, Selection 11b

Although *Aucassin and Nicolette* is much admired today, it appears that it was not highly esteemed, or at least not widely circulated in written form, in the Middle Ages, for only a single manuscript at the Bibliothèque Nationale in Paris (B.N. f. fr. 2168) has survived. This unique manuscript is in a small format and seems to have been hastily and somewhat carelessly written; it has no decoration whatsoever. It is possible that we are dealing with a transcription from memory of a dramatic performance by one or several *jongleurs*. Critics are very much divided on this question, but *Aucassin* has frequently been associated with dramatic literature. Grace Frank, in *Medieval French Drama*, suggests that the work might have been performed "with the aid of impersonation, voice-changes, and mimetic action" (237).

In the present selection, Count Garin goes to the viscount who has taken in Nicolette and demands that she be locked away so that Aucassin will no longer be distracted by her.

21:1a	Quant li quens Garins de Biaucare vit qu'il ne poroit Aucassin son fil retraire des amors Nicolete,
21:1b	il traist au visconte de le vile qui ses hon estoit, si l'apela:
21:2	"Sire quens, car ostés Nicolete vostre filole!
21:3	Que la tere soit maleoite dont ele fut amenee en cest païs!

21:4 C'or par li pert jou Aucassin, qu'il ne veut estre cevaliers ne faire point de quanque faire doie.

21:5a Et saciés bien que, se je le puis avoir, que je l'arderai en un fu,

21:5b et vous meïsmes porés avoir de vos tote peor."

21:6 "Sire," fait li visquens, "ce poise moi qu'il i va ne qu'il i vient ne qu'il i parole.

21:7a Je l'avoie acatee de mes deniers, si l'avoie levee et bautisie et faite ma filole,

21:7b si li donasse un baceler qui du pain li gaegnast par honor: de ce n'eüst Aucassins vos fix que faire.

21:8a Mais puis que vostre volentés est et vos bons,

21:8b je l'envoierai en tel tere et en tel païs que ja mais ne le verra de ses ex."

21:9 Nicole est en prison mise

21:10 En une canbre vautie,

21:11 Ki faite est par grant devisse,

21:12 Panturee a miramie.

21:13 A la fenestre marbrine

21:14 La s'apoia la mescine.

21:15 Ele avoit blonde la crigne

21:16 Et bien faite la sorcille,

21:17 La face clere et traitice:

21:18 Ainc plus bele ne veïstes.

21:19 Esgarda par le gaudine

21:20 Et vit la rose espanie

21:21 Et les oisax qui se crient,

21:22 Dont se clama orphenine:

21:23 "Ai mi! Lasse moi, caitive!

21:24 Por coi sui en prison misse?

21:25 Aucassins, damoisiax sire,

21:26 Ja sui jou li vostre amie

21:27 Et vos ne me haés mie!

21:28 Por vos sui en prison misse

21:29 En ceste canbre vautie

21:30 U je trai molt male vie;

21:31 Mais, par Diu le fil Marie,

21:32 Longement n'i serai mie,

21:33 Se jel puis fare."

21:34 Nicolete fu en prison, si que vous avés oï et entendu, en le canbre.

21:35a   Li cris et le noise ala par tote le terre et par tot le païs que Ni-
          colete estoit perdue:
21:35b   li auquant dient qu'ele est fuïe fors de la terre,
21:35c   et li auquant dient que li quens Garins de Biaucaire l'a faite
          mordrir.
21:36a   Qui qu'en eüst joie, Aucassins n'en fu mie liés, ains traist au
          visconte de la vile, si l'apela:
21:36b   "Sire visquens, c'avés vos fait de Nicolete ma tresdouce
          amie, le riens en tot le mont que je plus amoie?
21:37   Avés le me vos tolue ne enblee?
21:38a   Saciés bien que, se je en muir, faide vous en sera demandee;
          et ce sera bien drois,
21:38b   que vos m'arés ocis a vos deus mains, car vos m'avés tolu la
          riens en cest mont que je plus amoie."

21:8b   After this line I have omitted a short section in which the viscount imprisons
        Nicolette in a tower of his castle with an old woman as her only companion.
21:12   *miramie*: probably the best-known *hapax legomenon* in Old French. The word occurs
        only here, and the context gives no real clue to its meaning.

---

89. Conjunctions

Conjunctions relate one part of a sentence to another part or one
sentence to another. Coordinating conjunctions relate two elements between which no relationship of dependence is perceived; subordinating
conjunctions relate a dependent proposition to an independent one. In
Old French, the line of demarcation between the two is often unclear, and
Old French conjunctions are as difficult to classify as Old French adverbs.

89.1. Types and forms.   There are a limited number of true conjunc-
tions: *et* 'and,' *ou* 'or,' *ne* 'nor,' *se* 'if,' *quant* 'when, if, since,' *que* 'that.' Just as
many adverbs could double as prepositions in Old French, so could many
adverbs serve as conjunctions: *ainz* 'rather,' *car* 'for, because,' *mais* 'but,' *si*
'and, thus, therefore,' *com* 'as,' *donc* 'then.' Finally, there are a great number
of conjunctive phrases ending with *que* or *com(me)*: *ainsi comme* 'just as,' *ainz*
que 'before,' *de ço que* 'because,' *des que* 'as soon as,' *lors que* 'when,' *mais que*
'unless,' *puis que* 'since,' *por ce que* 'because, since,' *si que* 'as,' *si tost com* 'as
soon as,' *tant com* 'as much as,' among others. Many conjunctions, like
many adverbs and prepositions, had multiple forms, such as: *ains, ainsi,*
ainsi que, des, deci, desique, desdont, tres dont, tres dont que.

90. Coordinating Conjunctions

Coordinating conjunctions may connect parts of sentences (nouns, adjectives, verbs) or entire phrases together:

Je l'avoie acatee de mes deniers, *si* l'avoie levee *et* bautisie *et* faite ma filole, *si* li donasse un baceler qui du pain li gaegnast par honor. (21:7a–b)
I bought her with my money, (and) I held her over the font and had her baptized and made my god-daughter, and I would give her a young man who would earn her bread for her honorably

The conjunction *si* is used here to coordinate three separate independent clauses, whereas *et* is used in the second clause to coordinate the three past participles. This example illustrates the most common function of the coordinating conjunctions: to accumulate elements. *Ne* is also used in this manner whenever there is any aura of doubt (negation, hypothesis, question, fear):

Avés le me vos tolue *ne* enblee? (21:37)
Have you taken or stolen her from me?

"Sire," fait li visquens, "ce poise moi qu'il i va ne qu'il
i vient *ne* qu'il i parole" (21:6)
"Sir," said the viscount, "it troubles me that
he comes and goes and speaks to her."

Note that in an accumulation, the coordinating conjunction is almost always included before each item (see 20.87 on punctuation).
A second common function of the coordinating conjunction is to introduce an alternative, which may be either positive (*ou*) or negative (*ne*):

eles ont deus amis *ou* trois avoc leur barons (22:11a)
they have two or three lovers in addition to their husbands

il ne voloit estre cevalers, *ne* les armes prendre,
n'aler au tornoi, *ne* fare point de quanque il deüst. (20:24a–b)
he didn't want to be a knight, nor take up arms, nor go
to the tourneys, nor do anything that he should.

Mais and *ains* indicate a distinction between the terms coordinated: *mais* usually introduces an idea that is different from or overrides the preceding, whereas *ains* indicates a contradiction or a concept in direct opposition to that previously expressed:

Por vos sui en prison misse
En ceste canbre vautie
U je trai molt male vie;
Mais, par Diu le fil Marie,
Longement n'i serai mie. (21:28–32)

On your account am I thrown
Into prison in this vaulted room
Where I suffer greatly;
But, by God the Son of Mary,
I'll not be here long.

tant n'atenderoie je mie; *ains* m'esquelderoie (23:5a)
I'll not wait so long; rather, I'll hurl myself (against a wall)

As here, *ains* usually introduces in positive form the opposite of the idea expressed negatively in the preceding clause. The distinction between *mais* and *ains* can be seen clearly in the following example from a later passage in *Aucassin*:

Oïl, nos savions bien que vos estes Aucassins nos damoisiax,
mais nos ne somes mie a vos, *ains* somes au conte (30:11)
Yes, we were well aware that you are our master Aucassin,
but we do not belong to you; rather, we (belong to) the count
(your father).

Here, *mais* introduces a notion in the second clause that diverges from that in the first. *Ains* introduces a third clause that gives the positive in contrast to the negative of the second clause. In some cases, however, *ains* does not imply a contradiction and differs very little from *si*, *et*, or *mais*:

Aucassins n'en fu mie liés, *ains* traist au visconte de la vile, si l'apela.
(21:36a)
Aucassin was not at all happy, so he went to the viscount of the town
and spoke to him.

Car as a coordinating conjunction introduces the explanation for the action of the preceding clause. Since it does not require postpositioning of the subject (a property of adverbs), it is best classified in Old French as a conjunction:

et ce sera bien drois, *que* (= *car*) vos m'arés ocis a
vos deus mains, *car* vos m'avés tolu la riens en
cest mont que je plus amoie. (21:38a–b)
and this will be only right, for you will have
killed me with your two hands, because you have
taken from me that being whom I most loved in this world.

Nicolete laise ester, *que* (= *car*) ce est une caitive (20:29a)
Forget about Nicolette, for she is a captive

As can be seen in the preceding examples, *que* often functions as a conjunction equivalent to *car* 'for, because.' More rarely, one finds *car* equivalent to *que* in certain dialects:

mais les nes estoient si bien couvertes de mairien et de sarment
de vingne *ker* (= car) ne leur faisoient mie grant mal. (24,
13–15)
but the ships were so well covered with cask wood and vine
stock
that they did not do them much harm.

91.   Subordinating Conjunctions

There are well over a hundred subordinating conjunctions and conjunctive phrases in Old French, of which only the most important are considered here: *que, com, quant,* and *se.*

91.1.   *Que.*

(A)   The syntax of Old French (as we have had occasion to note) is
extremely free, and there is a tendency to use *que* as a linking conjunction whenever the relationship between two parts of a sentence is
unclear:

Et s'i vont les beles dames cortoises *que* eles ont
deus amis ou trois avoc leur barons. . . . (22:11a)
And the beautiful courtly ladies likewise go there,
those who have two or three lovers besides their husband. . . .

Toz seus, *que* conpaignon n'i ot (*Erec*, 3688)
All alone, without any companion

Que alone often indicates manner ("in such a way that, so that"),
intensity ("to such an extent that, so that"), or result ("in order that, so
that"):

Carles se dort, *qu'*il ne s'esveillet mie. (*Roland*, 724)
Charles sleeps, (in such a way that) he does not wake up.

Souef le traist *qu'*el ne se mut. (13, 210)
Gently he pulled it (the ring) off, in such a way that she didn't move.
(i.e., He pulled it off *so* gently *that* she didn't realize it)

Hüe le fiert tut a bandon,
Que mort l'abat as piez Gormund. (7, 88–89)
Hugh struck him violently,
To such an extent that he struck him dead at Gormund's feet.
(i.e., Hugh struck him *so* violently *that* he fell dead at Gormund's feet)

Prist l'olifan, *que* reproce n'en ait (*Roland*, 2263)
He took the olifant, *so as* not to incur any blame

Que may simply be the equivalent of "and":

> Morz est li quens, *que* plus ne se demuret. (*Roland*, 2021)
> The count is dead, (and) he lingers no more.

It may also introduce exclamations in the indicative or subjunctive:

> E! lasse, *que* n'en ai un hume ki m'ociet! (*Roland*, 2723)
> What a pity there is no one here to kill me!

> *Que* la tere soit maleoite dont ele fut amenee en cest païs! (21:3)
> May the land be damned from whence she was brought into this
> country!

In many texts *que* is used with the meaning of *car*, 'for, because' (see
Section 90):

> Nicolete laise ester, *que* ce est une caitive (20:29a)
> Forget about Nicolette, for she is a captive

> *Que* vus arsistes sun mustier,
> Mesavenir vus en deit bien. (7, 157–58)
> Since you burned his church,
> Misfortune will surely come to you.

It may replace *com* in comparisons (see 19.83):

> "Or as *que* bris parlé!" (8, 135)
> "Now you've spoken like a fool!"

From the beginning, Old French tended to anticipate the subordinate
clause by a correlative in the principal clause. This correlative was most
often the neuter pronoun *ce*, *ço*, but one can also find *en*, *le*, *il*, *chose*, *rien*:

> A un riche homme seroit grief
> D'esligier *ce* qu'il despendirent (15:516–17)
> It would be hard for a rich man
> To pay for what they spent

> faites de mei sul *ço que* faire en devez (18:44)
> do to me alone what you must do

> *Por ce* qu'el fresne fu trovee,
> Le Fresne li mistrent a non (7:228–29)
> Because she was found in the ash tree,
> They named her "Fresne"

> *Il* nen est dreiz *que* paiens te baillisent (6, 332)
> It is not right that pagans lay hold of you

> D'une *chose* s'est afichié . . .
> *Que* einz se lerreit detrenchier
> Que mes pur home le perdi[e]st. (7, 109–12)

On one thing he prided himself . . .
That he would rather let himself be cut to pieces
Than ever again to lose (the horse) to any man.

In the course of the Old French period, *que* combined with a number of prepositions and adverbs to form a rich system of compound conjunctions (such as *si que, ainz que, por ço que, san ce que, tant que, puis que*), many of which have survived into modern French:

Nicolete fu en prison, *si que* vous avés oï (21:34)
Nicolette was in prison, as you have heard

Quant no fille ravon trovee,
Grant joie nos a Deus donnee,
Ainz que li pechiez fust doublez. (14:491–93)
Since we have found our daughter
Before the sin was doubled,
God has given us great joy.

For additional examples, consult the Glossary under *que*.

(B)   As a general rule, *que* may be omitted in Old French whenever its elimination would cause no confusion in the syntax. *Que* is often not expressed, particularly in epic texts and in colloquial style, when the subordinate clause derives logically from the independent clause. Frequently it is introduced by *tant, tel, si*:

Jo vos plevis ˄ ja returnerunt Franc. (6,14)
I give you my word (that) the Franks will return at once.

Il l'aiment *tant* ˄ ne li faldrunt nïent (*Roland*, 397)
They love him so much they will never fail him

Tant i donra terre et avoir,
˄ Bon gré l'en devroit l'en savoir (8:273–74)
He will give (the abbey) so much land and wealth
(That) they will have to be grateful to him for it.

Dunc out *tel* doel ˄ unkes mais n'out si grant. (*Roland*, 2223)
He suffered greater anguish than ever before.

It was regularly omitted after verbs of knowing, thinking, saying, wishing, and promising (*savoir, dire, voloir, jurer, prometre, demander, prier*, and the like):

A l'abaesse *demandoient*
˄ Sa bele niece lor mostrast. (7:250–51)
To the abbess (they) asked (that)
Her beautiful niece (she) them show.
They asked the abbess
To show them her beautiful niece.

E or *sai* ben ⌃ n'avons guaires a vivre. (6, 233)
And I know very well now (that) we have not long to live.

Bien *set* ⌃ de Deu ad bon guarant (4, 280)
He knows well (that) in God he has a good protector.

Pensa et *dist* ⌃ s'ele seüst
La maniere et que ele fust (11:393–94)
(She) pondered and said (that) if she knew
Her background and who she was

It may also be omitted after verbs of fear (*criembre, redouter*), prevention (*garder, ne laissier*), and opinion (*croire, cuidier, penser, sembler*):

Ne *laira* pas ⌃ ne lor mesface (13, 116)
He will not stop without harming them

Gardez ⌃ nel me celez vos mie (11, 140)
See (that) you don't keep it from me

Pensa et *dist* ⌃ s'ele seüst
La maniere et que el fust,
Ja por sa fille nel perdist
Ne son seignor ne li tolist. (11:393–96)
(She) thought and said (that), if she knew
The situation and from what background she came,
(That) she would never cause her to be lost on her daughter's account
Nor would she take her lord from her.

(C)   The preceding examples suggest that the use of *que* in Old French is akin to the use of *that* in modern English. Whereas modern French requires *que* before all subordinate clauses, both Old French and English can and often do omit the conjunction. Similarly, both colloquial modern English and Old French permit a redundant use of the subordinate when a noun clause interrupts the flow of the principal clause:

saciés bien *que*, se je le puis avoir, *que* je l'arderai en un fu (21:5a)
know well that, if I can have her, that I will burn her in a fire

Li rois les refusa et dist *que*, quant il seroient d'iluec parti,
que chascuns feist del mieuz qu'il poist. (14, 104–06)
The king refused (their request) and said that, when they would be gone
   from that place, that each should do the best he could.

For *que* as a temporal conjunction, see 16.70.3.

91.2.   Com (comme, con, cum).   *Com* introduces a subordinate clause whose action is simultaneous with that of the principal clause:

> *Cum* apresmout vers le primseir,
> Dunc vit Brandans que cil dist veir (4, 255–56)
> As nightfall approached,
> Brendan saw that he told the truth

It is also used as a modal and in comparisons of equality, frequently in conjunction with *aussi* (*ainsi, si*):

> Cil estoit tex *con* je vos dirai. (20:19)
> He was as I shall tell you.
>
> De tantes teres *cume* li bers cunquist (6, 361)
> The many lands he conquered as a brave knight
>
> L'abaesse li commanda
> Que devant li soit aportez
> Tout *ainsi comme* il fu trovez. (7:216–18)
> The abbess ordered
> That he be brought before her
> Just as he had been found.

For *com* as an adverb of manner, see 17.74.2.

91.3. Quant. *Quant* situates an action in time and is usually translated "when." Often the time introduced by *quant* is reiterated at the beginning of the principal clause by an adverb (such as *atant, donc, lors,* or *si*):

> *Quant* li quens Garins de Biaucare vit qu'il ne poroit
> Aucassin son fil retraire des amors Nicolete,
> il traist au visconte de le vile (21:1a–b)
> When Count Garin of Beaucaire realized that he could
> not cure his son Aucassin of his love for Nicolette,
> he went to the viscount of the city
>
> *Quant* il l'oï dire et retrere,
> Dolenz en fu (2:59–60)
> When he heard it said and discussed,
> He was sad
>
> *Quant* asseür fu de s'amor,
> *Si* la mist a reson un jor (9:285–86)
> When he was sure of her love,
> (Then) he spoke to her one day
>
> *Quant* l'orent al mustier li moine einsi porté,
> *Dunc* sunt li chevalier dedenz l'encloistre entré (17:11–12)
> When the monks had carried him thus to the church,
> (Then) the knights entered the cloister

In many instances it is difficult to distinguish whether *quant* is functioning as a true conjunction or as an adverb of time.

Quant is likewise found as a conjunction of causality meaning "since, if, if ever":

> "Sire, *quant* pardonné l'avez,
> Jel vos dirai, si m'escoutez." (13:469–70)
> "Milord, since you have pardoned it,
> I will tell you; listen to me."

> Ja Dix ne me doinst riens que je li demant, *quant*
> ere cevaliers, ne monte a ceval. . . . (20:27a)
> May God never give me anything I ask of him, if ever
> I become a knight, nor mount a horse. . . .

91.4. *Se.* *Se* is usually a conjunction introducing a hypothetical subordinate clause:

> Longement n'i serai mie,
>   *Se* jel puis fare. (21:32–33)
> I'll not be here long at all,
>   If I can manage it.

> Saciés bien que, *se* je en muir, faide vous en sera
>   demandee (21:38a)
> Know well that, if I should die, you'll be called to pay
>   for it in blood

It may also function as an interrogative adverb (see 20.88.1). Often, as in line 22:4, it is difficult to know how to classify it.

After a negative principal clause, *se* is frequently combined with the adverb *non* to form a restrictive, "except, only":

> Si estoit enteciés de bones teces qu'en lui n'en avoit nule mauvaise
> *se* bone *non*. (20:23)
> He was so endowed with good traits that there were no bad, but only
> good (traits) in him (i.e., nothing except good traits).

For further examples and discussion, see 13.54.1.

92. Special Auxiliaries

Through the use of special endings to indicate tenses, the morphology of the Old French verb permits one to indicate the relative time of an action. The use of simple versus compound tenses distinguishes completed action from action in process; the use of the subjunctive mode versus the indicative allows the expression of virtual versus actual time (see 23.97).

There are, however, certain modal relationships for which special auxiliary verbs must be employed:

(A) The notion of imminence is expressed by *devoir* or *estre a*:

> Puis en *dut* estre maubaillïe (2:54)
> Afterwards she was to be ill-treated because of it

> Il savoit bien que *ert a* estre. (Béroul, 325)
> He knew well what was to happen.

> Cist hom fu en peril de mort
> En la mer, ou *devoit* noier. (18, 40–41)
> This man was in danger of death
> In the sea, where he was about to drown.

(B) The beginning of an action is expressed by *prendre a* or *(en)commencier a* + infinitive:

> Par mautalent li *prist a* dire (5, 38)
> In anger he began to say to him

> autre genz *comence a* entrer aprés als (25, 89–90)
> other people begin to enter after them

(C) The continuity of an action is expressed by the periphrase *aler* + gerund (*-ant* form):

> "Ovrez," fait sainz Thomas, quis *ala atendant* (17:22)
> "Open," said St. Thomas, who was waiting for them.

> Pur un sul levre *vat* tute jur *cornant*. (6, 90)
> He sounds his horn all day long for a mere hare.

(D) Repeated or habitual action in the past is expressed by the auxiliary *soloir*:

> Ovrir *soloit* l'uis du mostier (6:178)
> He was accustomed to open the church door
> He regularly opened the church door

(E) The end of an action is expressed by the verbs *finir de, laissier (a)* + infinitive:

> Totes ses roiz *laissa* a tendre (18, 12)
> He stopped casting his nets

(F) An action that almost occurred is denoted by locutions of the type *pres (que) ne, por poi (que) ne, par un petit (que) ne, a poi (que) ne* plus a verb in the indicative:

L'une le fert, *pur poi ne* funt (4, 21)
One (wave) strikes him, he almost perishes

Pres ne m'ont mort. (16e, 28)
They almost killed me.

A ben petit que il *ne* chiét. (7, 203)
He very nearly fell.

A po que de duel *n'*en ardoit. (12, 2)
He practically burned with grief.

Phonology 21

Picard phonological characteristics

This section describes the principal phonological differences between Picard and Francien. The development of sounds not specifically mentioned here was generally the same in both areas.

(A)   EL + consonant gave *-iau* rather than *-eau*:

LATIN ETYMON	EARLY OLD FRENCH	PICARD	FRANCIEN
BĔ́LLŬS	> bels	> biaus	beaus
*HĔ́LMŬ	> helme	> hiaume	heaume

(B)   As in Anglo-Norman, nasal *ẽ* was maintained as distinct from nasal *ã* (see Phonology 17.G).

(C)   Accented checked open *ę* often diphthongized to *ie*:

BĔ́STAM	> beste	> bieste	beste
CASTĔ́LLŬM	> chastel	> castiel	chastel

(D)   The Latin nominal ending -ÁTICU gave *-aige* and *-ache* alongside Francien *-age*:

*AETÁTĬCŬM	> eage	> eaige	eage, aage
*SALVÁTĬCŬM	> salvage	> sauvaige/ sauvache	sauvage

(E)   The diphthong *ie* was sometimes reduced to *i* (cf. Anglo-Norman, which leveled *ie* to *e*):

LATIN ETYMON	EARLY OLD FRENCH	PICARD	FRANCIEN
DENÁRĬŬS	> deniers	> denirs	deniers
*PĔTTĬA	> piece	> pice	piece

(F)   Francien *-iee* and *-ieu* were reduced to *-ie* and *-iu* in Picard:

MANSĬONÁTA	> /maisnieδe/	> maisnie	maisniee
LĂNCĔÁTA	> /lantsieδe/	> lanchie	lanciee
LŎCŬM	> lieu	> liu	lieu
DĔŬS	> Dieus	> Dius	Dieus

(G)   Francien *-ue* and *-ueu* were reduced to *-u* in Picard:

*PŎTENT	> /*pueδent/	> puent	pueent
PÓPŬLŬM	> poble	> pule	pueple (= pueule)

(H)   Pretonic *ei* became *i* in Picard (*oi* in Francien):

*PĬSCĬŌNE	> peisson	> pisson	poisson
*SEXÁNTA	> seissante	> sissante	soissante
*ORATĬŌNE	> oreison	> orison	oroison

(I)   A weak *-e-* was introduced between *p, b, v* and a following *r*, particularly in the future and conditional of certain verbs: *esperit* for *esprit*, *marberin* for *marbrin*, *avera* for *avra*, *aprendera* for *aprendra*.

(J)   The treatment of the velar consonants *c* and *g* before *a, e, i* is the single most characteristic development in Picard. Before *a*, Picard *c* and *g* did not palatalize:

CANTÁRE		> canter	chanter
CÁPRAM		> kievre	chievre
*GÁMBA		> gambe	jambe

Before *e, i,* and *yod,* Picard *c* palatalized to /tʃ/ (spelled *ch* or *c*):

CÁELŬM	>	/tsiel/	>	chiel ciel
LÁNCĔAM	>	lance	>	lanche lance

There was considerable confusion in the spellings of these sounds.

(K) -ÁBŬLŬ, -ÁBĬLE > *-aule, -avle*:

TÁBŬLAM	> table	> taule, tavle	table
DIÁBŎLŬM	> diaule	> diavle, diaule	diable
*MŪTÁBĬLE	> /muðab'lə/	> muavle	muable

(L) The groups *l'r, n'r, m'l* did not as a rule develop the glide sound as in Francien:

MŎLÉRE	> /mól'rə/	> molre	moldre, moudre
GĔNĔRŬM	> /gén'rə/	> genre	gendre
*SĬMĬLÁRE	> /sèm'lárə/	> sanler	sembler
TRĔMŬLÁRE	> /trèm'lárə/	> tranler	trembler

(M) As in Anglo-Norman, the initial Germanic *w-* was retained: *warder* for *garder, Wautier* for *Gautier, were* for *guerre.*

(N) Spellings varied greatly, particularly in the representation of sounds from Latin C, which might be written *c, k, qu, ch, s,* or *z* (< T'S). Thus, in *Aucassin and Nicolette* we find *asis* for *assis, Aucasins* for *Aucassins, Nicholete* for *Nicolete, laise* for *laisse, assés* for *assez, ostés* for *ostez, quens* for *cuens, ki* for *qui.*

The influence of Francien, especially in literary texts, often obscures certain dialectal traits. In the thirteenth century, provincial scribes like the poet Conon de Béthune (quoted in Phonology 20), began to realize that their language was not quite that of Paris or the court, and they constantly sought, with varying degrees of success, to conform to the accepted norm.

chapter 22

Reading and Textual Analysis, Selection 11c

This reading selection contains one of the most celebrated passages of *Aucassin and Nicolette,* in which the hero expresses his preference for hell over heaven. It is surprising to find such a sentiment proclaimed in the Middle Ages, dominated as it was by Christianity. Here and elsewhere in the *chantefable*—most notably in the "Torelore" section, which describes a land where the men stay in bed with newborn infants while the women make war on one another with eggs and cheeses—the author seems to be conjuring up a topsy-turvy world in which everything works in ways quite unexpected, which has led most modern critics to propose ironic, satiric, or parodic interpretations of the work. Aucassin in particular seems to represent a sort of medieval antihero—lovesick, refusing to fight, constantly upstaged by the resourcefulness of Nicolette. Such a perspective may explain the singular lack of popularity accorded the work during the medieval period. In the words of Jean-Charles Payen, the story may have been one "qui offusque le confort intellectuel du public médiéval . . . , qui bouscule trop de poncifs."

22:1	"Biax sire," fait li quens, "car laisciés ester.
22:2a	Nicolete est une caitive que j'amenai d'estrange tere, si l'acatai de mon avoir a Sarasins,
22:2b	si l'ai levee et bautisie et faite ma fillole, si l'ai nourie, si li donasce un de ces jors un baceler

22:2c	qui del pain li gaegnast par honor: de ce n'avés vos que faire.
22:3	Mais prendés le fille a un roi u a un conte.
22:4	Enseurquetot, que cuideriés vous avoir gaegnié, se vous l'aviés asognentee ne mise a vo lit?
22:5	Mout i ariés peu conquis, car tos les jors du siecle en seroit vo arme en infer, qu'en paradis n'enterriés vos ja."
22:6	"En paradis qu'ai je a faire?
22:7a	Je n'i quier entrer, mais que j'aie Nicolete ma tresdouce amie que j'aim tant,
22:7b	c'en paradis ne vont fors tex gens con je vous dirai:
22:8a	il i vont ci viel prestre et cil viel clop et cil manke qui tote jor et tote nuit cropent devant ces autex
22:8b	et en ces viés cruutes, et cil a ces viés capes ereses et a ces viés tatereles vestues,
22:8c	qui sont nu et decauc et estrumelé, qui moeurent de faim et de soi et de froit et de mesaises.
22:9	Icil vont en paradis: aveuc ciax n'ai jou que faire.
22:10a	Mais en infer voil jou aler, car en infer vont li bel clerc,
22:10b	et li bel cevalier qui sont mort as tornois et as rices gueres,
22:10c	et li buen sergant, et li franc home: aveuc ciax voil jou aler.
22:11a	Et s'i vont les beles dames cortoises que eles ont deus amis ou trois avoc leur barons,
22:11b	et s'i va li ors et li argens et li vairs et li gris, et si i vont herpeor et jogleor et li roi del siecle:
22:11c	avoc ciax voil jou aler, mais que j'aie Nicolete ma tresdouce amie aveuc mi."
22:12a	"Certes," fait li visquens, "por nient en parlerés, que ja mais ne le verrés. Et se vos i parlés
22:12b	et vos peres le savoit, il arderoit et mi et li en un fu, et vos meïsmes porriés avoir toute paor."
22:13	"Ce poise moi," fait Aucassins. Se se depart del visconte dolans.

22:1   *quens* for *visquens* (cf. 21:2).
22:8a   *ci* for *cil*.
22:8b   The ms has something resembling *cuutes*; some editors read *creutes* or *croutes*.
22:11a   *que*: see 21.91.1.
22:11b   *li roi del siecle*: poets whose work was adjudged the best at local poetry competitions were designated *roi* or king of the circle. The context suggests that Aucassin is referring to these crowned poets rather than to royalty.
22:12b   *vos peres* for *vostres peres* (see 4.11).

93. Past Participles

Past participles, like preterites, are divided into two classes in Old French—weak or strong—depending upon whether they receive the tonic accent or not. All past participles, weak and strong, are declined as Type I adjectives (see 12.49.1):

	MASCULINE	FEMININE		MASCULINE	FEMININE
	durer			boillir	
NS	durez	duree	NS	boilliz	boillie
OS	duré	duree	OS	boilli	boillie
NP	duré	durees	NP	boilli	boillies
OP	durez	durees	OP	boilliz	boillies
	laissier			veoir	
NS	laissiez	laissiee	NS	veüz	veüe
OS	laissié	laissiee	OS	veü	veüe
NP	laissié	laissiees	NP	veü	veües
OP	laissiez	laissiees	OP	veüz	veües
	proisier			voloir	
NS	prisiez	prisiee	NS	voluz	volue
OS	prisié	prisiee	OS	volu	volue
NP	prisié	prisiees	NP	volu	volues
OP	prisiez	prisiees	OP	voluz	volues

Strong past participles whose oblique masculine singular ends in -s are indeclinable in the masculine (see 12.49.3):

	MASCULINE	FEMININE
	prendre	
NS	pris	prise
OS	pris	prise
NP	pris	prises
OP	pris	prises

93.1. Weak past participles. All verbs with weak preterites (17.73) as well as some with strong preterites (18.77) have weak past participles—that is, i.e., past participles accented on the ending in Vulgar Latin. The following are the principal classifications of weak past participles:

(A)   *-ez* (NS) and *-é* (OS) for infinitives in *-er*; *-iez* (NS) and *-ié* (OS) for infinitives in *-ier*:

	MASCULINE	FEMININE		MASCULINE	FEMININE
	chanter			baillier	
NS	chantez	chantee	NS	bailliez	bailliee
OS	chanté	chantee	OS	baillié	bailliee
NP	chanté	chantees	NP	baillié	bailliees
OP	chantez	chantees	OP	bailliez	bailliees

(B)   *-iz* (NS) and *-i* (OS) for most verbs in *-ir* (with and without the *-iss-* infix):

	norir			sentir	
NS	norriz	norrie	NS	sentiz	sentie
OS	norri	norrie	OS	senti	sentie
NP	norri	norries	NP	senti	senties
OP	norriz	norries	OP	sentiz	senties

(C)   *-uz* (NS) and *-u* (OS) for some verbs in *-ir* without infix and many verbs in *-oir* and *-re*:

	ferir			paroir	
NS	feruz	ferue	NS	paruz	parue
OS	feru	ferue	OS	paru	parue
NP	feru	ferues	NP	paru	parues
OP	feruz	ferues	OP	paruz	parues

	vendre	
NS	venduz	vendue
OS	vendu	vendue
NP	vendu	vendues
OP	venduz	vendues

Like weak preterites, weak past participles can be identified by their characteristic vowel: *-é*, *-i*, or *-u*.

93.2. Strong past participles.   Many Old French verbs had past participles that had been accented on the stem in Vulgar Latin. These were of two types:

(A)   *-z* (NS) and *-t* (OS), with feminine in *-te*:

	MASCULINE	FEMININE		MASCULINE	FEMININE
	faire			plaindre	
NS	faiz	faite	NS	plainz	plainte
OS	fait	faite	OS	plaint	plainte
NP	fait	faites	NP	plaint	plaintes
OP	faiz	faites	OP	plainz	plaintes

(B)   *-s* (NS) and *-s* (OS), with feminine in *-se*:

	metre			prendre	
NS	mis	mise	NS	pris	prise
OS	mis	mise	OS	pris	prise
NP	mis	mises	NP	pris	prises
OP	mis	mises	OP	pris	prises

93.3. Alternative past participles.   Just as many verbs had two or more infinitives (see 10.37), a number had two or more past participles, frequently corresponding to different infinitives. One (or two) of the past participles might be strong while the other(s) might be weak:

asoudre	asouz (strong A, f.: asoute), asous (strong B, f.: asouse), assolu (weak C)
beneïr, benoïstre	beneïz, beneoiz
bolir, boillir	boliz, boluz, boilliz
cheoir	cheoiz, cheüz
coillir, cueldre	coilloiz, coilliz, coilluz
cosdre	cosuz, cosiz
covrir	coverz, covriz
cremir, criembre	cremiz, cremuz, crienz
ester	estez, esteüz
falir, faillir	fali, failli
issir	issiz, issuz
lire	liz, leüz
maleïr	maleïz, maleoiz
manoir, maindre	manuz, masuz, mes
naistre	nascuz, nez
nuisir, nuire	nuiz, neüz
pondre	pons, pos, poz, ponuz, ponduz

rompre	rompuz, roz
sentir	sentiz, sentuz
sivre, sevir, etc.	seviz, siviz, seüz
soloir, soudre	souz, sous, soluz
tolir, toudre	toloiz, toliz, toluz
veoir	veüz, vis

93.4. Homographs. Occasionally two verbs had the same past participle:

croire 'to believe' and croistre 'to grow':	creüz
ester 'to stand' and estovoir 'to be necessary':	esteüz
pooir 'to be able' and paistre 'to feed, to graze':	peüz
plaisir 'to please' and plovoir 'to rain':	pleüz
savoir 'to know' and sivre 'to follow':	seüz

94. Past Participles Used Actively

The past participle in Old French was used as a verbal form and, in an active sense, as an adjective indicating an agent who is doing or regularly performs an action:

> Aucasins s'en est tornés
> Molt dolans et *abosmés*. (15.7.1–2)
> Aucassin turned away
> Very sorrowful and distressed.

> Je sui tes homs *fianciés* et *plevés* (*Raoul*, 6732)
> I am your faithful and sworn man.

Among the more common past participles used as adjectives are *apris* 'skilled,' *araisnié* 'loquacious,' *baé* 'idler,' *celé* 'discreet,' *coneü* 'intelligent,' *destroit* 'cruel, ruthless, severe,' *forfait* 'guilty,' *juré* 'sworn by oath,' *mescreü* 'miscreant,' *osé* 'bold,' *porveü* 'prudent,' *recreü* 'recreant,' *trespensé* 'pensive,' *tressüé* 'bathed in sweat.'

95. Agreement of Past Participles

Participial agreement in Old French is not nearly so systematized as it is in the modern language. In verbs conjugated with *estre*, the past participle serves as a sort of verbal adjective (predicate nominative) and regularly agrees in case, number, and gender with the subject:

li bel cevalier (NP) qui *sont mort* (NP) (22:10b)
the fair knights who are dead

Nicole (NS, f.) *est* en prison *mise* (NS, f.) (21:0)
Nicolette is put in prison

Quant il (NS) en la chambre *est entrez* (NS) (13:460)
When he entered the room

With the auxiliary *avoir*, agreement is made not with the subject but with the direct object. There is agreement whether the object precedes the past participle, follows it, or is intermediary between it and the auxiliary:

si l'*ai* (FS) *levee* (FS) et *bautisie* (FS) (22:2b)
and I have raised her up and baptized her

S'espouse (FS) li *ont amenee.* (FS) (11:371)
They brought his wife to him.

sa fame *a eüz* (OP) deus fiz (OP) (2:35; cf. 1:15)
his wife has had two sons

(Il) *ont* molt grant joie (FS) *demenee* (FS) (15:522)
They were exceedingly joyful

s'avoient les espees (FP) *traites* (FP) desos les capes (23:10b)
and they had drawn their swords beneath their cloaks

The past participle also agrees with the object of an infinitive:

Li quens Garins de Biaucaire l'*a faite* mordrir (21:35c)
Count Garin of Beaucaire had her killed

A past participle may even agree with an unexpressed direct object (for omission see 7.26):

L'abaesse ⌃ li *a mostree* (8:262)
The abbess showed (the girl) to him

Et le pere ⌃ li *a donnee.* (15:510)
And the father gave (her) to him.

The past participle of an impersonal verb is usually neuter, whether or not the neuter pronoun *il* is expressed:

comme *est mesavenu* (10:353)
how unfortunate it is

um les (OP) *out* ainz *fait* (OS) aprés els bien barrer (16:36)
they had earlier had them locked behind them

But in Old French there is frequently no agreement where one would expect it:

> Sor moi en *est torné* (OS) li pis (NS) (3:86)
> The worst has turned upon me
>
> L'abaesse l'(FS) *a fet* (OS) aprendre. (7:238)
> The abbess had her educated.
>
> L'anel et le paille *ai trové*. (14:482)
> I have found the ring and the cloth.

Conversely, there is often agreement where there is no grammatical reason for it:

> Estroitement li *a baisiez* (NS? OP?) (13:462)
> She kissed him ardently

Phonology 22

Picard morphological characteristics

The following morphological characteristics appear in most Picard texts, although they all coexist with more common standard forms. Their presence in literary texts is often for purposes of meter or rhyme.

A. Picard generally uses *le* for the feminine singular article, both nominative and oblique, although *la* also occurs. Compare 21:36b *le riens* with 21:38b *la riens*. One occasionally encounters an analogical feminine nominative *li*:

> ja sui jou *li vostre amie* (21:26)

B. Among the pronouns, Picard frequently has *jou* for *je* and *mi, ti, si* for *moi, toi, soi*:

> avoc ciax voil *jou* aler, mais que j'aie Nicolete ma
> tresdouce amie aveuc *mi*. (22:11c)

C. Among the possessives, one encounters *men, ten, sen* for *mon, ton, son*; *me, te, se* for *ma, ta, sa*; and *no, vo* for *nostre, vostre*:

> par l'ame *ten* pere (22:185)
> *me* teste (23:5b); *te* tere (20:25b); *se* mere (20:25a)
> *vo* lit (22:4); *vo* arme (22:5)

D. Type IIIS preterites frequently have the alternation *eu/e* rather than *o/e*: *eu, euc* for *oi*; *eut* for *ot*; *eurent* for *orent*; *seut* for *sot*; *pleut* for *plot*; *peu, peuc* for *poi*; *peurent* for *porent*; and so forth. (See paradigms in 18.80.1.)

E. Certain verbal endings are typical of Picard: *-c* for the first singular present indicative and preterite (*je fac* [23:8], *cuic* [5, 66], *siec* [15,10.17]); *-omes* for the first person plural present indicative and future (*faisomes, alommes, seronmes, diromes*); *-iemes* for the first person plural imperfect indicative and conditional; *-ge, -che* in the present subjunctive (*prenge, diche, demeurche*); *-és* for *-ez* (see Phonology 17).

F. Picard (and Walloon) have special infinitive forms for *veoir, seoir,* and *cheoir*: *veïr, vir; seïr, sir*; and *cheïr, caïr*.

chapter 23

Reading and Textual Analysis, Selection 12

Aucassin returns grieving from his conversation with the viscount. While Aucassin is in his room feeling sorry for himself, Count Bougar launches his attack. Desperate, Count Garin promises that if Aucassin will fight with him, he may have Nicolette. Aucassin hastens to the attack and captures Count Bougar. He asks his father to free Nicolette in exchange for the count, but when his father refuses to keep his promise, Aucassin frees Bougar. Garin, realizing that he cannot cure Aucassin's lovesickness, has his son thrown into prison. Soon afterwards, Nicolette eludes her jailors and comes to the foot of the tower in which Aucassin is still lamenting his fate. She tells him that she can never be his and that therefore it is better for her to flee across the sea. There follows the amusing conversation found in our final reading selection.

23:1   Qant Aucassins oï dire Nicolete qu'ele s'en voloit aler en autre païs, en lui n'ot que courecier.

23:2   "Bele douce amie," fait il, "vos n'en irés mie, car dont m'ariis vos mort;

23:3a   et li premiers qui vos verroit ne qui vous porroit,

23:3b   il vos prenderoit lués et vos meteroit a son lit, si vos asoignenteroit.

23:4a   Et puis que vos ariiés jut en lit a home, s'el mien non, or ne quidiés mie que j'atendisse

23:4b	tant que je trovasse coutel dont je me peüsce ferir el cuer et ocirre.
23:5a	Naie voir, tant n'atenderoie je mie; ains m'esquelderoie de si lonc que je verroie une maisiere u une bisse pierre,
23:5b	s'i hurteroie si durement me teste que j'en feroie les ex voler et que je m'escerveleroie tos.
23:6	Encor ameroie je mix a morir de sifaite mort que je seüsce que vos eüsciés jut en lit a home, s'el mien non."
23:7	"A!" fait ele, "je ne quit mie que vous m'amés tant con vos dites; mais je vos aim plus que vos ne faciés mi."
23:8	"Avoi!" fait Aucassins, "bele douce amie, ce ne porroit estre que vos m'amissiés tant que je fac vos:
23:9a	fenme ne puet tant amer l'oume con li hom fait le fenme;
23:9b	car li amors de le fenme est en son oeul et en son le cateron de sa mamele et en son l'orteil del pié,
23:9c	mais li amors de l'oume est ens el cué plantee, dont ele ne puet iscir."
23:10a	La u Aucassins et Nicolete parloient ensanble, et les escargaites de le vile venoient tote une rue,
23:10b	s'avoient les espees traites desos les capes,
23:10c	car li quens Garins lor avoit conmandé que, se il le pooient prendre, qu'i l'ocesissent.
23:11	Et li gaite qui estoit sor le tor les vit venir, et oï qu'il aloient de Nicolete parlant et qu'il le maneçoient a occirre.
23:12	"Dix!" fait il, "con grans damages de si bele mescinete, s'il l'ocient!
23:13a	Et molt seroit grans aumosne, se je li pooie dire, par quoi il ne s'aperceüscent et qu'ele s'en gardast;
23:13b	car s'i l'ocient, dont iert Aucassins mes damoisiax mors, dont grans damages ert."

23:14	Li gaite fu mout vaillans,
23:15	Preus et cortois et saçans.
23:16	Il a comencié uns cans
23:17	Ki biax fu et avenans:
23:18	"Mescinete o le cuer franc,
23:19	Cors as gent et avenant,
23:20	Le poil blont et reluisant,
23:21	Vairs les ex, ciere riant.
23:22	Bien le voi a ton sanblant:
23:23	Parlés as a ton amant
23:24	Qui por toi se va morant.
23:25	Jel te di et tu l'entens:

23:26   Garde toi des souduians
23:27   Ki par ci te vont querant,
23:28   Sous les capes les nus brans;
23:29   Forment te vont maneçant,
23:30   Tost te feront messeant,
23:31   S'or ne t'i gardes."

23:1   Between the end of the preceding reading selection and the beginning of this, several episodes have been omitted. They are summarized in the Reading and Textual Analysis section.
23:2   *ariis*: some editors correct to *ariés* or *ariiés*.
23:9b   *cateron*: another *hapax legomenon* (cf. note to 21:12), but one whose meaning is perfectly clear.
23:10a   "While Aucassin and Nicolette were speaking in this manner, the watchmen . . ."
23:10c   *qu'i = qu'il*; the *l* has been lost by assimilation.
23:13a   *se je li pooie dire = se je le li pooie dire*. For the regular omission of *le* in this construction, see 7.26.
23:13b   *s'i = s'il*; see note to 23:10c.
23:16   *uns cans* for *un cant*. The scribe perhaps wrote NS *uns cans* in anticipation of *biax* and *avenans* in line 17, rather than the proper OS dir. obj. form *un cant*.

96. Old French Versification

With the exception of a few scientific treatises, all Old French compositions from the early period until the late twelfth century were in verse. The system of versification was based upon the number of syllables in a line. Eight-, ten-, and twelve-syllable lines were the most common, but the verse passages in *Aucassin and Nicolette* are in seven-syllable lines, and lyric poets on occasion used lines ranging from one to as many as sixteen syllables. Eight-syllable lines are usually referred to as **octosyllables**, ten-syllable lines as **decasyllables**, and twelve-syllable lines as **alexandrines** after the popular *Roman d'Alexandre*, one of the earliest works composed in this meter.

96.1. Counting syllables.   For syllable division, see Phonology 4. The principal difficulty in syllable counting is determining the value of a final unstressed feminine -*e*. If it occurs at the end of a line it is not counted, and such lines are said to be **feminine**:

En sa des-tre main tint chas-cuns s'es-pe- e nu-(e) (18:2)
 1   2   3   4   5   6   7   8   9 10 11 12

If interior before a consonant (e.g., syllables 4 and 11 in the example just cited), it is counted—except at the caesura (see Section 96.4). When interior before a vowel, the -e is generally not counted:

Con-tr(e) els tuz le re-tint, de rien ne s'es-ba-hi (19:3)
1   2 3 4 5 6   7   8   9   10 11 12

Al mar-tyr saint De-nis, quidul-ce Fran-c(e) a - pent (19:13)
1   2   3   4   5   6   7   8 9 10   11 12

Note that the verbal ending -ent is treated as unstressed -e:

Ce-le pa-ro-le ra-con-ter(ent) (2:50)
1   2   3 4 5   6   7   8

All lines that do not end in unstressed feminine -e are termed **masculine**.

96.2. Assonance. Early French epic poems (and a few nonepic works such as *Aucassin and Nicolette*) were written in assonant verse. Assonance requires the repetition in succeeding lines of the final stressed vowel, which may or may not be followed by random consonants and/or unstressed -e. Assonant lines are grouped in strophes of varying length termed *laisses*. The following words form a masculine assonance in -o- in *laisse* 136 of the *Song of Roland* (6, 106–16): *corns, cors, or, forz, blois, ost, port, parolt, mort, colps, trop.* A feminine assonance in -u:e is found in *laisse* 133 (6, 63–70): *buche, sunet, lunge, respundre, tutes, hume, encuntre, mençunge.* Note that the stressed element of a diphthong (e.g., *o* of the diphthong *oi* in *blois*) may assonate with a single vowel.

The verse portions of *Aucassin and Nicolette* consist of seven-syllable assonant lines arranged in *laisses* of irregular length. In the reading selection for Chapter 20, the assonance is masculine -i; in that for Chapter 21, it is feminine -i:e.

96.3 Rhyme. Rhyme was gradually introduced in the course of the twelfth century and eventually supplanted assonance altogether. Two lines must have the same final stressed vowel and succeeding consonant(s) in order to rhyme properly. Rhymes with vowels only are termed "poor": *quida : ira : buta : rehusa : sacha; nue : besague : veüe*. Rhymes with a vowel and following consonant are considered "sufficient": *ordonez : armez : savrez : remuez : vendrez.* Most Old French verse has poor or sufficient rhyme, although occasionally richer rhymes are encountered: *ameront : orront* (3:77–78), *seroiz : verroiz* (4:111–12). In Old French versification there was no requirement that masculine and feminine rhymes alternate, and most texts have a preponderance of masculine rhymes; there are, for example, 6,180 masculine rhyming lines in the *Life of St. Thomas Becket* versus 580 feminine.

All of Marie de France's *lais*, including "Fresne," were written in the meter that was to become associated with narratives in the courtly manner: octosyllabic rhyming couplets. Guernes' *Life of St. Thomas Becket* is composed of alexandrine (12-syllable) lines divided into stanzas of five lines each. The rhyme generally changes with each succeeding stanza, but occasionally two or more consecutive stanzas have the same rhyme.

96.4. The caesura. Decasyllabic (10-syllable) and alexandrine (12-syl-lable) lines are regularly divided into two parts, called **hemistichs**, by a pause or **caesura**. In decasyllabic lines, the caesura falls most frequently after the fourth syllable but occasionally after the fifth or sixth. In alexandrines, the caesura occurs regularly after the sixth syllable:

E mais-tr(e) E-du-vard Grim // l'a-veit for-ment sai-si (19:1)
1 2   3   4   5   6   7 8 9 10 11 12

En-bra-cié par de-sus // quant l'o-rent en-va-ï (19:2)
1 2 3 4 5 6   7   8 9 10 11 12

Con-tr(e) els tuz le re-tint // de rien ne s'es-ba-hi (19:3)
1   2 3 4 5 6   7 8 9 10 11 12

A feminine -*e* at the caesura is not counted in the meter, even when the following hemistich begins with a consonant. A line in which such a feminine -*e* occurs is said to have an **epic caesura**, since such caesuras are common in epic verse:

Main sur vos-tr(e) ar-ce-vesqu(e) // me-tez a grant pe-chié (19:9)
1   2 3   4 5 6   7 8 9 10   11 12

E as sainz de l'i-glis(e) // se co-man-d(e) er-ram-ment (19:14)
1 2 3   4 5 6   7 8 9   10   11   12

Car la hors le vo-lei(ent) // u os-ci-r(e) u lï-er (18:54)
1 2 3 4 5 6   7 8 9   10 1112

In the last example, remember that in versification the verbal ending -*ent* is treated like unstressed -*e*.

97. The -*ant* Form: Present Participle and Gerund

Modern French distinguishes a present participle, which refers to a transitory state and is invariable (*une mère aimant son fils*); a verbal adjective, which translates a permanent state and agrees in gender and number with the noun it modifies (*une mère aimante*); and a gerund, which indicates means or manner and is always preceded by the preposition *en* (*en aimant*). The situation in Old French, however, was much less clear. There was a tendency to confuse the present participle and the verbal adjective, since both were declined, and the "gerund" in Old French was often not preceded by *en*. To avoid the introduction of unnecessary subtleties, we proceed on the assumption that "present participles" modify nouns and "gerunds" modify verbs.

97.1. Present participle: forms. Used as a present participle or verbal adjective, the *-ant* form agrees in gender, number, and case with the noun or pronoun to which it refers. It is declined as a Type II adjective (see 12.49.2):

	MASCULINE	FEMININE
NS	dolanz	dolant, dolanz*
OS	dolant	dolant
NP	dolant	dolanz
OP	dolanz	dolanz

*Feminine NS often ends in *-z* by analogy with masculine NS. Feminine present participles occasionally were declined like Type I adjectives but never became generalized in Old French. In "Fresne" we find *mesdisante* (2:28) for *mesdisant* and *dolente* (3:71) for *dolant*.

97.2. Present participle: functions. The *-ant* form functions principally as a verbal adjective:

> . . .enfant avoit
> Petit em berz et *alaitant* (6:194–95)
> . . .she had a child
> (Which was) tiny in the cradle and nursing

> . . .Ele ert fainte et orgueilleuse
> Et *mesdisante* et envieuse. (2:27–28)
> . . .She was deceitful and proud
> And slandering and envious.

It is frequently found as a predicate nominative after *estre*:

> Nus hom n'est si esbahis,
> Tant *dolans* ni entrepris (20:10–11)
> No one is so troubled,
> So sad or overwhelmed

In reference to the subject, *oiant* and *veant* form an invariable circumstantial complement meaning "before, in front of, in the presence of" (literally: "within hearing/sight of"):

Oiant toz dit, nu cele mie:
"Tu es ma fille." (13:453–54)
(Her mother) before everyone said, she did not hide it at all:
"You are my daughter."

Voiant le pueple, nos veut prendre,
Faire ardoir et venter la cendre. (13, 285–86)
In the presence of the people he wants to capture us,
Have us burned, and scatter our ashes to the winds.

98. Gerund: Functions

Used most commonly in a verbal paraphrase with *aler* or *estre*, the *-ant* form indicates an action in progress:

Parlé as a ton amant
Qui por toi se *va morant* (23:23–24)
You have spoken to your lover
Who is dying because of you

Forment te *vont manecant* (23:29)
They are threatening you very much

Si l'orrat Carles, ki *est* as porz *passant*. (6, 13)
Charles, who is going through the pass, will hear it.

As the contexts of these examples show, this construction was particularly useful to poets writing assonant *laisses*. Occasionally the durative aspect is overlooked and it functions as a simple tense:

Car chevalcez! Pur qu'*alez arestant*? (6, 93)
Ride on! Why are you stopping?

De sun cervel le temple en *est rumpant*. (6, 74)
The temple of his brain has burst.

It may function as a circumstantial complement to the principal verb:

il fut mort *cunquerant* (6, 346)
he died conquering (i.e., victorious)

il vindrent, *ferant* des esperons, vers nous. (26, 77)
they came, striking with their spurs, toward us.

It is often encountered after prepositions, in which case it usually takes a direct object, which is generally placed between the preposition and the gerund:

> Servi vos ai *par* mes armes *portant* (*Raoul*, 682)
> I have served you by carrying my weapons
>
> S'en eissirent *al coc chantant* (*Brut*, 997)
> They left at the crowing of the cock

The *-ant* forms of a few verbs can function as verbal nouns:

> En mon *dormant*
> In my sleep
>
> Tot mon *vivant*
> All my life

Compare the use of the infinitive after prepositions and as a verbal noun (10.38.2).

99. The Subjunctive

(For the forms of the subjunctive, see 5.17.2.)

Whereas the indicative actualizes a process and situates it in time, the subjunctive shows that the process is only potential—envisaged but not actualized. Therefore, although there are four tenses for the subjunctive in Old French—present, imperfect, perfect, and pluperfect—they do not serve to situate an action in time. The present subjunctive conceives of a process as potential from the perspective of the present looking toward the future:

> Ja Dix ne me *doinst* riens que je li demant, quant ere cevaliers,
>   ne monte a ceval, ne que *voise* a estor ne a bataille,
>   la u je *fiere* cevalier ni autres mi. . . . (20:27a–b)
> May God never give me anything I ask of him were I to become a
>   knight, and mount a horse, and go into a skirmish or battle,
>   in which I might slay a knight or be slain. . . .

The imperfect subjunctive envisages an event from the perspective of the present looking toward the past:

> puis que vos ariiés jut en lit a home, s'el mien non, or
> ne quidiés mie que *j'atendisse* tant que je *trovasse* coutel. . . . (23:4a–b)
> after you have slept in another man's bed, don't think
> that I would wait until I had found a knife. . . .

The compound subjunctive tenses view an action as accomplished:

> il ne *fust* uns seux jors *ajornés* qu'il ne fust
>   as portes . . . de le vile (20:16c)
> Not a single day dawned that he wasn't
>   at the gates . . . of the town
> Cuida qu'aucuns les *eüst pris*
> En larrecin (6:185–86)
> He thought that someone
> Had stolen them

As this last example shows, the compound subjunctive tenses can incidentally indicate anteriority; however, their principal function is to mark the desired or perceived accomplishment of the action. In 7:216–17, the intent of the abbess' command is the completion of the action; there is no anteriority, since the action is to be accomplished in the immediate future.

Old French writers particularly favored the imperfect subjunctive, and it is often found where one would anticipate a present subjunctive:

> A l'abaesse demandoient
> Sa bele niece lor *mostrast*
> Et que *sofrist* qu'a eus *parlast* (7:250–52)
> They asked the abbess
> To show them her fine niece
> And permit her to speak with them

Here the action envisages the future, and one would therefore expect the present subjunctive in Old French. In our texts the ratio of imperfect subjunctive to present subjunctive is better than two to one.

100.   The Subjunctive in Independent Clauses

In principal clauses the subjunctive expresses a wish, desire, command, or exclamation. The clause is occasionally introduced by *que*, *si*, or *car*:

Son non *face* l'enfant nommer (1:18)
Let him give the child his name

Que la tere *soit* maleoite dont ele fut amenee en cest païs! (21:3)
May the land be damned from whence she was brought to this country!

Venget li reis, si nus purrat venger. (6, 54)
Let the king come, he will be able to avenge us.

It may express simple intention:

si li *donasse* un baceler qui du pain li gaegnast par honor (21:7b)
and (I intend) to give her a young husband who will provide her an
     honorable living

In the second person the subjunctive functions as a polite form of the
imperative:

> nes *deüssiez* laissier (16:30)
> you should not leave them
> (or) you ought not to have left them

For certain verbs (*avoir, estre, savoir, voloir, pooir*) the forms of the subjunctive are always used for the imperative;

> N'*aiez* pas paor! (16b, 26)
> Don't be afraid!
>
> Or *soies* liés (5, 199)
> Now be happy
>
> *Saciés* bien que, se je en muir. . . . (21:38a)
> Know well that, should I die. . . .

101.   The Subjunctive in Dependent Clauses

Since the subjunctive views a process as potential rather than actualized, it occurs regularly in Old French in dependent clauses after many
verbs and conjunctions that imply some hesitation regarding the eventual
realization of the process.

101.1. After verbs of desire, obligation, request, command.   The subjunctive is used after verbs of desire, obligation, request, command,
advice, fear, or prohibition such as *voloir, doner, plaire, sofrir, consentir, prier,
demander, parler, dire, mander, comander, enorter, conseillier, loer, criembre, doter,
garder, defendre*:

> Ge *criem* qu'il ne me *face* ennui. (*Béroul*, 2422)
> I fear that he may harm me.
>
> Sovente foiz a lui *parlerent*,
> C'une gentil fame *espousast*
> Et de cele se *delivrast*. (10:324–26)
> They often urged him (lit.: spoke to him)
> To wed a well-born woman
> And free himself from (Fresne).

> Li arcevesque *a conseillié*
> Que *soit* ainsi la nuit *lessié* (15:503–04)
> The archbishop advised
> That it be left as it was for the night

The syntax of Old French is flexible enough to allow most of these verbs to be followed by the indicative when the realization of the process is implied:

> Et *crient* que, s'il vit longement,
> Qu'il ne l'en *laissera* neient. (Troie, 747–48)
> And they are afraid that if he lives long
> He will not leave him any of it.

101.2. After verbs of opinion. The subjunctive may appear after verbs of opinion (such as *penser, croire, cuidier, sembler, estre a vis*) as a grammatical reflex (as in modern French after certain conjunctions), whether or not uncertainty is implied:

> *Cuida* qu'aucuns les *eüst pris*
> En larrecin (6:185)
> He thought that someone
> Had stolen them

> Ome *senbles* qui *core* a chiens,
> Qui *chast* sa beste por ataindre. (13, 40–41)
> You look like a man who runs dogs,
> Who pursues his game in order to capture it.

When, however, these verbs assert the speaker's certainty of a state or action, they are followed by the indicative:

> Je *cuit* que li pailles *est* sons. (12:430)
> I believe that the cloth is hers.

> Ne doute rien, bien set et *croit*
> Que le Fresne sa fille *estoit*. (13:451–52)
> She had no doubt, she knew and believed firmly
> That Fresne was her daughter.

101.3. After impersonal verbs of necessity, possibility, or doubt. The subjunctive is used after impersonal verbs of necessity, possibility, or doubt (such as *covenir, estovoir, chaloir, estre droiz, estre mestier*):

> *Dame, il couvient que* vos *railliez* au roi Artu vostre seignor
>   (14, 10–11)
> Milady, you must return to your husband King Arthur

Ne li *chalt*, sire, de quel mort nous *murjuns*. (*Roland*, 227)
He does not care, sir, how we die.

. . . et ne *fu* pas *mestier* que il *feust* avant *venu*. (*Joinville*, 182)
. . . and it was not necessary that he come forward.

101.4. After negative, interrogative, or hypothetical main clauses.   The
subjunctive is used after negative, interrogative, or hypothetical main
clauses:

"Sire," fet Lancelos au roi, "*vos plest* il que ge le *face* issi?" (14, 80–81)
"Sir," said Lancelot to the king, "does it please you that I do so?"

Lié seroient, *s'il avoit oir*
Qui aprés lui *peüst* avoir
Sa terre (10:327–29)
They would be happy if he had an heir
Who could inherit his land after (his death)

For the widespread use of the subjunctive in conditional sentences, see
10.41.

101.5. Following superlatives or their equivalents.   The subjunctive is
used following superlatives or their equivalents:

Nus hom n'est si esbahis . . .
Se il l'oit, ne *soit garis* (20:10–13)
No one is so troubled . . .
That he would not be healed if he heard it

il n'a si rice home en France, se tu vix sa fille avoir, que tu ne l'*aies* (20:30b)
there is no man so powerful in France, if you wish to have his
        daughter, that you'll not have her

N'i ot un seul . . .
Por sa franchise ne l'*amast*
Ne la *servist* et l'*anorast*. (9:318–20)
There was not a single person . . .
Who did not love, serve and honor
Her because of her noble actions.

Ausi ert Enyde *plus bele*
Que nule dame ne pucele
Qui *fust trovee* an tot le monde. (11, 33–35)
Thus was Enide more beautiful
Than any lady or maiden
Who might be found in all the world.

101.6. After hypothetical comparatives.   The subjunctive is used after many hypothetical comparatives (introduced by conjunctions such as *si com*, *ensement com*, *tant com*, *plus que*):

> *Ensement cum* la mort *atendist* de sun gré (17:2)
> Just as if he were willingly awaiting death
>
> je vos aim *plus que* vos ne *faciés* mi (23:7)
> I love you more than you do me

101.7. In adverbial clauses of time.   The subjunctive is used in adverbial clauses of time when the event has not yet been realized:

> Quant no fille ravon trovee . . .
> *Ainz que* li pechiez *fust doublez*. (14:491–93)
> Since we have found our daughter . . .
> Before the sin was doubled.
>
> E prient Deu qu'il guarisset Rollant
> *Josque il vengent* el camp cumunement (6, 147–48)
> And they pray God to protect Roland
> Until they arrive together on the battlefield.

101.8. In adverbial clauses suggesting alternatives.   The subjunctive is used in adverbial clauses suggesting alternatives, often introduced by indefinite expressions like *qui que*, *quel que*, *quanque*, *quoique*, *ou que*:

> Dunc l'en unt al mustier, *u voille u nun*, mené (17:1)
> Then they brought him to the church, whether he wished it or not
>
> *Qui qu'en eüst* joie, Aucassins n'en fu mie liés (21:36a)
> Although someone else might rejoice about it, Aucassin was not at all
>   happy
>
> il ne veut estre cevaliers, ne faire point de *quanque* faire *doie* (21:4)
> he did not want to be a knight, nor do anything he should do

Phonology 23

Picard was the major northern dialect of Old French. It shared traits both with Norman and Anglo-Norman to the west and with dialects to the east, notably Walloon and Lotharingian, the dialect of Lorraine. This final phonology section discusses traits common to Picard, Norman, Anglo-Norman, Walloon, Lotharingian, Champenois, and the southeastern dialects (Burgundian, Bourbonnais, Nivernais, Franche-Comté).

The following chart lists the characteristics that distinguish Picard and its neighboring dialects:

TRAITS	P	N	A-N	W	L	C	SE
1. a > ei (ai)	x	xx		x	xx	x	xx
2. -el + consonant > -iau	xx	x		x		x	
3. e + nasal stays /ẽ/	xx	x	xx	xx			
4. -aige, -ache for -age	xx	x		xx	xx	x	xx
5. ie > i	x			xx	xx	x	
6. iee > ie	xx	x		xx	xx	x	xx
7. introduction of weak e /ə/	x	x		x			
8. c, g + a does not palatalize	xx	xx	x				
9. c, g palatalizes before e, i	xx	xx	x				
10. absence of glide sound	xx			xx	xx	x	xx
11. Germanic w-	xx	x	x	xx	xx	x	x
12. o > ou, o, u		xx	xx	x	x	x	xx

xx — Occurs in most texts.
x — Occurs in certain texts only or scattered through a number of texts.

1. See Phonology 19.1.
2. Common in Picard, this trait can be found occasionally in texts in most other dialects, including Francien.
3. See Phonology 19.7.
4. It is not clear whether -aige represents the pronunciation /ɛ ǰ ə/; the i may simply be "parasitic" (see section on Norman in Phonology 19).
5. The reduction of the diphthong -ie- to -i- in Picard, Walloon, and Lotharingian is similar to the leveling of that same diphthong to -e- in the west, south, and southwest (Phonology 19.4).
6. This development is more widespread than the reduction of -ie- to -i-, which occurred principally in Walloon and Lotharingian. The shift from /ieə/ to /iə/ is important in Picard, Walloon, Lotharingian, and the southeastern dialects, and it is found also in some Norman and Champenois texts.
8 and 9. These changes, typical of Picard, are common also in Norman but not in Anglo-Norman.
10. Walloon, Lotharingian, and Burgundian, like Picard, did not develop a glide sound between l'r, n'r and m'l: polre, poure (=poudre); cenre (=cendre); ensanle (=ensemble). Owing to the influence of the central French scriptoria, ml is rarely found in written texts.
12. For the dialectal treatments of accented o, see Phonology 19.2.

Norman

A comparison of the traits shared with Anglo-Norman (outlined in Phonology 19) and those shared with Picard (listed above) shows that the principal distinction between Norman and Anglo-Norman is the treatment of the consonants *c* and *g* before *a, e, i,* and *yod* (traits 8 and 9).

Walloon

In addition to sharing all the aforementioned traits (except 8 and 9) with Picard, Walloon also incorporates most Picard morphological traits:

le for feminine *la*
me, te, se for *ma, ta, sa*
me(n), te(n), se(n) for *mon, ton, son*
mi, ti, si for *moi, toi, soi*
no, vo for *nostre, vostre*
-omes for the first person plural present indicative and future

Developments that distinguish Walloon from Picard include: *lh* for palatal *l* (*conselh* = *conseil*), *ju* rather than *jou* for *je*, and the palatalized nominative pronouns *ilh, cilh*. Imperfect indicative endings in *-(i)eve* were maintained. The diphthongs *ai, oi, ui* were reduced to *a, o, u*: *fare* = *faire*, *avoent* = *avoient, destrure* = *destruire. e* (< Latin accented free *A*) > *ei*:

TÁLEM > tel > teil
PÁTREM > pere > peire

o (< Latin accented free *O*) occasionally diphthongized to *oi*:

DǪS > dos, dous > dois
HÓRAM > ore, oure > oire

"Parasitic" *i* after *e* and *a* was frequent: *queil, abbei, freire* for *quel, abbé, frere*. This *i* was also common in Lotharingian (see next section) and Norman (Phonology 19).

Lotharingian

Lotharingian shares most phonological characteristics with Picard and Walloon, but it does not favor many of their morphological traits. It does not regularly use *men, ten, sen; le* for feminine *la*; or the ending *-omes*. It prefers *jeu, ceu* as the stressed forms of *je, ce*, and it often has *lo* for the masculine article *le*.

In Lotharingian, *a* palatalized to *e* before the palatals and dentals and sometimes before *r* (spelled *ai, ei, e: vaiches, maleides, perle* for *vaches, malades, parle*). *A* velarized before *l* and *bl* (spelled *au: loiaul, corporaul, tauble, honorau-*

ble). *U* + nasal did not palatalize to /y/ but became /õ/ *chascon, common, aukon, londi*).

L was lost before a consonant (*atre, assi, chade, mavais* for *autre, aussi, chaude, mauvaise*).

Final *-r* was lost after the high vowels *e, i, u* in the thirteenth century. This led to considerable scribal confusion, especially in the spellings of verbal forms.

The imperfect indicative endings were *-eve (-eive), -ieve*.

Particularly prevalent is the introduction of a "parasitic" *i* after *a* and *e* (*jai, praiel, teil* for *ja, prael, tel*).

The first person singular present indicative of *estre* and *pooir* was often *seux* and *peux* (for Francien *sui* and *puis*).

In orthography, there was constant confusion between *s* and *x, s* and *c, s* and *z*: *plux, medixant, ces* (= *ses*), *se* (= *ce*), *mors*.

Burgundian

Although Burgundian, Bourbonnais, Nivernais, and Franche-Comté were all spoken in the southeastern region, Burgundian was by far the principal dialect of the area, and the others are generally subsumed under this name.

Burgundian is particularly characterized by three traits: development of accented E to *ei* (see Phonology 19.8), the reduction of *iee* (< ATA) to *ie* (see Picard trait 5), and the absence of a glide consonant in the groups *n'r, l'r, m'l* (see Picard trait 10).

Burgundian shares many important characteristics with Lotharingian: velarization of *a* before *bl* (*tauble, convenaubles*), the insertion of "parasitic" *i* after *e* and *a*, preference for the masculine singular article *lo*, nasalization of *u* > /õ/, and development of *a* > *ei*.

Traits that distinguish Burgundian from Lotharingian include the lack of Germanic *w-* (although it is found in some texts from the Franche-Comté); the use of initial *h-* before forms of *avoir* (*havoir, ha, havoye, hont*); the introduction of *-h-* to indicate hiatus (*hehu, recehu, vehoir,* for Francien *eü, receü, vëoir*); and the development of the -ÁRĬŬM ending to *-er, -eir*. The development of the diphthong *ei* to *oi* was not checked by a following nasal:

PÓENAM > /péna/ > *peine* > *poine* (Francien *peine*)
SENĬÓREM > *seignor* > *soignor* (Francien *seignour, seigneur*)

Checked *e* was sometimes diphthongized to *ei* and *oi*, then reduced to *o*:

SĬCCŬM > *sécco* > *seic* > *soic* > *soc* (Francien *sec*)
Similarly: *troze, soze* (for Francien *treize, seize*)

Champenois

The important annual fairs at Lagny, Troyes, Bar-sur-Aube, and Pro-vins and the active patronage of the local nobility made the region of Champagne around Troyes a major center of literary activity during the twelfth century. One of the leading writers of Old French, Chrétien de Troyes, composed his Arthurian romances in Champenois. It was also used by the lyric poet Gace Brulé, by the chronicler Villehardouin, and by the epic poet Bertrand de Bar-sur-Aube; and manuscripts of such impor-tant works as the *Roman de Renart*, Joinville's *Chronicles*, and *La Mort le roi Artu* were copied in Champenois.

The dialect of Champagne is phonologically close to that of the Ile-de-France. The area, however, was a crossroads for language as well as for trade: manuscripts from its southern parts may show the influence of Burgundian, those from the east and southeast may reveal traces of Lotharingian, and those from the north occasionally display Picard, Wal-loon, and Lotharingian traits.

The following Champenois traits do not appear in the table at the beginning of this section: differentiation of *eau* to *iau* (*biau, miaudres*); lowering of *e* to *a* before a nasal or before *l* and *r* (*ofrande, jame, als = eus, pardirent*); lowered forms *en, an* for the indefinite pronoun *on*; *ein* for Francien *ain* and *ain* for Francien *ein* (*einsi, seint, ataindre, frain*); "parasitic" *i*, particularly in eastern Champagne (*compaigne, Gascoigne, barraige*); occasion-al use of the masculine singular oblique article *lo* for *le* (cf. Burgundian).

textual emendations

I.

The lay of "Fresne" exists in two manuscripts: British Museum, Harley 978, folios 148d–152c (referred to as "H"); and Bibliothèque Nationale, f. fr. 1104, folios 39d–43a ("S"). H, written in England in the mid-thirteenth century, is widely regarded as the better; it has been faithfully edited by Alfred Ewert, *Marie de France: Lais*. H is, nonetheless, a very corrupt text, and an excellent critical edition, based on H but using S where needed, has been prepared by Jean Rychner, *Les Lais de Marie de France*, which preserves the Anglo-Norman orthography. A hybrid text edited by Ernest Hoepffner, *Marie de France: Les Lais*, is based on H but uses the Francien orthography of S. My edition of "Fresne" is based on S and departs from it only where that manuscript is manifestly less satisfactory than H:

12	sires	97	feroient
16	Ditant de force	158	arestue
17	Lentremetra	187	nen ot
45	mester	190	Il en avoit dieu mercie
46	si	191	Jus lavoit mis
47	est de ceste	207	virent
60	nen pot plus fere	214	il va c.
67	enceintee	220	Lenfanz
69	*Lines 65–66 are repeated in error after this line*	221	A la dame lavoit m.
		247	voit
76	sires	252	soufist
78	Ceus qui ceste	254	coit
85	Or ai .ii.	268	car il i r.

279	Molt i	423	o soi
283	la parla	432	lui
291	vo dame	435	ne me
322	Que molt la tint en grant	441	Lab. le me b.
	chierte	443	anel li b.
323	Tant que sa gent len ont	447	avoit a.
	blasme	466	ce
324	A molt grant mal li ont	470	Je vos
	torne	480	a eus p.
372	i est o lui	489	ce sui je liez
376	preist	494	fet ele
386	tant *repeated*	511	lui
389–92 *omitted*			

II.

The selections from Guernes de Pont-Sainte-Maxence's *Life of St. Thomas Becket* essentially follow Emmanuel Walberg's critical edition of manuscript B (Wolfenbüttel). I have, however, restored the manuscript readings in a number of instances (my lines 16:17, 16:32, 17:13, 17:21, 18:8, 18:20, and 19:35), and I have modernized the punctuation. The texts in this volume correspond to Walberg's lines 5121–25, 5146–50, 5161–63, 5176–80, 5371–75, 5381–410, 5456–555, 5566–95, 5606–15, and 5631–45. The following rejected readings from B have been replaced by Walberg's critical readings:

16.38	il quidouent prendre le	18:25	le corn
	saint u d.	18:30	granz malveistiez
17:3	altre i unt b.	18:31	le ele
17:5	se *omitted*	18:33	mesurez
17:16	Quant vindrent icil q.	18:35	Beneit est le altres o.
17:20	aveit	18:45	prestres
17:24	qui sunt fol n.	18:47	Desuz
17:26	hum *omitted*	18:48	quil pristrent
17:27	nostre v.	18:58	ne sevrer
17:35	Jo irai	19:1	Edward
18:6	le pilier	19:6	Mais maistre Edward
18:11	Del nun	19:10	Mais nest pur nul feirie
18:15	Le col del m.		ne pur mustier laissie
18:22	qua cele feiz sainz	19:12	a ses oilz
	Thomas saira	19:16	vint premiers
18:23	e sacha	19:25	E le braz maistre Edward

III.

Aucassin and Nicolette exists in a single manuscript, Bibliothèque Natio-nale, f. fr. 2168, written in the late thirteenth century. It has been frequently and well edited. My edition is faithful to the manuscript except in the following instances, which most editors agree to emend:

20:8	biax est li dis
21:2	Sire visquens
21:5a	puis et avoir
21:33	far
21:34	*The rubricator mistakenly painted a capital* A, *rather than* N *of* Nicolete
22:1	visquens
22:10c	li bien s.
22:13	ise se d.
23:20	blont et avenant

glossary

Abbreviations

1	first person
2	second person
3	third person
= = >	spelling variant of
adj.	adjective
adv.	adverb
art.	article
aux.	auxiliary
comp.	comparative
cond.	conditional
conj.	conjunction
dem.	demonstrative
f.	feminine
FP	feminine plural
FS	feminine singular
fut.	future
imperf.	imperfect
indef.	indefinite
inf.	infinitive
interj.	interjection
interrog.	interrogative
m.	masculine
n.	neuter
nom.	nominative

NP   masculine nominative plural
NS   masculine nominative singular
num.   number
obj.   object
OP   masculine oblique plural
OS   masculine oblique singular
phr.   phrase
pl.   plural
poss.   possessive
pp.   past participle
prep.   preposition
pres.   present (indicative, unless otherwise stated)
pret.   preterite
pron.   pronoun
sg.   singular
subjunc. subjunctive

Indented subordinate entries are orthographic or morphological variants of their unindented headword. Such forms are also entered in the
main alphabetical sequence when they are not adjacent to their headword.

a #1 1:14, 2:33, 2:58, 3:72, 3:88, 4:106,
5:140, 5:174, 6:192, 7:213, 7:219,
7:221, 7:250, 7:252, 8:253, 8:259,
8:282, 10:324, 10:340, 11:375, 11:378,
11:379, 11:385, 12:423, 12:424,
14:477, 15:516, 16:6, 16:7, 16:10,
16:12, 16:44, 16:47, 16:48, 17:7, 17:35,
17:37, 18:19, 18:32, 18:34, 18:59,
19:12, 19:26, 19:34, 19:39, 19:40,
19:44, 20:27a, 21:13, 22:2a, 22:4,
23:3b, 23:23. [prep. denoting
direction toward] to, toward, at, in,
before, with, on <enclitic in *al, as
#1, au #1*>.
a #2 2:40, 10:337, 16:15, 16:50, 21:38b,
23:22. [prep. indicating means,
manner, cause] by, with, by means
of, in, on, in accord with, according
to <enclitic in *al, as #1, au #1*>.
a #3 16:16, 18:22, 18:45, 18:47. [prep.
denoting point in time] at, upon
<enclitic in *al, au #1*>.

a #4 10:340, 18:51, 20:16c, 20:16d,
20:30a, 22:3, 22:8b, 23:4a, 23:6.
[prep. indicating possession,
association, accompaniment, or a
characteristic trait] of, on, with,
having <enclitic in *al, as #3, au
#1*>.
a #5 5:147, 6:209, 11:389, 19:9, 19:35,
21:12. [prep. introducing an
adverbial complement] with, by,
for, -ly.
a #6 1:17, 3:90, 8:258, 12:416, 13:442,
13:444, 16:37, 17:8, 17:40, 18:40,
18:48, 18:52, 19:18, 22:6, 23:6, 23:11.
[untranslated prep. introducing an
inf.] <enclitic in *au #2*>.
a #7 8:265, 10:341, 10:343, 10:348,
13:455. [3 sg. pres. of *avoir #1*].
a #8 1:23, 1:24, 2:33, 2:35, 2:48, 2:58,
5:140, 5:171, 6:176, 6:189, 6:190,
6:191, 6:205, 6:206, 7:221, 7:222,
7:225, 7:227, 7:238, 8:261, 8:262,

8:278, 9:302, 10:321, 10:336, 10:358, 11:384, 11:391, 12:408, 12:414, 13:447, 13:448, 13:449, 13:462, 14:487, 14:488, 14:492, 15:503, 15:509, 15:510, 17:14, 20:29b, 21:35c, 23:16. [3 sg. pres. of *avoir* #2 (aux.)].

  ad 16:50, 17:31, 18:4, 18:8, 18:9, 18:24, 18:45, 19:33, 19:34. == > *a* #8.

a #9 10:344, 10:347, 13:466, 20:30b. [3 sg. pres. of *avoir* in *i avoir* construction] there is, there are.

a #10 23:7. [interjection] Ah!

a #11 occurs within idiomatic expressions in 5:163, 7:229, 8:266, 9:286, 10:323, 20:20.

a escient 6:209. [adv. phr.] with certainty.

a grant esploit 5:147. [adv. phr.] rapidly.

a miramie 21:12. [adv. phr.] admirably(?).

abaesse 5:154, 7:212, 7:216, 7:238, 7:250, 8:262, 8:269, 9:305, 13:441. [FS] abbess.

abaïe 5:151, 6:177, 7:233, 8:260. [FS] abbey.

abaier 5:145. [inf.] to bark.

abati 19:22, 19:28. [3 sg. pret. of *abatre*, to strike down or off].

abatu 16:46, 19:31. [pp. m. of *abater*] struck down or off.

achater [inf.] to buy.
  acata 20:29a. == > *achata*.
  acatai 22:2a. [1 sg. pret.].
  acatee 21:7a. [pp. f.].
  achata 13:437. [3 sg. pret.].

achoison 8:279. [FS] motive, reason.

acier 16:25. [OS] steel.

acommença 8:258. [3 sg. pret. of *acommencier*, to begin].

acor 18:15, 18:25. [OS] tail, flap (of a cloak or mantle).

'acostez 18:32. [pp. m. of *(s')acoster*] stayed beside.

acumplirez 18:30. [2 pl. fut. of *acumplir*, to carry out, to accomplish].

ad 16:50, 17:31, 18:4, 18:8, 18:9, 18:24, 18:45, 19:33, 19:34. [3 sg. pres. of *avoir* #2 (aux.)].

adés 17:29. [adv.] always.

adesez 18:43. [2 pl. imperative of *adeser*, to touch].

adont 12:421. [adv.] then.

aé 7:236, 7:241. [OS] age (cf. *en tel aé que*).

afaitie 8:264. [pp. f. of *afaitier*] properly raised.

afetiement 11:388. [adv.] properly.

afichier 17:7. [inf.] to place firmly, to affix.

afiert 2:37. [3 sg. pres. of *aferir*, to imply].

'agenoilla 1:21, 5:160. [3 sg. pret. of *(s')agenoillier*, to kneel].

ai #1 3:85, 22:6. [1 sg. pres. of *avoir* #1].

ai #2 6:199, 6:200, 14:474, 14:482, 14:483, 14:484, 18:16, 18:39, 22:2b. [1 sg. pres. of *avoir* #2 (aux.)].

ai #3 22:9. [1 sg. pres. of *avoir* #1] in *n'avoir . . . que faire*, q.v.

ai #4 21:23. [interjection] Ah!

aie 22:7a, 22:11c. [1 sg. pres. subjunc. of *avoir* #1].

aïe 20:25a. [2 sg. imperative of *aidier*, to help].

aies 20:30b. [2 sg. pres. subjunc. of *avoir* #1].

aim 20:27b, 22:7a, 23:7. [1 sg. pres. of *amer*].

ainc (+ ne) 21:18. [adv.] never.
  ainz (+ ne) 8:254. == > *ainc* (+ *ne*).

ains 21:36a, 23:5a. [adv.] rather.

ainsi 9:287, 15:504. [adv.] thus.
  einsi 17:11, 17:14, 18:46. == > *ainsi*.
  einsint 15:507. == > *ainsi*.
  issi #1 2:46, 7:232. == > *ainsi*.

ainsi comme 7:218. [conj. adv. phr.] just as.

ainz 16:36, 19:54, 19:55. [adv.] before, earlier.

ainz (+ ne) 8:254. = = >*ainc* (+ *ne*).

ainz qu(e) 14:493. [conj. phr.] before.

aire 20:32b. [FS] breeding (cf. *de bon aire*).

aït 2:31. [3 sg. pres. subjunc. of *aidier*, to help].

ait 2:41. [3 sg. pres. subjunc. of *avoir* #*1*].

ajornés 20:16c. [pp. m. of *ajorner*] dawned.

al 16:11, 17:1, 17:10, 17:11, 17:20, 18:1, 18:12, 18:56, 18:60, 19:13, 19:24, 19:35. = = >*au* #*1*.

ala 8:259, 16:28, 17:22, 18:46, 21:35a. [3 sg. pret. of *aler* #*1*].
  alad 17:18. = = >*ala*.

alaitant 6:195. [pres. participle OS of *aletier*.] nursing.

Alemaigne 20:32a. [FS] Germany.

aler #**1** 17:36, 18:43, 18:50, 20:24b, 22:10a, 22:10c, 22:11c. [inf.] to go.
  ala 8:259, 16:28, 17:22, 18:46, 21:35a. [3 sg. pret.].
  alad 17:18. = = >*ala*.
  alé 16:47, 18:6. [pp. m.].
  alee #**1** 11:372, 12:399, 13:432. [pp. f.].
  alez #**1** 16:29, 17:40. [2 pl. imperative].
  aloient 7:249, 23:11. [3 pl. imperf.].
  irai 17:25, 17:35. [1 sg. fut.].
  irés 23:2. [2 pl. fut.].
  va #**1** 14:498, 21:6, 22:11b, 23:24. [2 sg. pres.].
  vait 6:175, 6:192, 7:219, 19:20. [3 sg. pres.].
  vet 5:147, 7:213. = = >*vait*.
  voise 20:27a. [1 sg. pres. subjunc.].
  vont 22:7b, 22:8a, 22:9, 22:10a, 22:11a, 22:11b, 23:27, 23:29. [3 pl. pres.].
  vunt 16:35. = = >*vont*.

'aler #**2**, i.e., **(s'en) aler** 23:1. [inf.] to go away, to depart.
  'alee #**2** 9:301. [pp. f.].
  'alerent 15:523. [3 pl. pret.].
  'alez #**2** 18:31. [pp. m.].
  'alum 19:45. [1 pl. imperative].

aletié 6:206. [pp. m. of *aletier*] nursed.

aletiez 6:201. [2 pl. imperative of *aletier*, to nurse (an infant)].

alez #**1** 16:29, 17:40. [2 pl. imperative of *aler* #*1*].

'alez #**2** 18:31. [pp. m. of *(s'en) aler*] gone away, departed.

aloient 7:249, 23:11. [3 pl. imperf. of *aler* #*1*].

alquant 17:21. See *li alquant*.

alteus 18:33. [OP] altars.
  autex 22:8a. [OP].

altre #**1** 16:42 [OS], 17:17 [NP], 18:8 [OS]. = = >*autre* #*1*.

altre #**2** 17:3 [NP], 18:35 [NS]. = = >*autre* #*2*.

altresi 16:4. [adv.] likewise.

'alum 19:45. [1 pl. imperative of *(s'en) aler*].

alumer to light. [inf.]
  aluma 6:182. [3 sg. pret.].
  alume 6:204. [3 sg. pres.].
  alumez 6:198. [2 pl. imperative].

ama 9:316. [3 sg. pret. of *amer*].

amaladis 20:12. [pp. m. of *amaladir*] grown ill with.

amant 23:23. [OS] beloved, friend.

amast 7:247, 9:319. [3 sg. imperf. subjunc. of *amer*].

amender 3:93. [inf.] to make amends.

amener [inf.] to bring (a person).
  amena 14:499, 20:29b. [3 sg. pret.].
  amenai 22:2a. [1 sg. pret.].
  amenee 11:371, 12:414, 20:29a, 21:3. [pp. f.].

amer 8:258, 23:9a. [inf.] to love.
  aim 20:27b, 22:7a, 23:7. [1 sg. pres.].
  ama 9:316. [3 sg. pret.].
  amast 7:247, 9:319. [3 sg. imperf. subjunc.].

amee 4:102, 11:392, 14:487. [pp. f.].

ameroie 23:6. [1 sg. cond.].

ameront 3:77. [3 pl. fut.].

amés 23:7. [2 pl. pres.].

amissiés 23:8. [2 pl. imperf. subjunc.].

amoie 21:36b, 21:38b. [1 sg. imperf.].

amoit 7:239. [3 sg. imperf.].

amot 9:299. = = >amoit.

ami 9:288. [OS] lover, friend.

amie #1 15:509, 20:7, 20:27b, 20:31a, 21:26, 21:36b, 22:7a, 22:11c. [FS].

amis 10:358 [NS], 11:368 [OP], 22:11a [OP].

amie #2 13:435, 13:454, 23:2, 23:8. in bele amie, Miss (form of address for an unmarried woman).

amissiés 23:8. [2 pl. imperf. subjunc. of amer].

amoie 21:36b, 21:38b. [1 sg. imperf. of amer].

amoit 7:239. [3 sg. imperf. of amer].

amot 9:299. = = >amoit.

Amor 20:24a. [FS] Love.

amor 8:265, 9:285, 11:374. [FS] love.

amors 21:1a [OP], 23:9b [NS], 23:9c [NS]. [f. noun, declines as m.].

amur 16:21. = = >amor.

amot 9:299. = = >amoit.

an 3:66. [OS] year.

anz 7:235. [OP].

andui 1:07. [indef. pron., NP] both.

anel 4:128, 6:207, 9:303, 9:309, 13:443, 13:445, 13:447, 14:479, 14:482. [OS] ring.

angoisseusement 4:105. [adv.] deeply, with true anxiety.

anorast 9:320. [3 sg. imperf. subjunc. of anorer, to honor].

ante 9:291, 13:440. [FS] aunt (here: foster mother).

antif 20:2. [OS] ancient (man).

anz 7:235. [OP of an].

'aparcevoir, i.e., (s')aparcevoir [inf.] to notice.

'aperceüscent 23:13a. [3 pl. imperf. subjunc.].

'aparcevoit 9:291. [3 sg. imperf.].

'aparcevroit 8:269. [3 sg. cond.].

apareillier 12:397. [inf.] to prepare.

apeler [inf.] to call.

apela 6:196, 12:401, 21:1b, 21:36a. [3 sg. pret.].

apele 7:230, 12:423. [3 sg. pres.].

apelee 13:431. [pp. f.].

apelent 8:256. [3 pl. pres.].

apent 19:13. [3 sg. pres. of apendre, to belong to, to be under the protection of].

'aperceüscent 23:13a. [3 pl. imperf. subjunc. of (s')aparcevoir)].

'apoia 21:14. [3 sg. pret. of (s')apoiier, to lean (on)].

aporter [inf.] to bring (other than persons).

aporta 12:427. [3 sg. pret.].

aporte 7:220. [3 sg. pres.].

aporté 4:124, 6:199, 13:447. [pp. m.].

aportez 7:217. = = >aporté.

aprendre 7:238. [inf.] to learn.

aprés #1 10:328, 16:36, 19:41. [prep.] after.

emprés 7:211. = = >aprés.

aprés #2 15:509. [adv.] afterwards.

apresté 12:405, 16:22, 16:27. [pp. m. of aprester] ready, readied, prepared.

aprestez 18:42. = = >apresté.

apuié 19:40. [pp. m. of apuier] entrusted to.

'apuiez 18:56. [pp. m. of (s')apuier] leaned against.

arcevesque #1 14:499, 16:14, 16:28, 18:5, 18:9, 18:12, 19:9. [OS] archbishop.

arcevesques 11:369, 16:16. [NS].

arcevesque #2 15:503. = = >arcevesques.

ardoir [inf.] to burn.

arderai 21:5a. [1 sg. fut.].

arderoit 22:12b. [3 sg. cond.].
ardoit 20:16d. [3 sg. imperf.].
arés 21:38b. [2 pl. fut. of *avoir* #2 (aux.)].
aresona 13:434. [3 sg. pret. of *aresoner, aresnier*, to speak (to)].
'aresté 17:5. [pp. m. of *(s')arester*] stopped.
'aresteüe 5:158. [pp. f. of *(s')arester*] stopped.
argens 22:11b. [NS] silver.
argoit 20:16d. [3 sg. imperf. of *ardoir*].
ariere #1 5:166. [prep.] behind.
ariere #2 6:175, 13:456, 17:32, 18:24, 19:52. [adv.] back.
ariés 22:5. [2 pl. cond. of *avoir* #2 (aux.)].
  ariiés 23:4a. = = >*ariés*.
  ariis 23:2. = = >*ariés*.
arme 22:5. [OS] soul.
armé 16:26, 16:34, 17:13. [pp. m. of *armer*] armed.
  armez 17:34, 18:17. = = >*armé*.
'armerent 16:24. [3 pl. pret. of *(s')armer*, to arm (oneself)].
armes 20:24a, 20:25a. [OP] arms, weapons.
armez 17:34, 18:17. = = >*armé*.
aroit 20:32a. [3 sg. cond. of *avoir* #1].
as #1 13:461, 15:513, 16:35, 16:37, 17:37, 17:38, 19:14, 20:16c, 20:29b, 22:10b. [enclitic form of *a* #1 and *les* #1,2].
as #2 18:51. [enclitic form of *a* #2 and *les* #2].
as #3 16:51. [enclitic form of *a* #4 and *les* #1].
as #4 20:29c, 23:19. [2 sg. pres. of *avoir* #1].
as #5 18:10, 18:14, 23:23. [2 sg. pres. of *avoir* #2 (aux.)].
asemblé 16:10. [pp. m. of *assembler*] assembled, gathered.
  asemblez 17:32. = = >*asemblé*.
aseri 5:137. [pp. m. of *asserir*] grown calm.
asez 16:28. [indef. pron.] many.

asis 20:9. = = >*assis*.
asognentee 22:4. [pp. f. of *assoignanter*] taken as a mistress.
asoignenteroit 23:3b. [3 sg. cond. of *assoignanter*, to take as a mistress].
asolez 18:37. [2 pl. imperative of *assoler*, to absolve].
assés 20:32a. = = >*assez*.
asseür 9:285. [adj., NS] sure, certain.
assez 2:51. [adv.] very much, very.
  assés 20:32a. = = >*assez*.
assis 20:22b. [pp. m. of *asseoir*] placed, set.
  asis 20:9. = = >*assis*.
atant 1:20, 5:136. [adv.] thereupon.
atendre 14:497. [inf.] to await, to wait.
  atendant 17:22. [gerund].
  atenderoie 23:5a. [1 sg. cond.].
  atendi 18:12. [3 sg. pret.].
  atendisse 23:4a. [1 sg. imperf. subjunc.].
  atendist 17:2. [3 sg. imperf. subjunc.].
  atendrai 16:33. [1 sg. fut.].
atornerent a mal 10:323. [3 pl. pret. of *atorner a mal*, to attribute, to impute ill (to)].
atuchier 17:6. [inf.] to touch.
au #1 1:10, 1:19, 2:25, 2:26, 4:128, 5:172, 7:225, 11:367, 15:518, 20:16b, 20:24b, 21:1b, 21:36a. [prep., enclitic form of *a* #1,2,3,4 and *le* #1].
  al 16:11, 17:1, 17:10, 17:11, 17:20, 18:1, 18:12, 18:56, 18:60, 19:13, 19:24, 19:35. = = >*au* #1.
au #2 12:397. [prep., enclitic form of *a* #6 and *le* #1].
Aucassins #1 20:26, 20:31a, 21:7b, 21:25, 21:36a, 22:13, 23:1, 23:8, 23:10a, 23:13b. [NS] hero of *Aucassin and Nicolette*.
  Aucassin 21:1a, 21:4. [OS].
  Aucasins 20:20. = = >*Aucassin*.
  Aucassins #2 20:4. = = >*Aucassin*.
aucun 4:115. [adj., NS] some.
aucuns 6:185. [indef. pron., NS] someone.

aumosne 23:13a. [FS] good deed.
auquant 21:35b, 21:35c. See *li auquant*.
aürer 19:16. [inf.] to worship.
autex 22:8a. [OP of *alteus*].
autre #1 6:187 [FS], 8:279 [FS], 23:1
  [OS]. [adj.] other, another.
  altre #1 16:42 [OS], 17:17 [NP],
  18:8 [OS]. = = > *autre #1*.
  autres #1 19:33. [OP].
autre #2 10:358 [FS], 18:3 [FS], 19:47
  [OS]. [pron.] the other.
  altre #2 17:3 [NP], 18:35 [NS].
  = = > *autre #2*.
  autres #2 20:27b. [NS].
autrui 3:87. [indef. pron., OS]
  someone else.
avant 6:196, 14:494, 17:16, 17:25, 19:16.
  [adv.] forward.
aveient 17:20. [3 pl. imperf. of *avoir
  #2*].
aveit 16:16, 18:15, 18:19, 19:1, 19:4,
  19:26, 19:38, 19:39. [3 sg. imperf. of
  avoir #1].
avenant 23:19. [adj., OS] pleasant,
  agreeable.
  avenans 23:17. [NS].
avenir [inf.] to happen, to come to
  pass.
  avendra 2:39. [3 sg. fut.].
  avenu 9:306, 16:9. [pp. m.].
  avenue 15:528. [pp. f.].
  avint 18:46. [3 sg. pret.].
aventure 2:39, 7:214, 14:496, 14:500,
  15:527, 17:33. [FS] story, event;
  adventure.
aversier 17:19, 18:51. [OS] the devil.
avés #1 21:34, 21:36b, 21:37, 21:38b.
  = = > *avez #1*.
avés #2 22:2c. = = > *avez #2*.
avesprer 18:47. [OS] nightfall, dusk.
aveuc 22:9, 22:10c, 22:11c. [prep.]
  with.
  avoc 22:11a, 22:11c. = = > *aveuc*.
avez #1 9:288, 13:469. [2 pl. pres. of
  avoir #2 (aux.)].
  avés #1 21:34, 21:36b, 21:37,
  21:38b. = = > *avez #1*.

avez #2 17:39. [2 pl. pres. of *avoir
  #1*] in *n'avoir . . . que faire*, q.v.
  avés #2 22:2c. = = > *avez #2*.
avïens 3:82. [1 pl. imperf. of *avoir #2*
  (aux.)].
aviés 22:4. [2 pl. imperf. of *avoir #2*
  (aux.)].
avint 18:46. [3 sg. pret. of *avenir*].
avis 3:85. in *ce m'est avis*, I believe; it is
  my opinion (that).
avoc 22:11a, 22:11c. = = > *aveuc*
avoi 20:31a, 23:8. [interjection] Hey!
avoient 23:10b. [3 pl. imperf. of *avoir
  #2*].
avoir #1 8:275, 8:277, 10:328, 10:342,
  20:30a, 20:30b, 21:5a, 21:5b, 22:12b.
  [inf.] to possess, to own, to have.
  a #7 8:265, 10:341, 10:343, 10:348,
  13:455. [3 sg. pres.].
  ai #1 3:85, 22:6. [1 sg. pres.].
  aie 22:7a, 22:11c. [2 sg. pres.
  subjunc.].
  aies 20:30b. [2 sg. pres. subjunc.].
  ait 2:41. [3 sg. pres. subjunc.].
  aroit 20:32a. [3 sg. cond.].
  as #4 23:19. [2 sg. pres.].
  aveit 16:16, 18:15, 18:19, 19:1,
  19:4, 19:26, 19:38, 19:39.
  = = > *avoit #1*.
  avoit #1 4:99, 6:194, 10:327,
  20:18, 20:22a, 20:31a, 21:15. [3 sg.
  imperf.].
  avrai 3:74. [1 sg. fut.].
  avroit 4:120. [3 sg. cond.].
  avroiz 10:346. [2 pl. fut.].
  eüst #1 3:83, 10:332, 21:36a. [3
  sg. imperf. subjunc.].
  eüz 1:15, 2:35. [pp. m.].
  oi 14:476. [1 sg. pret.].
  ont #1 22:11a. [3 pl. pres.].
  ot #1 1:11, 1:13, 3:70, 4:118,
  6:187, 6:193, 11:374, 15:502,
  15:511. [3 sg. pret.].
avoir #2 22:4. [inf.] to have (aux.).
  a #8 1:23, 1:24, 2:33, 2:35, 2:48,
  2:58, 5:140, 5:171, 6:176, 6:189,
  6:190, 6:191, 6:205, 6:206, 7:221,

7:222, 7:225, 7:227, 7:238, 8:261,
8:262, 8:278, 9:302, 10:321, 10:336,
10:358, 11:384, 11:391, 12:408,
12:414, 13:447, 13:448, 13:449,
13:462, 14:487, 14:488, 14:492,
15:503, 15:509, 15:510, 17:14,
20:29b, 21:35c, 23:16. [3 sg. pres.].
ai #2 6:199, 6:200, 14:474, 14:482,
14:483, 14:484, 18:16, 18:39, 22:2b.
[1 sg. pres.].
arés 21:38b. [2 pl. fut.].
ariés 22:5. [2 pl. cond.].
ariiés 23:4a. = = >*ariés*.
ariis 23:2. = = >*ariés*.
as #5 18:10, 18:14, 23:23. [2 sg.
pres.].
aveient 17:20. = = >*avoient*.
avés #1 21:34, 21:36b, 21:37,
21:38b. = = >*avez #1*.
avez #1 9:288, 13:469. [2 pl.
pres.].
avïens 3:82. [1 pl. imperf.].
aviés 22:4. [2 pl. imperf.].
avoie 21:7a. [1 sg. imperf.].
avoient 23:10b. [3 pl. imperf.].
avoit #2 1:08, 2:43, 2:44, 5:144,
5:165, 7:235, 12:404, 13:431, 20:17,
23:10c. [3 sg. imperf.].
eüsciés 23:6. [2 pl. imperf.
subjunc.].
eüst #2 6:185. [3 sg. imperf.
subjunc.].
ont #2 2:42, 10:351, 11:371,
12:406, 15:507, 15:521, 15:522,
15:529, 15:530. [3 pl. pres.].
orent 4:126, 10:354, 12:405, 16:12,
17:11, 19:2. [3 pl. pret.].
ot #2 1:15, 2:57, 4:101, 4:124,
9:305, 11:367, 13:450. [3 sg. pret.].
out #1 16:36, 16:45, 19:40.
= = >*ot #2*.
unt 16:52, 17:1, 17:3, 17:10, 17:21,
17:36, 18:7, 18:36, 18:40, 18:51,
19:6, 19:10, 19:36, 19:53. [3 pl.
pres. of *avoir #2* (aux.)].
avoir #3 8:273, 22:2a. [OS]
possessions, wealth.
avoirs 20:25b. [OP].

avoir peor 21:5b. [inf.] to be afraid.
avoir paor 22:12b. = = >*avoir
peor*.
avoit peor 11:373. [3 imperf. of
avoir peor].
avoirs 20:25b. [OP of *avoir #3*].
avoit #1 4:99, 6:194, 10:327, 20:18,
20:22a, 20:31a, 21:15. [3 sg. imperf.
of *avoir #1*].
aveit 16:16, 18:15, 18:19, 19:1,
19:4, 19:26, 19:38, 19:39.
= = >*avoit #1*.
avoit #2 1:08, 2:43, 2:44, 5:144, 5:165,
7:235, 12:404, 13:431, 20:17, 23:10c.
[3 sg. imperf. of *avoir #2* (aux.)].
avoit #3 4:129, 7:243, 8:253, 8:279,
20:23. [3 sg. imperf. of *avoir* in *i avoir*
construction] there was, there were.
avoit a non 20:20. [3 sg. imperf. of
avoir a non, to be named, to be
called].
avoit peor 11:373. [3 sg. imperf. of
avoir peor].
avrai 3:74. [1 sg. fut. of *avoir #1*].
avroient 10:330. [3 pl. cond. of *avoir* in
i avoir construction].
avroit 4:120. [3 sg. cond. of *avoir #1*].
avroiz 10:346. [2 pl. fut. of *avoir #1*].

baceler 20:29c, 21:7b, 22:2b. [OS]
young man.
bacheler 16:34. [NP] knights.
baigniez 6:202. [2 pl. imperative of
baignier, to bathe].
baillier [inf.] to give, to entrust.
bailla 9:309, 13:441. [3 sg. pret.].
baillierent 13:443. [3 pl. pret.].
bailliez 4:109. [2 pl. imperative].
baingnié 6:205. [pp. m. of *baignier*]
bathed.
baise 19:35. [3 sg. pres. of *baisier*, to
kiss].
baisiez 13:462. [pp. m. of *baisier*]
kissed.
bares 20:16c. [OP] barriers.
barons 22:11a. [OP] brave men;
husbands (cf. *bers*).

barrer 16:36. [inf.] to bar closed.

bataille 20:27a. [OS] battle.

bautisie 20:29b, 21:7a, 22:2b. [pp. f. of *bautisier*] baptized.

bel #1 4:121, 6:208, 12:418. [adj., OS] beautiful, handsome.

    bel #2 22:10a, 22:10b. [NP].

    bele 5:149, 7:236, 7:243, 7:251, 8:263, 10:344, 13:445, 14:486, 21:18, 23:12. [FS].

    beles 22:11a. [FP].

    biax #1 20:3. [OP].

    biax #2 20:8, 20:21, 22:1, 23:17. [NS].

bel #3 9:304. in *estre molt bel*, to please. 13:446. in *ce m'est molt bel*, gladly, willingly (lit.: this pleases me very much).

bele amie 13:435, 13:454, 23:2, 23:8. [FS] Miss (form of address for an unmarried woman).

Beneeit in *saint Beneeit*, St. Benedict.

bers 18:31. [NS] brave man (cf. *baron*).

berz 6:195. [OS] crib.

besague 18:3. [OS] twibill, mortising axe.

    besagues 16:52 [OP]

bescoz 19:33. in *en bescoz* [adv. phr.], obliquely, slantingly.

biauté 7:242, 15:520. [FS] beauty.

biax #1 20:3. [adj., OP of *bel* #1].

biax #2 20:8, 20:21, 22:1, 23:17. [adj., NS of *bel* #1].

bien #1 2:37, 4:108, 4:133, 5:144, 5:168, 6:209, 9:311, 12:409, 12:426, 13:449, 13:451, 16:36, 18:22, 19:11, 20:9, 20:22b, 20:31b, 21:5a, 21:16, 21:38a, 23:22. [adv.] well, a lot.

bien #2 13:466. [OS] good.

    bienz 18:16. [OP] good deeds.

bien garnie 5:152. [idiom] well provided for.

bien tailliés 20:21. [pp. phr.] well-formed.

bisse 23:5a. [adj., FS] gray, dark-hued.

blanc 19:49. [adj., OS] white.

blanchir 19:50. [inf.] to be white.

blasmee 2:44. [pp. f. of *blasmer*] reproached, rebuked.

blont 23:20. [adj., OS] blond.

    blonde 21:15. [FS].

    blons 20:22a. [OP].

bofu 12:407. [OS] quilting(?), silk material stitched with gold thread.

bois 5:141. [OS] woods.

bon #1 1:14, 1:24, 4:120, 4:126, 8:253, 15:511, 20:32b. [adj., OS] good.

    bone #1 2:48, 20:23. [FS].

    bones 20:23, 20:32b. [FP].

    bons #1 12:425, 12:429, 13:436, 18:45, 21:8a. [NS].

    bons #2 20:1. [OP].

    buen 22:10c. == > *bon* #1.

    buens 18:16. == > *bons* #1.

    meillor 8:254. [OS, comparative] better.

bon #2 8:274. See *savoir bon gré*.

bone #2 7:245. in *de bone escole* [idiom], well-raised, properly educated.

bonement 5:160, 11:387. [adv.] graciously, properly.

Bougars de Valence 20:16b. [NS] Count of Valence, who makes war on Aucassin's father, Garin de Biaucaire.

brait 19:38. [pp. m. of *braire*] cried out, brayed.

branchu 5:167. [adj., OS] branching.

brant 19:34. [OS] sword.

    brans 23:28. == > *branz*.

    branz 16:25. [OP].

braz #1 4:128, 6:207, 19:25. [OS] arm.

    bras 20:21. == > *braz* #2.

    braz #2 5:171. [OP].

Bretaingne 2:52, 7:243. [OS] Brittany.

    Bretaigne 1:03. == > *Bretaingne*.

brisié 19:34. [pp. m. of *brisier*] broken.

Bruron 8:256. [OS] Fresne's lover and eventual husband.

buen 22:10c. == > *bon* #1.

buens 18:16. == > *bons* #1.

buter 16:37. [inf.] to strike (against), to knock; to push.

    buta 17:32, 18:23. [3 sg. pret.].

    buté 17:3. [pp. m.].

c' #1 2:38, 3:81, 10:325, 21:36b.
== >qu(e) #4.

c' #2 3:75. == >ce #1.

c' #3 21:4, 22:7b. == >car #1.

ça 4:109, 6:200, 18:20. [adv.] here.

caitive 20:29a, 21:23, 22:2a. [FS]
captive; wretch.

canbre 21:10, 21:29, 21:34.
== >chambre.

cans 20:8, 23:16. [NS] song.

Cantorbire 16:12. [FS] Canterbury.

capes 22:8b, 23:10b, 23:28. [FP] capes.

car #1 2:27, 3:79, 7:239, 8:268, 8:275,
12:404, 16:26, 16:36, 16:38, 17:6,
17:19, 18:21, 18:54, 18:56, 19:40,
19:49, 21:38b, 22:5, 22:10a, 23:2,
23:9b, 23:10c, 23:13b. [conj.]
because, for.

    c' #3 21:4, 22:7b. == >car #1.

    qu(e) #7 20:29a, 21:4, 21:38b,
22:5, 22:12a. == >car #1.

car #2 13:438, 17:38, 20:25a, 21:2,
22:1. [special use to introduce a
request] Please; do now.

carpentier 16:47. [NP] carpenters.

cateron 23:9b. [OS] nipple.

cause 19:15. [FS] cause, case.

caviax 20:22a. [OP] hair.

ce #1 3:85, 9:290, 9:304, 10:338,
11:380, 12:409, 13:446, 14:485,
14:489, 20:28, 20:29a, 20:29c, 21:6,
21:7b, 21:38a, 22:2c, 22:13, 23:8.
[dem. pron., 3 sg. n.] this.

    c' #2 3:75. == >ce #1.

    ço #1 16:32. [OS].

    ço #2 8:254, 16:5. [NS, stressed
form].

ce #2 10:351, 13:464. == >cel #1.

ce #3 2:64. See san ce qu(e).

ce #4 7:228, 10:366. See por ce qu(e).

ce m'est avis 3:85. [idiom] I believe, it
is my opinion (that).

ce m'est molt bel 13:446. [idiom]
gladly, willingly (lit.: this to me is
very pleasing).

ce qu(e) 4:117, 8:284, 15:517. [relative
pron.] what.

ço qu(e) 16:33, 18:44. == >ce
qu(e).

    qu(e) #8 2:37, 2:60, 3:88, 6:176,
11:394. == >ce qu(e).

ceinstrent 16:25. [3 pl. pres. of ceindre,
to strap on].

cel #1 4:119, 16:29, 16:48, 19:26. [dem.
adj., OS] that.

    ce #2 10:351, 13:464. == >cel
#1.

    cel #3 16:16. == >cele #1.

    cele #1 2:39, 2:50, 5:147, 6:188,
14:500, 18:22. [FS].

    ces 20:29c, 22:2b, 22:8a, 22:8b.
[OP].

    icele 6:181. == >cele #1.

cel #2 [dem. pron., OS]. that one.

    cele #2 4:103, 6:203, 9:299,
10:326, 10:357, 13:432, 15:506. [FS].

    celes 4:95, 11:390. [FP].

    cels 18:37, 18:38, 19:44. [OP].

    celui 12:419. [stressed form].

    ciax 22:9, 22:10c, 22:11c.
== >cels.

cel #3 16:16. == >cele #1.

cela 12:420. [3 sg. pret. of celer].

celai 14:476. [1 sg. pret. of celer].

cele #1 2:39, 2:50, 5:147, 6:188,
14:500, 18:22. [dem. adj., FS of cel
#1].

    cel #3 16:16. == >cele #1.

    icele 6:181. == >cele #1.

cele #2 4:103, 6:203, 9:299, 10:326,
10:357, 13:432, 15:506. [dem. pron.,
FS of cel #2].

celer [inf.] to hide.

    cela 12:420. [3 sg. pret.].

    celai 14:476. [1 sg. pret.].

    cele #3 13:453. [3 sg. pres.].

    celé 14:481. [pp. m.].

    celee 7:232, 10:357. [pp. f.].

    celez 13:435. [2 pl. imperative].

celes 4:95, 11:390. [dem. pron., FP of
cel #2].

cels 18:37, 18:38, 19:44. [dem. pron.,
OP of cel #2].

    ciax 22:9, 22:10c, 22:11c. == >cels.

celui 12:419. [dem. pron., stressed form of *cel* #2].

cent 20:16c. [num.] one hundred.

certes 3:77, 9:297, 18:18, 22:12a. [adv.] indeed.

cervel 19:43, 19:46, 19:49, 19:50. [OS] brain.

ces 20:29c, 22:2b, 22:8a, 22:8b. [dem. adj., OP of *cel* #1].

cest #1 2:32, 4:108, 5:164, 10:344, 21:3, 21:38b. [dem. adj., OS] this.
    ceste 2:47, 3:78, 20:29a, 20:29b, 21:29. [FS].

cest #2 13:443. [dem. pron., OS] this.

ceston 4:130. [OS] mounting, setting.

ceval 20:16d, 20:25a, 20:27a.
    = = > *cheval*.

cevalers 20:24a. = = > *chevaliers* #2.

cevalier #1 20:27b. = = > *chevalier* #1.

cevalier #2 22:10b. = = > *chevalier* #2.

cevaliers #1 20:16c. = = > *chevaliers* #1.

cevaliers #2 20:27a, 21:4. = = > *chevaliers* #2.

chainsil 4:121. [OS] linen cloth.

chaïr 19:46. [inf.] to fall.
    chaï 13:461, 19:30. [3 sg. pret.].
    chaü 19:55. [pp. m.].
    chiet 13:456. [3 sg. pres.].

chambellenc 12:423. [OS] chamberlain.
    chambellans 12:401. [OP].

chambre 4:95, 5:136, 12:413, 13:460, 16:17, 16:44. [FS] room.
    canbre 21:10, 21:29, 21:34. = = > *chambre*.
    chambres 11:383, 16:49. [FP].

chandoille 6:198. [FS] candle.
    chandoilles 6:182. [FP].

chanter 5:145, 17:40. [inf.] to sing.
    chantent 16:30. [3 pl. pres. of *chanter*].

chardin 16:45. [OS] garden.

chascuns 1:08, 16:26, 18:2. [indef. pron., NS] each.

chastel 9:302, 17:26. [OS] castle.

chaü 19:55. [pp. m. of *chaïr*] fallen.

chemin 5:139, 5:143. [OS] road, highway.

cherir [inf.] to cherish.
    chieri 9:316. [3 sg. pret.].
    chierie 4:102. [pp. f.].
    chierissoit 7:239. [3 sg. imperf.].

cheval 1:24. [OS] horse.
    ceval 20:16d, 20:25a, 20:27a.
    = = > *cheval*.

chevalier #1 2:25. [OS] knight.
    cevalers 20:24a. = = > *chevaliers* #2.
    cevalier #1 20:27b.
    = = > *chevalier* #1.
    cevalier #2 22:10b.
    = = > *chevalier* #2.
    cevaliers #1 20:16c.
    = = > *chevaliers* #1.
    cevaliers #2 20:27a, 21:4.
    = = > *chevaliers* #2.
    chevalier #2 1:04, 10:322, 10:363, 16:24, 16:31, 16:41, 16:48, 17:12, 17:17, 19:54. [NP].
    chevalier #3 9:315.
    = = > *chevaliers* #2.
    chevaliers #1 16:50, 17:34, 19:4. [OP].
    chevaliers #2 10:336, 14:487, 15:501. [NS].
    chevaliers #3 1:06.
    = = > *chevalier* #2.

chief 4:121, 19:20, 19:43. [OS] piece, endpiece; end; head.

chiens 5:145, 5:148. [OP] dogs.

chieri 9:316. [3 sg. pret. of *cherir*].

chierie 4:102. [pp. f. of *cherir*] cherished.

chierissoit 7:239. [3 sg. imperf. of *cherir*].

chiet 13:456. [3 sg. pres. of *chaïr*].

choisi 6:184. [3 sg. pret. of *choisir*, to perceive].

chose 6:187, 8:271. [FS] thing.

ci #1 6:199, 10:339, 14:483, 16:33, 17:34, 17:39, 18:10, 18:14, 18:49, 23:27. [adv.] here.

ci #2 22:8a. = = >cil #2.
ciax 22:9, 22:10c, 22:11c. = = >cels.
ciel 5:174. [OS] heaven.
ciere 23:21. [FS] face.
cil #1 2:32, 17:18, 18:23, 18:33, 19:41.
[dem. adj., NS] this, that.
    ci #2 22:8a. = = >cil #2.
    cil #2 16:1, 16:31, 22:8a. [NP].
    cis 12:425, 13:436. = = >cil #1.
cil #3 2:57, 9:310, 11:370, 18:34, 20:19.
[dem. pron., NS] this, that.
    cil #4 11:390, 13:444, 16:12, 17:19,
    18:48, 22:8b. [NP].
    icil 22:9. = = >cil #4.
ciu 17:24. [adj., NP] blind.
'clama 21:22. [3 sg. pret. of (se) clamer,
to call oneself].
cler 20:7. [adj., OS] clear,
unblemished.
    clere 20:22b, 21:17. [FS].
clerc 17:28, 19:5, 22:10a. [NP] clerks,
religious clerics.
    clers 17:15. [NS].
clergié 16:17. [OS] clergy.
clers 17:15. [adj., NS of cler].
clochier 5:156. [OS] bell tower.
cloistre 17:5, 17:20. [OS] cloister.
clop 22:8a. [NP] lame persons,
cripples.
clos #1 7:233. [OS] cloister,
enclosure.
clos #2 17:21. [pp. m. of clore] closed.
ço #1 16:32. [OS of ce #1].
ço #2 8:254, 16:5. [NS, stressed form
of ce #1].
ço #3 18:23. in de ço qu(e) [connective
phrase], because.
ço qu(e) 16:33, 18:44. = = >ce qu(e).
cochiee 9:308. [pp. f. of couchier] gone
to bed.
coffre 9:312, 9:313, 12:411. [OS] small
coffer, chest.
coi 21:24. in por coi [interrogative adv.
phr.], why?
col 18:53, 19:42. [OS] neck.
colp 19:20, 19:26. [OS] blow.
    colps 19:33. [OP].

colpa 19:25. [3 sg. pret. of couper, to
cut].
Colstentinoble 20:32a.
    = = >Costentinoble.
'comande 19:14. [3 sg. pres. of (se)
comander, to commend oneself (to
God, to the saints)].
comander [inf.] to order, to command;
to commend.
    comant 17:23. [1 sg. pres.].
    commanda 5:174, 7:216, 13:442. [3
    sg. pret.].
    commande 12:416. [3 sg. pres.].
    conmandé 23:10c. [pp. m.].
comencier 16:27, 17:16. [inf.] to begin.
    comença 17:8. [3 sg. pret.].
    comence 19:18. [3 sg. pres.].
    comencent 16:37, 18:52. [3 pl.
    pres.].
    comencié 18:39, 23:16. [pp. m.].
comencierent 18:48. [3 pl. pret.].
commanda 5:174, 7:216, 13:442. [3 sg.
pret. of comander].
commande 12:416. [3 sg. pres. of
comander].
commandement 6:203. [OS] order.
comme #1 7:218. in ainsi comme
[conjunctive adv. phr.], just as.
15:514. in si comme [adv. phr.], just
as.
comme #2 10:353. [adv. of manner,
introduces an exclamation]
How . . . !
    con #2 23:12. = = >comme #2.
comment 7:215, 7:226, 8:267, 9:306,
12:403, 15:528. [adv. of manner]
how.
con #1 20:19, 22:7b. [adv. of manner]
as, just as.
con #2 23:12. = = >comme #2.
con #3 1:11. in si con. = = >si comme,
q.v.
con #4 23:7, 23:9a. See tant con.
conforta 4:106. [3 sg. pret. of conforter,
to comfort].
confortoient 4:96. [3 pl. imperf. of
conforter, to comfort].

conmandé 23:10c. [pp. m. of *comander*]
ordered, commanded.
conoistre [inf.] to know, recognize.
    conneüe 2:51, 14:483. [pp. f.].
    conneüst 3:84. [3 sg. imperf.
    subjunc.].
    connurent 6:209. [3 pl. pret.].
conquis 22:5. [pp. m. of *conquerre*]
gained.
conseil 2:32, 9:295, 10:337. [OS] idea;
advice.
conseiller [inf.] to advise.
    conseillera 11:378. [3 sg. fut.].
    conseillerai 9:298. [1 sg. fut.].
    conseillié 15:503. [pp. m.].
conta 1:22, 14:500. [3 sg. pret. of
conter].
conte #1 1:02. [OS] tale.
conte #2 20:16b, 20:30a, 22:3. [OS]
count.
    quens 20:16b, 20:17, 21:1a, 21:2,
    21:35c, 22:1, 23:10c. [NS].
conter 7:214. [inf.] to recount, to tell.
    conta 1:22, 14:500. [3 sg. pret.].
    conte #3 6:176. [3 sg. pres.].
    conté 2:58. [pp. m.].
    content 20:16a. [3 pl. pres.].
contre 17:21, 17:30, 19:3. [prep.]
against.
contree 1:07, 15:525. [FS] country,
land.
corage 12:410, 15:511, 19:40. [OS]
heart.
    corages 12:422. [NS].
    curages 16:23. = = > *corages*.
'coroçast 11:386. [3 sg. imperf.
subjunc. of *(se) courecier*, to grow
angry].
coroucie 9:294. [pp. f. of *courecier*]
angered.
cors #1 17:30, 20:21, 23:19. [OS] body.
    cors #2 17:37, 20:25b. [OP].
cortois 20:9, 23:15. [adj., OS] noble,
refined, gracious; endowed with
courtly graces.
    cortoise 7:244, 8:264, 20:32b. [FS].
    cortoises 22:11a. [FP].

corune 19:21. [FS] crown (of head).
corunez 18:26. [pp. m. of *coronner*]
crowned.
cos 5:145. [NP] roosters.
Costentinoble 4:125. [FS]
Constantinople.
    Colstentinoble 20:32a.
    = = > *Costentinoble*.
cotes 16:25. [OP] capes.
couchier 12:398, 12:415. [inf.] to go to
bed.
Coudre 10:343, 10:346, 15:524. [FS]
Coudre (Hazel), sister of Fresne.
coudre 10:347. [OS] hazelnut tree.
courecier 23:1. [inf.] to get angry (cf.
n'avoir qu(e) courecier).
coutel 23:4b. [OS] knife.
couvertor 12:406, 12:428. [OS] cover.
couvine 15:518. [OS] assembly, feast,
party.
coveneit 18:59. [3 sg. imperf. of *covenir*,
to be necessary].
creanté 10:336. [pp. m. of *creanter*]
promised.
crei 18:22. [1 sg. pres. of *croire*].
cremez 17:33. [2 pl. pres. of *creimbre*, to
fear].
creüz 1:16. [pp. m. of *croistre*]
increased, grown.
crïer 18:48. [inf.] to cry.
    crïé 19:38, 19:53. [pp. m.].
    crient 21:21. [3 pl. pres.].
crigne 21:15. [FS] hair.
cris 21:35a. [NS] cry.
croire 9:295. [inf.] to believe.
    crei 18:22. = = > *croi*.
    croi 9:290. [1 sg. pres.].
    croit 13:451. [3 sg. pres.].
cropent 22:8a. [3 pl. pres. of *cropir*, to
crouch, to huddle].
cruiz 18:57. [OS] cross.
cruutes 22:8b. [FP] crypts.
cuer 11:392, 23:4b, 23:18. [OS] heart.
    cué 23:9c. = = > *cuer*.
cui 11:374. [relative pron., stressed
form of *qui #1*] whom, to whom.
cuidier [inf.] to believe.

cuida 6:185. [3 sg. pret.].

cuideriés 22:4. [2 pl. cond.].

cuit 8:254, 9:290, 12:430. [1 sg. pres.].

quida 18:21. = = > *cuida.*

quidiés 23:4a. [2 pl. imperative].

quit 23:7. = = > *cuit.*

cuignies 16:52, 18:3. [FP] axes, hatchets.

cula 19:23. [3 sg. pret. of *culer,* to flow].

cum 17:2. in *ensement cum.* 17:6. in *si tost cum.* 17:25. in *tant cum,* q.v.

cupel 19:21. [OS] top of the head.

curages 16:23. = = > *corages.*

curt 16:5, 16:14. [FS] court.

d' #1 1:07, 4:127, 18:6, 18:26, 20:29a, 22:2a. = = > *de #1.*

d' #2 4:127, 6:187, 8:271, 10:332, 20:24a. = = > *de #2.*

d' #3 4:121, 4:127, 10:341, 12:407, 16:25, 17:15, 18:12, 19:51, 20:32a. = = > *de #3.*

d' #4 4:98, 15:517. = = > *de #6.*

d' #5 4:123 See *dedesus d(e).*

damages 23:12, 23:13b. [NS] shame, pity.

dommage 10:330. [OS].

dame 2:45, 2:47, 2:53, 3:65, 4:99, 4:103, 4:107, 4:117, 6:176, 7:221, 7:231, 9:287, 11:387, 12:414, 12:426, 13:431, 13:440, 13:446, 13:461, 13:465, 15:530. [FS] lady (generally married).

dames 1:09, 22:11a. [FP].

Damnedeu 19:12. [OS] the Lord God.

damoisele 5:135, 5:150, 6:175, 7:234, 7:244, 8:261, 8:282, 10:343, 11:383, 12:399, 12:408, 12:427, 14:485. [FS] young lady (generally unmarried).

damoiseles 10:355. [FP].

damoisiax 20:20, 21:25, 23:13b. [NS] young man, youth.

danz 19:28. [NS] sir.

de #1 4:100, 4:120, 4:125, 4:134, 5:136, 6:210, 7:212, 10:326, 10:352, 10:363,

11:370, 11:377, 11:384, 12:400, 13:433, 13:457, 16:5, 17:8, 17:17, 18:8. [prep. indicating movement away from] from, of < enclitic in *del #2, des #1, du >.*

d' #1 1:07, 4:127, 18:6, 18:26, 20:29a, 22:2a. = = > *de #1.*

de #2 1:16, 3:67, 4:129, 6:201, 6:206, 13:455, 14:496, 15:519, 16:2, 18:41, 18:44, 18:46, 19:3, 19:20, 20:12, 20:14, 20:23, 20:32b, 21:7a, 21:8b, 22:2a, 22:8c, 23:6. [prep. introducing a circumstantial complement of means, manner, measure, or cause] by, with, of, for, in, about, on account of, by means of < enclitic in *del #2, des #2, du >.*

d' #2 4:127, 6:187, 8:271, 10:332, 20:24a. = = > *de #2.*

de #3 2:48, 3:80, 3:89, 7:215, 7:233, 7:236, 7:245, 8:257, 8:265, 9:285, 9:288, 9:304, 10:339, 11:370, 11:373, 12:421, 13:463, 13:464, 14:472, 14:473, 14:489, 15:520, 16:11, 16:20, 16:21, 16:35, 16:44, 17:27, 18:11, 18:34, 19:14, 19:21, 20:3, 20:16c, 20:21, 20:24b, 20:29a, 20:29c, 20:32a, 20:32b, 21:1b, 21:4, 21:5b, 21:7b, 21:36a, 21:36b, 22:2b, 22:2c, 23:9b, 23:9c, 23:10a, 23:11, 23:12. [prep. indicating possession, attribution, association, qualification, composition] of, about, in, with, for, by < enclitic in *del #2, des #3, du >.*

d' #3 4:121, 4:127, 10:341, 12:407, 16:25, 17:15, 18:12, 19:51, 20:32a. = = > *de #3.*

de #4 17:2. [prep. introducing an adv. complement] of, -ly.

de #5 3:90. [prep. used in comparisons] than.

de #6 3:91, 5:164, 8:280, 16:27. [untranslated prep. introducing an inf.] < enclitic in *del #3 >.*

d' #4 4:98, 15:517.

de #7 19:48 See *sovenir de.*

de #8 5:138, 21:35b see *fors de(l).*

de ço qu(e) 18:23. [conjunctive phr.] because.

de desuz 18:34. [adv. phr.] above.

de si lonc qu(e) 23:5a. [adv. phr.] from as far as (here: as soon as).

de sun gré 17:2. [adv. phr.] willingly, of his own accord.

de totes pars 10:352. [adv. phr.] on all sides.

decauc 22:8c. [pp. m. of *dechausser*] unshod.

decolé 16:13. [pp. m. of *decoler*] beheaded.

decolper 16:38. [inf.] to behead.

dedenz 7:233, 17:4, 17:12. [prep.] within.

dedesus d(e) 4:123. [compound prep.] on top of; within(?).

deduiz 10:347. [OP] pleasures.

defendeür 17:29. [NP] defenders.

defendre [inf.] to defend, to forbid.
   defenderont 20:25b. [3 pl. fut.].
   defendu 7:225. [pp. m.].
   deffent 20:25a. [2 sg. imperative].

defors 6:179. [compounded adv.] outside, without.

degré 16:46 [NP], 18:13 [OS] stairway(s).
   degrez 16:51, 17:36. [OP].

dei 18:27. [1 sg. pres. of *devoir*].

deïst 7:226. [3 sg. imperf. subjunc. of *dire*].

deit 17:26. [3 sg. pres. of *devoir*].

del #1 8:278, 17:30, 17:36, 18:5, 18:6, 18:13, 18:15, 18:21, 18:25, 18:31, 18:55, 18:60, 19:19, 19:43, 20:2, 22:2c, 22:11b, 22:13, 23:9b. == > *du*.

del #2 16:22, 19:37. [enclitic form of *de #1,2,3* and *le #4*].

del #3 16:23, 18:42. [enclitic form of *de #6* and *le #1*].

del tut 18:42, 19:40. == > *du tout*.

delivra 1:10. [3 sg. pret. of *delivrer*, to give birth].

'delivrast 10:326. [3 sg. imperf. subjunc. of *(se) delivrer*, to free, to rid (oneself) of].

delivree 12:413. [pp. f. of *delivrer*] cleared out (room).

'delivrera 11:380. [3 sg. fut. of *(se) delivrer*, to free, to rid (oneself) of].

delivrerai 4:110. [1 sg. fut. of *delivrer*, to get rid of].

demain 7:211, 15:505, 15:508. [adv.] tomorrow.

demander 19:18. [inf.] to ask (for).
   demanda 18:9. [3 sg. pret.].
   demandé 18:7. [pp. m.].
   demandee 8:261, 21:38a. [pp. f.].
   demandoient 7:250. [3 pl. imperf.].
   demant 20:27a. [1 sg. pres.].

demenee 15:522. [pp. f. of *demener*] displayed.

'demente 3:72. [3 sg. pres. of *(se) dementer*, to lament].

deniers 21:7a. [OP] small coins, pennies.

Denis in *saint Denis*, St. Denis, patron of France.

'depart 22:13. [3 sg. pres. of *(se) departir*, to leave].

departira 15:505. [3 sg. fut. of *departir*, to separate].

depecier 16:39, 16:53. [inf.] to destroy, to break into pieces.

deport 20:2. [OS] amusement, sport.

derechief 15:515. [adv.] immediately.

des #1 16:18, 21:1a, 23:26. [enclitic form of *de #1* and *les #1,2*].

des #2 8:270, 17:13, 17:21, 19:33. [enclitic form of *de #2* and *les #1,2*].

des #3 1:09, 3:92, 4:109, 5:148, 10:355, 11:367, 16:6, 20:5, 20:6. [enclitic form of *de #3* and *les #1,2*].

des #4 18:25. See *hors des*.

des qu(e) 3:78, 7:237. [temporal conjunctive phr.] as soon as.

desachier 17:9. [inf.] to tear apart, to tear away.
   desachié 19:6. [pp. m.].

desbarez 17:31. [pp. m. of *desbarer*] unbarred.

descendi 18:13. [3 sg. pret. of *descendre*, to descend].

descendu 16:15. [pp. m. of *descendre*] descended.

deservoit 2:64. [3 sg. imperf. of *deservir*, to deserve].

desfendre 3:91. [inf.] to defend.

desfubla 13:433. [3 sg. pret. of *desfubler*, to take off, to remove].

desfublee 12:400. [pp. f. of *desfubler*] taken off, removed.

desi qu(e) 5:172. [compound prep.] up (to), as far as.

desonor 2:34. [FS] dishonor.

desos 23:10b. [prep.] beneath.

despendirent 15:517. [3 pl. pret. of *despendre*, to spend].

despoillier 12:416. [inf.] to undress.

desqu'a 3:69. [prep.] to the end of.

dessevré 15:508. [pp. m. of *dessevrer*] separated.

destre #1 5:144. [FS] right, right side.

destre #2 18:2. [adj., FS] right.

destrier 16:26. [OS] warhorse.

destroit 2:63. in *tenoit en destroit*, held imprisoned.

desturbé 16:7. [pp. m. of *desturber*] disrupted, disturbed.

desur 18:47, 19:44. = = > *desus* #1.

desus #1 5:173, 9:308. [prep.] in, on.

desus #2 19:2. in *par desus* [compound prep.], above (here: by the shoulders[?]).

desuz 18:34. in *de desuz* [adv. phr.], below.

detraire 17:9. [inf.] to quarter (a person), to rip apart; to pull.
   detraist 18:23. [3 sg. pret.].

detrenchier 16:31. [inf.] to slay (with knives), to cut open.
   detrenchié 19:36. [pp. m.].

Deu en laissiez penser 17:39 leave it in God's hands (lit.: let God think about it).

Deus 1:11, 5:162, 14:492, 16:33, 18:50. [NS] God.

Deu 4:116, 10:350, 16:1, 16:2, 16:21, 17:27, 17:39, 18:34, 18:46, 19:16, 19:40. [OS].

Dieu 1:23, 3:93, 5:174, 6:190. = = > *Deu*.

Dieus 2:31. = = > *Deus*.

Diu 21:31. = = > *Deu*.

Dix 20:27a, 23:12. = = > *Deus*.

deus 1:11, 1:15, 2:35, 2:41, 3:67, 3:70, 3:83, 3:84, 3:85, 14:473, 14:476, 20:3, 21:38b, 22:11a. [num. OP] two.
   dous 17:5, 17:7, 18:33, 19:25, 19:34. = = > *deus*.
   dui 1:04, 2:42, 16:6, 16:7. [NP].

deüssiez 16:30. [2 pl. imperf. subjunc. of *devoir*].

deüst 20:24b. [3 sg. imperf. subjunc. of *devoir*].

devant 1:21, 5:158, 7:217, 13:432, 16:15, 22:8a. [prep.] before.

devers #1 16:45, 18:31. [prep.] toward.

devers #2 16:43. in *par devers* [compound prep.], by way of.

devez 2:46 [2 pl. imperative]. 18:44 [2 pl. pres. of *devoir*].

devisé 15:507. [pp. m. of *deviser*] arranged.

devisse 21:11. in *par grant devisse* [adv. phr.], carefully, artfully.

devoir. [modal inf.] should, ought, be necessary, have to; to be about to.
   dei 18:27. [1 sg. pres.].
   deit 17:26. [3 sg. pres.].
   deüssiez 16:30. [2 pl. imperf. subjunc.].
   deüst 20:24b. [3 sg. imperf. subjunc.].
   devez 2:46. [2 pl. imperative]. 18:44. [2 pl. pres.].
   devoient 10:366. [3 pl. imperf.].
   devrium 17:29. [1 pl. cond.].
   devroit 8:274. [3 sg. cond.].
   doie 21:4. [3 sg. pres. subjunc.].
   durent 15:514. [3 pl. pret.].
   dut 2:54, 12:398. [3 sg. pret.].

di 3:81, 23:25. [1 sg. pres. of *dire*].
di va 12:424. [interjection to get someone's attention] Say there! Hey!
dient 20:16a, 21:35b, 21:35c. [3 pl. pres. of *dire*].
Dieu 1:23, 3:93, 5:174, 6:190. = = > *Deu*.
Dieus 2:31. = = > *Deus*.
digné 16:12. [pp. m. of *disner* (sic)] dined, eaten.
dire 2:59, 23:1, 23:13a. [inf.] to say, to tell.
   deïst 7:226. [3 sg. imperf. subjunc.].
   di 3:81, 23:25. [1 sg. pres.].
   dient 20:16a, 21:35b, 21:35c. [3 pl. pres.].
   dirai 1:01, 13:470, 20:19, 22:7b. [1 sg. fut.].
   dis #1 14:472. [1 sg. pret.].
   disoient 4:96, 20:25a. [3 pl. imperf.].
   dist 6:197, 8:284, 11:393. [3 sg. pret.].
   dit #1 2:30, 4:117, 7:223, 9:306, 11:380, 13:453, 14:489. [3 sg. pres.].
   dite 2:51. [pp. f.].
   dites #1 13:465. [2 pl. pres.].
   dites #2 13:438, 13:468, 23:7. [2 pl. imperative].
dis #2 20:8. [NS] narrative, story.
dis #3 20:16d [num.] ten.
disner 16:47. [OS] dinner.
disoient 4:96, 20:25a. [3 pl. imperf. of *dire*].
dist 6:197, 8:284, 11:393. [3 sg. pret. of *dire*].
dit 2:30, 4:117, 7:223, 9:306, 11:380, 13:453, 14:489. [3 sg. pres. of *dire*].
dite 2:51. [pp. f. of *dire*] said, told.
dites #1 13:465. [2 pl. pres. of *dire*].
dites #2 13:438, 13:468, 23:7. [2 pl. imperative of *dire*].
Diu 21:31. = = > *Deu*.
Dix 20:27a, 23:12. = = > *Deus*.

doie 21:4. [3 sg. pres. subjunc. of *devoir*].
doinst 20:27a. [3 sg. pres. subjunc. of *doner*].
dois 1:21. [OS] dais (raised platform).
Dol 8:253, 11:370. [OS] city in Brittany.
dolans 20:11, 22:13. [pres. participle, NS, of *doloir*, to grieve, to lament] grief-stricken, sorrowful, sad.
   dolenz 2:60. = = > *dolans*.
dolente 3:71. [pres. participle, FS, of *doloir*] grief-stricken, sad.
dolenté 19:55 in *chaü en dolenté*, fallen on hard times.
dolenz 2:60. = = > *dolans*.
dolouser 4:104. [inf.] to grieve.
dommage 10:330. [OS of *damages*].
donasse 21:7b. [1 sg. imperf. subjunc. of *doner*].
   donasce 22:2b. = = > *donasse*.
donastes 14:479. [2 pl. pret. of *doner*].
donc 13:447. [adv.] then, at that time, at that moment; next; thus, therefore, consequently.
   dont #3 3:81, 21:22, 23:2, 23:13b. = = > *donc*.
   dunc 16:19, 16:37, 16:46, 17:1, 17:10, 17:12, 18:9, 18:40, 18:51, 19:26, 19:46, 19:49. = = > *donc*.
   idunc 19:27, 19:29, 19:51. = = > *donc*.
doner. [inf.] to give.
   doinst 20:27a. [3 sg. pres. subjunc.].
   donasce 22:2b. = = > *donasse*.
   donasse 21:7b. [1 sg. imperf. subjunc.].
   donastes 14:479. [2 pl. pret.].
   donés 20:27b. [2 pl. pres.].
   donna 12:419, 13:438. [3 sg. pret.].
   donné 1:24, 8:278. [pp. m.].
   donnee 14:492, 15:510, 15:526. [pp. f.].
   donra 8:272, 8:273, 20:29c. [3 sg. fut.].

donrai 20:30a. [1 sg. fut.].
donron 10:350. [1 pl. fut.].
duner 19:20. = = > *doner*.
dont #1 23:4b, 23:13b. [relative pron.]
of, by, or with whom/which.
dont #2 13:437, 21:3, 23:9c. [relative
and interrogative adv. of place]
from whence, from where.
dont #3 3:81, 21:22, 23:2, 23:13b.
= = > *donc*.
doublez 14:493. [pp. m. of *doubler*]
doubled.
douce 20:15, 20:27b, 23:2, 23:8. [adj.,
FS] sweet, fair.
  dox (= *dous*) 20:8. [NS].
  dulce 19:13. = = > *douce*.
dous 17:5, 17:7, 18:33, 19:25, 19:34.
= = > *deus*.
doute 13:451. [1 sg. pres. of *douter*, to
doubt].
Dovre 16:6. [FS] Dover (England).
dox 20:8. [adj., NS of *douce*].
drap 12:407. [NS] cover, cloth,
clothing.
  dras 6:184, 19:24. [OP].
'drecié 16:18. [pp. m. of *(se) drecier*]
gotten up.
dreit 16:15, 16:45. [adv.] right,
directly.
drois 21:38a. [adj., NS] right, proper,
just.
du 1:01, 5:143, 5:174, 6:178, 8:272,
15:529, 20:2, 20:29c, 21:7b, 22:5.
[enclitic form of *de* #1,2,3 and *le*
#1].
  del #1 8:278, 17:30, 17:36, 18:5,
  18:6, 18:13, 18:15, 18:21, 18:25,
  18:31, 18:55, 18:60, 19:19, 19:43,
  20:2, 22:2c, 22:11b, 22:13, 23:9b.
  = = > *du*.
du tout 9:289. [adv. phr.] completely,
altogether.
  del tut 18:42, 19:40. = = > *du tout*.
duel 4:108, 10:365. [OS] lamentation.
dui 1:04, 2:42, 16:6, 16:7. [num. NP of
deus].
dulce 19:13. = = > *douce*.

dunc 16:19, 16:37, 16:46, 17:1, 17:10,
17:12, 18:9, 18:40, 18:51, 19:26, 19:46,
19:49. = = > *donc*.
duner 19:20. = = > *doner*.
durement 2:44, 2:62, 3:71, 4:104, 5:152,
9:292, 9:294, 9:299, 16:37, 19:37,
23:5b. [adv.] strongly, much,
greatly.
durent 15:514. [3 pl. pret. of *devoir*].
dut 2:54, 12:398. [3 sg. pret. of *devoir*].

e all occurrences. = = > *et*.
Eduvard (Grim) 19:1 [NS], 19:6 [NS],
19:25 [OS]. Edward Grim, clerk, St.
Thomas' only defender. Author of
the principal Latin source about St.
Thomas.
  Eduvarz 19:26. = = > *Eduvard*
  [NS].
Engletere 20:32a. [FS] England.
eglise 7:212. [FS] church.
  iglise 18:17, 18:57, 19:14, 19:15.
  = = > *eglise*.
einsi 17:11, 17:14, 18:46. = = > *ainsi*.
einsint 15:507. = = > *ainsi*.
  el #1 4:117, 11:394, 12:415.
  = = > *ele #1*.
el #2 4:130, 6:200, 7:211, 7:228, 8:256,
15:505, 15:508, 16:43, 17:18, 17:20,
17:40, 18:1, 18:35, 19:49, 19:50,
20:25a, 23:4a, 23:4b, 23:6. [enclitic
form of *en #1* and *le #1*].
el #3 17:5, 19:20, 23:9c. in *enz el*
[compound prep.], in, within.
ele #1 1:10, 2:27, 2:29, 2:64, 3:73,
4:107, 4:134, 5:159, 5:161, 5:162,
6:176, 6:210, 7:222, 7:227, 7:235,
7:237, 7:241, 8:284, 10:359, 11:376,
11:386, 11:393, 12:419, 12:420,
12:424, 13:448, 13:449, 13:450,
13:455, 14:496, 15:528, 20:31b,
20:32a, 21:3, 21:15, 21:35b, 23:1, 23:7,
23:9c, 23:13a. [3 sg. personal subject
pron., FS] she.
  el #1 4:117, 11:394, 12:415.
  = = > *ele #1*.
  elle 2:36. = = > *ele #1*.

ele #2 18:31. [FS] wing.

eles 4:97, 22:11a. [3 pl. personal subject pron., FP] they.

elle 2:36. = = > *ele* #1.

els 16:36, 16:52, 17:18, 17:21, 17:35, 19:3, 19:41. = = > *eus.*

em #1 6:195. = = > *en* #1.

em #2 7:246. = = > *en* #2.

em #3 9:292, 12:410. = = > *en* #3.

emmenerent 15:524. [3 pl. pret. of *emmener,* to lead away].

empainst 17:8. [3 sg. pret. of *empaindre,* to shove].

emporte 9:303. [3 sg. pres. of *emporter,* to carry, to take].

emprés 7:211. = = > *aprés* #1.

en #1 1:03, 2:49, 3:66, 4:95, 4:113, 4:121, 5:139, 5:149, 5:151, 6:177, 7:243, 9:302, 9:312, 10:344, 10:347, 11:392, 12:410, 13:460, 15:523, 15:525, 16:13, 16:14, 16:17, 16:29, 18:2, 18:3, 18:17, 18:57, 19:55, 20:23, 20:29b, 20:30b, 20:31a, 20:31b, 20:32a, 21:3, 21:5a, 21:8b, 21:9, 21:10, 21:24, 21:28, 21:29, 21:34, 21:36b, 21:38b, 22:5, 22:6, 22:7b, 22:8b, 22:9, 22:10a, 22:12b, 23:1, 23:4a, 23:6, 23:9b. [prep. localizing temporally or spatially] in(to), on(to), at, before < enclitic in *el* #2, *es* #2 >.

    em #1 6:195. = = > *en* #1.

en #2 2:63, 5:169, 6:186, 7:246, 10:346, 19:25, 19:34. [prep. of manner, means, attribution] in, by < enclitic in *es* #2 >.

    em #2 7:246. = = > *en* #2.

en #3 1:12, 1:13, 1:23, 2:25, 2:36, 2:53, 2:54, 2:60, 3:71, 3:85, 3:86, 4:110, 4:111, 4:118, 6:190, 8:274, 9:294, 11:380, 11:386, 13:455, 14:476, 15:523, 15:529, 17:28, 17:29, 17:39, 18:27, 18:39, 18:44, 20:23, 20:26, 21:36a, 21:36a, 21:38a, 21:38a, 22:5, 22:12a, 23:5b, 23:13a. [invariable pron. standing for a noun governed by *de* #3] about, for, or of it, him, her, or them.

em #3 9:292, 12:410. = = > *en* #3.

en #4 5:136, 5:138, 5:142, 6:192, 9:289, 9:296, 9:301, 9:302, 16:52, 17:1, 18:6, 18:20, 18:31, 18:43, 18:50, 18:58, 18:59, 19:5, 19:21, 19:45, 19:51, 19:52, 23:1, 23:2. [invariable, untranslated adv. particle used with verbs of motion or direction to indicate movement away from].

en #5 3:89, 8:274. = = > *on.*

en bescoz 19:33. [adv. phr.] obliquely, slantingly.

en present 19:11. [idiom] before him.

en tel aé qu(e) 7:241 to that age when.

enblee 21:37. [pp. f. of *embler*] stolen.

enbracié 19:2. [pp. m. of *embracier*] embraced, taken in (one's) arms.

enceinter, enceintier. [inf.] to become pregnant.

    ençaintai 14:475. [1 sg. pret.].

    enceinta 1:09, 3:66. [3 sg. pret.].

    enceintie 9:293. = = > *enceintiee.*

    enceintiee 3:67. [pp. f.].

enchargier 18:53. [inf.] to load.

encisa 19:24. [3 sg. pret. of *enciser,* to cut].

encloistre 17:4, 17:12, 19:52. [OS] enclosure, cloister, monastery.

encomence 5:161. [3 sg. pres. of *encommencier,* to begin].

encontre 18:13. [prep.] toward.

encontré 18:8. [pp. m. of *encontrer*] encountered.

    encontrez 17:20. = = > *encontré.*

encor 23:6. [adv.] yet, still.

endemain 16:13. [OS] the next day.

endementres 16:24. [adv.] meanwhile.

enemi 16:1. [NP] enemies.

enfant 1:18, 4:98, 4:122, 5:135, 5:142, 5:159, 5:164, 5:171, 6:189, 6:194, 6:199, 6:204, 7:215, 7:220, 10:332. [OS] child, infant.

    enfans 20:3. = = > *enfanz.*

    enfanz 1:11, 1:16, 2:41, 3:67, 3:83, 3:92, 4:109, 14:473. [OP].

enferma 9:312. [3 sg. pret. of *enfermer*, to enclose].

enginnier 16:40. [inf.] to contrive, to devise.

enhaï 2:61. [3 sg. pret. of *enhair*, to hate].

enhaïrent 2:56. [3 pl. pret. of *enhair*, to hate].

enmena 9:315. [3 sg. pret. of *emmener*, to lead away].

ennore 10:362. [3 sg. pres. of *ennorer*, to honor].

enpaint 18:24. [pp. m. of *empaindre*] shoved.

enpereris 20:32a. [FS] empress.

enploiie 20:31b. [pp. f. of *emploier*] used, employed.

enragié #1 16:14. [NP] madmen.

enragié #2 18:36, 19:7. [pp. m. of *enragier*] mad, besotted.

ens el 23:9c. = = > *enz el*.

ensaingna 12:402. [3 sg. pret. of *enseignier*, to teach].

ensaingnie 8:263. [pp. f. of *enseignier*] well-bred, well-mannered.

ensemble 9:296, 9:301, 18:40. [adv.] together.

    ensanble 23:10a. = = > *ensemble*.

ensement 19:15, 19:50. [adv.] likewise.

ensement cum 17:2. [conjunctive phr.] just as (if).

enseurquetot 22:4. [adv.] especially.

entama 19:22. [3 sg. pret. of *entamer*, to penetrate, to cut into].

entecie 20:32b. [pp. f. of *entechier*] endowed with.

enteciés 20:23. [pp. m. of *entechier*] endowed with.

entendre 7:237. [inf.] to understand, to hear.

    entendi 18:11. [3 sg. pret.].

    entendu 21:34. [pp. m.].

    entens 23:25. [2 sg. pres.].

    entent 12:424. [2 sg. imperative].

enterriés 22:5. [2 pl. cond. of *entrer*].

entor #1 6:207, 9:293, 11:387. [prep.] around.

entor #2 4:131. [adv.] around.

entra 17:18, 19:41. [3 sg. pret. of *entrer*].

entre 5:171, 13:466, 18:33. [prep.] in, among, between.

    entr' 20:25b. = = > *entre*.

entrepris 20:11. [pp. m. of *entreprendre*] crushed, overwhelmed.

entrer 16:35, 22:7a. [inf.] to enter.

    enterriés 22:5. [2 pl. cond.].

    entra 17:18, 19:41. [3 sg. pret.].

    entré 16:43, 17:4, 17:12. [pp. m.].

    entree 5:139, 5:150. [pp. f.].

    entrerent 17:19. [3 pl. pret.].

    entrez 13:460, 16:49. = = > *entré*.

envaï 19:2. [pp. m. of *envaïr*] attacked.

envelopent 4:122. [3 pl. pres. of *enveloper*, to wrap up].

enveoit 13:458. [3 sg. imperf. of *envoier*].

envïeuse 2:28. [adj., FS] envious.

envoier [inf.] to send, to send for.

    enveoit 13:458. [3 sg. imperf.].

    envoia 9:310. [3 sg. pret.].

    envoiee 9:307. [pp. f.].

    envoierai 21:8b. [1 sg. fut.].

    envoierent 13:444. [3 pl. pret.].

enz el 17:5, 19:20. [compound prep.] in, within.

    ens el 23:9c. = = > *enz el*.

ere 20:27a. [1 sg. fut. of *estre* #2].

erent #1 16:46, 16:47, 19:5, 19:52. [3 pl. imperf. of *estre* #1 (aux.)].

erent #2 2:49, 19:54, 19:55. [3 pl. imperf. of *estre* #2].

ereses 22:8b. [adj., FP] threadbare.

erramment 19:14. [adv.] at once.

errant 5:172. [adv.] quickly.

ert #1 4:132, 6:194, 6:210, 9:294, 9:306, 17:32. [3 sg. imperf. of *estre* #1 (aux.)].

ert #2 2:27, 17:15. [3 sg. imperf. of *estre* #2].

    iert #1 12:409. = = > *ert* #2.

ert #3 23:13b. [3 sg. fut. of *estre* #2].

    iert #2 2:38, 23:13b. = = > *ert* #3.

es #1 13:454. [2 sg. pres. of *estre* #*2*].

es #2 11:383, 16:49, 17:13, 19:53. [enclitic form of *en* #*1,2* and *les* #*1,2*] in (the).

es vos 1:20. [deictic] Look! Behold! There is. . . .

esbahi 19:3. [3 sg. pret. of *(s')esbahir,* to be frightened, to be astonished].

esbahis 20:10. [pp. m. of *esbahir*] troubled, frightened.

esbanoiement 11:382. [OS] good times, joy, festivity.

escargaites 23:10a. [NP] night watchmen.

escervelad 19:30. [3 sg. pret. of *escerveler,* to cut (his) brains out].

escerveleroie 23:5b. [1 sg. cond. of *escerveler,* to cut (his) brains out].

eschange 10:346. [OS] exchange.

eschaufé 6:205. [pp. m. of *eschaufer*] warmed.

eschaufez 6:202. [2 pl. imperative of *eschaufer,* to warm].

eschieles 16:50. [FS] ladder.

escïent 5:153. in *mien escïent* [idiom], I believe, in my opinion. 6:209. in *a escïent* [adv. phr.], with certainty.

escole 7:245. in *de bone escole* [idiom], well-raised, properly educated.

escoutez 13:470. [2 pl. imperative of *escouter,* to listen (to)].

'escria 19:44. [3 sg. pret. of *(s')ecrier,* to cry out, to shout].

escu 17:30. [OS] shield.

escumengié 18:37. [pp. m. of *escumengier*] excommunicated.

'esforcié 19:37. [pp. m. of *(s')esforcier*] striven, done (their) utmost.

esfreez 13:459. [pp. m. of *esfreer*] frightened.

esgarder [inf.] to look, to look at.

  esgarda 21:19. [3 sg. pret.].

  esgarde 12:417. [3 sg. pres.].

  esgardé 7:222, 13:448. [pp. m.].

  esgardee 11:391. [pp. f.].

  esgardent 10:338. [3 pl. pres.].

  esguardez 19:8. [2 pl. imperative].

esgarez 8:267. [pp. m. of *esgarer*] troubled.

'esjoï 14:495. [3 sg. pret. of *(s')esjoïr,* to cheer up, to become happy].

esligier 15:517. [inf.] to pay for.

esluignier 18:55, 18:58. [inf.] to move someone away from something.

esmaier 16:32. [inf.] to become frightened.

espanie 21:20. [pp. f. of *espanir*] in bloom, open.

espaule 19:23. [FS] shoulder.

espee 18:2, 19:20, 19:23, 19:43. [FS] sword.

  espees 17:13, 19:53, 23:10b. [FP].

espés 5:168. [adj., OS] thick.

esploit 5:147. in *a grant esploit* [adv. phr.], rapidly.

espöentez 18:41. [pp. m. of *espoenter*] frightened.

espousast 10:325. [3 sg. imperf. subjunc. of *espouser*].

espouse 10:332, 11:371. [FS] wife.

espousee #1 12:398. [FS] bride.

espouser [inf.] to marry, to wed.

  espousast 10:325. [3 sg. imperf. subjunc.].

  espousee #2 1:08, 10:358, 14:488, 15:509. [pp. f.].

  espousera 15:506. [3 sg. fut.].

'esquelderoie 23:5a. [1 sg. cond. of *(s')escoillir,* to hurl, to throw (oneself)].

est #1 3:67, 3:68, 3:86, 4:134, 5:139, 5:150, 5:157, 5:158, 5:166, 8:267, 9:301, 10:353, 11:372, 12:399, 12:400, 13:432, 13:460, 16:9, 16:49, 18:1, 18:31, 18:32, 18:34, 18:35, 21:9, 21:35b, 23:9c. [3 sg. pres. of *estre* #*1* (aux.)].

est #2 2:47, 3:75, 4:98, 9:287, 10:340, 12:430, 14:475, 14:485, 14:486, 16:23, 18:33, 18:49, 20:8, 20:10, 20:15, 20:29a, 20:31a, 20:32b, 21:8a, 21:11, 22:2a, 23:9b. [3 sg. pres. of *estre* #*2*].

est #3 3:85. See *ce m'est avis.* 13:446. See *ce m'est molt bel.*

esté 2:48, 10:321, 16:45. [pp. m. of *estre* #2] been.

    esteient 16:18. = = > *estoient* #1.

esteit 18:56. = = > *estoit* #1 (aux.).

estendu 19:32. [pp. m. of *estendre*] stretched out.

ester 2:45, 17:38, 20:29a, 22:1. [inf.] to stand, to be.

estes #1 9:293, 19:7. [2 pl. pres. of *estre* #1 (aux.)].

estes #2 18:20, 19:8. [2 pl. pres. of *estre* #2].

estoient #1 [3 pl. imperf. of *estre* #1 (aux.)].

    esteient 16:18. = = > *estoient* #1.

estoient #2 1:04, 4:95, 10:356. [3 pl. imperf. of *estre* #2].

estoit #1 1:16, 4:131, 5:169, 5:170, 15:528, 20:23, 20:24a, 21:35a. [3 sg. imperf. of *estre* #1 (aux.)].

    esteit 18:56. = = > *estoit* #1 (aux.).

estoit #2 4:100, 6:193, 7:245, 11:369, 12:407, 13:452, 20:17, 20:19, 20:21, 20:32a, 21:1b, 23:11. [3 sg. imperf. of *estre* #2].

estor 20:27a. [OS] skirmish.

estorer 18:57. [inf.] to establish.

estrange 20:29a, 22:2a. [adj., FS] foreign.

estre #1 2:54, 14:481, 18:27. [inf.] to be (aux.).

    erent #1 16:46, 16:47, 19:5, 19:52. [3 pl. imperf.].

    ert #1 4:132, 6:194, 6:210, 9:294, 9:306, 17:32. [3 sg. imperf.].

    est #1 3:67, 3:68, 3:86, 4:134, 5:139, 5:150, 5:157, 5:158, 5:166, 8:267, 9:301, 10:353, 11:372, 12:399, 12:400, 13:432, 13:460, 16:9, 16:49, 18:1, 18:31, 18:32, 18:34, 18:35, 21:9, 21:35b, 23:9c. [3 sg. pres.].

    esteient 16:18. = = > *estoient* #1.

    esteit 18:56. = = > *estoit* #1

    estes #1 9:293, 19:7. [2 pl. pres.].

    estoient #1. [3 pl. imperf.].

estoit #1 1:16, 4:131, 5:169, 5:170, 15:528, 20:23, 20:24a, 21:35a. [3 sg. imperf.].

fu #1 2:51, 2:53, 5:137, 7:218, 7:228, 7:232, 7:234, 9:307, 9:308, 10:357, 12:413, 12:425, 13:436, 15:526, 15:527, 18:19, 18:28, 20:29a. [3 sg. pret.].

furent #1 15:508, 16:2, 16:7, 16:13, 16:27, 16:34. [3 pl. pret.].

fust #1 14:493, 20:16c, 20:31b. [3 sg. imperf. subjunc.].

fut 21:3. = = > *fu* #1.

sera #1 21:38a. [3 sg. fut.].

soit 7:217, 13:467, 15:504, 20:13, 21:3. [3 sg. pres. subjunc.].

sont #1 22:10b. [3 pl. pres.].

sunt #1 16:5, 16:6, 16:10, 16:11, 16:15, 16:43, 16:48, 17:4, 17:5, 17:12, 18:6, 19:37, 19:51, 19:55. = = > *sont* #1.

estre #2 17:29, 19:17, 20:24a, 20:28, 21:4, 23:8. [inf.] to be (as copula).

    ere 20:27a. [1 sg. fut.].

    erent #2 2:49, 19:54, 19:55. [3 pl. imperf.].

    ert #2 2:27, 17:15. [3 sg. imperf.].

    ert #3 23:13b. [3 sg. fut.].

    es #1 13:454. [2 sg. pres.].

    iert #1 12:409. = = > *ert* #2.

    iert #2 2:38, 23:13b. = = > *ert* #3.

    est #2 2:47, 3:75, 4:98, 9:287, 10:340, 12:430, 14:475, 14:485, 14:486, 16:23, 18:33, 18:49, 20:8, 20:10, 20:15, 20:29a, 20:31a, 20:32b, 21:8a, 21:11, 22:2a, 23:9b. [3 sg. pres.].

    esté 2:48, 10:321, 16:45. [pp. m.].

    estes #2 18:20, 19:8. [2 pl. pres.].

    estoient #2 1:04, 4:95, 10:356. [3 pl. imperf.].

    estoit #2 4:100, 6:193, 7:245, 11:369, 12:407, 13:452, 20:17, 20:19, 20:21, 20:32a, 21:1b, 23:11. [3 sg. imperf.].

fu #2 1:12, 2:38, 2:60, 3:71, 3:81, 4:125, 7:226, 7:236, 9:285, 11:383, 16:5, 16:28, 21:34, 21:36a, 23:14, 23:17. [3 sg. pret.].

fui #1 14:490. [1 sg. pret.].

furent #2 1:05, 1:07, 15:513. [3 pl. pret.].

fust #2 11:394, 20:16c. [3 sg. imperf. subjunc.].

sera #2 10:338, 21:38a. [3 sg. fut.].

serai 21:32. [1 sg. fut.].

seroient 10:327. [3 pl. cond.].

seroit 15:516, 22:5, 23:13a. [3 sg. cond.].

seroiz 4:111. [2 pl. cond.].

sont #2 2:36, 22:8c. [3 pl. pres.].

sui 3:75, 14:489, 18:27, 18:41, 18:42, 21:24, 21:26, 21:28. [1 sg. pres.].

sumes 17:28. [1 pl. pres.].

sunt #2 16:22, 17:24, 18:37, 18:38, 19:8, 19:54. = = >*sont #2*.

estre (molt) bel 9:304. [phrasal verb] to please.

estroitement 13:462. [adv.] ardently, fervently.

estrumelé 22:8c. [pp. m. of *estrumeler*] barelegged.

estuet 3:92, 16:19. [3 sg. pres. of *estovoir* (modal), to have to, to be necessary to].

et (all occurences). [conj.] and.

e all occurrences. = = >*et*.

eulz 8:270. [OP of *oeul*] eyes.

ex #2 21:8b, 23:5b, 23:21, 20:22a. = = >*eulz*.

eus 7:252. [3 pl. obj. pron. m.] them.

els 16:36, 16:52, 17:18, 17:21, 17:35, 19:3, 19:41. = = >*eus*.

ex #1 20:25b. = = >*eus*.

eüsciés 23:6. [2 pl. imperf. subjunc. of *avoir #2* (aux.)].

eüst #1 3:83, 10:332, 21:36a. [3 sg. imperf. subjunc. of *avoir #1*].

eüst #2 6:185. [3 sg. imperf. subjunc. of *avoir #2* (aux.)].

eüst #3 21:7b. [3 sg. imperf. subjunc. of *avoir #1*] in *n'avoir . . . que faire*, q.v.

eüz 1:15, 2:35. [pp. m. of *avoir #1*] had.

ex #1 20:25b. = = >*eus*.

ex #2 21:8b, 23:5b, 23:21, 20:22a. = = >*eulz*.

fablent 20:16a. [3 sg. pres. of *fabler*, to narrate].

fac 23:8. [1 sg. pres. of *faire #1*].

face #1 1:18. [3 sg. pres. subjunc. of *faire #2*].

face #2 20:22b, 21:17. [FS] face.

faciés 23:7. [2 pl. pres. subjunc. of *faire #1*].

faide 21:38a. [FS] night of blood vengeance (for a death).

faim 22:8c. [FS] hunger.

fainte 2:27. [adj., FS] deceitful.

faire #1 17:24, 17:27, 17:30, 18:44, 19:7, 21:4, 22:6. [inf.] to do, to make.

fac 23:8. [1 sg. pres.].

faciés 23:7. [2 pl. pres. subjunc.].

faisoit 4:119, 20:16b. [3 sg. imperf.].

fait #1 2:42, 6:176, 18:16, 21:36b. [pp. m.].

fait #3 23:9a. [3 sg. pres.].

faite #1 20:29b, 21:7a, 21:11, 21:16, 22:2b. [pp. f.].

faites 18:44. [2 pl. imperative].

fare 20:24b, 21:33. = = >*faire #1*.

ferai 3:73, 18:29, 18:39. [1 sg. fut.].

fere #1 2:60. = = >*faire #1*.

ferez #1 4:108, 17:35. [2 pl. fut.].

feront 23:30. [3 pl. fut.].

fesoient 10:365. [3 pl. imperf.].

fet #1 9:288, 15:507. = = >*fait #1*.

fet #3 3:90, 6:203, 10:335. = = >*fait #3*.

firent 15:518, 16:51. [3 pl. pret.].

fist #1 10:360, 11:385, 20:6. [3 sg. pret.].

faire #2. [inf.] to cause (when followed by an inf.).
   face #1 1:18. [3 sg. pres. subjunc.].
   fait #2 16:36, 17:36. [pp. m.].
   faite #2 21:35c. [pp. f.].
   fera 7:223. [3 sg. fut.].
   fere #2 12:415. == >*faire #2*.
   feroie 23:5b. [1 sg. cond.].
   fet #2 7:238. == >*fait #2*.
   fis 14:477. [1 sg. pret.].
   fist #2 9:313. [3 sg. pret.].
faire #3 [inf.] to say.
   fait #4 16:19, 16:32, 16:41, 17:9, 17:22, 17:23, 17:33, 17:35, 17:38, 18:10, 18:14, 18:16, 18:18, 18:20, 18:26, 18:28, 18:29, 18:39, 18:41, 19:7, 19:27, 19:45, 20:26, 20:28, 20:31a, 21:6, 22:1, 22:12a, 22:13, 23:2, 23:7, 23:8, 23:12. [3 sg. pres.].
   fet #4 2:45, 3:73, 5:162, 4:107, 9:287, 12:424, 12:426, 13:465, 14:494. == >*fait #4*.
   fist #3 18:50. [3 sg. pret.].
   font 10:339. [3 pl. pres.].
   funt 16:29, 17:34, 17:35, 18:37. == >*font*.
faire #4 17:39, 20:29c, 21:7b, 22:2c, 22:9. in *n'avoir . . . que faire* [idiom], not to be of any interest/concern to someone.
fame #1 1:08, 1:15, 2:25, 2:35, 2:41, 2:61, 3:83, 10:325, 10:337. [FS] wife, woman.
   fames 2:55, 3:80. [FP].
   fenme 20:30a, 23:9a, 23:9a, 23:9b. == >*fame*.
fame #2 2:48. reputation.
fare 20:24b, 21:33. == >*faire #1*.
faudrai 9:297. [1 sg. fut. of *faillir*, to fail].
feirié 19:8 [NP], 19:10 [OS] feast day(s).
feiz #1 18:22. [FS] time, occasion.
feiz #2 17:5. == >*foiz*.
felonies 18:30. [FP] treacheries,

felonies (i.e., acts of disloyalty or treason against an overlord).
felun 16:1, 19:36. [NP] traitors, felons.
fenestre 21:13. [FS] window.
fenme 20:30a, 23:9a, 23:9a, 23:9b. == >*fame #1*.
fera 7:223. [3 sg. fut. of *faire #2*].
ferai 3:73, 18:29, 18:39. [1 sg. fut. of *faire #1*].
fere #1 2:60. == >*faire #1*.
fere #2 12:415. == >*faire #2*.
ferez #1 4:108, 17:35. [2 pl. fut. of *faire #1*].
ferir 16:22, 19:37, 23:4b. [inf.] to strike, to hit.
   ferez #2 19:27. [2 pl. imperative].
   feri 19:27. [3 sg. pret.].
   feru 19:33, 19:36. [pp. m.].
   fiere 20:27b. [1 sg. pres. subjunc.].
fermé 16:44. [pp. m. of *fermer*] closed.
   fermez 16:53. == >*fermé*.
fermeté 17:26. [FS] stronghold.
feroie 23:5b. [1 sg. cond. of *faire #2*].
feront 23:30. [3 pl. fut. of *faire #1*].
feru 19:33, 19:36. [pp. m. of *ferir*] struck, hit.
fesoient 10:365. [3 pl. imperf. of *faire #1*].
fet #1 9:288, 15:507. [pp. m. of *faire #1*].
fet #2 7:238. [pp. m. of *faire #2*].
fet #3 3:90, 6:203, 10:335. [3 sg. pres. of *faire #1*].
fet #4 2:45, 3:73, 4:107, 5:162, 9:287, 12:424, 12:426, 13:465, 14:494. [3 sg. pres. of *faire #3*].
feu 6:198, 6:204. [OS] fire.
   fu #3 21:5a, 22:12b. == >*feu*.
ficha 19:42. [3 sg. pret. of *fichier*, to shove, to kick, to thrust].
fiefé 10:322. [adj., NP] enfeoffed (endowed with a fief).
fiere 20:27b. [1 sg. pres. subjunc. of *ferir*].
fil #1 20:18, 21:1a, 21:31. [OS] son.
   fil #2 17:19, 18:51. [NP].

filz 1:15. [OP].

fix 20:25a, 20:28, 21:7b. [NS].

fiz 2:35. = = >*filz.*

fille 6:193, 6:197, 10:341, 11:375,
11:395, 12:414, 12:420, 13:452,
13:454, 14:483, 14:491, 14:494,
15:514, 15:524, 20:18, 20:30b, 22:3.
[FS] daughter.

   file 20:30a. = = >*fille.*

   filles 3:70, 14:476. [FP].

fillole 20:29b, 22:2b. [FS] goddaughter.

   filole 21:2, 21:7a. = = > *fillole.*

filz 1:15 [OP] of *fil #1*].

   fiz 2:35. = = >*filz.*

fin 4:129. [adj., OS] pure.

finee 5:165. [pp. f. of *finer*] ended, died.

firent 15:518, 16:51. [3 pl. pret. of *faire*
#1].

fis 14:477. [1 sg. pret. of *faire #2*].

fist #1 10:360, 11:385, 20:6. [3 sg.
pret. of *faire #1*].

fist #2 9:313. [3 sg. pret. of *faire #2*].

fist #3 18:50. [3 sg. pret. of *faire #3*].

fix 20:25a, 20:28, 21:7b. [NS of *fil #1*].

fiz 2:35. = = >*filz.*

flechir 16:20. [inf.] to bend.

foillu 5:168. [adj., OS] leafy.

foiz 8:281, 10:324, 12:404. [FP] times,
occasions.

   feiz #2 17:5. = = >*foiz.*

folement 2:29. [adv.] foolishly, rashly.

folie 14:472. [FS] folly, madness.

font 10:339. [3 pl. pres. of *faire #3*].

   funt 16:29, 17:34, 17:35, 18:37.
   = = >*font.*

force 16:39. [FS] (strength of) force.

forest 5:140. [FS] forest.

forme 7:242. [3 sg. pres. of *former*, to
form, to create].

forment 18:52, 19:1, 23:29. [adv.]
strongly, tightly, very much.

fors #1 5:138, 6:200, 16:24 (*la fors*),
18:21, 21:35b. [adv.] outside.

   hors 18:54. in *la hors.* 19:19.
   = = >*fors #1.*

fors #2 5:169. [OP] forks (of tree).

fors #3 12:419, 20:18, 22:7b. [prep.]
except.

frales 20:17. [adj., OP] frail.

franc 16:41 [NP], 22:10c [NP], 23:18
[OS]. [adj.] noble.

   france 20:32b. = = >*franche.*

   franche 7:245. [FS].

France 19:13, 20:30b, 20:32a. [FS]
France.

franchise 9:319. [FS] noble actions.

fraternité 8:277. [FS] company,
opportunity to fraternize.

fremi 12:422. [3 sg. pret. of *fremir*, to
shudder].

Fresne 1:01, 7:229, 7:230, 10:345,
10:348, 10:357, 13:452, 15:529. [FS]
Fresne (Ash Tree), eponymous
heroine of Marie de France's *lai.*

fresne 5:167, 5:172, 6:184, 6:200, 7:228,
9:308. [OS] ash tree.

froit 22:8c. [OS] cold.

fruiz 10:348. [OP] fruit(s).

fu #1 2:51, 2:53, 5:137, 7:218, 7:228,
7:232, 7:234, 9:307, 9:308, 10:357,
12:413, 12:425, 13:436, 15:526,
15:527, 18:19, 18:28, 20:29a. [3 sg.
pret. of *estre #1* (aux.)].

   fut 21:3. = = >*fu #1.*

fu #2 1:12, 2:38, 2:60, 3:71, 3:81,
4:125, 7:226, 7:236, 9:285, 11:383,
16:5, 16:28, 21:34, 21:36a, 23:14,
23:17. [3 sg. pret. of *estre #2*].

fu #3 21:5a, 22:12b. = = >*feu.*

fui #1 14:490. [1 sg. pret. of *estre #2*].

fuïr [inf.] to flee.

   fui #2 18:26. [2 sg. imperative].

   fuï 19:5. [pp. m.].

   fuïe 21:35b. [pp. f.].

   fuiez 18:28. [2 pl. imperative].

funt 16:29, 17:34, 17:35, 18:37. [3 pl.
pres. of *faire #3*].

furent #1 15:508, 16:2, 16:7, 16:13,
16:27, 16:34. [3 pl. pret. of *estre #1*
(aux.)].

furent #2 1:05, 1:07, 15:513. [3 pl.
pret. of *estre #2*].

fust #1 14:493, 20:16c, 20:31b. [3 sg. imperf. subjunc. of *estre #1* (aux.)].
fust #2 11:394, 20:16c. [3 sg. imperf. subjunc. of *estre #2*].
fut 21:3. [3 sg. pret. of *estre #1* (aux.)].

gaaigner [inf.] to earn, to gain.
    gaaignera 20:29c. [3 sg. fut.].
    gaegnast 21:7b, 22:2c. [3 sg. imperf. subjunc.].
    gaegnié 22:4. [pp. m.].
gaite 23:11, 23:14. [NS] watchman.
ganbes 20:21. [FP] legs.
garçon 10:364. [NP] young boys, valets.
'gardast 23:13a. [3 sg. imperf. subjunc. of *(se) garder*, to be careful].
garder 13:442. [inf.] to watch over, to guard, to safekeep.
    garda 9:311. [3 sg. pret.].
    garde 5:164. [3 sg. pres.]. 23:26. [2 sg. imperative].
    gardee 4:101. [pp. f.].
    gardes 23:31. [2 sg. pres.].
    gardot 5:154. [3 sg. imperf.].
Garins (de Biaucaire) 20:17, 21:35c, 23:10c. [NS] Aucassin's father.
    Garin 20:16b. [OS].
    Garins de Biaucare 21:1a.
    = = > *Garins (de Biaucaire)*.
garis 20:13. [pp. m. of *garir*] healed.
garnie 5:152. in *bien garnie* [idiom], well provided for.
gas 4:98. [NS] joke, jest, laughing matter.
gastoit 20:16d. [3 sg. imperf. of *gaster*, to lay waste].
gaudine 21:19. [FS] copse.
ge 3:81, 13:445. = = > *je*.
gendre 11:378, 14:498. [OS] son-in-law.
gent #1 2:30, 2:49, 4:134, 6:179, 6:210, 10:362, 16:12. [FS] people, lineage.
    gens #1 22:7b. [FP].
gent #2 23:19. [adj., OS] fair, handsome, noble.
    gens #2 20:21. [NS].

gentil 4:122 [OS], 10:325 [FS]. [adj.] noble, genteel.
gesir 19:32, 19:47. [inf.] to lie.
geter 14:477, 19:19. [inf.] to throw.
    geta 12:428, 19:43. [3 sg. pret.].
    getera 11:377. [3 sg. fut.].
    geterai 4:113. [1 sg. fut.].
grande 20:16b. = = > *grant #2*.
granment 19:22. [adv.] greatly, deeply.
    grantment 8:278. = = > *granment*.
grant #1 5:139, 5:143, 9:318, 10:323, 10:329, 10:330, 15:518, 16:27, 19:9, 19:20, 20:12. [adj., OS] great.
    grande 20:16b. = = > *grant #2*.
    grans #1 20:5. = = > *granz #1*.
    grans #2 23:13a. = = > *grant #2*.
    grans #3 20:21, 23:12, 23:13b. [NS].
grant #2 2:34, 4:100, 4:118, 11:389, 14:471, 14:492, 15:502, 15:522. [FS].
    granz #1 15:515, 18:30. [FP].
    granz #2 7:236. = = > *grant #2*.
grant #3 occurs in adverbial expressions in 5:147 (*a grant esploit*), 21:11 (*par grant devisse*), 17:4 (*le grant pas*), q.v.
grant piece 7:232. [adv. phr.] for a long while.
grantment 8:278. = = > *granment*.
granz #1 15:515, 18:30. [adj., FP of *grant #1*].
    grans #1 20:5. = = > *granz #1*.
granz #2 7:236. = = > *grant #2*.
gré 8:274, 17:2. [OS] desire, pleasure (cf. *savoir bon gré, de sun gré*).
grief 15:516. [adj., OS] difficult.
gris 22:11b. [NP] gray fur.
groni 19:38. [pp. m. of *grondre*] groaned.
gros 4:128. [adj., OS] large.
guarant 17:37. [OS] protection.
guere 20:16b. [FS] war.
    gueres 22:10b. [FP].
guerpi 19:4, 19:26. [pp. m. of *guerpir*] abandoned.
guerredon 4:120. [OS] reward.

ha 10:353. [interjection] Ah!

haés 21:27. [2 pl. pres. of *haïr*, to hate].

haï 16:2. [pp. m. of *haïr*] hated.

haïe 2:53. [pp. f. of *haïr*] hated.

haitiez 14:490. [adj., NS] happy.

hastivement 5:157. [adv.] quickly.

hauberc 19:17. [OS] hauberk (a defensive shirt of mail extending to the knees).

> haubercs 17:13. [OP].

haut 20:22b. [adj., OS] exalted, high.

> haute 4:134, 6:210, 20:31a. [FS].

heritage 10:329, 15:512. [OS] inheritance, heritage.

herpeor 22:11b. [NP] musicians who sing while playing the harp.

homme #1 3:89, 15:516. [OS] man.

> hom 1:19, 20:10, 23:9a. [NS].
>
> home #1 20:30b, 23:4a, 23:6. = = > *homme* #1.
>
> home #2 22:10c. = = > *homme* #2.
>
> homes #1 2:42. = = > *homme* #2.
>
> homes #2 20:16d, 20:25a. = = > *hommes*.
>
> homme #2 1:05, 7:249, 9:317. [NP].
>
> hommes 3:84. [OP].
>
> hon 21:1b. = = > *hom*.
>
> huem 18:58. = = > *hom*.
>
> hum 17:26, 18:26. = = > *hom*.
>
> oume 23:9a, 23:9c. = = > *homme* #1.

honers 20:31a. = = > *honor* #1.

honnie 4:111. [pp. f. of *honnir*] shamed.

> honie 3:75. = = > *honnie*.

'honnir, i.e., (se) honnir 3:91, 3:94. [inf.] to shame (oneself); to be ashamed.

honniz 2:36. [pp. m. of *honnir*] shamed.

honor #1 3:74. [FS] honor, possession, wealth.

> honers 20:31a. = = > *honor* #1.

honor #2 20:29c, 21:7b. in *par honor* [adv. phr.], honorably.

honte 2:34. [FS] shame.

hors 18:54. in *la hors.* 19:19. = = > *fors* #1.

hors del 19:19, 19:43. [compound prep.] out of (with sg. obj.).

hors des 18:25. [compound prep.] out of (with pl. obj.).

huchié 19:38. [pp. m. of *huchier*] called out.

Hue de Morevile 16:3. [NS] one of the murderèrs of Thomas Becket.

Hue (Mauclerc) 17:14, 17:18. [NS] Hugh of Horsea, clerk to Robert del Broc.

> Hue Malclerc 19:41. = = > *Hue Mauclerc*.

hué 19:54. [pp. m. of *huer*] decried.

huem 18:58. = = > *hom*.

huis 6:183. [OP] doors.

hum 17:26, 18:26. = = > *hom*.

hure 19:22. [FS] head.

hurteroie 23:5b. [1 sg. cond. of *hurter*, to dash, to ram].

i #1 6:191, 8:275, 8:281, 11:368, 11:369, 12:399, 12:401, 12:406, 13:459, 14:497, 14:499, 16:33, 16:35, 16:45, 16:50, 17:3, 17:19, 17:32, 19:16, 19:17, 21:32, 22:5, 22:7a, 22:8a, 22:11a, 22:11b, 23:5b. [adv.] there.

i #2 4:129, 5:153, 8:254, 8:279, 9:318, 10:330, 11:382. [invariable adv. particle used in *i avoir* construction].

i #3 2:37, 8:273, 21:6, 22:12a, 23:31. [invariable pron. standing for a noun governed by *a* #1-4] of/about/to him/her/it/them.

i #4 23:10c, 23:13b. = = > *il* #2.

i #5 5:163. = = > *il* #3.

i avoir. [idiomatic expression used in all tenses but only in 3rd sg.] there is, there are.

> (i) a #9 10:344, 10:347, 13:466, 20:30b. [3 sg. pres.].
>
> (i) avoit #3 4:129, 7:243, 8:253, 8:279, 20:23. [3 sg. imperf.].
>
> (i) avroient 10:330. [3 sg. cond.].

(i) ot #3 4:130, 5:151, 5:153, 6:177, 8:254, 9:318, 11:382, 18:4, 23:1. [3 sg. pret.].

(i) out #2 16:44. == >*ot* #3.

icele 6:181. == >*cele* #1.

ici 8:255, 18:26, 18:29, 18:30. [adv.] here.

icil 22:9. == >*cil* #4.

idunc 19:27, 19:29, 19:51. == >*donc*.

iert #1 12:409. [3. sg. imperf. of *estre* #2].

iert #2 2:38, 23:13b. [3 sg. fut. of *estre* #2].

iglise 18:17, 18:57, 19:14, 19:15. == >*eglise* [FS].

il #1 1:13, 2:36, 2:45, 2:59, 4:125, 6:187, 6:190, 6:197, 7:218, 7:226, 8:265, 8:268, 8:272, 8:275, 8:284, 9:287, 10:327, 10:331, 10:335, 10:359, 11:367, 12:426, 12:429, 13:437, 13:459, 13:460, 13:464, 13:465, 14:494, 14:498, 15:501, 15:513, 16:32, 16:41, 17:7, 17:9, 17:23, 17:31, 17:33, 17:35, 17:38, 18:10, 18:14, 18:20, 18:39, 18:41, 18:46, 19:7, 19:27, 19:45, 20:5, 20:6, 20:13, 20:16c, 20:18, 20:22a, 20:24a, 20:24b, 20:32a, 21:1a, 21:1b, 21:4, 21:6, 22:12b, 23:2, 23:3b, 23:12, 23:16. [3 sg. personal subject pron., NS] he.

il #2 10:339, 15:514, 15:517, 15:518, 15:521, 16:22, 16:30, 16:38, 17:4, 17:5, 17:34, 17:35, 18:37, 19:6, 20:25b, 22:8a, 23:10c, 23:11, 23:12, 23:13a. [3 pl. personal subject pron. NP] they.

  i #4 23:10c, 23:13b. == >*il* #2.

il #3 2:37, 7:226, 20:16c, 20:30b. [3 sg. n. impersonal subject pron.] it.

  i #5 5:163. == >*il* #3.

iluec 18:4. [adv.] there, at that place.

  ilec 5:146. == >*iluec*.

  illec 5:170, 6:186. == >*iluec*.

  iloec 16:49. == >*iluec*.

infer 22:5, 22:10a, 22:10a. [OS] hell.

iniquité 17:15, 19:51. [FS] iniquity.

Innocent 16:13. [NP] Holy Innocents (infants in Bethlehem slaughtered by Herod after the birth of Christ).

'ira 18:22. [3 sg. pret. of *(s')irer*, to become enraged].

irai 17:25, 17:35. [1 sg. fut. of *aler*].

irés 23:2. [2 pl. fut. of *aler*].

iscir 23:9c. [inf.] to leave, to go out of.

  ist #2 7:212. [3 sg. pres.].

issi #1 2:46, 7:232. == >*ainsi*.

'issir, i.e., **(s'en) issir** [inf.] to go out of, to leave.

  'issi #2 5:138, 5:143. [3 sg. pret.].

  'ist #1 5:136. [3 sg. pres.].

ist #2 7:212. [3 sg. pres. of *iscir*].

j' 17:35, 22:2a, 22:7a, 22:7a, 22:11c, 23:4a, 23:5b. == >*je*.

ja #1 4:110. [adv.] at once.

ja #2 14:485, 21:26. [adv.] indeed.

ja #3 16:18. [adv.] just (now).

ja (+ ne) 2:38, 11:395, 13:466, 20:27a, 22:5. [adv.] never.

ja mais (+ ne) 19:45, 21:8b, 22:12a. [adv.] never(more).

  jamés (+ ne) 3:74, 3:77, 4:112, 8:270, 9:297, 10:333. == >*ja mais (+ ne)*.

jadis 1:03, 14:471. [adv.] formerly, once, of old.

jargonce 4:130. [FS] precious stone, probably of bluish hue (hyacinth, jacounce, jacinth).

je 1:02, 3:79, 4:110, 12:430, 14:475, 18:39, 20:19, 20:27a, 20:27b, 20:30a, 21:5a, 21:7a, 21:8b, 21:30, 21:36b, 21:38a, 21:38b, 22:6, 22:7a, 22:7b, 23:4b, 23:5a, 23:5b, 23:6, 23:7, 23:8, 23:13a. [1 sg. subject pron.] I < enclitic in *jel*>.

  ge 3:81, 13:445. == >*je*.

  j' 17:35, 22:2a, 22:7a, 22:7a, 22:11c, 23:4a, 23:5b. == >*je*.

  jo 16:42, 18:27. == >*je*.

  jou 21:4, 21:26, 22:9, 22:10a, 22:10c, 22:11c. == >*je*.

jel 13:470, 21:33, 23:25. [enclitic form of *je* and *le* #3].

jeté 12:406. [pp. m. of *jeter*] thrown.

jo 16:42, 18:27. == >*je*.

jogleor 22:11b. [NP] entertainers, jongleurs.

joianz 1:12. [adj., NS] joyful.

joie 1:13, 4:118, 14:492, 15:502, 15:519, 15:522, 20:14, 21:36a. [FS] joy.

jor 9:286, 11:367, 16:45, 22:8a. [OS] day.

    jors 20:16c [NS], 20:29c [OP], 22:2b [OP], 22:5 [OP].

    jur 16:11. == >*jor.*

joste 2:26. [prep.] beside.

jou 21:4, 21:26, 22:9, 22:10a, 22:10c, 22:11c. == >*je.*

jugier 16:33. [inf.] to ordain (for); to adjudge, to assign.

juint 19:12. [pp. m. of *joindre*] joined.

'jujai 3:79. [1 sg. pret. of *(se) jugier*, to judge (oneself)].

jumeles 10:356. [adj., FP] twin.

jur 16:11. == >*jor.*

jus 5:159. [adv.] down.

justise 16:20. in *mort de justise* [idiom], death by execution.

jut 23:4a, 23:6. [pp. m. of *gesir*] lain.

ki 21:11, 23:17, 23:27. == >*qui* #*1.*

l' **#1** 1:17, 1:18, 3:66, 3:88, 3:92, 4:109, 4:122, 5:135, 5:142, 5:158, 5:159, 5:171, 6:178, 6:189, 6:204, 6:207, 7:215, 7:220, 7:230, 8:265, 8:274, 9:309, 13:445, 13:447, 14:479, 14:482, 14:499, 16:13, 16:14, 16:16, 16:21, 16:28, 16:44, 17:19, 18:9, 18:15, 18:25, 18:47, 18:51, 19:47, 23:9a, 23:9b, 23:9c. == >*le* #*1.*

l' **#2** 2:43, 2:44, 2:55, 2:56, 4:101, 5:140, 6:196, 7:227, 7:230, 7:238, 7:239, 7:247, 7:249, 8:258, 9:302, 9:315, 9:316, 9:319, 9:320, 11:391, 13:431, 13:434, 20:29a, 20:29b, 20:30b, 21:5a, 21:7a, 21:8b, 21:35c, 22:2a, 22:2b, 22:4, 23:10c, 23:12, 23:13b. == >*la* #*2.*

l' **#3** 5:154, 6:177, 7:212, 7:216, 7:233, 7:238, 7:250, 8:260, 8:262, 8:269, 9:305, 10:358, 12:398, 13:441, 14:476, 14:496, 15:527, 17:4, 17:12, 17:33,

18:3, 18:8, 18:31, 19:14, 19:20, 19:23, 19:43, 19:52. == >*la* #*1.*

l' **#4** 2:59, 3:82, 6:191, 6:200, 6:205, 6:206, 7:221, 7:222, 8:256, 8:274, 9:292, 9:299, 12:404, 12:408, 12:410, 12:427, 13:437, 13:448, 13:449, 13:469, 15:507, 15:530, 17:1, 17:10, 17:11, 17:14, 17:36, 18:15, 18:19, 18:20, 18:36, 18:40, 18:51, 18:58, 19:1, 19:2, 19:4, 19:6, 19:10, 19:26, 19:28, 19:30, 19:33, 19:36, 20:13, 20:31a, 21:1b, 21:36a, 23:25. == >*le* #*4.*

la **#1** 1:13, 2:25, 2:30, 2:49, 2:53, 3:65, 4:95, 4:99, 4:103, 4:117, 4:131, 4:132, 5:135, 5:136, 5:137, 5:138, 5:140, 5:148, 5:150, 5:151, 5:155, 6:175, 6:179, 7:221, 7:231, 7:234, 8:257, 8:261, 8:277, 8:282, 9:311, 10:343, 10:346, 10:347, 10:349, 10:355, 10:363, 11:373, 11:383, 11:387, 11:394, 12:397, 12:399, 12:402, 12:408, 12:413, 12:414, 12:427, 13:431, 13:434, 13:439, 13:455, 13:460, 13:461, 14:485, 14:495, 15:504, 15:513, 15:519, 15:524, 15:526, 15:530, 16:5, 16:11, 16:14, 16:15, 16:21, 16:35, 16:43, 16:44, 17:2, 17:6, 17:7, 17:27, 18:1, 18:4, 18:5, 18:34, 18:45, 18:47, 19:15, 19:21, 19:22, 19:34, 19:35, 21:3, 21:13, 21:14, 21:15, 21:16, 21:17, 21:20, 21:35b, 21:36a, 21:38b. [FS definite art.] the.

    l' **#3** 5:154, 6:177, 7:212, 7:216, 7:233, 7:238, 7:250, 8:260, 8:262, 8:269, 9:305, 10:358, 12:398, 13:441, 14:476, 14:496, 15:527, 17:4, 17:12, 17:33, 18:3, 18:8, 18:31, 19:14, 19:20, 19:23, 19:43, 19:52. == >*la* #*1.*

la **#2** 2:62, 2:63, 4:96, 4:106, 4:112, 4:113, 4:114, 4:115, 4:116, 7:224, 7:231, 7:240, 7:247, 7:248, 8:263, 8:270, 9:286, 9:316, 9:320, 10:350, 10:366, 11:377, 11:379, 11:390, 12:415, 12:416, 14:477. [3 sg. direct obj. pron., FS] her, it.

    l' **#2** 2:43, 2:44, 2:55, 2:56, 4:101, 5:140, 6:196, 7:227, 7:230, 7:238,

7:239, 7:247, 7:249, 8:258, 9:302,
9:315, 9:316, 9:319, 9:320, 11:391,
13:431, 13:434, 20:29a, 20:29b,
20:30b, 21:5a, 21:7a, 21:8b, 21:35c,
22:2a, 22:2b, 22:4, 23:10c, 23:12,
23:13b. = = > *la* #2.
la #3 4:132, 5:157, 17:40, 18:36,
20:27b, 21:14, 23:10a. [adv.] there.
la fors 16:24. = = > *fors*.
la hors 18:54. = = > *fors*.
lacié 18:38. [pp. m. of *lacier*] tied up.
laienz 16:42. [adv.] in there.
laissier 16:30. [inf.] to abandon, to let
(be); to allow, to permit, to let.
    laisciés 22:1. = = > *laissiez* #1.
    laise 20:29a. [2 sg. imperative].
    laissié 19:10. [pp. m.].
    laissiez #1 17:10, 17:24, 17:38,
    18:43, 18:50. [2 pl. imperative].
    lait #1 6:191. [3 sg. pres.].
    lerai 4:114. [1 sg. fut.].
    lessa 5:173. [3 sg. pret.].
    lessié 15:504. = = > *laissié*.
    lessier 9:314. = = > *laissier*.
    lessiez 2:45, 4:108. = = > *laissiez*
    #1.
    lessoit 10:331. [3 sg. imperf.].
laissiez #2 17:39. in *Deu en laissiez*
penser, leave it in God's hands.
lait #2 6:201. [OS] milk.
    let 6:206. = = > *lait* #2.
lampes 6:182. [FP] lamps.
larrecin 6:186. [OS] theft.
las 10:353. [interjection] Alas!
lasse 3:73, 21:23. [interjection, f.] woe
is me! (lit.: weary, unfortunate
[one]).
lay 1:01, 15:529. [OS] lay, short verse
narrative.
laz 4:127. [OS] ribbon, tie, lace.
le #1 1:02, 1:20, 1:21, 2:57, 5:141,
5:155, 5:156, 6:180, 6:184, 6:204,
16:208, 7:211, 7:229, 7:230, 7:233,
8:276, 8:280, 9:308, 9:309, 9:313,
10:345, 12:405, 12:411, 12:412,
12:417, 12:423, 12:428, 13:450,
14:482, 15:529, 16:38, 16:40, 16:45,

17:4, 17:16, 17:27, 17:30, 17:32, 18:7,
18:11, 18:20, 18:53, 18:60, 19:18,
19:19, 19:21, 19:24, 19:25, 19:32,
19:42, 19:43, 19:44, 19:46, 19:47,
19:49, 19:50, 20:7, 20:22b, 21:31,
21:35a, 21:36b, 21:36b, 23:9b, 23:18,
23:20. [OS definite art.] the
< enclitic in *al, au, del* #3, *du, el*
#2 >.
    l' #1 1:17, 1:18, 3:66, 3:88, 3:92,
    4:109, 4:122, 5:135, 5:142, 5:158,
    5:159, 5:171, 6:178, 6:189, 6:204,
    6:207, 7:215, 7:220, 7:230, 8:265,
    8:274, 9:309, 13:445, 13:447,
    14:479, 14:482, 14:499, 16:13,
    16:14, 16:16, 16:21, 16:28, 16:44,
    17:19, 18:9, 18:15, 18:25, 18:47,
    18:51, 19:47, 23:9a, 23:9b, 23:9c.
    = = > *le* #1.
    lu 19:18. = = > *le* #1.
le #2 9:315, 10:348, 10:357, 12:407,
13:452, 15:510. [NS definite art.] the.
le #3 20:16c, 20:19, 20:22b, 20:25b,
20:30a, 21:1b, 21:34, 21:35a, 21:36b,
22:3, 23:9a, 23:9b, 23:10a, 23:11. [FS
definite art.] the < enclitic in *jel* >.
le #4 1:14, 3:93, 5:173, 5:174, 6:201,
6:202, 7:215, 7:223, 10:359, 11:389,
12:403, 12:412, 12:426, 12:428,
13:442, 15:501, 17:23, 17:37, 18:18,
18:21, 18:23, 18:53, 18:54, 19:3, 19:6,
19:27, 19:29, 19:31, 22:12b, 23:22. [3
sg. direct obj. pron., OS] him, it
< enclitic in *del* #2, *nel, nu, quil, sel,*
sil >.
    l' #4 2:59, 3:82, 6:191, 6:200,
    6:205, 6:206, 7:221, 7:222, 8:256,
    8:274, 9:292, 9:299, 12:404, 12:408,
    12:410, 12:427, 13:437, 13:448,
    13:449, 13:469, 15:507, 15:530,
    17:1, 17:10, 17:11, 17:14, 17:36,
    18:15, 18:19, 18:36, 18:40, 18:51,
    18:58, 19:1, 19:2, 19:4, 19:6, 19:10,
    19:26, 19:28, 19:30, 19:33, 19:36,
    20:13, 20:31a, 21:1b, 21:36a, 23:25.
    = = > *le* #4.
le #5 21:5a, 21:8b, 21:37, 22:12a,

23:10c, 23:11. [3 FS direct obj. pron.] her.

le grant pas 17:4. [adv. phr.] swiftly.

lé 5:167. [adj., OS] wide.

legiers 19:17. [adj., NS] agile, light.

lerai 4:114. [1 sg. fut. of *laissier*].

les #1 6:183, 6:184, 12:401, 16:25, 16:39, 16:50, 16:51, 16:53, 17:21, 17:25, 17:31, 17:34, 17:36, 18:43, 18:45, 18:50, 19:4, 19:24, 20:22a, 21:21, 22:5, 23:5b, 23:10a, 23:21, 23:28 [OP definite art.] the < enclitic in *as #1,3, des, es #2* >.

les #2 2:55, 5:156, 11:381, 16:25, 18:3, 19:53, 20:24a, 22:11a, 23:10b, 23:28. [FP definite art.] the < enclitic in *as #2, des, es #2* >.

les #3 3:69, 6:185, 9:311, 9:312, 15:505, 16:36, 17:8, 17:17, 17:20, 23:11. [3 OP direct obj. pron.] them < enclitic in *nes, ques, quis #2, ses #3* >.

lessa 5:173. [3 sg. pret. of *laissier*].

lessié 15:504. [pp. m. of *laissier*].

lessier 9:314. = = > *laissier*.

lessiez 2:45, 4:108. [2 pl. imperative of *laissier*].

lessoit 10:331. [3 sg. imperf. of *laissier*].

let 6:206. = = > *lait #2*.

letree 4:131. [adj., FS] inscribed.

leur 22:11a. = = > *lor #3* [OP].

'leva 6:181. [3 sg. pret. of *(se) lever*].

lever #1 1:17. [inf.] to raise, to bring up, to educate.

  levee 7:227, 20:29b, 21:7a, 22:2b. [pp. f.] served as godparent for someone (lit.: lifted him/her over the baptismal font).

'lever #2 i.e., (se) lever. [inf.] to get up, to arise.

  'leva 6:181. [3 sg. pret.].

  'levez 6:197. [2 pl. imperative].

  'levoit 13:457. [3 sg. imperf.].

li #1 1:19, 1:23, 3:86, 6:196, 7:213, 7:219, 7:229, 10:336, 11:368, 11:369, 11:374, 12:422, 12:430, 14:487, 14:489, 14:493, 15:501, 15:503, 16:4,

17:6, 18:9, 18:26, 18:29, 18:31, 18:35, 18:45, 18:49, 20:8, 20:16b, 20:17, 20:20, 20:28, 20:29a, 21:1a, 21:6, 21:35a, 21:35c, 22:1, 22:11b, 22:12a, 23:3a, 23:9a, 23:9b, 23:9c, 23:10c, 23:11, 23:14. [NS definite art.] the.

li #2 7:249, 10:322, 10:354, 10:363, 10:364, 16:1, 16:6, 16:14, 16:18, 16:24, 16:29, 16:34, 16:46, 16:47, 16:48, 17:3, 17:11, 17:12, 17:16, 17:19, 17:21, 18:3, 18:6, 18:36, 18:51, 19:8, 19:36, 19:51, 21:35b, 21:35c, 22:10a, 22:10b, 22:10c, 22:11b. [NP definite art.] the.

li #3 21:26. [FS definite art.] the.

li #4 1:17, 1:22, 1:24, 3:88, 4:105, 7:216, 8:262, 9:300, 10:323, 11:371, 13:461, 13:462, 13:463, 14:500, 16:19, 16:29, 17:34, 17:35, 18:16, 18:25, 18:28, 18:48, 19:20, 19:23, 19:43, 19:48, 20:16d, 20:25a, 20:27a, 23:13a. [3 sg. indirect obj. pron., OS] (to) him.

li #5 2:42, 3:70, 4:118, 4:119, 4:124, 4:128, 7:214, 8:272, 8:283, 8:284, 9:304, 9:305, 9:307, 9:309, 9:310, 11:396, 12:409, 12:421, 12:422, 12:429, 13:439, 13:447, 15:510, 20:29c, 21:7b, 22:2b, 22:2c. [3 FS indirect obj. pron.] (to) her.

li #6 4:106, 4:120, 7:213, 7:217, 8:265, 9:293, 10:342, 10:365, 11:372, 11:385, 12:421, 13:432, 14:478, 15:511, 15:512, 20:31b, 20:32a, 21:4, 22:12b. [stressed obj. pron., FS] her.

li alquant 17:21. [pl. indef. pron.] some, certain ones.

li auquant . . . li auquant 21:35b–c. [pl. indef. pron.] some . . . others.

lie 4:128. [3 sg. pres. of *lïer*].

lié 10:327. [adj., OS] happy.

  liés 21:36a. = = > *liez*.

  liez 1:12, 14:489. [NS].

lïer 18:54. [inf.] to tie.

lilies 19:48. [FP] lilies.

lit 12:397, 12:405, 12:412, 12:417, 22:4, 23:3b, 23:4a, 23:6. [OS] bed.

livrer 18:59. [inf.] to deliver (over).

löer 3:90. [inf.] to praise.
loing 5:144. [adv.] far.
    loinz 17:17. = = > *loing.*
lonc 23:5a. in *de si lonc qu(e)* [adv. phr.]
    (here: as soon as).
lonc tens 4:101. [adv. phr.] for a long
    time.
longuement 10:321. [adv.] for a long
    while.
    longement 21:32.
    = = > *longuement.*
lor #1 7:251, 12:402, 23:10c. [3 pl.
    indirect obj. pron., OP, FP] (to)
    them.
    lur #1 16:9, 17:24, 17:33, 18:5,
    18:50. = = > *lor #1.*
lor #2 10:335, 15:514, 15:524, 15:525.
    [3 pl. poss. adj., FS] their.
    lur #2 16:2, 16:9. = = > *lor #2.*
lor #3 10:337 [OS], 15:523 [OS],
    20:25b [OP]. [3 pl. poss. adj.] their.
    leur 22:11a. = = > *lor #3* [OP].
    lur #3 16:47, 17:24. = = > *lor #3*
    [OS].
lu 19:18. = = > *le #1.*
lués 23:3b. [adv.] at once.
lui 2:26, 3:90, 9:301, 10:321, 10:324,
    10:328, 11:370, 15:506, 20:23, 23:1. [3
    sg. stressed obj. pron., OS] him.
lur #1 16:9, 17:24, 17:33, 18:5, 18:50.
    = = > *lor #1.*
lur #2 16:2, 16:9. = = > *lor #2.*
lur #3 16:47, 17:13, 17:24. = = > *lor
    #3* [OS].

m' #1 13:440. = = > *ma.*
m' #2 2:31, 3:77, 3:85, 3:92, 6:198,
    6:201, 13:444, 13:446, 13:470, 16:33,
    18:10, 18:14, 21:38b, 23:2, 23:5a,
    23:5b, 23:7, 23:8. = = > *me #2.*
ma 13:454, 14:471, 14:472, 20:31a,
    21:7a, 21:36b, 22:2b, 22:7a, 22:11c. [1
    sg. poss. adj., FS] my.
    m' #1 13:440. = = > *ma.*
    me #3 20:27b, 23:5b. = = > *ma.*
main 18:2, 19:9, 19:39. [FS] hand.
    mains 18:25, 19:12, 21:38b. [FP].

maint 16:45. [adj., OS] many a.
    meintes 12:404. [OP].
mais #1 16:1, 16:35, 17:5, 17:17, 17:28,
    18:12, 18:43, 18:50, 18:55, 18:59,
    19:10, 19:27, 19:28, 19:31, 20:24a,
    21:8a, 21:31, 22:3, 22:10a, 23:7, 23:9c.
    [conj.] but.
    mes #2 8:279. = = > *mais #1.*
mais #2 19:45, 21:8b, 22:12a. [forms
    negative adv. with *ne, ja, onques*]
    more.
mais qu(e) 22:7a, 22:11c. [conjunctive
    phr.] unless.
maiserez 18:33. [pp. m. of *maiserer*]
    constructed (of masonry).
maisiere 23:5a. [FS] wall.
maisnie 18:1. [FS] household,
    retainers, followers.
maistre 19:1, 19:6, 19:26. [NS] master.
maisun 17:27. [FS] house.
mal #1 16:27, 16:40, 17:16, 20:12.
    [OS] evil; sickness.
mal #2 11:375 in *tenist mal vers*, might
    speak ill of.
mal #3 10:323 in *atornerent a mal*,
    attributed or imputed ill (to).
malbailli 8:266. [pp. m. of *maubaillir*]
    unfortunate.
male 21:30. [adj., FS] wicked, evil.
maleoite 21:3. [adj., FS] cursed,
    accursed.
malfaitur 17:30. [OS] evildoer,
    malefactor.
malvaise 16:2. = = > *mauvaise.*
malveis 18:26. [adj., NS of *mauvaise*]
    evil, wicked, bad.
mamele 23:9b. [FS] breast.
manaces 18:41. [FP] threats.
mananz 1:05. [adj., NP] well-to-do.
mandé 2:33. [pp. m. of *mander*]
    announced.
mandot 1:14. [3 sg. imperf. of *mander*,
    to announce].
maneçant 23:29. [gerund of *menacier*]
    threatening.
manecié 18:40. [pp. m. of *menacier*]
    threatened.

maneçoient 23:11. [3 pl. imperf. of *menacier*].

mangié 16:16. [pp. m. of *mangier*] eating.

maniere #1 11:394. [FS] situation; background, upbringing.

maniere #2 12:402. [FS] manner, way.

manke 22:8a. [NP] maimed, one-armed person.

manoient 1:03. [3 pl. imperf. of *manoir*, to live, to dwell].

mantel 12:400, 13:433, 18:15, 18:25, 19:24. [OS] cloak, mantle.

marbrine 21:13. [adj., FS] marble-encased.

mariage 10:351. [OS] marriage.

Marie 21:31. [FS] Mary, mother of Jesus.

marit 11:379. [3 sg. pres. subjunc. of *marier*, to wed].

Martir 19:35. [OS] area of Canterbury cathedral where Thomas Becket was martyred (north arm of west transept).

martire 16:23, 18:42, 19:11. [OS] martyrdom.

martyr 19:13. [OS] martyr.

maubaillie 2:54. [pp. f. of *maubaillir*] unfortunate.

mauvaise 20:23. [adj., FS] evil, wicked, bad.

    malvaise 16:2. = = > *mauvaise*.

    malveis 18:26. [NS].

    pis 3:86. [NS, superlative].

    poior 10:360. [OS, comparative].

me #1 2:31, 23:4b. [1 sg. reflexive pron. (often omitted in translation)] myself.

me #2 3:79, 4:109, 13:435, 13:438, 13:440, 13:441, 13:442, 13:443, 14:479, 16:20, 16:32, 16:41, 17:9, 17:38, 18:10, 18:14, 18:29, 18:49, 20:27a, 20:27b, 21:27, 21:37. [1 sg. obj. pron.] me, myself; to me, from me.

    m' #2 2:31, 3:77, 3:85, 3:92, 6:198, 6:201, 13:444, 13:446, 13:470,

16:33, 18:10, 18:14, 21:38b, 23:2, 23:5a, 23:5b, 23:7, 23:8. = = > *me* #2.

me #3 20:27b, 23:5b. = = > *ma*.

meesmes 17:31. = = > *meïsmes* #1.

mei 17:10, 18:17, 18:44. = = > *moi*.

meillor 8:254. [adj., OS, comparative of *bon*] better.

meintes 12:404. [OP of *maint*].

meïsmes #1 3:79, 14:498, 21:5b, 22:12b. [adj., NS] (one)self.

    meesmes 17:31. = = > *meïsmes* #1.

    meïsme 7:227. [FS].

    meïsmes #2 3:72, 14:474. [OS].

meïsmes #3 3:66. [adj., OS] same, very.

menacier. [inf.] to threaten.

maneçant 23:29. [gerund].

manecié 18:40. [pp. m.].

maneçoient 23:11. [3 pl. imperf.].

mener 17:37. [inf.] to lead, to take.

    mené 17:1, 18:36. [pp. m.].

    menee 5:140, 9:302. [pp. f.].

mengier 1:19, 2:26. [OS] meal.

ment 3:87. [3 sg. pres. of *mentir*, to lie].

menus 20:22a. [adv.] tightly.

mer 16:6. [FS] sea.

merciê 1:23, 6:190. [pp. m. of *mercïer*] thanking.

mere 11:372, 11:391, 13:434, 15:513, 18:34, 20:25a. [FS] mother.

'merveil 2:31. [1 sg. pres. of *(se) merveiller*, to wonder].

merveille #1 7:248. [adv.] marvelously, wonderfully, greatly.

merveille #2 11:389. [FS] marvel, wonder.

merveilleus 10:365. [adj., OS] extreme, great, singular.

    mervelleuse 20:16b. [FS].

mes #1 3:76 [NS], 3:76 [NP], 21:7a [OP], 23:13b [NS]. [1 sg. poss. adj.] my.

    mis #2 16:23. = = > *mes* #1 [NS].

mes #2 8:279. = = > *mais* #1.

mes #3 12:418, 14:490, 15:502 in
onques mes. [adv.] nevermore.
mesage 1:22, 2:57. [OS] message.
mesagier 1:20. [OS] messenger.
mesaises 22:8c. [FP] misery.
mesavenu 10:353. [pp. m. of *mesavenir*]
happening in an unfortunate
manner.
meschine 4:99, 4:132, 5:155, 9:311,
11:373, 13:439, 14:495, 15:519. [FS]
(young) girl.
    mescine 21:14. = = > *meschine.*
    mescinete 23:12, 23:18 [FS,
    diminutive].
mescreï 2:62. [pp. m. of *mescroire*]
mistrusted.
mesdisante 2:28. [pres. participle, FS,
of *mesdire*] slandering.
mesdit #1 3:87. [3 sg. pres. of *mesdire*,
to slander].
mesdit #2 14:474. [pp. m. of *mesdire*]
slandered.
mesfet 13:463. [OS] error, crime.
meson 2:49, 7:219, 10:363, 11:377. [FS]
house.
mesparla 3:65. [3 sg. pret. of *mesparler*,
to speak ill of, to lie about].
mesparlai 3:80, 14:473. [1 sg. pret. of
mesparler, to speak ill of, to lie
about].
messeant 23:30. [adj., OS]
uncomfortable.
metre. [inf.] to put.
    meteroit 23:3b. [3 sg. cond.].
    metez 19:9. [2 pl. pres.].
    metrai 16:42. [1 sg. fut.].
    mis #1 6:186. [pp. m.].
    mise 21:9, 22:4. [pp. f.].
    misse 21:24, 21:28. = = > *mise.*
    mist 5:159, 5:173, 12:412, 19:42. [3
    sg. pret.] See also *mist a reson.*
    mistrent 7:229. [3 pl. pret. in
    mistrent a non, q.v.].
mi #1 20:27b, 21:23, 22:11c, 22:12b,
23:7. = = > *moi.*
mi #2 15:512 in *par mi.* [adv. phr.] in
half.

mie 2:46, 3:88, 12:409, 12:429, 13:453,
14:481, 21:27, 21:32, 21:36a, 23:2,
23:4a, 23:5a, 23:7. [particle used
with *ne* (to reinforce negative)].
mielz 16:22. = = > *mieus.*
mien 23:4a, 23:6. [1 sg. poss. pron.,
OS] mine.
    miens 18:43, 18:50. [OP].
mien escient 5:153. [idiom] I believe;
in my opinion.
mieus 3:90, 3:93. [adv.] better (comp.
of *bon*).
    mielz 16:22. = = > *mieus.*
    mix 20:25b, 23:6. = = > *mieus.*
mile 20:16d. [num.] thousand.
ministre 17:28, 18:36. [NP] clergymen.
miramie 21:12 in *a miramie.* [adv. phr.]
admirably (?).
mis #1 6:186. [pp. m. of *metre*] put.
mis #2 16:23. = = > *mes #1.*
mise 21:9, 22:4. [pp. f. of *metre*] put.
    misse 21:24, 21:28. = = > *mise.*
mist 5:159, 5:173, 12:412, 19:42. [3 sg.
pret. of *metre*].
mist a reson 9:286. [3 sg. pret. of *metre
a reson,* to speak to (someone)].
mistrent a non 7:229. [3 pl. pret. of
metre a non, to name].
miue 20:25b. [1 sg. poss. pron., FS]
mine.
mix 20:25b, 23:6. = = > *mieus.*
moeurent 22:8c. [3 pl. pres. of *morir*].
moi 3:86, 3:91, 3:94, 9:288, 9:289,
9:296, 12:424, 13:468, 14:474, 14:480,
21:6, 21:23, 22:13. [1 sg. stressed obj.
pron.] me.
    mei 17:10, 18:17, 18:44. = = > *moi.*
    mi #1 20:27b, 21:23, 22:11c,
    22:12b, 23:7. = = > *moi.*
moine #1 18:8. [OS] monk.
    moine #2 16:29, 17:11, 19:5.
    [NP].
    moines 17:21, 17:38. [OP].
molt #1 2:29, 2:31, 2:44, 2:48, 2:53,
2:63, 3:70, 3:71, 4:100, 4:102, 4:121,
5:160, 5:168, 6:190, 7:222, 7:225,
7:239, 7:240, 8:263, 8:266, 9:316,

10:323, 10:361, 11:382, 11:388,
11:391, 13:448, 14:495, 15:511,
15:522, 15:525, 21:30, 23:13a. [adv.]
much, very much, exceedingly,
very, often.
>   **mout** 22:5, 23:14. $= = >$ *molt* #1.
>   **mult** 16:40, 17:15. $= = >$ *molt* #1.

molt #2 4:118, 10:342. [adj.] much,
many.

molt #3 9:304. See *estre molt bel.*
13:446. See *ce m'est molt bel.*

molu 19:34. [adj., OS] sharp, keen.

mon 2:33, 9:295, 14:484, 22:2a. [1 sg.
poss. adj., OS] my.

mont 21:36b, 21:38b. [OS] world.

monte 20:25a [2 sg. imperative].
20:27a. [1 sg. pres. of *monter,* to
mount].

morant 23:24. [gerund of *morir*] dying,
killing.

mordrir 21:35c. [inf.] to murder.
>   **murdrir** 3:92. $= = >$ *mordrir.*

morir 23:6. [inf.] to die; to kill.
>   **moeurent** 22:8c. [3 pl. pres.].
>   **morant** 23:24. [gerund].
>   **mors** 23:13b. $= = >$ *mort* #1.
>   **mort #1** 6:194, 22:10b, 23:2. [pp.
>   m.].
>   **muir** 21:38a. [1 sg. pres. subjunc.].
>   **murir** 16:19. $= = >$ *morir.*

mort #2 16:21, 17:2, 18:45, 18:57,
18:59, 23:6. [FS] death.

mort de justise 16:20. [idiom] death
by execution.

mortel 20:16b. [adj., FS] mortal,
deadly.

mostier 4:113, 5:155, 6:178, 14:477.
[OS] monastery, convent.
>   **mustier** 16:29, 17:1, 17:10, 17:11,
>   17:18, 18:1, 18:21, 18:60, 19:10,
>   19:19. $= = >$ *mostier.*

mostrast 7:251. [3 sg. imperf. subjunc.
of *mostrer,* to show].

mostré 7:221. [pp. m. of *mostrer*]
shown.

mostree 8:262. [pp. f. of *mostrer*]
shown.

mout 22:5, 23:14. $= = >$ *molt* #1.

muir 21:38a. [1 sg. pres. subjunc. of
morir].

mult 16:40, 17:15. $= = >$ *molt* #1.

Munt Olivete 18:47. [OS] Mount of
Olives, associated with Christ's
Passion.

muntez 16:50. [pp. m. of *monter*]
mounted.

mur 5:156. [OS] wall.
>   **murs** 20:16c. [OP].

murdrir 3:92. $= = >$ *mordrir.*

murir 16:19 . $= = >$ *morir.*

murs 20:16c. [OP of *mur*].

mustier 16:29, 17:1, 17:10, 17:11, 17:18,
18:1, 18:21, 18:60, 19:10, 19:19.
$= = >$ *mostier.*

n' except for idioms, *n'* is merged with
ne as *n(e)* #1.

n'avoir que courecier 23:1. [idiom] to
feel very angry.

n'avoir . . . que faire 17:39. [idiom]
not to be of any interest/concern to
someone.
>   **n'ai . . . que faire** 22:9. [1 sg.
>   pres.].
>   **n'as . . . que faire** 20:29c. [2 sg.
>   pres.].
>   **n'avés . . . que faire** 22:2c.
> $= = >$ *n'avez ... que faire.*
>   **n'avez . . . que faire** 17:39. [2 pl.
>   pres.].
>   **n'eüst . . . que faire** 21:7b. [3 sg.
>   imperf. subjunc.].

naie voir 23:5a. [adv. phr.] indeed not.

Nativité 16:11. [FS] feast of the
Nativity, Christmas.

nature 7:242. [FS] nature.

Nazareus 18:49. [NS] Nazarene (i.e.,
Jesus Christ).

n(e) #1 2:38, 2:39, 2:42, 2:46, 2:60,
3:74, 3:77, 3:81, 3:82, 3:84, 3:88, 4:98,
4:107, 4:111, 4:112, 4:126, 5:143,
6:187, 6:191, 7:226, 7:243, 7:247,
7:248, 8:254, 8:267, 8:270, 9:297,
9:318, 9:319, 9:320, 10:332, 10:335,

10:341, 10:344, 10:348, 10:354, 11:385, 11:396, 12:409, 12:418, 12:429, 13:451, 13:464, 13:466, 14:481, 14:490, 14:497, 15:502, 16:7, 16:20, 16:22, 16:32, 16:35, 16:39, 17:19, 17:25, 17:26, 17:39, 18:11, 18:27, 18:39, 18:41, 18:45, 18:58, 19:3, 19:4, 19:10, 19:16, 19:17, 19:19, 19:28, 19:38, 19:39, 19:45, 20:10, 20:13, 20:16c, 20:18, 20:23, 20:24a, 20:24b, 20:27a, 20:27b, 20:28, 20:29c, 20:30b, 20:31b, 21:1a, 21:4, 21:7b, 21:8b, 21:18, 21:27, 21:32, 21:36a, 22:2c, 22:5, 22:7a, 22:7b, 22:9, 22:12a, 23:2, 23:4a, 23:5a, 23:7, 23:8, 23:9a, 23:9c, 23:13a, 23:31. [negative adv. (often in combination with *onques, mais, pas, mie, ja, plus*] not < enclitic in *nel, nes, nu #2*>.
    nen 2:38, 8:265, 10:360. == > *n(e) #1*.
ne #2 2:38, 2:39, 3:74, 3:82, 3:94, 4:112, 7:244, 9:314, 9:318, 10:334, 11:396, 16:8, 16:20, 16:22, 17:26, 18:55, 18:58, 19:4, 19:10, 19:38, 19:39, 20:24a, 20:24b, 20:27a, 21:4, 21:6, 21:37, 22:4, 23:3a. [conj.] nor, and.
ne . . . ne 19:39, 20:18. [conj.] neither . . . nor.
ne . . . qu(e) 23:1. [adv.] only.
ne set mie qu'a l'ueil li pent 3:88. [proverb] he cannot see beyond the end of his nose (lit.: he does not know what is hanging before his eye).
nee 4:134, 6:210. [pp. f. of *naistre*] born.
nef 16:8. [OS] ship.
nel 11:395, 13:435, 17:35, 18:29, 18:55. [enclitic form of *ne #1* and *le #4*].
    nu #2 2:64, 4:97, 9:314, 10:333, 10:334, 13:453. == > *nel*.
nen 2:38, 8:265, 10:360. == > *n(e) #1*.
nes 16:30, 18:43. [enclitic form of *ne #1* and *les #3*].
nés 20:22b. [OS] nose.

Nicolete 20:29a, 20:31a, 21:1a, 21:2, 21:34, 21:35a, 21:36b, 22:2a, 22:7a, 22:11c, 23:1, 23:10a, 23:11. [FS] heroine of *Aucassin and Nicolete*.
    Nicholete 20:4, 20:27b.
    == > *Nicolete*.
    Nicole 21:9. == > *Nicolete*.
ni 20:11, 20:27b. [conj.] nor.
niece 7:224, 7:231, 7:251. [FS] niece.
nient 22:12a (in *por nient* [adv. phr.], uselessly, for nothing) == > *noient*.
nis 16.18. [adv.] not even.
no 14:491. == > *nostre*.
noblement 10:361. [adv.] in a noble manner.
noces 11:367, 11:381, 15:513, 15:515. [FS] wedding (ceremony).
noient 13:464. [indef. pron.] nothing.
    nient 22:12a. == > *noient* (in *por nient* [adv. phr.], uselessly, for nothing).
noise 5:148, 21:35a. [FS] noise; rumor, report.
noiz 10:347. [FP] nuts.
nommer 1:18. [inf.] to name.
    nomé 15:530. [pp. m.].
    nomerai 8:255. [1 sg. fut.].
    numé 17:14. == > *nomé*.
non #1 1:18, 5:162, 7:229, 8:255, 10:343. [OS] name.
    nun #1 18:11, 18:12, 18:35. == > *non #1*.
non #2 13:466, 20:23, 23:4a, 23:6 in *s(e) . . . non*, q.v.
    nun #2 17:1, 17:24. == > *non #2*.
non #3 20:20 in *avoit a non*, was named, was called.
nonains 5:153. [FP] nuns.
norrir 7:223, 13:444. [inf.] to nourish, to raise.
    norri 13:440. [pp. m.].
    norrie 4:101, 7:234. [pp. f.].
    norrira 4:116. [3 sg. fut.].
    nourie 22:2b. == > *norrie*.
nort 17:36, 18:31. [OS] north.

nos #1 2:37, 3:82. [1 pl. subject pron.] we.
  nus #4 17:28. = = >nos #1.
nos #2 10:339, 13:466, 14:492. [1 pl. obj. pron.] us, to us.
  nus #5 16:19, 19:45. = = >nos #2.
nostre 14:483. [1 pl. poss. adj., FS] our.
  no 14:491. = = >nostre.
nourie 22:2b. [pp. f. of norrir].
nu #1 19:35, 22:8c. [adj., OS] uncovered, naked.
  nue 18:2. [FS].
  nus #6 23:28. [OP].
nu #2 2:64, 4:97, 9:314, 10:333, 10:334, 13:453. = = >nel.
nuit 5:137, 6:181, 12:397, 15:504, 18:47, 22:8a. [FS] night.
nul #1 12:418. [indef. pron., OS] no one.
  nus #1 7:247. [NS].
nul #2 20:18. [adj., OS] no, not one.
  nule 20:23. [FS].
  nuls 17:26, 18:58. [NS].
  nus #2 10:348. [OP].
  nus #3 20:10. = = >nuls.
numé 17:14. [pp. m. of nommer] named.
nun #1 18:11, 18:12, 18:35. = = >non #1.
nun #2 17:1, 17:24. = = >non #2.
nuncier 16:28. [inf.] to announce.
nus #1 7:247. [indef. adj., NS of nul #1].
nus #2 10:348. [adj., OP of nul #2].
nus #3 20:10. = = >nuls.
nus #4 17:28. = = >nos #1.
nus #5 16:19, 19:45. = = >nos #2.
nus #6 23:28. [adj., OP of nu #1].

o #1 9:289, 9:296, 9:301, 9:313, 10:321, 10:342, 11:372, 11:374, 12:420, 14:478, 14:480, 15:514, 20:7, 23:18. [prep.] with.
  od 16:17, 16:52, 17:18, 19:43, 19:46, 19:47. = = >o #1.

o #2 5:148. = = >ou #1.
o tout 5:142, 6:192. [compound prep.] with.
obedïence 17:23. [FS] obedience (to holy vows).
oblïez 18:45. [pp. m. of oublier] forgotten.
ocirre 4:98, 23:4b. [inf.] to slay, to kill.
  occirre 23:11. = = >ocirre.
  ocesissent 23:10c. [3 pl. imperf. subjunc.].
  ocient 23:12, 23:13b. [3 pl. pres.].
  ocioit 20:16d. [3 sg. imperf.].
  ocis 21:38b. [pp. m.].
  oscire 18:40, 18:54. = = >ocirre.
od 16:17, 16:52, 17:18, 19:43, 19:46, 19:47. = = >o #1.
oeul 23:9b. [OS] eye.
  eulz 8:270. [OP].
  ex #2 21:8b, 23:5b, 23:21, 20:22a. = = >eulz.
oï #1 2:59, 4:103, 4:117, 8:257, 14:496, 23:1, 23:11. [3 sg. pret. of oïr].
oï #2 5:144, 21:34. [pp. m. of oïr] heard.
oi 14:476. [1 sg. pret. of avoir #1].
oiant 2:30, 13:453. [pres. participle of oïr] before, in front of.
oïl 13:446. [adv.] yes.
oir 10:327, 10:341, 20:18. [OS] heir.
oïr 6:180, 20:1. [inf.] to hear.
  oï #1 2:59, 4:103, 4:117, 8:257, 14:496, 23:1, 23:11. [3 sg. pret.].
  oï #2 5:144, 21:34. [pp. m.].
  oiant 2:30, 13:453. [pres. participle].
  oïrent 2:55. [3 pl. pret.].
  oit 20:13. [3 sg. pres.].
  ooit 5:148. = = >oit.
  orront 3:78. [3 pl. fut.].
oisax 21:21. [OP] birds.
oit 20:13. [3 sg. pres. of oïr].
  ooit 5:148. = = >oit.
Olivete 18:47 in Munt Olivete. [OS] Mount of Olives, associated with Christ's Passion.

ombre 5:170. [FS] shade.
on 7:230. [3 sg. indef. subject pron.]
one.
    en #5 3:89, 8:274. $==>on$.
    um 16:36, 17:14. $==>on$.
    un #4 19:35. $==>on$.
once 4:129. [FS] ounce.
onques (+ ne) 2:38, 3:81, 4:126,
5:143, 10:348, 10:360, 11:384. [adv.]
never.
onques mes (+ ne) 12:418, 14:490,
15:502. [adv.] nevermore.
ont #1 22:11a. [3 pl. pres. of *avoir*
#1].
ont #2 2:42, 10:351, 11:371, 12:406,
15:507, 15:521, 15:522, 15:529,
15:530. [3 pl. pres. of *avoir* #2
(aux.)].
    unt 16:52, 17:1, 17:3, 17:10, 17:21,
    17:36, 18:7, 18:36, 18:40, 18:51,
    19:6, 19:10, 19:36, 19:53.
    $==>ont$ #2.
ooit 5:148. [3 sg. pres. of *oïr*].
or #1 3:85, 9:287, 10:338, 16:41, 19:11,
19:54, 19:55, 20:16a, 21:4, 23:4a,
23:31. [adv.] now.
    ore 3:68, 16:30, 18:59, 20:26,
    20:31a. $==>or$ #1.
or #2 4:129. [OS] gold.
    ors 22:11b. [NS].
ordenez #1 18:16. [NS] ordained
man.
ordenez #2 18:35. [pp. m. of *ordener*]
set up, established, ordained.
ore 3:68, 16:30, 18:59, 20:26, 20:31a.
$==>or$ #1.
oré 16:8. [OS] storm.
orent 4:126, 10:354, 12:405, 16:12,
17:11, 19:2. [3 pl. pret. of *avoir* #2
(aux.)].
orer 18:46. [inf.] to pray.
orgueilleuse 2:27. [adj., FS] proud.
orinne 4:100. [FS] origin, lineage.
oriol 16:44, 16:48. [OS] porch, covered
walkway.
orphenine 21:22. [FS] orphan.
orront 3:78. [3 pl. fut. of *oïr*].

ors 22:11b. [NS of *or* #2].
orteil 23:9b. [OS] toe.
oscire 18:40, 18:54. $==>ocirre$.
ostel 6:192. [OS] house, lodging.
oster 18:55, 18:58. [inf.] to take away,
to remove.
    osterent 16:25. [3 pl. pret.].
    ostés 21:2. [2 pl. imperative].
ot #1 1:11, 1:13, 3:70, 4:118, 6:187,
6:193, 11:374, 15:502, 15:511. [3 sg.
pret. of *avoir* #1].
ot #2 1:15, 2:57, 4:101, 4:124, 9:305,
11:367, 13:450. [3 sg. pret. of *avoir*
#2 (aux.)].
    out #1 16:36, 16:45, 19:40. $==>$
    ot #2.
ot #3 4:130, 5:151, 5:153, 6:177, 8:254,
9:318, 11:382, 18:4, 23:1. [3 sg. pret.
of *avoir* #1 in *i avoir*. construction].
there was, there were.
    out #2 16:44. $==>ot$ #3.
otroia 8:284, 9:300. [3 sg. pret. of
otroier, to grant].
otroié 10:352. [pp. m. of *otroier*]
granted.
ou #1 2:32, 4:125, 4:132, 10:338,
12:398. [adv. of place] where.
    o #2 5:148. $==>ou$ #1.
    u #1 19:8, 20:27b, 21:30, 23:10a.
    $==>ou$ #1.
ou #2 12:425, 13:436, 20:31a.
[interrogative adv.] where?
    u #2 18:49. $==>ou$ #2.
ou #3 22:11a. [conj.] or.
    u #3 20:30a, 20:32a, 22:3, 23:5a.
    $==>ou$ #3.
ou #4 6:179 in *par ou*. [conjunctive
adv. phr.] through which.
oublier 9:314. [inf.] to forget.
oume 23:9a, 23:9c. $==>homme$ #1.
out #1 16:36, 16:45, 19:40. $==>ot$
#2.
out #2 16:44. [3 sg. pret. of *avoir* #1
in *i avoir* construction].
outre 5:142. [adv.] beyond, further.
ouvri 12:411. [3 sg. pret. of *ovrir*].
ovriers 16:51. [OP] workers.

ovrir 6:178. [inf.] to open.
  ouvri 12:411. = = >ovri.
  overt 17:31. [pp. m.].
  ovrez 17:22. [2 pl. imperative].
  ovri 6:183. [3 sg. pret.].

paille 4:123, 6:208, 9:303, 9:309, 12:411,
  12:417, 13:450, 14:478, 14:482. [OS]
  cloth, usually of silk with gold
  threads.
    pailles 12:425, 12:430, 13:436.
    [NS].
pain 20:29c, 21:7b, 22:2c. [OS] bread.
paines 20:5. [FP] pains.
païs 8:256, 10:344, 15:523, 20:16d, 21:3,
  21:8b, 21:35a, 23:1. [OS] country,
  land.
panturee 21:12. [pp. f. of panturer]
  painted.
paor 22:12b. = = >peor in avoir peor, to
  be afraid.
par #1 16:49, 23:27. [prep. of
  movement through space] through.
par #2 2:52, 21:19, 21:35a. [prep. of
  distance covered] throughout,
  across.
par #3 14:471, 14:484, 15:512, 16:39,
  18:15, 21:11. [prep. of manner or
  means] by.
par #4 5:162, 17:23, 21:31. [prep. in
  formulating oaths] by . . . !
par #5 8:260, 16:42. [prep. of route
  taken] by way of.
par #6 18:38, 21:4. [prep. of agent
  (usually after a passive verb)] by,
  through, on account of.
par #7 20:15. [augmentative adv.
  conveying notion of superlative in
  tant par, so very much].
par desus 19:2. [compound prep.]
  above (here: by the shoulders[?]).
par devers 16:43. [compound prep.]
  by way of.
par grant devisse 21:11. [adv. phr.]
  carefully, artfully.
par honor 20:29c, 21:7b, 22:2c. [adv.
  phr.] honorably.

par mi 15:512. [adv. phr.] in half.
par ou 6:179. [conjunctive adv. phr.]
  through which.
par quoi 23:13a. [conjunctive adv.
  phr.] in such a manner that.
par tens 6:181. [adv. phr.] early.
paradis 22:5, 22:6, 22:7b, 22:9. [OS]
  paradise.
pardon 8:280, 13:463. [OS] pardon.
pardonné 13:467, 13:469. [pp. m. of
  pardonner] pardoned.
parentez 3:76. [NS] relatives
  (conceived of collectively).
parler 2:46, 3:89, 7:213, 8:257. [inf.] to
  speak.
    parla 2:29, 8:282, 8:283. [3 sg.
    pret.].
    parlant 23:11. [gerund].
    parlast 7:252. [3 sg. imperf.
    subjunc.].
    parlastes 14:480. [2 pl. pret.].
    parlé 18:9. [pp. m.].
    parlerent 10:324. [3 pl. pret.].
    parlerés 22:12a. [2 pl. fut.].
    parlés #1 20:26, 22:12a. [2 pl.
    pres.].
    parlés #2 23:23. = = >parlé.
    parloient 23:10a. [3 pl. imperf.].
    parole #1 21:6. [3 sg. pres.].
parmi 5:141, 19:52. [prep.] through.
parole #1 21:6. [3 sg. pres. of parler].
parole #2 2:50, 3:78, 7:246. [FS] word,
  speech.
pars 10:352 in de totes pars. [adv. phr.]
  on all sides.
part #1 15:512. [3 sg. pres. of partir, to
  leave, depart; to share].
part #2 5:147, 6:188, 18:6, 18:8. [FS]
  side.
parti #1 16:5. [pp. m. of partir] left.
'parti #2 19:51. [pp. m. of (s'en) partir]
  departed.
pas #1 4:97, 4:98, 6:191, 16:22, 17:19,
  17:25, 18:27, 19:4, 19:28. [particle
  used with ne (to reinforce
  negative)].
pas #2 17:4 in le grant pas, swiftly.

'pasma 13:456. [3 sg. pret. of (se)
pasmer, to faint].

pasmoisons 13:457. [FP] fainting fit,
swoons.

passage 16:8. [OS] passage.

passé 7:235, 16:6. [pp. m. of passer]
passed.

pastre 18:45. [NS] shepherd.

pavement 19:32, 19:44, 19:47. [OS]
stone floor.

pechié 14:484, 19:9. [OS] sin.
pechiez 14:493. [NS].

pensa 11:393. [3 sg. pret. of penser, to
think, to reflect].

penser 17:39. See Deu en laissiez penser.

pent 3:88 in ne set mie qu'a l'ueil li pent
[proverb], he cannot see beyond the
end of his nose (lit.: he does not
know what is hanging before his
eye).

peor 11:373, 21:5b in avoir peor, to be
afraid.
paor 22:126. = = > peor.

per 10:340. [NS] peer, equal; friend.

perdre 10:366. [inf.] to lose, to
destroy.
perdist 11:395. [3 sg. imperf.
subjunc.].
perdroiz 10:345. [2 pl. fut.].
perdue 14:484, 21:35a. [pp. f.].
pert 21:4. [1 sg. pres.].

pere 14:497, 15:510, 20:25a, 20:26. [NS]
father.
peres 20:28, 20:31a, 22:12b.
= = > pere.

perir 5:164. [inf. used as substantive]
danger, peril, death.

pert 21:4. [1 sg. pres. of perdre].

peser. [inf.] to grieve, to worry, to
weigh upon one's mind.
pesa 3:70, 4:105, 12:410. [3 sg.
pret.].
pesast 11:385. [3 sg. imperf.
subjunc.].
peseroit 9:292. [3 sg. cond.].
poise 21:6, 22:13. [3 sg. pres.].

peseroit 9:292. [3 sg. cond. of peser].

petit 6:195, 9:318. [adj., OS] little.
petis 20:3. [OP].

peu 20:32a, 22:5. = = > poi.

peüsce 23:4b. [1 sg. imperf. subjunc.
of pooir].

peüst 10:328, 19:48. [3 sg. imperf.
subjunc. of pooir].
poïst 11:376. = = > peust.

peut 17:6, 17:7. [3 sg. pres. of pooir].

pié 16:15, 19:39, 19:42, 20:16d, 23:9b.
[OS] foot.
piés 20:21. = = > piez.
piez 13:461, 17:7. [OP].

piece #1 4:127, 19:35. [FS] piece.

piece #2 7:232 in grant piece [adv.
phr.], for a long while.

pierre 19:34, 23:5a. [FS] stone.

piez 13:461, 17:7. [OP of pié].
piés 20:21. = = > piez.

pilier 18:4, 18:6, 18:32, 18:55. [OS]
pillar.
piler 18:56, 18:60. = = > pilier.
piliers 18:33. [NS].

pis 3:86. [NS, superlative of mauvais]
worst.

pitié 13:455. [FS] pity.

plaidier 17:8. [inf.] to speak (to), to
address.

plaindre 4:104. [inf.] to lament.

plains 17:15. [adj., NS] full.

plantee 23:9c. [pp. f. of planter] planted.

plantez 5:170. [pp. m. of planter]
planted.

plesir 5:163. [OS] pleasure, delight (cf.
vient a plesir).

plet #1 4:116, 10:350, 13:467. [3 sg.
pres. of plaire, to please].

plet #2 13:464. [OS] situation, matter.

plorer 4:103. [inf.] to weep.

plot 1:11, 9:300. [3 sg. pret. of plaire, to
please].

plus 6:188, 10:341, 14:497, 18:39, 19:17,
21:18, 21:36b, 21:38b, 23:7. [adv.]
more.

pöeit 18:58. [3 sg. imperf. of pooir].

pöez 9:290, 10:342, 18:49. [2 pl. pres.
of pooir].

poi 19:33. [pron., adv.] little, a little, slightly.
    peu 20:32a, 22:5. = = > *poi.*
poil 23:20. [OS] hair.
point 20:24b, 21:4. [particle used with *ne* (to reinforce negative)].
poinz 17:13, 19:53. [OP] fists, hands.
    puinz 18:51. = = > *poinz.*
poior 10:360. [adj., OS, comparative of *mauvais*] worse.
poise 21:6, 22:13. [3 sg. pres. of *peser*].
pooir [inf.] to be able; can.
    peüsce 23:4b [1 sg. imperf. subjunc.].
    peüst 10:328, 19:48 [3 sg. imperf. subjunc.].
    peut 17:6, 17:7. = = > *puet.*
    pöeit 18:58. [3 sg. imperf.].
    pöez 9:290, 10:342, 18:49. [2 pl. pres.].
    poïst 11:376. = = > *peüst.*
    pooie 23:13a. [1 sg. imperf.].
    pooient 23:10c. [3 pl. imperf.].
    porent 16:35, 16:39, 18:55, 19:19. [3 pl. pret.].
    porés 21:5b. [2 pl. fut.].
    poroit 20:28, 21:1a. = = > *porroit.*
    porra 5:146. [3 sg. fut.].
    porriés 22:12b. [2 pl. cond.].
    porroit 23:3a, 23:8. [3 sg. cond.].
    pot 6:188, 7:237. [3 sg. pret.].
    puet 3:89, 9:304, 14:481, 23:9a, 23:9c. [3 sg. pres.].
    puis #1 13:445, 21:5a, 21:33. [1 sg. pres.].
por #1 5:170, 10:331, 10:345, 11:395, 15:530, 20:7. [prep. of aim or intention] for.
    pur #1 16:21. = = > *por* #1.
por #2 3:91, 8:277. [(followed by inf.) prep. of aim, consequence, or cause of an action] for, in order to.
    pur #2 16:46, 16:53, 17:16, 17:33, 18:57, 18:60, 19:17. = = > *por* #2.
por #3 1:13, 9:319, 10:365, 15:519, 21:28, 23:24. [prep.] on account of, because of.

pur #3 16:2, 16:8, 16:20, 16:32, 19:4, 19:10. = = > *por* #3.
por #4 7:224, 7:231, 10:333. See *tenir por.*
por #5 13:458, 14:498. [after *aler, envoier,* prep. indicating person sent for].
por ce qu(e) 7:228, 10:366. [conjunctive phr.] because, since.
por coi 21:24. [interrogative adv. phr.] why?
por nient 22:12a. [adv. phr.] uselessly, for nothing.
porchaceron 10:349. [1 pl. fut. of *porchacer,* to seek to win; to procure].
porchacié 10:351. [pp. m. of *porchacer*] sought to win; procured.
porent 16:35, 16:39, 18:55, 19:19. [3 pl. pret. of *pooir*].
porés 21:5b. [2 pl. fut. of *pooir*].
poroit 20:28, 21:1a. [3 sg. cond. of *pooir*].
'porpensa 8:271. [3 sg. pret. of *(se) porpenser,* to reflect (upon)].
porra 5:146. [3 sg. fut. of *pooir*].
porriés 22:12b. [2 pl. cond. of *pooir*].
porroit 23:3a, 23:8. [3 sg. cond. of *pooir*].
    poroit 20:28, 21:1a. = = > *porroit.*
porter 9:313, 14:478, 19:17. [inf.] to carry.
    porta 3:69, 5:159, 19:21. [3 sg. pret.].
    porté 2:57, 17:10, 17:11. [pp. m.].
    portez 16:52. = = > *porté.*
portes 20:16c. [FP] doors.
porteüre 2:40. [FS] pregnancy.
portez 16:52. [pp. m. of *porter*].
portier 6:177, 7:225. [OS] doorman, guard.
    portiers 7:213, 7:219. [NS].
pot 6:188, 7:237. [3 sg. pret. of *pooir*].
povres 2:56. [adj., FP] poor.
premiers 23:3a. [adj., NS] first.
prendre 16:31, 16:38, 20:24a, 23:10c. [inf.] to take.
    pren 20:25a. [2 sg. imperative].

prenderoit 23:3b. [3 sg. cond.].
prendés 22:3. [2 pl. imperative].
prendra 10:337. [3 sg. fut.].
prent 6:204. [3 sg. pres.].
pris #1 5:171, 6:185, 6:191,
11:367, 17:10. [pp. m.].
prist 2:32, 5:135, 10:359, 12:411. [3
sg. pret.].
pres 19:25. [adv.] almost.
pres de 10:339. [compound prep.]
near.
present 19:11 in *en present* [idiom],
before him.
prestre 22:8a. [NP] priests.
preu [adj., OS] bold, brave, good,
noble.
    preude 2:61. [FS].
    preus 23:15. [NS].
    preuz 1:06 [OP], 14:486 [FS].
preudome 11:379. [OS] an honest,
good man of proper upbringing.
    preudom #1 10:340.
    = = > *preudome*.
    preudom #2 10:354. [NP].
    preudons 2:32, 4:115, 6:196. [NS].
preus (= **preuz**) 23:15. [NS of *preu*].
priere 5:165. [FS] prayer.
primes 9:307, 9:310, 14:480. [adv.]
first, for the first time.
pris #1 5:171, 6:185, 6:191, 11:367,
17:10. [pp. m. of *prendre*] taken.
pris #2 3:74. [OS] worth, esteem.
prison 21:9, 21:24, 21:28, 21:34. [FS]
prison.
prist 2:32, 5:135, 10:359, 12:411. [3 sg.
pret. of *prendre*].
privé 16:17. [adj., OS] private.
proisast 7:248. [3 sg. imperf. subjunc.
of *prisier*, to value].
proisiee 11:392. [pp. f. of *prisier*]
valued.
promist 8:283. [3 sg. pret. of *prometre*,
to promise].
    promit 4:118. = = > *promist*.
proueces 20:6. [FP] brave deeds, feats
of valor.
pucele 8:257, 10:349, 15:526. [FS]
maiden.

pueple 17:32, 18:60. [OS] people.
puet 3:89, 9:304, 14:481, 23:9a, 23:9c.
[3 sg. pres. of *pooir*].
    peut 17:6, 17:7. = = > *puet*.
puinz 18:51. = = > *poinz*.
puis #1 13:445, 21:5a, 21:33. [1 sg.
pres. of *pooir*].
puis #2 2:54, 5:173, 8:254, 15:526.
[adv.] afterwards.
puis #3 6:191, 6:205, 6:206. [adv.]
then, next (in a succession of
events).
puis qu(e) #1 23:4a. [adv. phr.] after.
puis qu(e) #2 21:8a. [conjunctive
phr.] since.
pur #1 16:21. = = > *por #1*.
pur #2 16:46, 16:53, 17:16, 17:33,
18:57, 18:60, 19:17. = = > *por #2*.
pur #3 16:2, 16:8, 16:20, 16:32, 19:4,
19:10. = = > *por #3*.
'purpensez 18:28. [pp. m. of *(se)
porpenser*] reflected (upon).

qanque 11:384. = = > *quanque*.
qant 15:501, 23:1. = = > *quant*.
qu' is combined with *que* as *qu(e)*.
quanque 9:300, 13:467, 20:24b, 21:4.
[compound n. relative pron.]
whatever, as much as, all that.
    qanque 11:384. = = > *quanque*.
quant 2:59, 5:137, 5:165, 7:212, 7:235,
7:241, 9:285, 9:307, 10:359, 12:405,
12:413, 13:457, 13:460, 13:469,
14:480, 14:491, 15:523, 15:527, 16:12,
16:34, 16:39, 17:11, 18:28, 18:46, 19:2,
19:19, 19:31, 20:27a, 21:1a. [conj.]
when, since.
    qant 15:501, 23:1. = = > *quant*.
quarrez 5:169. [pp. m. of *quarrer*, to
quarter; to square] divided.
quarz 16:4, 18:3. [ordinal num., NS]
(the) fourth.
quatre 5:169, 16:1, 16:6, 16:34, 17:16,
17:17. [num.] four.
qu(e) #1 5:159, 10:345, 12:420, 14:484,
14:487, 15:520, 15:521, 18:24, 20:27b,
22:2a, 22:7a, 22:11a. [relative pron.
(of persons)] whom, who, that.

qu(e) #2 1:02, 1:13, 7:242, 12:419, 13:450, 13:455, 14:479, 14:496, 15:518, 15:521, 16:13, 16:45, 20:5, 20:6, 20:27a, 20:31b, 21:36b, 21:38b. [relative pron. (of things)] which, that.

qu(e) #3 3:73, 13:465, 17:9, 17:33, 18:17, 19:7, 20:26, 22:4, 22:6. [n. interrogative pron.] what?

qu(e) #4 1:10, 1:15, 2:35, 2:40, 2:47, 3:83, 4:97, 4:111, 4:112, 4:134, 6:185, 6:210, 7:217, 7:223, 7:226, 7:252, 8:272, 9:292, 10:332, 10:337, 10:354, 10:359, 11:367, 11:375, 11:379, 11:385, 12:429, 12:430, 13:452, 15:504, 18:19, 18:22, 19:21, 19:30, 19:34, 20:16b, 20:16c, 20:23, 20:24a, 20:27a, 20:30b, 21:1a, 21:5a, 21:6, 21:8b, 21:34, 21:35a, 21:35b, 21:35c, 21:38a, 23:1, 23:4a, 23:5b, 23:6, 23:7, 23:8, 23:10c, 23:11, 23:13a. [conj.] that.

   c' #1 2:38, 3:81, 10:325, 21:36b. ==>*qu(e)* #4.

qu(e) #5 3:94, 6:188, 8:280, 16:23, 18:39, 23:5a, 23:6, 23:7. [conj. used in comparisons] than, as.

qu(e) #6 21:3. [conj. introducing independent propositions in the subjunctive] may....

qu(e) #7 20:29a, 21:4, 21:38b, 22:5, 22:12a. ==>*car* #1.

qu(e) #8 2:37, 2:60, 3:88, 6:176, 11:394. ==>*ce qu(e)*.

qu(e) #9 14:493 in *ainz qu(e)*, q.v.

qu(e) #10 4:117, 8:284, 15:517 in *ce qu(e)*, q.v.

qu(e) #11 16:33, 18:44 in *ço qu(e)* ==>*ce qu(e)*, q.v.

qu(e) #12 18:23 in *de ço qu(e)*, q.v.

qu(e) #13 3:78, 7:237 in *des qu(e)*, q.v.

qu(e) #14 5:172 in *desi qu(e)*, q.v.

qu(e) #15 22:7a, 22:11c in *mais qu(e)*, q.v.

qu(e) #16 17:39, 20:29c, 21:7b, 22:2c, 22:9, 23:1 in *n'avoir ... qu(e) faire*, q.v.

qu(e) #17 7:228, 10:366 in *por ce qu(e)*, q.v.

qu(e) #18 21:8a, 23:4a in *puis qu(e)*, q.v.

qu(e) #19 21:36a in *qui qu(e)*, q.v.

qu(e) #20 2:64 in *san ce qu(e)*, q.v.

qu(e) #21 11:386 in *sol tant qu(e)*, q.v.

qu(e) #22 10:322, 17:4, 23:4b in *tant qu(e) #1*, q.v.

qu(e) #23 23:8 in *tant qu(e) #2*, q.v.

qu(e) (+ negative) 23:1. [restrictive adv.] only. .

que qu(e) 19:6, 19:36. [conjunctive phr.] while.

quel 19:8. [relative pron., NP] what.

quens 20:16b, 20:17, 21:1a, 21:2, 21:35c, 22:1, 23:10c. [NS of *conte #2*].

quer 17:40. [OS] choir.

querre. [inf.] to seek.
   querant 23:27. [gerund].
   quier 22:7a. [1 sg. pres.].
   quiers 18:10, 18:14, 18:17. [2 sg. pres.].
   quiert 13:463. [3 sg. pres.].
   quis #1 18:7. [pp. m.].
   quistrent 18:48. [3 pl. pret.].

ques 5:154. ==>*quis #2*.

qui #1 2:26, 2:33, 2:49, 2:55, 2:57, 3:65, 3:90, 4:95, 4:100, 4:116, 5:140, 6:180, 6:193, 7:247, 9:299, 9:310, 9:315, 10:328, 10:356, 11:370, 11:390, 13:440, 13:444, 14:486, 14:488, 15:511, 16:28, 16:40, 16:51, 17:28, 17:32, 18:5, 18:37, 18:38, 19:41, 20:1, 20:24a, 20:29a, 20:29c, 21:1b, 21:7b, 21:21, 22:2c, 22:8a, 22:8c, 22:10b, 23:3a, 23:11, 23:24. [relative pron.] who, whom, which <enclitic in *ques*, *quil*, *quis #2*>.
   cui 11:374. [stressed form].
   ki 21:11, 23:17, 23:27. ==>*qui #1*.

qui #2 13:437. [interrog. pron.] who?

qui #3 18:57, 19:13. [relative pron.] (of him) to whom.

qui #4 3:87, 19:46. [relative pron.] he who, anyone who.

qui qu(e) 21:36a. [relative pron.] whoever.

quida 18:21. [3 sg. pret. of *cuidier*].
quidiés 23:4a. [2 pl. imperative of
cuidier].
quier 22:7a. [1 sg. pres. of *querre*].
quiers 18:10, 18:14, 18:17. [2 sg. pres.
of *querre*].
quiert 13:463. [3 sg. pres. of *querre*].
quil 13:438, 13:441, 18:48. [enclitic
form of *qui* #*1* and *le* #*4*].
quint 16:11. [ordinal num.] fifth.
quir 19:24. [OS] skin.
quis #1 18:7. [pp. m. of *querre*]
sought.
quis #2 17:22. [enclitic form of *qui*
#*1* and *les* #*3*].
   ques 5:154. == >*quis* #*2*.
quisine 16:43. [FS] kitchen.
quistrent 18:48. [3 pl. pret. of *querre*].
quit 23:7. [1 sg. pres. of *cuidier*].
quoi 23:13a in *par quoi*. [conjunctive
adv. phr.] in such a manner that.

raconterent 2:50. [3 pl. pret. of *raconter*,
to recount].
raison 5:161. [FS] discourse.
   reson #1 7:237. == >*raison*.
ravon 14:491. [2 pl. pres. of *ravoir*, to
have once again (found).
Reaus 19:53. [rallying cry] Royal! (i.e.,
Long live the king!).
recercelés 20:22a. [adj., OP] curled.
reçoivre 8:280. [inf.] to receive.
reconneü 13:449. [pp. m. of *reconoistre*]
recognized.
Reinalz (li fiz Urs) 16:4, 18:8, 18:10,
18:14, 18:15, 18:16, 18:18, 18:23,
18:28, 19:28. [NS] Renald fitz Ours,
one of the murderers of Thomas
Becket.
   Reinalt 18:13, 18:24. [OS of
   Reinalz].
refaire 16:46. [inf.] to reconstruct, to
redo.
   refont 15:515. [3 pl. pres.].
referi 19:29. [3 sg. pret. of *referir*, to
strike again or in turn].
regardee #1 2:43. [pp. f. of *regarder*]
looked at.

'regardee #2 5:166. [pp. f. of *(se)*
regarder] looked around (oneself).
regart 6:187. [OS] concern.
rehusa 18:24. [3 sg. pret. of *rehuser*, to
move back, to draw back].
rei 18:7, 18:20, 19:18. == >*roi* #*1*.
reluisant 23:20. [adj., OS] shining.
remembra 12:421. [3 sg. pret. of
remembrer, to remember, to recall].
remüez 18:19. [pp. m. of *remuer*]
excited, inflamed, impassioned.
rendu 9:305. [pp. m. of *rendre*]
returned, given back.
'rent 19:12. [3 sg. pres. of *(se) rendre a*,
to render (oneself) unto}.
repairier 17:20. [OS] return.
repera 8:260, 8:281. [3 sg. pret. of
repairier, to return].
repere 8:276. [OS] the opportunity to
lodge there.
reperoit 8:268. [3 sg. imperf. of
repairier, to return].
resbaudis 20:14. [adj., NS] cheered up.
reson #1 7:237. == >*raison*.
reson #2 9:286 in *mist a reson*, spoke
to (someone).
respondi 13:439. [3 sg. pret. of
respondre, to reply].
restut 18:12. [3 sg. pret. of *rester*, to
stop, to stand still].
resurdra 19:45. [3 sg. fut. of *resurdre*, to
get up again; to resuscitate].
retez 18:27. [pp. m. of *reter*] held,
restrained.
retint 19:3. [3 sg. pret. of *retenir*, to
hold; to restrain; to defend].
retor 8:275. [OS] the opportunity to
visit or return there.
retraire #1 21:1a. [inf.] to pull away
from, to snatch away from.
retraire #2. [inf.] to tell, to recount,
to narrate.
   retrere 2:59. == >*retraire* #*2*.
returné 19:52. [pp. m. of *returner*]
returned.
rians 20:22a. [adj., OP] laughing.
   riant 23:21. [FS].
rice 20:30b. == >*riche* #*1*.

rices 22:10b. $==>$ *riches* [FP].
Richarz li Brez 16:5, 19:31. [NS]
Richard the Breton, one of the
murderers of Thomas Becket.
riche #1 6:208, 15:516. [adj., OS] rich,
powerful; magnificent.
> **rice** 20:30b. $==>$ *riche #1*.
> **rices** 22:10b. $==>$ *riches* [FP].
> **riche #2** 5:149, 5:152. [FS].
> **riche #3** 1:05, 7:249, 19:55. [NP].
> **riches** 1:19 [NS], 2:56 [FP].

richement 7:240, 9:298, 11:381, 15:525.
[adv.] splendidly, well.
rien 16:32. [adv.] at all.
rien (+ ne) 4:107, 13:451, 19:3. [FS]
nothing.
riens #1 20:27a. [indef. pron.]
anything.
riens #2 21:36b, 21:38b. [FS] thing,
object, being.
'rist 2:25. [3 sg. pret. of *(se) rire de*, to
laugh (about)].
Robert del Broc 17:15. [OS] nephew
of Randel of Broc; twice
excommunicated by Thomas Becket.
> **Roberz del Broc #1** 16:49.
> $==>$ *Robert del Broc*.
> **Roberz del Broc #2** 16:40. [NS].

roé 4:123. [adj., OS] wheel-shaped or
round design (on material).
roi #1 20:30a, 22:3. [OS] king.
> **rei** 18:7, 18:20, 19:18. $==>$ *roi
> #1*.
> **roi #2** 22:11b. [NP].

roïne 15:520, 20:32a. [FS] queen.
rose 21:20. [FS] rose.
> **roses** 19:48. [FP]

rovir 19:49. [inf.] to be red.
rue 23:10a in *tote une rue* [adv. phr.],
(all) along the road.

s' #1 1:21, 2:25, 5:136, 5:138, 5:142,
5:158, 5:160, 5:166, 6:192, 8:269,
9:291, 9:301, 11:380, 11:386, 12:400,
14:495, 15:523, 16:18, 16:24, 18:22,
18:31, 18:32, 18:56, 19:3, 19:5, 19:44,
19:51, 19:52, 21:14, 23:1, 23:13a.
$==>$ *se #1*.

s' #2 5:163, 9:293, 10:327, 11:376,
11:393, 20:25b, 20:32a, 23:12, 23:13b,
23:31. $==>$ *se #2*.
s' #3 7:214, 9:285, 11:371, 15:509, 18:2,
18:57, 20:7. $==>$ *sa*.
s' #4 22:11a, 22:11b, 23:5b, 23:10b.
$==>$ *si #1,3*.
s' #5 23:4a, 23:6. $==>$ *s(e)* in *s(e) . . .
non*, q.v.
sa 1:15, 2:34, 2:35, 2:61, 3:68, 5:141,
5:161, 5:165, 6:176, 7:219, 7:224,
7:231, 7:251, 9:319, 10:329, 10:331,
10:362, 11:372, 11:375, 11:377,
11:391, 11:395, 12:414, 12:420,
13:452, 14:488, 18:2, 20:16d, 20:29b,
20:30b, 23:9b. [3 FS poss. adj.] his,
her.
> **s' #3** 7:214, 9:285, 11:371, 15:509,
> 18:2, 18:57, 20:7. $==>$ *sa*.
> **se #3** 20:25a. $==>$ *sa*.

saçans 23:15. [adj., NS] wise.
sachent 4:133. [3 pl. pres. of *savoir*].
sachier 18:52. [inf.] to pull, to grab, to
snatch.
> **sacha** 18:25. [3 sg. pret.].
> **saché** 17:3. $==>$ *sachié*.
> **sachié** 18:19, 19:39. [pp. m.].

saciés 21:5a, 21:38a. [2 pl. imperative
of *savoir*].
sacrez 18:34. [pp. m. of *sacrer*]
dedicated.
sage 8:264, 14:486. [adj., FS] wise,
clever, well-educated.
sai 1:02. [1 sg. pres. of *savoir*].
sain et sauf 4:114. [adj. phr.] safe and
sound.
sains 6:183. [OP] bells.
saint #1 5:162 [OS], 18:5 [OS], 18:17
[FS], 18:21 [OS], 19:15 [FS]. [adj.]
holy.
> **sainte** 17:23. [FS].
> **sainz #1** 17:37. [OP].

saint #2 16:38, 19:19. [OS] saint, holy
man.
> **sainz #2** 17:6, 18:9, 18:26, 18:29.
> [NS].
> **sainz #3** 19:14. [OP].

saint Beneeit 18:35. St. Benedict.

saint Denis 19:13. St. Denis, patron of France.

saint Thomas 19:42. [OS] St. Thomas Becket, archbishop of Canterbury (1162-70).

   sainz Thomas 16:19, 17:22, 18:11, 18:22, 18:56, 19:11, 19:30. [NS].

saisi 18:15, 18:51, 19:1. [pp. m. of *saisir*] seized.

sale 16:15, 16:35. [FS] main hall.

Saltewode 16:10. [OS] Saltwood Castle (fief of Canterbury).

salver 18:60. [inf.] to save.

san ce que 2:64. [adv. phr.] without.

sanblant 23:22. == > *semblant*.

sanc 19:46, 19:49, 19:50. [OS] blood.

Sarasins 20:29b, 22:2a. [OP] Saracens.

Satan 18:1. [OS] Satan.

sauf 4:114 in *sain et sauf* [adv. phr.], safe and sound.

savant 17:24 in *nun savant* [adv. phr.], unwise, foolish.

savoir 9:290. [inf.] to know.

   saciés 21:5a, 21:38a. [2 pl. imperative].

   sai 1:02. [1 sg. pres.].

   savoit 22:12b. [3 sg. imperf.].

   savon 2:37. [2 pl. pres.].

   savrez 12:426, 18:18. [2 pl. fut.].

   set #2 8:267, 13:451. [3 sg. pres.] (cf. *ne set mie qu'a l'ueil li pent*).

   seü 10:354. [pp. m.].

   seüe 2:52, 15:527. [pp. f.].

   seüsce 23:6. [1 sg. imperf. subjunc.].

   seüst 11:393. [3 sg. imperf. subjunc.].

   sot 2:60, 10:359, 13:464, 15:501. [3 sg. pret.].

   sout 16:40. == > *sot*.

savoir bon gré 8:274. [idiom] to thank.

se #1 3:72, 8:266, 8:271, 10:326, 13:433, 13:456, 13:457, 16:34, 17:5, 18:28, 19:12, 19:14, 19:37, 21:21, 21:22, 22:13, 23:24. [reflexive particle associated with verb,

indicating that its subject is also in some actual or figurative sense the object; usually remains untranslated in English].

   s' #1 1:21, 2:25, 5:136, 5:138, 5:142, 5:158, 5:160, 5:166, 6:192, 8:269, 9:291, 9:301, 11:380, 11:386, 12:400, 14:495, 15:523, 16:18, . 16:24, 18:22, 18:31, 18:32, 18:56, 19:3, 19:5, 19:44, 19:51, 19:52, 21:14, 23:1, 23:13a. == > *se #1*.

se #2 2:42, 3:84, 4:116, 4:119, 8:265, 8:268, 9:291, 9:295, 10:331, 10:335, 10:350, 18:10, 18:14, 20:13, 20:27b, 20:30a, 20:30b, 20:31a, 21:5a, 21:33, 21:38a, 22:4, 22:12a, 23:10c, 23:13a. [conj.] if < enclitic in *ses #3*>.

   s' #2 5:163, 9:293, 10:327, 11:376, 11:393, 20:25b, 20:32a, 23:12, 23:13b, 23:31. == > *se #2*

se #3 20:25a. == > *sa*.

se #4 22:13. == > *si #4*.

s(e) . . . non 13:466, 20:23, 23:4a, 23:6. [locution functioning as prep.] except.

seeit 16:17. [3 sg. imperf. of *seoir*, to be seated, sitting].

sei 17:8, 18:19, 19:39. == > *soi #1*.

seignor 2:33, 2:58, 8:253, 10:333, 10:361, 11:376, 11:396, 12:412, 13:458. [OS] lord, husband.

   seignur 16:41 [NP], 17:27 [OP], 17:38 [NP]. == > *seignor*.

   sire 1:12, 1:23, 3:76, 4:124, 5:163, 6:194, 10:339, 11:368, 11:374, 12:403, 13:469, 16:29, 21:2, 21:6, 21:25, 21:36b, 22:1. [NS].

   sires 1:12, 2:43, 14:489. == > *sire*.

sejor 8:276. [OS] the opportunity to sojourn there.

sel 6:202. == > *sil*.

selonc 1:02. [prep.] according to.

   selunc 16:9. == > *selonc*.

sembla 12:409, 12:429. [3 sg. pret. of *sembler*, to seem].

semble 15:520. [3 sg. pres. of *sembler*, to seem].

semblant 7:246, 10:360, 11:385. [OS]
appearance; face, expression;
attitude, manner.
  sanblant 23:22. = = >*semblant*.
senestre 19:23. [adj., FS] left.
sentier 16:42. [OS] path.
sera #1 21:38a. [3 sg. fut. of *estre* #1
(aux.)].
sera #2 10:338, 21:38a. [3 sg. fut. of
estre #2].
serai 21:32. [1 sg. fut. of *estre* #2].
serf 19:51. [NP] servants.
sergant 16:18, 19:5, 22:10c. [NP]
servants.
  sergens 20:16d. [OP].
  serjant 9:317. = = >*sergant*.
seroient 10:327. [3 pl. cond. of *estre*
#2].
seroit 15:516, 22:5, 23:13a. [3 sg. cond.
of *estre* #2].
seroiz 4:111. [2 pl. cond. of *estre* #2].
seror 14:488. [OS] sister.
  serors 10:356. [OP].
servir [inf.] to serve.
  sert 10:361. [3 sg. pres.].
  serviront 10:334. [3 pl. fut.].
  servist 9:320. [3 sg. imperf.
  subjunc.].
  servoit 11:388. [3 sg. imperf.].
servise 4:119, 6:180, 7:211. [OS]
service, favor; religious service,
mass.
servitur 17:28. [NP] servants.
servoit 11:388. [3 sg. imperf. of *servir*].
ses #1 1:12, 2:43, 10:358, 20:25a, 21:1b.
[3 NS poss. adj.] his, her, its.
ses #2 5:171, 11:368, 14:473, 17:7,
19:12, 20:16d, 21:8b. [3 OP and
FP poss. adj.] his, her, its.
ses #3 16:53. [enclitic form of *se* #2
and *les* #3].
set #1 7:235. [num.] seven.
set #2 3:88, 8:267, 13:451. [3 sg. pres.
of *savoir*].
seü 10:354. [pp. m. of *savoir*] known.
seüe 2:52, 15:527. [pp. f. of *savoir*]
known.

seul 9:318, 12:419, 20:18. [adj., OS]
only, alone, single.
  seule 2:40. [FS].
  seux 20:16c. [NS].
  sul 18:44, 18:59. = = >*seul*.
seüsce 23:6. [1 sg. imperf. subjunc. of
savoir].
seüst 11:393. [3 sg. imperf. subjunc. of
savoir].
seux 20:16c. [adj., NS of *seul*].
si #1 3:65, 4:108, 6:189, 10:350,
11:380, 12:416, 15:530, 18:24, 20:25b,
20:32a, 21:1b, 21:36a, 22:11b. [adv.]
thus.
  s' #4 22:11a, 22:11b, 23:5b,
  23:10b. = = >*si* #1, #3.
si #2 2:31. [adv. introducing an oath]
so (help me God)!
si #3 4:111, 4:126, 7:243, 7:244,
12:418, 14:490, 15:502, 19:21, 19:31,
20:10, 20:16b, 20:23, 20:24a, 20:30b,
20:31a, 23:5b, 23:12. [adv. followed
by an adj. or adv.] so <enclitic in
sel, sil>.
si #4 4:106, 7:221, 8:258, 9:286,
10:341, 13:456, 13:470, 20:16d, 20:17,
20:25a, 20:29a, 20:29b, 20:29c, 21:7a,
21:7b, 22:2a, 22:2b, 23:3b.
[conjunctive adv.] and.
  se #4 22:13. = = >*si* #4.
si #5 9:317. [3 NP poss. adj.] his, her,
its.
si #6 23:5a. See *de si lonc que*.
si comme 15:514. [adv. phr.] just as.
  si con 1:11. = = >*si comme*.
si qu(e) 21:34. [conjunctive phr.] as.
si tost cum 17:6. [temporal
conjunctive phr.] as soon as.
siecle 22:5, 22:11b. [OS] world.
sien #1 4:127. [3 sg. stressed poss.
adj., OS] his, her.
sien #2 8:272, 8:278. [3 OS poss.
pron.] his or her wealth/goods/
land/possessions.
  sue 19:15. [FS].
  sons 12:430. [NS].
  suens 18:45. [OP].

sifaite 23:6. [adj. phr.] such a.

sifaitement 15:521. [adv.] in this manner, in this way; thus.

sil 18:52. [enclitic form of si #3 and le #4].

    sel 6:202. = = >sil.

sire 1:12, 1:23, 3:76, 4:124, 5:163, 6:194, 10:339, 11:368, 11:374, 12:403, 13:469, 16:29, 21:2, 21:6, 21:25, 21:36b, 22:1. [NS of seignor].

    sires 2:43, 14:489. = = >sire.

sist 1:19, 2:26. [3 sg. pret. of seoir, to be seated, sitting].

siwez 16:41. [2 pl. imperative of siure, to follow].

siwirent 17:17. [3 pl. pret. of siure, to follow].

soferroient 4:97. [3 pl. cond. of suffrir].

sofrist 7:252. [3 sg. imperf. subjunc. of suffrir].

soi #1 3:72, 5:166, 9:313, 12:423. [3 sg. stressed reflexive pron.] (him)self, (her)self.

    sei 17:8, 18:19, 19:39. = = >soi #1.

soi #2 22:8c. [FS] thirst.

soignant 10:331. [FS] mistress.

soit 7:217, 13:467, 15:504, 20:13, 21:3. [3 sg. pres. subjunc. of estre #1 (as aux.)].

sol tant qu(e) 11:386. [conjunctive adv. phr.] not even to the extent that.

soloit 6:178. [3 sg. imperf. of soloir, to have as a duty or custom].

son #1 1:14, 1:18, 1:22, 2:58, 3:69, 6:192, 6:203, 6:206, 6:207, 7:236, 8:255, 9:302, 9:303, 10:329, 10:361, 11:376, 11:378, 11:392, 11:396, 12:400, 12:410, 12:412, 13:433, 13:458, 13:463, 14:498, 15:512, 20:16d, 20:17, 21:1a, 23:3b, 23:9b. [3 OS poss. adj.] his, her.

    sun 16:17, 16:26, 17:2, 19:11, 19:12, 19:34, 19:40, 19:42. = = >son #1.

son #2 4:124, 6:194, 12:403, 14:497. [3 NS poss. adj.] his, her.

son #3 23:9b. [OS] tip, top, end.

sonna 6:183. [3 sg. pret. of sonner, to sound, to ring].

sons 12:430. [3 sg. stressed poss. pron., NS] hers, his.

sont #1 22:10b. [3 pl. pres. of estre #1 (aux.)].

    sunt #1 16:5, 16:6, 16:10, 16:11, 16:15, 16:43, 16:48, 17:4, 17:5, 17:12, 18:6, 19:37, 19:51, 19:55. = = >sont #1.

sont #2 2:36, 22:8c. [3 pl. pres. of estre #2].

    sunt #2 16:22, 17:24, 18:37, 18:38, 19:8, 19:54. = = >sont #2.

sor 3:86, 3:87, 5:144, 6:184, 12:412, 12:417, 12:428, 23:11. [prep.] on; against.

    sur 16:26, 17:36, 18:17, 18:53, 19:9, 19:23, 19:32, 19:42, 19:47. = = >sor.

sorcille 21:16. [FS] eyebrow.

sot 2:60, 10:359, 13:464, 15:501. [3 sg. pret. of savoir].

    sout 16:40. = = >sot.

souduians 23:26. [OP] soldiers.

soufri 20:5. [3 sg. pret. of suffrir].

soupris 20:24a. [adj., NS] overcome.

sous 23:28. [prep.] beneath.

sout 16:40. [3 sg. pret. of savoir].

sovenir de 19:48. [inf.] to remember, to recall.

sovent 8:268. [adv.] often.

soventes 8:281. [adj., FP] many, frequent.

    sovente 10:324. = = >soventes.

sue 19:15. [FS of sien #2].

suens 18:45. [OP of sien #2].

suffrir 16:23, 18:42. [inf.] to suffer; to tolerate.

    soferroient 4:97. [3 pl. cond.].

    sofrist 7:252. [3 sg. imperf. subjunc.].

    soufri 20:5. = = >suffri.

    suffri 18:57. [3 sg. pret.].

sui 3:75, 14:489, 18:27, 18:41, 18:42, 21:24, 21:26, 21:28. [1 sg. pres. of estre #2].

sul 18:44, 18:59. = = >*seul.*

sumes 17:28. [1 pl. pres. of *estre* #2].

sun 16:17, 16:26, 17:2, 19:11, 19:12, 19:34, 19:40, 19:42. = = >*son* #1.

sunt #1 16:5, 16:6, 16:10, 16:11, 16:15, 16:43, 16:48, 17:4, 17:5, 17:12, 18:6, 19:37, 19:51, 19:55. [3 pl. pres. of *estre* #1 (aux.)].

sunt #2 16:22, 17:24, 18:37, 18:38, 19:8, 19:54. [3 pl. pres. of *estre* #2].

sur 16:26, 17:36, 18:17, 18:53, 19:9, 19:23, 19:32, 19:42, 19:47. = = >*sor.*

sus 17:40 in *la sus* [adv. phr.], up there.

suspendu 18:38. [pp. m. of *suspendre*] suspended, hung.

sustenir 16:21. [inf.] to undergo, to endure; to support, to hold up.
    sustenue 18:4. [pp. f.].

t' #1 23:31. = = >*te* #1.

t' #2 18:16. = = >*te* #3.

tables 16:18. [FP] tables.

tailliés 20:21 in *bien tailliés* [pp. phr.], well-formed.

tans 20:17. = = >*tens* time (but here: "prime" of life).

tant #1 8:272, 8:273, 8:283, 10:344, 14:486, 20:11, 20:15, 20:27b, 20:32b, 22:7a, 23:5a. [adv.] so, so much, so many.

tant #2 11:386 in *sol tant que* [conjunctive adv. phr.], not even to the extent that.

tant con 23:7, 23:9a. [conjunctive phr.] as much as.
    tant qu(e) #2 23:8. = = >*tant con.*

tant cum 17:25. [conjunctive phr.] as long as.

tant par 20:15. [adv. phr.] so very much.

tant qu(e) #1 10:322, 11:386, 17:4, 23:4b. [conjunctive phr.] until.

tant qu(e) #2 23:8. = = >*tant con.*

tanz 1:16, 18:16. [indef. adj., OP] so many.

tasta 6:189. [3 sg. pret. of *taster*, to feel].

tatereles 22:8b. [FP] tatters, old worn clothes.

te #1 [2 sg. reflexive pron.] you, yourself.
    t' #1 23:31. = = >*te* #1.

te #2 (= *ta*) 20:25a, 20:25b. [2 FS poss. adj.] your.

te #3 5:163, 20:30a, 23:25. [2 sg. indirect obj. pron.] to you.
    t' #2 18:16. = = >*te* #3.

te #4 20:25b, 23:27, 23:29, 23:30. [2 sg. direct obj. pron.] you.

teces 20:23, 20:32b. [FP] qualities, marks of distinction.

tel #1 3:89. [indef. adj., OS] such a(n).
    tel #2 21:8b. = = >*tele.*
    tele 11:374. [FS].
    tex 20:19 [NS], 22:7b [OP].

tel #3 7:241. See *en tel aé qu(e).*

tendra (+ por) 7:224. [3 sg. fut. of *tenir (+ por)*].

'tendra (+ a) 8:266. [3 sg. fut. of *tenir* in *(se) tenir a*, to consider oneself (to be)].

tendrez 17:25. [2 pl. fut. of *tenir*].

tendront (+ por) 10:333. [3 pl. fut. of *tenir (+ por)*].

tenir [inf.] to hold.
    tendrez 17:25. [2 pl. fut.].
    tenoient 11:389. [3 pl. imperf.].
    tenoit 11:370. [3 sg. imperf.] (here: to hold a benefice).
    tindrent 11:381. [3 pl. pret.].
    tint 5:141, 18:2, 19:6. [3 sg. pret.].

tenir (+ por) [idiom] to consider (someone) to be.
    tendra (+ por) 7:224. [3 sg. fut.].
    tendront (+ por) 10:333. [3 pl. fut.].
    tint (+ por) 7:231. [3 sg. pret.].

tenist mal vers 11:375–76. [3 sg. imperf. subjunc. of *tenir mal vers*, to speak ill of].

tenoient 11:389. [3 pl. imperf. of *tenir*].

tenoit 11:370. [3 sg. imperf. of *tenir*] (here: to hold a benefice).

tenoit en destroit 2:63. [3 sg. imperf. of *tenir en destroit*, to imprison].

tens 4:101, 6:181. [OS] time (cf. *tans*, *lonc tens, par tens*).

'tenuz (+ a) 18:32. [pp. m. of *tenir* in *(se) tenir a*] held to.

terme 1:10, 3:69. [OS] term, (appointed) time.

terre 8:273, 10:329, 10:342, 17:6, 17:7, 20:16d, 20:25a, 20:29a, 20:31a, 21:35a, 21:35b. [FS] land.

    tere 20:25b, 21:3, 21:8b, 22:2a. == > *terre*.

tes 20:25a, 20:25a. [OP of *ton*].

teste 23:5b. [FS] head.

tex 20:19 [NS], 22:7b [OP of *tel* # *1*].

Thomas in *saint Thomas*, St. Thomas Becket, archbishop of Canterbury (1162–70).

tindrent 11:381. [3 pl. pret. of *tenir*].

tint 5:141, 18:2, 19:6. [3 sg. pret. of *tenir*].

tint (+ por) 7:231. [3 sg. pret. of *tenir (+. por)*].

toi 23:24, 23:26. [2 sg. stressed personal pron.] you.

tolir [inf.] to take away.

    toli 18:5. [3 sg. pret.].

    tolist 11:396. [3 sg. imperf. subjunc.].

    tolu 21:38b. [pp. m.].

    tolue 21:37. [pp. f.].

ton 5:162, 23:22, 23:23. [2 OS poss. adj.] your.

    tes 20:25a, 20:25a. [OP].

tor 23:11. [FS] tower.

    tors 5:156. [FP].

    tur 17:26. == > *tor*.

torné 3:86. [pp. m. of *torner*] turned.

    turné 16:48. == > *torné*.

tornoi 20:24b. [OS] tournament, joust.

    tornois 22:10b. [OP].

tornoiement 8:259. [OS] tournament, joust.

tors 5:156. [FP of *tor*].

tos # 1 22:5. [OP of *tot* # *1*].

tos # 2 23:5b. == > *tot* # *2*.

tost # 1 6:188, 13:458, 16:27, 23:30. [adv.] quickly, at once.

tost # 2 17:6 in *si tost cum* [temporal conjunctive phr.], as soon as.

tot # 1 1:22, 21:35a, 21:36b. [adj., OS] all.

    tos # 1 22:5. [OP].

    tote # 1 21:35a, 22:8a. [FS].

    tote # 3 22:8a. == > *tot* # *1*.

    totes 2:55, 3:80, 10:352. [FP].

    tout # 1 10:344. == > *tot* # *1*.

    toute # 1·2:30, 2:52, 10:362. == > *tote* # *1*.

    toz # 1 3:76, 12:422. [NS].

    tuit # 1 9:317. [NP].

tot # 2 4:114. [adv.] completely, entirely.

    tos # 2 23:5b. == > *tot* # *2*.

    tote # 2 21:5b. == > *tot* # *2*.

    tout # 2 7:218. == > *tot* # *2*.

    toute # 2 22:12b. == > *tote* # *2*.

    toz # 2 13:459. == > *tot* # *2*.

    tut # 2 16:15, 19:25, 19:30, 19:32, 19:35. == > *tot* # *2*.

    tuz # 2 18:19. == > *tot* # *2*.

tot # 3 [indef. pron., OS] all, everything, everyone.

    tout # 3 2:58, 5:137, 20:24a. == > *tot* # *3*.

    toz # 3 13:453. [OP].

    tuit # 2 4:133, 19:5. [NP].

    tut # 3 16:9 [NS], 16:26 [NP], 16:33 [OS]. == > *tot* # *3*.

    tuz # 1 16:19, 17:8, 18:50, 19:3. == > *toz* # *3*.

tote # 1 21:35a, 22:8a. [adj., FS of *tot* # *1*].

    toute # 1 2:30, 2:52, 10:362. == > *tote* # *1*.

tote # 2 21:5b. == > *tot* # *2*.

tote # 3 22:8a. == > *tot* # *1*.

tote une rue 23:10a. [adv. phr.] (all) along the road.

totes 2:55, 3:80, 10:352. [adj., FP of *tot* # *1*].

    toutes 20:32b. == > *totes*.

tout # 1 10:344. == > *tot* # *1*.

tout # 2 7:218. == > *tot* # *2*.

tout # 3 2:58, 5:137, 20:24a. == > *tot* # *3*.

tout #4 5:142, 6:192 in *o tout*
[compound prep.], with.

tout #5 9:289 in *du tout* [adv. phr.],
completely, altogether.

toute #1 2:30, 2:52, 10:362. = = > *tote*
#*1*.

toute #2 22:12b. = = > *tot* #*2*.

toutes 20:32b. = = > *totes*.

toz #1 3:76, 12:422. [adj., NP of *tot*
#*1*].

toz #2 13:459. = = > *tot* #*2*.

toz #3 13:453. [OP of *tot* #*3*].

  tuz #1 16:19, 17:8, 18:50, 19:3.
  = = > *toz* #*3*.

traïnier 18:21. [inf.] to drag.

traire 18:52. [inf.] to pull, to draw; to
lead (a life); to go.

  trai 21:30. [1 sg. pres.].

  traist 21:1b, 21:36a. [3 sg. pret.].

  trait 18:36, 19:39. [pp. m.].

  traites 23:10b. [pp. f.].

traitice 20:22b, 21:17. [adj., FS] oval
(in describing shape of face).

traïtur 18:7, 18:11, 19:18. [OS] traitor.

  traïtres 18:20, 18:27. [NS].

trametra 1:17. [3 sg. fut. of *trametre*, to
send].

trei 18:6. [NP of *trois*].

tresdouce 20:31a, 21:36b, 22:7a, 22:11c.
[adj., FS] dearest.

trespassé 20:17. [pp. m. of *trespasser*]
outlived.

tresqu(e) 17:36, 19:24. [adv.] right (up)
to.

trois 22:11a. [num. OP] three.

  trei 18:6. [NP].

trop 10:330. [adv.] very.

trover 18:49. [inf.] to find.

  trouver 5:146. = = > *trover*.

  trova 7:215. [3 sg. pret.].

  trovasse 23:4b. [1 sg. imperf.
  subjunc.].

  trovassent 16:53. [3 pl. imperf.
  subjunc.].

  trové 6:189, 6:200, 14:482, 15:529,
  18:10, 18:14. [pp. m.].

  trovee 4:132, 7:228, 14:491, 15:521.
  [pp. f.].

trovera 4:115. [3 sg. fut.].

troverez 18:29. [2 pl. fut.].

trovez 7:218, 12:425, 13:436.
= = > *trové*.

trueve 6:207. [3 sg. pres.].

tu 13:454, 18:10, 18:14, 18:17, 20:29c,
20:30a, 20:30b, 20:30b, 23:25. [2 sg.
subject pron.] you.

tuit #1 9:317. [NP of *tot* #*1*].

tuit #2 4:133, 19:5. [NP of *tot* #*3*].

tur 17:26. = = > *tor*.

turné 16:48. = = > *torné*.

tut #1 18:42, 19:40 in *del tut* = = > *du
tout*, q.v.

tut #2 16:15, 19:25, 19:30, 19:32,
19:35. = = > *tot* #*2*.

tut #3 16:9 [NS], 16:26 [NP], 16:33
[OS]. = = > *tot* #*3*.

tuz #1 16:19, 17:8, 18:50, 19:3.
= = > *toz* #*3*.

tuz #2 18:19. = = > *tot* #*2*.

u #1 19:8, 20:27b, 21:30, 23:10a.
= = > *ou* #*1*.

u #2 18:49. = = > *ou* #*2*.

u #3 20:30a, 20:32a, 22:3, 23:5a.
= = > *ou* #*3*.

u voille u nun 17:1. [idiom] whether
he wished (it) or not.

u . . . u 18:54. [compound conj.] either
. . . or.

ueil 3:88 in *ne set mie qu'a l'ueil li pent*,
[proverb] he cannot see beyond the
end of his nose (lit.: he does not
know what is hanging before his
eye).

uis #1 5:158, 6:178, 16:44. [OS] door.

  uis #2 16:35, 16:37, 16:39, 16:53,
  17:21, 17:25, 17:31. [OP].

um 16:36, 17:14. = = > *on*.

un #1 1:17, 3:92, 4:109, 19:47, 20:29c,
22:2b. [num., OS] one.

  uns #1 17:14. [NS].

un #2 1:24, 4:113, 4:121, 4:123, 4:127,
4:128, 5:139, 5:167, 6:177, 6:199,
8:253, 8:259, 9:286, 9:312, 9:318,
10:340, 11:379, 12:406, 12:407,
12:411, 13:443, 14:477, 15:516, 16:42,

16:44, 17:25, 18:4, 18:8, 18:32, 18:59, 19:33, 20:18, 20:29c, 20:30a, 21:5a, 21:7b, 22:2b, 22:3, 22:12b. [OS indef. art.] a, an.
    uns #2 20:16c. [NS].
uns #3 23:16. $==>un$ #2.
un #3 17:3. [indef. pron., NP] the ones.
un #4 19:35. $==>on$.
une #1 14:476, 18:6. [num., FS] one.
    unes 1:09. $==>une$ #1.
une #2 1:07, 2:40, 2:41, 4:99, 4:127, 4:129, 4:130, 5:149, 5:151, 6:193, 8:271, 10:325, 10:341, 20:29a, 21:10, 22:2a, 23:5a, 23:10a. [FS indef. art.] a, an.
uns #1 17:14. [NS of *un* #1].
uns #2 20:16c. [NS of *un* #2].
uns #3 23:16. $==>un$ #2.
unt 16:52, 17:1, 17:3, 17:10, 17:21, 17:36, 18:7, 18:36, 18:40, 18:51, 19:6, 19:10, 19:36, 19:53. [3 pl. pres. of *avoir* #2 (aux.)].
ure 16:16. [FS] hour.
ustilz 16:51. [OP] tools.

va #1 14:498, 21:6, 22:11b, 23:24. [2 sg. imperative of *aler*].
va #2 12:424 in *di va* [interjection to get someone's attention], say there! hey!
vaillanz 1:06. [adj., NS] valiant, brave, noble.
    vaillans 23:14. $==>vaillanz$.
vaint 20:24a. [3 sg. pres. of *veintre*, to vanquish, to conquer, to win].
vairs #1 20:22a, 23:21. [adj., OP] bright (applied to eyes).
vairs #2 22:11b. [NS] fur (squirrel fur, popular for lining or trimming: cf. Eng. *miniver*).
vait 6:175, 6:192, 7:219, 19:20. [3 sg. pres. of *aler*].
    vet 5:147, 7:213. $==>vait$.
vallet 20:18. [OS] young boy.
vauroit 20:1. [3 sg. cond. of *voloir*].
vaut 4:107. [3 sg. pres. of *valoir*, to be worth].

vautie 21:10, 21:29. [adj., FS] vaulted (i.e., with stone ceiling).
veer 17:33. $==>veoir$.
veez 17:34. [2 pl. imperative of *veoir*].
veïst 19:46, 19:49. [3 sg. imperf. subjunc. of *veoir*].
veïstes 21:18. [2 pl. pret. of *veoir*].
veit 19:11. [3 sg. pres. of *veoir*].
velt 7:214, 8:275. [3 sg. pres. of *voloir*].
vendrez 18:20. [2 pl. fut. of *venir*].
    venrez 9:296. $==>vendrez$.
venez 9:289, 14:494. [2 pl. imperative of *venir*].
vengiee 3:68. [pp. f. of *vanger*] avenged.
venir 23:11. [inf.] to come.
    vendrez 18:20. [2 pl. fut.].
    venez 9:289, 14:494. [2 pl. imperative].
    venoient 6:179, 23:10a. [3 pl. imperf.].
    venrez 9:296. $==>vendrez$.
    venu 16:10, 16:11. [pp. m.].
    venue 5:157, 18:1. [pp. f.].
    vient 13:459, 21:6. [3 sg. pres.].
    vindrent 16:14, 16:26, 17:16. [3 pl. pret.].
    vint #1 4:106, 5:172, 6:188, 7:241, 11:368, 13:437, 19:16. [3 sg. pret.].
vent 16:8. [OS] wind.
veoir 7:249, 13:445. [inf.] to see.
    veer 17:33. $==>veoir$.
    veez 17:34. [2 pl. imperative].
    veïst #1 19:49. [3 sg. imperf. subjunc.].
    veïstes 21:18. [2 pl. pret.].
    veit 19:11. $==>voit$.
    veoient 11:390. [3 pl. pres.].
    verra 21:8b. [3 sg. fut.].
    verrés 22:12a. $==>verrez$.
    verrez 16:20, 16:32. [2 pl. fut.].
    verroie 23:5a. [1 sg. cond.].
    verroit 8:270, 23:3a. [3 sg. cond.].
    verroiz 4:112. [2 pl. cond.].
    veü 3:82, 4:126, 11:384, 12:404, 12:408, 13:450. [pp. m.].
    veüe 18:5. [pp. f.].
    virent 6:208. [3 pl. pret.].

vit 5:155, 7:247, 12:418, 19:31, 21:1a, 21:20, 23:11. [3 sg. pret.].

voi 23:22. [1 sg. pres.].

voient 20:25b. = = > *veoient.*

voit 5:167, 8:263. [3 sg. pres.].

verai 17:27. [adj., OS] true.

veraiement 4:133. [adv.] truly.

verge 4:131. [FS] band.

vergier 16:43. [OS] orchard.

vergonder 3:94. [inf.] to disgrace.

verité 10:355. [FS] truth.

    veritez 2:47, 3:75, 14:475. [FS noun, declined as NS].

vermeil 19:50. [adj., OS] red.

verra 21:8b. [3 sg. fut. of *veoir*].

verrez 16:20, 16:32. [2 pl. fut. of *veoir*].

    verrés 22:12a. = = > *verrez.*

verroie 23:5a. [1 sg. cond. of *veoir*].

verroit 8:270, 23:3a. [3 sg. cond. of *veoir*].

verroiz 4:112. [2 pl. cond. of *veoir*].

vers #1 20:1. [OP] verses.

vers #2 3:93, 14:474, 15:511. [prep.] towards, to; against.

vers #3 11:376. See *tenist mal vers.*

vespres 16:30, 17:40. [OP] vespers (evening prayers).

vestoit 7:240. [3 sg. imperf. of *vestir*, to dress].

vestues 22:8b. [pp. f. of *vestir*] dressed.

vet 5:147, 7:213. = = > *vait.*

veü 3:82, 4:126, 11:384, 12:404, 12:408, 13:450. [pp. m. of *veoir*] seen.

veüe 18:5. [pp. f. of *veoir*] seen.

veut 21:4. [3 sg. pres. of *voloir*].

veve 6:193. [FS] widow.

vie 16:2, 21:30. [FS] life.

viel 12:407 [OS], 20:2 [OS], 22:8a [NP]. [adj.] old.

    viés 22:8b, 22:8b, 22:8b. [OP].

    vix #2 20:17. [NS].

vient 13:459, 21:6. [3 sg. pres. of *venir*].

vient a plesir 5:163. [3 sg. pres. of *venir a plesir*, to please].

viés 22:8b, 22:8b, 22:8b. [adj., OP of *viel*].

vil 19:54. [adj., NP] base.

vilain 10:364. [NP] townspeople.

vile 5:138, 5:146, 5:149, 5:151, 20:16c, 20:29a, 20:29b, 21:1b, 21:36a, 23:10a. [FS] town, villa, farm.

vilenie 14:471. [FS] contemptible action.

vindrent 16:14, 16:26, 17:16. [3 pl. pret. of *venir*].

vint #1 4:106, 5:172, 6:188, 7:241, 11:368, 13:437, 19:16. [3 sg. pret. of *venir*].

'vint #2 5:142. [3 sg. pret. of *(s'en) venir*, to come, to arrive].

virent 6:208. [3 pl. pret. of *veoir*].

vis 19:12, 20:7. [OS] face.

visconte 21:1b, 21:36a, 22:13. [OS] viscount.

    visquens 20:29a, 21:6, 21:36b, 22:12a. [NS].

vit 5:155, 7:247, 12:418, 19:31, 21:1a, 21:20, 23:11. [3 sg. pret. of *veoir*].

vix #1 20:30a, 20:30b. [2 sg. pres. of *voloir*].

vix #2 20:17. [NS of *viel*].

vo #1 22:4. = = > *vostre #1.*

vo #2 22:5. = = > *vostre #2.*

voi 23:22. [1 sg. pres. of *veoir*].

voie 5:141. [FS] path, way.

voient 20:25b. [3 pl. pres. of *veoir*].

voil #1 3:93, 16:21, 22:10a, 22:10c, 22:11c. [1 sg. pres. of *voloir*].

voil #2 17:24. [OS] desire, intent.

voille 17:1. [3 sg. pres. subjunc. of *voloir* in *u voille u nun* [idiom], whether he wished (it) or not].

voir 23:5a in *naie voir* [adv. phr.], indeed not.

voise 20:27a. [1 sg. pres. subjunc. of *aler*].

voisin 1:04 [NP], 1:14 [OS] neighbor(s).

    voisine 3:68, 14:472. [FS].

voit 5:167, 8:263. [3 sg. pres. of *veoir*].

    veit 19:11. = = > *voit.*

voldrent 18:53. [3 pl. pret. of *voloir*].

voleient 16:38, 17:37, 18:54. = = > *voloient.*

volent 16:31. [3 pl. pres. of *voloir*].

volenté 13:468, 16:9. [FS] will, desire.

volonté 10:335. = = > *volenté.*
volentés 21:8a. [FS noun, declined
as m. nom.].
volentiers 7:220, 10:334. [adv.]
willingly.
voler 23:5b. [inf.] to fly (out).
voloir [inf.] to wish, to want, to
desire.
    vauroit 20:1. [3 sg. cond.].
    velt 7:214, 8:275. = = > *volt.*
    veut 21:4. = = > *volt.*
    vix #1 20:30a, 20:30b. [2 sg.
    pres.].
    voil #1 3:93, 16:21, 22:10a,
    22:10c, 22:11c. [1 sg. pres.].
    voille 17:1. [3 sg. pres. subjunc. in
    u voille u nun, q.v.].
    voldrent 18:53. [3 pl. pret.].
    voleient 16:38, 17:37, 18:54.
    = = > *voloient.*
    volent 16:31. [3 pl. pres.].
    volez 9:295, 17:9, 19:7. [2 pl.
    pres.].
    voloient 6:180. [3 pl. imperf.].
    voloit 12:415, 20:24a, 23:1. [3 sg.
    imperf.].
    volt 9:314, 14:497, 16:33, 19:16,
    19:17. [3 sg. pres.].
    vouloit 12:403. = = > *voloit.*
volonté 10:335. = = > *volenté.*
volte 18:4. [FS] vault.
vont 22:7b, 22:8a, 22:9, 22:10a, 22:11a,
22:11b, 23:27, 23:29. [3 pl. pres. of
aler].
    vunt 16:35. = = > *vont.*
vos #1 10:345, 13:465, 14:479, 14:480,
20:26, 20:27b, 21:7b, 21:27, 21:36b,
21:37, 21:38b, 22:2c, 22:5, 22:12a,
22:12b, 23:2, 23:4a, 23:6, 23:7, 23:8.
[2 pl. subject pron.] you.
    vous #1 21:5b, 21:34, 22:4, 23:7.
    = = > *vos* #1.
    vus #1 17:39, 18:18, 19:7, 19:8.
    = = > *vos* #1.
vos #2 1:01, 8:255, 9:297, 9:298,
10:350, 13:437, 13:438, 13:467,
13:470, 14:481, 20:19 [2 pl. indirect
obj. pron.] (to) you.

vous #2 21:38a, 22:7b. = = > *vos*
#2.
vus #2 17:23. = = > *vos* #2.
vos #3 4:110, 23:3a, 23:3b, 23:7, 23:8.
[2 pl. direct obj. pron.] you.
    vous #3 23:3a. = = > *vos* #3.
    vus #3 16:31, 16:42. = = > *vos*
    #3.
vos #4 10:340, 21:5b, 21:28. [2 pl.
stressed obj. pron.] you.
    vus #4 18:38. = = > *vos* #4.
vos #5 9:289, 9:296. [2 pl. reflexive
pron. (untranslated)].
vos #6 21:8a [NS], 21:38b [FP], 22:12b
[NS]. [2 pl. poss. adj.] your.
    voz 17:40 [OP], 18:30 [FP], 18:41
    [FP]. = = > *vos* #6.
vos #7 1:20 in *es vos* [deictic], look!
behold! there is. . . .
vostre #1 6:201, 9:288, 14:478, 19:9. [2
pl. poss. adj., OS] your.
    vo #1 22:4. = = > *vostre* #1.
    vo #2 22:5. = = > *vostre* #2.
    vostre #2 9:291, 13:468, 21:2,
    21:8a, 21:26. [FS].
vouloit 12:403. = = > *voloit.*
vous #1 21:5b, 21:34, 22:4, 23:7.
= = > *vos* #1.
vous #2 21:38a, 22:7b. = = > *vos* #2.
vous #3 23:3a. = = > *vos* #3.
voz 17:40 [OP], 18:30 [FP], 18:41 [FP].
= = > *vos* #6.
vunt 16:35. [3 pl. pres. of *aler*].
Vuillaumes 19:16. = = > *Willaumes.*
vus #1 17:39, 18:18, 19:7, 19:8.
= = > *vos* #1.
vus #2 17:23. = = > *vos* #2.
vus #3 16:31, 16:42. = = > *vos* #3.
vus #4 18:38. = = > *vos* #4.

Willaumes (de Traci). 16:3, 19:29.
[NS] William of Tracy, one of the
murderers of Thomas Becket.
    Vuillaumes 19:16.
    = = > *Willaumes.*
    Williaume 18:53. [OS].
Wingelesé 16:7. [OS] Winchelsea,
seaport in Sussex.

general index

phonology index